Everyday Life and the "Reconstruction" of Soviet Russia During and After the Great Patriotic War, 1943–1948

The Allan K. Wildman Group for the Study of the Workers, Peasants, and Intelligentsia in the Revolutionary Era has established its *Historical Series* to promote research into the history of the workers, peasants, and intelligentsia in Late Imperial and Soviet Russia.

The Allan K. Wildman Group Historical Series

1. Michael Melancon and Alice K. Pate, eds., *New Labor History: Worker Identity and Experience in Russia, 1840–1918* (2002)

2. Page Herrlinger, *Working Souls: Russian Orthodoxy and Factory Labor in St. Petersburg, 1881–1917* (2007)

3. Jeffrey W. Jones, *Everyday Life and the "Reconstruction" of Soviet Russia during and after the Great Patriotic War, 1943–48*

Everyday Life and the "Reconstruction" of Soviet Russia During and After the Great Patriotic War, 1943–1948

Jeffrey W. Jones

Bloomington, Indiana, 2008

SLAVICA

ISBN 978-0-89357-348-5

Library of Congress Cataloging-in-Publication Data goes here

Slavica Publishers   [Tel.] 1-812-856-4186
Indiana University   [Toll-free] 1-877-SLAVICA
2611 E. 10th St.   [Fax] 1-812-856-4187
Bloomington, IN 47408-2603   [Email] slavica@indiana.edu
USA   [www] http://www.slavica.com/

To the memory of my mom and dad

Contents

From the Series Editors xi

Acknowledgments xiii

Introduction

"Everything here will have to change" 1

Chapter One

"Everything has to be rebuilt from scratch in this country, starting with our own Rostov": The Impact of the Great Fatherland War 16

Chapter Two

"I will have to hang myself now—life has become simply impossible": Living Conditions during "Reconstruction" 40

Chapter Three

"When will that 'near future' finally arrive?": The Myth of "Reconstruction" and the "Politics of Productivity" 77

Chapter Four

"When will we be able to feed our children?": National Identity, Gender, and Soviet "Family Rhetoric" 112

Chapter Five

"Every family has its freak": Perceptions of Collaboration in Occupied Soviet Russia 145

Chapter Six

"People Without A Definite Occupation": The Illegal Economy and "Speculation" 180

Chapter Seven

"What sort of democracy is this?": Political Rhetoric, Popular Perceptions, and Soviet Elections 212

Chapter Eight
"Right now you can't get anything done without a bribe": Problems in
and Perceptions of the Soviet Communist Party 244

Conclusion
"In my opinion, this is all a fraud!" 279

Bibliography 289

Index 303

From the Series Editors

The Wildman Group arose during the mid-1990s as an informal discussion forum for those interested in labor and social history, with special emphasis on the Russian revolutions of 1905 and 1917. The Allan K. Wildman Group for the Study of Russian Workers and Society, as it eventually called itself, came to encompass many persons whose scholarly interests revolved around the Russian Revolution and related phenomena at a time when academic publishers, journals, and those who led graduate programs had often moved to different research priorities. The group's interest in promoting continued research in revolutionary studies led to the 2002 publication by Slavica of *New Labor History: Worker Identity and Experience in Russia, 1840–1918*, a collection of new research about labor history from American and Russian scholars under the editorship of Michael Melancon and Alice Pate. The studies contained in the volume and the responses to them in the field demonstrated the continued vitality of late 19th- and 20th-century social history and its ability to place familiar historical episodes and phenomena in new perspectives. This factor gave rise to the idea of the *Allan K. Wildman Group Historical Series*, which Slavica agreed to publish. In order to broaden its scope to one more appropriate for a series, the group also renamed itself The Allan K. Wildman Group for the Study of Russian Workers, Peasants, and Intelligentsia during the Revolution and the Soviet Era. The *Wildman Series* now focuses on the entire revolutionary experience, especially in terms of the broad social strata most involved in making the Revolution and sustaining the state and society that resulted.

The Wildman Series' third volume and second monograph, Jeffrey W. Jones' *Everyday Life and the "Reconstruction" of Soviet Russia During and After the Great Patriotic War, 1943–1948*, reminds us of how little we know about the end of the war and the immediate post-war era in the Soviet Union. Jones uses the case of Rostov-na-Donu, totally devastated by the vast battles that raged around it, to reveal how people and party responded to the grim task that confronted them after the German forces were expelled. Society and state both strived to rebuild but comprehended the process differently. In the official "reconstruction" mythology, state and party leaders portrayed themselves as a vanguard, whereas local populations, mostly workers, saw them as a privileged elite. The chapters revolve around these conflicting interpretative ideologies, as expressed through official public sources, internal documents, police reports on the population, and interviews and memoirs. What emerges is a portrayal, compelling and persuasive, of the physical realities of rebuilding the infrastructures of modern life and the ways various elements of society perceived the process. The Wildman Group believes that Jones' study will help define our approaches to chronicling post-war Soviet life, the most exciting new field in Russian historiography.

Acknowledgments

A number of people assisted in a variety of ways in making this book happen. Donald J. Raleigh, my advisor at UNC-Chapel Hill, gave me a tremendous amount of support and advice from beginning to end with this project, and I owe him a profound gratitude. The staff of the Rostov Party and Rostov State Archives were always generous with their time and help. A number of people have taken the time to read and comment on earlier drafts of the manuscript, or sometimes separate chapters. I would like to thank David Griffiths, Michael Hunt, Sam Baron, who initially sparked my interest in Russian and Soviet history, Don Reid, and Gerald Surh for their input early in the process. James Heinzen, Michael Hickey, Diane Koenker, and Rex Wade all provided helpful comments on the latter stages of the manuscript. The invaluable input of "anonymous" readers Donald Filtzer and Matt Payne were *extremely* helpful in revising and clarifying certain aspects of the manuscript. I thank them both very much.

A number of colleagues in a variety of fields have read and commented on parts of the book, and I would like to thank them as well: Thomas Jackson, Watson Jennison, Betsy Jones-Hemenway, Susanna Lee, Lisa Levenstein, Paula Michaels, Karl Qualls, Michael Roberto, and James Wood. I want to thank Christopher Jacobsen for help in doing the bibliography. I am also very grateful to series' editors Michael Melancon and Alice Pate, and to Vicki Polansky at Slavica Publishers for her tremendous help through the onerous final stages of the project. George Fowler dealt with various technical snafus and saw the book through to light.

Earlier versions of parts of this book have been published and appear here by permission: "'Every family has its freaks': Perceptions of Collaboration in Occupied Soviet Russia, 1943–1948," *Slavic Review* 64: 4: 747–70 (© American Association for the Advancement of Slavic Studies, 2005); and "'People Without A Definite Occupation': Class Conflict and the Illegal Economy in Rostov-on-the-Don, 1943–1948," in *Provincial Landscapes: The Local Dimensions of Soviet Power 1917-1953*, ed. Donald J. Raleigh (Pittsburgh: University of Pittsburgh, 2001), 236–54.

Financial support for the research and writing of this book came from The International Research & Exchanges Board (IREX) and the University of North Carolina at Greensboro, for which I am of course very grateful.

Finally, I would like to thank Tatiana Jones for years of support, assistance, insight and encouragement. Our daughter Ellie is the light of my life, and I appreciate every moment we have together.

Introduction

"Everything here will have to change"

In 1943, on a cold winter day in Rostov-on-Don, nine-year-old Vadim Iakov-lev heard the approaching troops on Engels Street while he and a friend sifted through the rubble of a bombed-out store for canned goods. Quiet had descended on the city after a heated two-week battle between Soviet and German forces, and when the boys saw the red flag with the hammer and sickle at the head of the procession, they ran alongside yelling, "*Nashi! Nashi! Nashi!*" (Ours! Ours! Ours!)[1] At that moment of euphoria little did they know of the tremendous hardships and difficulties that lay ahead. On February 14, 1943, the Soviet Red Army reclaimed Rostov-on-Don, a major industrial center and strategically important city in southern Russia, ending more than six months of German occupation that left many lives in turmoil. Nazi forces killed thousands, executing Jews, communists, POWs, Armenians, and suspected partisans. When they retreated they burned everything in their path, wrecking an infrastructure of roads, railways, bridges, industry, housing, and public buildings that had taken decades to develop. In Rostov, the fighting reduced almost all of the buildings on Engels Street, the main thoroughfare of the city, to ruins. It severely damaged or destroyed the mass transit system, the railway station, the river port, the Rostov-Bataisk Dam, and a railway bridge across the Don River. The war left an indelible mark on the city and its residents, who faced a difficult challenge in rebuilding. In the following weeks and months local authorities set about changing the street names back from German to Russian and worried about the bodies of soldiers littered throughout the city — "reconstruction" had begun.[2]

This book examines how people put the pieces back together again, revealing the struggles and conflicts involved in the complex process that the regime labeled "reconstruction" (*vosstanovlenie*). In its official version, it is a

---

[1] Interview by author, 15 March 1995.

[2] On bodies in the city, see TsDNI f. 13, op. 4, d. 29, ll. 24–25. Genadii Ermolenko found "a lot of corpses" of Red Army and German troops in a shed and nearby field in June 1943, four months after liberation. Interview by author, 16 April 1995. An estimated 26.6 million Soviet citizens perished in the war. See E. M. Andreev, L. E. Darskii, and T. L. Khar'kova, *Naselenie Sovetskogo Soiuza: 1922–1991 gg.* (Moscow: Nauka, 1993), 73.

tale of a unified population following the "vanguard" party and overcoming all difficulties to rebuild the Soviet economy on a higher level than before the war. I analyze the symbolic and physical "reconstruction" of the USSR by examining how the Stalinist system operated, how the regime construed the official ideology of Marxism-Leninism—expressed as "socialism"—and wielded it to political advantage, and how perceptions and representations of Soviet "reality" differed in significant ways. Imbued with tones of sacrifice and heroism and couched in terms of collective unity and the family, "reconstruction" amounted to a discursive myth based on party ideology's configuration of social classes, gender, and national identity. This mythic portrayal trumpets the successes of the period, which were substantial, but ignores tensions in the political and social structure. A "myth" is an interpretation/construction of "what happened" preferred by those in power and thus imposed on society as *the* "true" story. Political myths obscure "reality" in all of its multifaceted complexities and operate to suppress other, conflicting (or more complex) and nuanced interpretations, while states manipulate and control myths to promote a collective goal, though not always successfully.[3] My aim is to expose the underlying assumptions and contradictions of the ruling ideology while bringing different representations of Soviet reality to light, to discover what "reconstruction" meant to people in Rostov, with a primary focus on the working class in this alleged "workers' state." I approach the subject thematically with an eye to "everyday life," defined as interactions that in some way involved the Stalinist state, be it through work, the buying and selling of goods, voting, bureaucratic encounters, or in less obvious ways, such as enduring shortages or having one's comments overheard and reported by an informant.[4]

---

[3] See Clifford Geertz, *The Interpretation of Cultures: Selected Essays* (New York: Basic Books, 1973), 142–46, 162–64; and Hayden V. White, *The Content of the Form: Narrative Discourse and Historical Representation* (Baltimore: Johns Hopkins University Press, 1987), x. On the structure and role of myth, see Leszek Kolakowski, *The Presence of Myth* (Chicago: University of Chicago Press, 1989); Oleg Kharkhordin, *The Collective and the Individual in Russia: A Study of Practices* (Berkeley: University of California Press, 1999). On the relationship between perception and memory, myth and reality, see S. E. Poliakov, *Mify i real'nost' sovremennoi psikhologii* (Moscow: Editorial URSS, 2004). For the importance of myth in Soviet political culture, see A. M. Beda, *Sovetskaia politicheskaia kul'tura cherez prizmu MVD: Ot "moskovskogo patriotizma" k idee "Bol'shogo Otechestva" (1946–1958)* (Moscow: Izdatel'stvo ob"edineniia Mosgorarkhiv, 2002). On the role of myth in Soviet history, see Rósa Magnúsdóttir, "Keeping Up Appearances: How the Soviet State Failed to Control Popular Attitudes Toward the United States of America, 1945–1959" (Ph.D. diss., University of North Carolina-Chapel Hill, 2006).

[4] See Michel de Certeau, *The Practice of Everyday Life*, trans. Steven Rendall (Berkeley: University of California Press, 2002); Sheila Fitzpatrick, *Everyday Stalinism: Ordinary Life in Extraordinary Times. Soviet Russia in the 1930s* (New York: Oxford University

I argue that while the party portrayed itself as the "vanguard" of society, many workers saw local leaders as a privileged elite whose position of dominance stemmed from control over the production and allocation of resources. Perceptive gaps and fundamental misunderstandings existed between party leaders and the workers for whom the party claimed to rule. Local leaders conceptualized society in terms of "us"—the party elite or *nomenklatura*[5]—and "them"—the population at large and especially workers in this urban setting—and devised discursive strategies to maintain and justify their power. Workers often expressed discontent with party policies and defined their interests in opposition to the goals of local authorities, expressing a shared identity and interests—a separate class consciousness—juxtaposed to an amorphous, omnipresent "they," the representatives of the local elite with whom they interacted, directly or indirectly, on a daily basis.[6] The gap or "disconnect" between the representatives of power and the populace at this critical juncture in Soviet history, moreover, points to some very *real*, systemic problems in the functioning of Stalinism—problems that could only be addressed—eventually—through reforms. The seeds of de-Stalinization were sown during the war and postwar years, although they would not bloom until the mid-1950s.[7] In his memoir, K. S. Karol records the words of his friend Kolia, a Don Cossack and Red Army veteran who, at a small gathering of friends in Rostov in 1946, compared Stalin to Hitler and said, "everything here [in the USSR] will have to change."[8] His (drunken) statement expresses my (more or less sober) argument: the criticism of Stalin suggests tension between state and society, while the latter comment presages de-Stalinization and the reforms of the post-Stalin era.

Press, 1999); and Christina Kiaer and Eric Naiman, eds., *Everyday Life in Early Soviet Russia: Taking the Revolution Inside* (Bloomington: Indiana University Press, 2006).

[5] The city party's nomenklatura consisted of all obkom, gorkom, and district (*raikom*) secretaries, heads of raikom departments such as *agitprop* (agitation and propaganda) departments, Komsomol (Communist Youth Organization) secretaries, newspaper editors and prosecutors.

[6] E. P. Thompson, *The Making of the English Working Class* (London: V. Gollancz, 1963). While adopting Thompson's broad definition of class that includes both its *economic and cultural* components, I agree with Gareth Stedman Jones that Thompson disregards the role of ideology as a mediating factor in consciousness, and with Joan Scott that Thompson fails to account for gender differences within the working class. I address these deficiencies. See Jones, *Languages of Class: Studies in English Working-Class History, 1832–1982* (Cambridge: Cambridge University Press, 1983), and Joan Wallach Scott, *Gender and the Politics of History* (New York: Columbia University Press, 1988).

[7] On this point, see, for example, Elena Iu. Zubkova, *Obshchestvo i reformy 1945–1964* (Moscow: Rossiia molodaia, 1993) or, in English, *Russia After the War: Hopes, Illusions, and Disappointments, 1945–1957*, trans. Hugh Ragsdale (Armonk, NY: M. E. Sharpe, 1998).

[8] K. S. Karol, *Solik: Life in the Soviet Union, 1939–1946* (London: Pluto Press, 1986), 129.

The focus of the case study is Rostov-on-Don, the "Gateway to the Caucasus," a major industrial and transportation center in southern Russia located along the Don River, about forty kilometers upstream from the Sea of Azov in formerly autonomous Cossack territory.[9] Nazi forces took the city for about ten days in late November 1941, and then again for about six and a half months beginning July 24, 1942. In early 1943 the tide of the war turned with the Soviet victory at Stalingrad and the front began moving west. The Red Army retook Rostov on February 14, which is the starting point of my study. As of that date, there were 150,000–300,000 people residing in Rostov, down from over a half million on the eve of war.[10] Thousands of demobilized soldiers, evacuees, and others returned to or settled in the city during and after the war;[11] by 1948 the population had climbed to about 450,000.[12] My study ends in 1948 with the officially proclaimed completion of reconstruction, declared by the regime as reaching prewar levels of production in heavy industry. While the physical reconstruction of the USSR continued into the 1950s, the narrative of "reconstruction" ended — the regime closed that chapter and moved on to promote itself as a Cold War rival "superpower" to the United States. The end of my study also coincides with the death in August 1948 of one of Stalin's key lieutenants, Andrei Zhdanov, whose campaign to revive ideological purity in the CPSU begun in 1946 underscores the importance of ideology in the postwar years.

The period officially dubbed "reconstruction" has not received due attention in the scholarly literature. The natural tendency is to look at the war years (1941–45) or concentrate on the period from the end of the war to

---

[9] I focus mainly on Rostov-on-Don, but where appropriate I consider developments in Rostov oblast.

[10] After the war an internal party document put the figure at 150,000. Tsentr Dokumentatsii Noveishei Istorii (TsDNI) f. 13, op. 4, d. 29, l. 12. A report from the occupying German forces to Berlin in August 1942 states that "the number of inhabitants who remained in Rostov comes to approximately 200,000–300,000." Yitzhak Arad et al., eds. *The Einsatzgruppen Reports: Selections from the Dispatches of the Nazi Death Squads' Campaign Against the Jews, July 1941–January 1943* (New York: Holocaust Library, 1989), 358. For the prewar figure, see *Narodnoe khoziaistvo Rostovskoi oblasti v 9oi piatiletke: Statisticheskii sbornik* (Rostov-on-Don: Statistika, Rostovskoe otdelenie, 1976), 10. The 1939 census put Rostov's population at 510,000.

[11] As of January 1946, 2,704 demobilized troops were in Rostov, and that number would increase steadily in subsequent months. Rossiiskii gosudarstvennyi arkhiv sotsial'noi i politicheskoi istorii (RGASPI) f. 17, op. 122, d. 146, l. 27.

[12] By the middle of 1947 there were an estimated 406,700 people in Rostov, and from that point the city's population grew gradually but steadily, reaching 552,000 in 1956. See V. K. Morkovin, "Rabochie Dona v poslevoennyi period (1946–1950)" (Kandidatskaia diss., Rostov State University, Rostov-on-Don, 1972). See also Statisticheskoe upravlenie Rostovskoi oblasti, *Rostovskaia oblast' za 50 let: Statisticheskii sbornik* (Rostov-on-Don: Statistika, Rostovskoe otdelenie, 1967), 21.

Stalin's death (1945–53). Yet the period of reconstruction (1943–48) is vitally important in part precisely because it bridges the war and postwar periods. The end of the war in Europe in May 1945 is, of course, highly significant, and I highlight its importance. Also, there is obviously change over the course of this five-year period, *especially* following victory, as the country did rebuild its destroyed industry and infrastructure to a significant degree. However, the end of the war is *not* the natural breaking point historians often designate it as because many of the issues facing societies in the immediate postwar period were rooted in the prewar and war years.[13] In addition, as we will see, the postwar famine (1946–48) continued the privations of the war years into reconstruction. The regime's heroic tale of "reconstruction" ended abruptly (and somewhat arbitrarily) in 1948, a year which many scholars in Soviet history have noted as an important turning point.[14] On the international front it is also clear by 1948—the year of the Soviet blockade of Berlin and the US and British airlift to end it—that relations with the USSR's wartime allies had turned cold.

A local study is one of the best ways to address reconstruction. I will not make a case for the "typicality" of Rostov;[15] in fact, my description of the

---

[13] On this point, see Tony Judt, "Preface," and Jan T. Gross, "Themes for a Social History of War Experience and Collaboration," in *The Politics of Retribution in Europe: World War II and Its Aftermath*, ed. Istvan Deak et al. (Princeton, NJ: Princeton University Press, 2000), ix, xi–xii and 22–23, 31 respectively. Also, Hanna Diamond's study of women and collaboration in Vichy France emphasizes strong currents of continuity to 1948. Diamond, *Women and the Second World War in France, 1939–1948: Choices and Constraints* (New York: Longman, 1999). See also Paul V. Dutton, "An Overlooked Source of Social Reform: Family Policy in French Agriculture, 1939–1945," *Journal of Modern History* 72: 2 (June 2000): 411; Jeffry M. Diefendorf, "Introduction: New Perspectives on a Rebuilt Europe," in *Rebuilding Europe's Bombed Cities*, ed. Diefendorf (New York: St. Martin's Press, 1990).

[14] See Julie Hessler, *A Social History of Soviet Trade: Trade Policy, Retail Practices, and Consumption, 1917–1953* (Princeton, NJ: Princeton University Press, 2004); Karl Qualls, "Imagining Sevastopol: History and Postwar Community Construction, 1942–1953," in *National Identities* 5: 2 (July 2003): 123–39; and idem, "Local-Outsider Negotiations in Postwar Sevastopol's Reconstruction, 1944–53," in *Provincial Landscapes: The Local Dimensions of Soviet Power*, ed. Donald J. Raleigh (Pittsburgh: University of Pittsburgh Press, 2001), 276–98; Donald Filtzer, *Soviet Workers and Late Stalinism: Labour and the Restoration of the Stalinist System after World War II* (Cambridge: Cambridge University Press, 2002); Zubkova, *Russia After the War*; and William O. McCagg, *Stalin Embattled, 1943–1948* (Detroit: Wayne State University Press, 1978).

[15] Here I am following the lead of Donald Raleigh in his study of the Civil War in Saratov. Donald J. Raleigh, *Experiencing Russia's Civil War: Politics, Society, and Revolutionary Culture in Saratov, 1917–1922* (Princeton, NJ: Princeton University Press, 2002), 4. The Civil War was followed by its own period of "reconstruction" (also described as *vosstanovlenie* in Soviet rhetoric). Diane P. Koenker notes that "a local approach permits the historian to explore particular histories, traditions, and personalities without

city—and the region it is located in—stresses its peculiarities. Yet most of the issues I explore are deeply rooted in Russian history and not unique to Rostov-on-Don or the lower Don region: poverty and exploitation; crime; gender inequality; corruption; and anti-Semitism. Other phenomena in the book are inherent to Soviet rule and the Stalinist system: "speculation," the buying and reselling of goods for profit; the election campaigns; and the informant system. Many of these issues, moreover, were common to war-torn Eurasia: material hardship; problems in production; illegal economic activity; elections; collaboration; corruption; and political and social divisions.[16] Like a single piece in a much larger puzzle, the "reconstruction" of Rostov has condensed within it more general experiences that are larger than the locality itself.[17] Also, as in the 1930s, the conceptual framework expressed in the regime's political discourse during reconstruction did not allow for an acknowledgment that corruption was inherent in the system, nor that there could be antagonism between the government and the working masses it was supposed to represent.[18] Thus there was an unbridgeable gap between official discourse and the way the system operated, between the existence of corruption and mass resistance and the ways the government interpreted these is-

---

losing sight of the larger issues at stake." Koenker, *Republic of Labor: Russian Printers and Soviet Socialism, 1918–1930* (Ithaca, NY: Cornell University Press, 2005), 2.

[16] See, for example, Christopher Lloyd, *Collaboration and Resistance in Occupied France: Representing Treason and Sacrifice* (New York: Palgrave Macmillan, 2003); Carola Hein, Jeffry M. Diefendorf, and Ishida Yorifusa, eds., *Rebuilding Urban Japan after 1945* (New York: Palgrave Macmillan, 2003); Deak et al., *Politics of Retribution in Europe*; Lynne Taylor, *Between Resistance and Collaboration: Popular Protest in Northern France, 1940–45* (New York: St. Martin's Press, 2000); John Dower, *Embracing Defeat: Japan in the Wake of World War II* (New York: W. W. Norton and Co./New Press, 1999); Padraic Kenney, *Rebuilding Poland: Workers and Communists, 1945–50* (Ithaca, NY: Cornell University Press, 1997); Gill Bennett, ed., *The End of the War in Europe, 1945* (London: HMSO 1996); Jeffry M. Diefendorf, *In the Wake of War: The Reconstruction of German Cities after World War II* (New York: Oxford University Press, 1993) and idem, *Rebuilding Europe's Bombed Cities*; Jan T. Gross, *Polish Society under German Occupation: Generalgouvernement, 1939–44* (Princeton, NJ: Princeton University Press, 1979).

[17] See Allan Pred, *Making Histories and Constructing Human Geographies: The Local Transformation of Practice, Power Relations, and Consciousness* (Boulder, CO: Westview Press, 1990), 15. For city-level studies in various periods, see also David Hoffmann, *Peasant Metropolis: Social Identities in Moscow, 1929–1941* (Ithaca, NY: Cornell University Press, 1994); Stephen Kotkin, *Magnetic Mountain: Stalinism as a Civilization* (Berkeley: University of California Press, 1995).

[18] Gábor Tamás Rittersporn, *Simplifications staliniennes et complications soviétiques: Tensions sociales et conflits politiques en U.R.S.S., 1933–1953* (Paris: Editions des archives contemporaines, 1988).

sues. By focusing on the disjuncture between the ruling elite and workers, my work provides a new perspective on Stalinism during Soviet reconstruction.[19]

The Role of Ideology in Soviet History

I define ideology as an "interpretive system" or "strategy of containment," a way of processing and comprehending "reality," of consciously categorizing and expressing perceptions of the material world. We produce, disseminate, and consume ideologies all our lives, whether or not we are aware of it, and we all have understandings of the political environment of which we are part, as well as views about the merits and/or failings of that environment.[20] Ideology plays a crucial role in political practices, shaping the means and ends to which rulers apply policies, and was an important instrument of power for the regime for most of Soviet history.[21] Of course, the Bolshevik regime was not made by ideology alone, but also by the tools of state it inherited to pur-

---

[19] Amir Weiner's study of Ukraine makes a strong case for the Great Fatherland War as the most important formative experience of the Soviet era and for the importance of local studies. Weiner, *Making Sense of War: The Second World War and the Fate of the Bolshevik Revolution* (Princeton, NJ: Princeton University Press, 2000). On late Stalinism and the 1940s, see also J. Eric Duskin, *Stalinist Reconstruction and the Confirmation of a New Elite, 1945–1953* (New York: Palgrave, 2001); Filtzer, *Soviet Workers and Late Stalinism*; Kees Boterbloem, *Life and Death under Stalin: Kalinin Province, 1945–1953* (Montreal: McGill-Queen's University Press, 1999); Juliane Fürst, ed., *Late Stalinist Russia: Society Between Reconstruction and Reinvention* (London: Routledge, 2006); and Joon-Seo Song, "The Legacy of World War II on the Stalinist Home Front: Magnitogorsk 1941–1953" (Ph.D. diss., Michigan State University, 2007).

[20] On this point, see Michael Freeden, *Ideology: A Very Short Introduction* (Oxford: Oxford University Press, 2003), 1.

[21] James P. Scanlan maintains that Marxism-Leninism occupied a central position in Soviet political culture. Ideology, he asserts, "establishes, among other things, the leadership's right to exist and defines the critical contribution that the Communist Party makes to society." Marxism-Leninism, he adds, is the "self-glorification of a ruling class, the theoretical expression of its own self-image." Scanlan, *Marxism in the USSR: A Critical Survey of Current Soviet Thought* (Ithaca, NY: Cornell University Press, 1985), 15. On the importance of ideology in the 1930s, see Kotkin, *Magnetic Mountain*, 152. Kotkin notes that "to dismiss or downplay the significance of ideology in the USSR in the 1930s because the ideological precepts were changed or violated in practice (or because they supposedly represented a degeneration of true Marxism-Leninism) is to render the behavior and thinking of contemporaries incomprehensible" (152). On the importance of ideology more generally, see David Harvey, *The Condition of Post-Modernity: An Enquiry into the Origins of Social Change* (Oxford: Blackwell Publishers, 1989); and James C. Scott, *Seeing Like a State: How Certain Schemes to Improve the Human Condition Have Failed* (New Haven: Yale University Press, 1998).

sue its ideological project—the tools of wartime coercion and mobilization.[22] Those tools were passed on to (and sharpened by) Stalin, who coerced and mobilized the Soviet population through collectivization and industrialization in the late 1920s and early 1930s. The tools of coercion and mobilization employed by the Stalinist regime became all the more relevant during the Great Fatherland War and after, when society needed to be rebuilt. Rather than disregard the ruling ideology as empty rhetoric, I focus on its importance in this process, showing how it operated as an interpretive system that both enabled and constrained people's comprehension of their society and their place within it.

The official ideology of the USSR was, of course, Marxism-Leninism, which took on very specific features under Stalin's attention (though it was never officially dubbed Marxism-Leninism-Stalinism). The 1936 Constitution declared the country "a socialist state of workers and peasants," conceiving of it as superior to and more purely democratic than capitalist states because it was based on the "social ownership" of the means of production en route to a "classless" society and because it eliminated economic and political repression—the "exploitation of man by man." However, there was a major fissure between ideology and practice in the Soviet system, between the lofty ideas of "socialism" and the corrupt, repressive, inefficient implementation of Stalinism. Determining whether "true" socialism is attainable or whether Soviet leaders themselves sincerely believed the theory is beyond the scope of this study, which emphasizes the concept because it formed the ideological boundaries for the way issues were interpreted and discussed. As we will see, the precepts of socialism (as the Stalinists understood them) shaped official definitions of such varied concepts as "the family," "care," "collaboration," "work," "speculation," "citizen," "corruption," etc.—terms laden with ideologically-determined meanings. Workers saw things differently, yet the ruling ideology shaped the parameters of their worldview as well. Illuminating the ideological context of the era against the backdrop of material conditions allows me to expose the gap between party ideology and conflicting representations of Soviet "reality" among workers and others.

State, Society, and Class in the Soviet Union

My examination of class relations in the USSR is not unlike a focus on "state" and "society," terms that are inherently amorphous, fluid, and imprecise.[23] In

---

[22] Peter Holquist, *Making War, Forging Revolution: Russia's Continuum of Crisis, 1914–1921* (Cambridge: Cambridge University Press, 2002), 6–7.

[23] On state and society, see Lynne Viola, "Introduction," in Viola, ed., *Contending with Stalinism: Soviet Power and Popular Resistance in the 1930s* (Ithaca, NY: Cornell University Press, 2002). On class in the early Soviet period, see Lewis H. Siegelbaum and

my configuration of the relationship between state and society, the state (mainly) governed on behalf of a ruling elite, the highest level party leadership or *nomenklatura*, while the key segment of urban society was the working class, on whose behalf the state claimed to rule. I see the underlying conflict of interests between the ruling elite and the working class as the most important social relationship of reconstruction (and of the Soviet era more generally), but I am not suggesting that the state is *equivalent to* the ruling elite nor that society is the *same as* the working class. Clearly the state is greater than *just* the ruling elite and society is greater than *just* the working class. Also, "state" and "society" overlap; white-collar workers employed by the state— *sluzhashchie* in Soviet parlance—are an important part of the postwar "middle class," who, along with elements of the intelligentsia and a labor aristocracy, strike a deal with the ruling elite.[24] Scholars note that the Soviet state and its ideology skewed "class" as a category; the regime constructed "the working class" to fit its own needs and purposes and thus the concept did not accurately reflect the reality of social or productive relations.[25] I agree, but I see this acknowledgement as the *beginning* of our discussion of class in Soviet society. Beneath the official definition of "the Soviet working class," for which the party considered itself a "vanguard," many people went to work in factories from day to day. My concern is for how they saw the world around them and their role and position therein, as well as for how they were depicted in state propaganda and perceived by local party leaders (those who went to work in offices from day to day).[26]

Ronald Grigor Suny, eds., *Making Workers Soviet: Power, Class, and Identity* (Ithaca, NY: Cornell University Press, 1994).

[24] On this point, see Vera Dunham, *In Stalin's Time: Middleclass Values in Soviet Fiction* (Durham, NC: Duke University Press, 1990). On the role of white-collar workers, defined as office workers, bookkeepers, typists, or higher specialists, in the early Soviet period, see Daniel Orlovsky, "The Hidden Class: White-Collar Workers in the Soviet 1920s," in Siegelbaum and Suny, *Making Workers Soviet*, 220–52.

[25] See, for example, Sheila Fitzpatrick, "Ascribing Class: The Construction of Social Identity in Soviet Russia," *Journal of Modern History* 65: 4 (1993): 745–70; and idem, *Everyday Stalinism*, 11.

[26] My understanding of class stresses the dialectical interaction between economics and cultural values, between the material and ideological elements of existence. I see class not as a purely economic category, nor as a solely linguistic construct, but as the meeting point between the material world and ways of comprehending it, between socioeconomic relations and the ways people consciously express their perceptions of those relations. If, as is often alleged, traditional Marxism defines class strictly by economic function, I see it as one's comprehension of everyday life—expressed through language, which Pierre Bourdieu calls "practical consciousness" or "articulated consciousness"—in all its forms, a definition that allows for change in the consciousness of individuals moving up or down the social structure. Bourdieu, *Outline of a Theory of Practice* (Cambridge: Cambridge University Press, 1993). For an under-

In focusing on class I am not diminishing the importance of other identities, nor am I suggesting one-dimensional images of the "working class" and "party elite" (or "nomenklatura"). Gender differences were particularly significant in postwar Soviet society because of the dramatic demographic imbalance, with women in Rostov outnumbering men roughly 2.5 to 1 following demobilization. National identity was also important, especially with regard to relations between Russians and Jews. The line between classes, moreover, is always blurry, like that between state and society. Many members of the nomenklatura were from working-class or peasant backgrounds, so that a symbiotic relationship existed between these social groups.[27] As noted there was also a "middle class" comprised of segments of the population such as the intelligentsia, and a sizable peasantry as well. Official interpretations of Soviet society won support among *all* segments of the population, which is the primary function of a ruling ideology—to "manufacture consent."[28] There were "true believers" from a variety of social groups, while at the same time there were members of the ruling party who did not believe their own rhetoric. Yet despite its complexity, amorphous character, and fluidity, at any given moment a Soviet working class existed as a separate and identifiable entity in people's consciousness of everyday life. In that consciousness, moreover, workers were juxtaposed to a ruling elite associated with the Communist Party, which controlled culture, politics, and economics, as is apparent in the variety of sources examined here.[29]

History From "Above" and "Below"

I utilize several distinct source bases (the press, internal archival documents, memoirs, and interviews) to highlight the underlying class conflict of Soviet society and reveal how workers perceived everyday life differently from

---

standing of class similar to my own, see Koenker, *Republic of Labor*, especially pp. 6–10 but also chaps. 3, 6, 9, and 10; see also S. A. Smith, "Workers against Foremen in St. Petersburg, 1905–1917," in Siegelbaum and Suny, *Making Workers Soviet*, 113–37. Smith emphasizes the middle position between the material and the linguistic, noting the "importance of discourse in constituting class relations, while not subscribing to the extreme view that discourse alone constitutes real objects" (11, 136–37).

[27] See Milovan Djilas, *The New Class: An Analysis of the Communist System* (New York: Praeger, 1957). Thompson also emphasizes the "fluency" of class, arguing that it is not a rigid "structure" or "category," but, above all, "an *historical* phenomenon" (*Making of the English Working Class*, 9).

[28] See Michael Burawoy, *Manufacturing Consent: Changes in the Labor Process Under Monopoly Capitalism* (Chicago: University of Chicago Press, 1982); Edward S. Herman and Noam Chomsky, *Manufacturing Consent: The Political Economy of the Mass Media* (New York: Pantheon Books, 1988).

[29] I agree with Djilas that, while not identical to it, the party is the core or base of the ruling class (Djilas, *New Class*, 39).

those in power. Authentic voices in their own way, these sources give us representations and reflections of reality, but not reality itself. The views expressed in these texts overlap to a significant degree but deal with the complex issues of reconstruction in nuanced ways, stressing different themes and asking different kinds of questions. I read these varying materials as distinct bodies of opinion or layers of discourse in order to elucidate the operation of power and ideology and to underscore the differing (and often conflicting) class perceptions of Soviet "reconstruction."[30] I begin each chapter after the first one with an analysis of the party's public record, the local organ of the Communist Party press, *Molot* (Hammer)—the open voice of power and authority—because it is a key link in the prevailing class dialogue between those in power and those below in the social structure. Second, I examine the party's record of discussions behind closed doors obtainable through city party organization reports and the minutes of meetings, material that provides invaluable insight on how local party leaders perceived society.[31] Third, I read informant reports (*svodki*), memoirs, interviews, and lists of questions posed by workers and others at meetings with party agitators for a qualified glance at popular opinion.[32]

Of course, all sources are flawed and limited in serious ways. The press and internal party documents—including *svodki*—originate from a single "source lens," referring to the particular biases inherent in *any* source that shape the ways in which a text is read. All of these sources flow, in other words, through a Stalinist administrative filter.[33] The flaws of the press are obvious; newspaper accounts are composed with the conscious goal of swaying the opinions and/or mood of the public on issues of importance to the regime, as well as to "explain" party policies and address public grievances—to "manufacture consent." The Soviet press contextualized everyday life, imposed a structure of thinking even among nonbelievers, and defined the

---

[30] James C. Scott notes with regard to his study of Malay society, "When I confined the issue to class relations alone ... it seemed that the poor sang one tune when they were in the presence of the rich and another tune when they were among the poor. The rich too spoke one way to the poor and another among themselves." Scott, *Domination and the Arts of Resistance: Hidden Transcripts* (New Haven: Yale University Press, 1990), ix.

[31] A classic example of a work based on this type of source material is J. Arch Getty, *Origins of the Great Purges: The Soviet Communist Party Reconsidered, 1933–1938* (Cambridge: Cambridge University Press, 1985).

[32] Among the most valuable sources we have for getting at popular opinion, *svodki* are also among the most problematic. For works that rely mostly or in part on *svodki*, see, for example, Sarah Davies, *Popular Opinion in Stalin's Russia: Terror, Propaganda, and Dissent, 1934-1941* (Cambridge: Cambridge University Press, 1997); Zubkova, *Russia After the War*; and Fitzpatrick, *Everyday Stalinism*.

[33] On "source lens," see Viola, *Contending with Stalinism*, 2.

parameters of public (and to some degree private) discussion in society.[34] The closed party record recounting meetings and conferences by those in power is, of course, likewise limited in what it can reveal about Soviet "reality." Shaped and constrained by the ruling ideology, discussions among those in power were influenced by several factors, including who was talking to whom within a strictly hierarchical structure, as well as the prevailing political winds nationally and the omnipresent local political cliques and conflicts. Such variables aside, however, obviously what those within the power structure said to each other *behind closed doors* differed from what they said publicly to those outside the exclusive group, and my intent is to highlight and analyze those differences.[35]

I examine popular views through *svodki*, lists of questions posed by workers and others to party representatives, memoir accounts, and interviews, all of which are flawed sources. Memoirs and interviews are shaped by historical memory, which constructs the past through the filter of the present. There are also pitfalls with oral history, especially in the Soviet context: the shroud of silence that surrounded many events for so long; the randomness (and selectivity) of individual memories; and the fact that people's recollections are often contradictory.[36] *Svodki*, of course, are particularly controversial sources.[37] The

---

[34] As Jeffrey Brooks notes, *Thank You, Comrade Stalin! Soviet Public Culture from Revolution to Cold War* (Princeton, NJ: Princeton University Press, 2000), xiv. On the role of the press, see also Matthew Lenoe, *Agitation, Propaganda, and the "Stalinization" of the Soviet Press, 1922–1930* (Pittsburgh: Center for Russian and East European Studies, University Center for International Studies, University of Pittsburgh, 1998); and Peter Kenez, *The Birth of the Propaganda State: Soviet Methods of Mass Mobilization, 1917–1929* (Cambridge: Cambridge University Press, 1985).

[35] The party never represented more than a small percentage of the overall population. On party membership, see T. H. Rigby, *Communist Party Membership in the U.S.S.R., 1917–1967* (Princeton, NJ: Princeton University Press, 1968).

[36] On these points, see Catherine Merridale, *Night of Stone: Death and Memory in Twentieth-Century Russia* (New York: Viking, 2000), 325.

[37] On the origins of the *svodki* during World War I and their importance during the Civil War, see Peter Holquist, "Anti-Soviet *Svodki* From the Civil War: Surveillance as a Shared Feature of Russian Political Culture," *Russian Review* 56: 3 (1997): 445–50, and idem, "'Information Is the Alpha and Omega of Our Work': Bolshevik Surveillance in Its Pan-European Context," *Journal of Modern History* 69: 3 (1997): 415–50. As historians of France have long warned, secret police reports are "shaped by the intentions of the observer, not the observed." Elizabeth Fox-Genovese and Eugene D. Genovese, "The Political Crisis of Social History: A Marxian Perspective," *Journal of Social History* 10: 2 (1976): 211, cited in Viola, "Popular Resistance in the Stalinist 1930s," in *Contending with Stalinism*, 27. Viola raises this point elsewhere as well: Viola, "Kollektivizatsiia i Riazanskaia okrug 1929–1930 gg.," translated from English by Elena Osokina, in *Riazanskaia derevnia v 1929–1930 gg.: Khronika golovokruzheniia. Dokumenty i materialy*, ed. L. Viola et al. (Moscow: ROSSPEN, 1998), xlii.

district party secretaries who wrote and edited these reports on the "mood of the population" selected and prioritized items while offering their analysis of the opinions expressed by workers and others.[38] It is not inconceivable that some informants lied about what they heard or from whom, and the party scribes certainly could have doctored reports to promote their own political goals. Yet, despite the many undeniable problems with *svodki*, it would be foolish to ignore these invaluable sources, especially given that *all* historical sources are constructed and problematic in some way. I agree with Jochen Hellbeck that we must not "treat this source body as an *unmediated* window to popular belief," but if read properly svodki can tell us something about popular opinion in Stalinist society—the window, one might say, is half open.[39] Faced with the potential for conflict in the process of "reconstruction," Soviet authorities wanted to know the views of the populace.[40] The party clearly did not collect this information solely for punitive purposes, although those whose comments crossed "the line," i.e., criticized Stalin by name or denounced the Soviet system, were punished.[41] These cases were exceptions, however; the main goal or intent of the *svodki* was to gauge the public's "mood" on important matters, *not* to catch and punish dissenters. I recognize the inherent flaws of my sources and concede that they originate from a single "source lens." However, I contend that we can piece together an accurate portrait of "reconstruction" by utilizing a wide range of sources and treating them as qualitatively different "bodies of opinion," each of which should be read and dealt with on its own terms.

---

[38] The reports emphasized examples that deviated from consensual opinion and the topics covered in these reports were imposed from above, thereby limiting their value as a gauge of "true" public opinion. On these points, see Zubkova, *Russia After the War*, 7; and Davies, *Popular Opinion in Stalin's Russia*, 13.

[39] Jochen Hellbeck, "Fashioning the Stalinist Soul: The Diary of Stepan Podlubnyi (1931–1939)," *Jahrbücher für Geschichte Osteuropas* 44: 3 (1996): 344–73, here 344n2 (emphasis mine).

[40] Mary Leder, an informant in the 1930s and 1940s, records her contact for the Soviet secret police (NKVD) as saying, "We need this information to help us shape policy"; his comment, of course, should not be taken as a literal truth, but it seems likely that the regime *did* want to know the genuine reactions of the populace to its policies. Getty discusses the regime's use of *svodki* during the 1936 election campaigns, noting that "Moscow seems to have been vitally interested in public reaction to the constitution." J. Arch Getty, "State and Society Under Stalin: Constitutions and Elections in the 1930s," *Slavic Review* 50: 1 (Spring 1991): 23.

[41] Several of the harsher criticisms were followed by the dire phrase "this information was passed on to the appropriate organs." See, for example, TsDNI f. 13, op. 4, d. 335, ll. 172–173; TsDNI f. 13, op. 4, d. 415, l. 73; TsDNI f. 13, op. 4, d. 343, ll. 109–110; TsDNI f. 13, op. 4, d. 214, l. 168; TsDNI f. 13, op. 4, d. 253, l. 69; TsDNI f. 13, op. 4, d. 259, ll. 25, 43, 75, and 128; and TsDNI f. 13, op. 4, d. 343, l. 10.

We only recently gained access to the *svodki*, but a number of scholars have used them effectively, including several identified above.[42] Lynne Viola sees the strength of the *svodki* as their "spatial and synchronic proximity (*especially lower down the regional hierarchy*) to the scene of action."[43] Thus the closer one is to the original, *least* edited version, as is the case for this study, the better—another good reason for working in regional as well as central archives. Also, similar opinions are recorded repeatedly (sometimes many times over) in the *svodki* and attributed to different speakers, adding weight to their legitimacy as beliefs held by the public. People making negative comments took some risk in doing so, which is why such statements seem like isolated, minority opinions. A lot of people might have held similar views, but few would have said so beyond a small trusted circle of family and friends. It is in the interests of those drawing up these reports, moreover, to portray criticism as rare and uncommon since part of their job is to "explain" party policy to workers and others in order to secure their support. In any case, a plethora of often *very* negative comments were recorded (as will become apparent in the chapters that follow), which shows that people did not always present themselves in a conformist way. There were many conformists; the *svodki* always begin with *positive* comments—invariably described as "the majority view"—that sound a lot like the party press. However, the scribes also recorded many harsh criticisms of the regime and its policies, and, as Lesley Rimmel notes, "the earthy, realistic, informal, and often unprintable language of the negative statements lends them an air of believability."[44] Balanced with the lists of questions and comments made by workers and others at meetings with party representatives, as well as with memoirs and interviews, *svodki* can tell us a great deal about popular opinion in the Soviet Union during "reconstruction."[45]

This book examines several slices of daily life during reconstruction from different angles—the workplace, the market, the polling booth, etc.—which allows me to highlight the underlying, ideologically-driven assumptions of those in power and contrast them with the often conflicting worldviews of workers and others. The first chapter provides background on Rostov and looks at the effects of the war and occupation on the city. Chapter 2 analyzes

---

[42] Davies, *Popular Opinion in Stalin's Russia*; and Zubkova, *Russia After the War*. Fitzpatrick also makes use of *svodki* in *Everyday Stalinism*.

[43] Viola, "Popular Resistance in the Stalinist 1930s," 29 (emphasis mine). For a similar point, see also Tracy MacDonald, "A Peasant Rebellion in Stalin's Russia: The Pitelinskii Uprising, Riazan, 1930," in Viola, *Contending With Stalinism*, 84–108.

[44] Lesley A. Rimmel, "Svodki and Popular Opinion in Stalinist Leningrad," in *Cahiers du Monde russe* 40 (1999): 222.

[45] I agree with Rimmel that one should "emphasize the importance of using a wide variety of sources in order to show the scope of responses to the policies of the Stalin government" (Rimmel, "Svodki and Popular Opinion," 221).

the varying perceptions and representations of material conditions, revealing how some people disagreed with the explanations the party gave for the postwar famine. Chapter 3 examines the "myth of reconstruction," exposing how the highly exploitative nature of productive relations at the factory level belied state officials' claims that they governed in workers' interests. Chapter 4 focuses on gender and nationality, illuminating how official rhetoric of the Soviet "family" masked serious rifts and divisions within society. Chapter 5 looks at the alleged traitors of Soviet society, showing that the regime applied concepts like "collaboration" very broadly and filtered social discontent in that direction, constructing one of a number of scapegoats or internal "others." Chapter 6 considers "speculation," the illegal economy, a widespread and systemic problem with which leaders dealt by demonizing individual speculators. Chapter 7 scrutinizes a series of postwar elections, portraying an active (though sometimes reluctant) electorate while revealing dissatisfaction with party rule. Chapter 8 examines the problems plaguing the local party organization, including widespread corruption, showing that while many workers revered Stalin, many also defined their own interests differently from those of local leaders. The material in these chapters reveals the differing perspectives of reconstruction locally within a national and international context, illuminating our understanding of Stalinism at a crucial juncture in Soviet history.

Chapter One

"Everything has to be rebuilt from scratch in this country, starting with our own Rostov": The Impact of the Great Fatherland War

Before looking at "reconstruction" we should examine what was being reconstructed—what was there before the devastation of the war swept much of it away. No country suffered more than the Soviet Union, especially the occupied territories. The desolation and poverty wrought by the war made a strong impression on N. S. Patolichev, who took over as First Secretary of the Rostov obkom in 1947. He recalls how he felt one year after victory: "Already several peaceful months were behind us, but you were still reminded of the war with every step. A lot of families in cities destroyed during the war still lived in mud huts, while many mothers and wives were still waiting for their sons and husbands to return from the front." Not enough time had elapsed since the end of the war, he adds, and "the war's impact was still too strong."[1] Former Soviet leader Mikhail Gorbachev remembers traveling between his southern home in Stavropol *krai* (territory) and Moscow, visiting Rostov, Kharkov, Voronezh, Orel, and Kursk along the way. He saw "ruins everywhere, deep scars left by the war."[2] Mary Leder likewise tells us that "life was hard at this time in the Soviet Union, especially in the war-ravaged towns and villages to which demobilized soldiers were returning throughout 1945 and 1946."[3] Justifying his decision to become a public works engineer after victory, in 1944 Karol's friend Kolia said, "Everything has to be rebuilt from scratch in this country, starting with our own Rostov."[4] Clearly the material devastation of the city was plain for all to see (and live), as was the dramatic demographic impact of the war.

This chapter describes Rostov and, relying mainly on memoirs, traces its history to the Great Fatherland War, depicting the harsh impact of the war on the city. Founded on the Don River in 1749 as a customs point on the site of a fortress built to ensure safe passage of Russian wares through Cossack country, by 1940 Rostov-on-Don had evolved into a major urban center in south-

---

[1] N. S. Patolichev, *Ispytanie na zrelost'* (Moscow: Politizdat, 1977), 285.

[2] Mikhail S. Gorbachev, *Memoirs* (London: Doubleday, 1996), 39.

[3] Leder, *My Life in Stalinist Russia*, 279.

[4] Karol, *Solik*, 263.

ern Russia. Of course, Rostov had known hard times prior to the outbreak of World War II: as elsewhere in the Russian Empire there were severe pogroms against the city's Jewish population in the waning weeks of the 1905 Revolution.[5] A decade later World War I, two revolutions, Civil War, and famine (1914–21) took a *very* heavy toll in the lower Don and especially on the local Cossack population because the White Army based its operations there and garnered some support among Cossacks. Several issues in the forefront of the Civil War era such as anti-Semitism, famine, a breakdown of rule and authority, extreme poverty endured by the population, etc., were apparent during and after the Second World War as well. The Stalinist purges (1936–39) also had a significant impact on Rostov's population and, coming as they did so close to the outbreak of the war, are highly relevant to our discussion of the 1940s, so I deal with that difficult era here in some detail as well.

Rostov-on-Don

Located along the steppe, Rostov, like many Soviet cities, was an interesting mix of old and new. The oldest part of the city grew up along the right side of the Don as it winds south toward the Sea of Azov, across from an island in the river. The city's streets ascend up from the river—parallel and perpendicular to it—the first ones built far enough from the shore to avoid flooding (which nonetheless was a periodic problem in Rostov). In 1834 Rostov's port opened, spurring steady economic growth and development over the remainder of the century and beyond. The city became a major site for exporting grain through the Black Sea and a significant industrial center. Entrepreneurs built Rostov's first factories in the mid-19th century, including the first iron-casting factory in 1846, the first textile factory seven years later, and in 1857 the Asmolov Tobacco Factory. As elsewhere in Russia, over the course of the next century, under both tsarist and Soviet suzerainty, peasants moved from the surrounding countryside to work in Rostov. As its population grew, the city became home to numerous plants producing iron, metals, machine tools, tractors, combines and other farm machinery, ships and maritime equipment, as well as shoes, dishes, beer, leather goods, and other consumer items. Its thriving port employed numerous dockworkers, and the city became *the* vital hub in southern Russia's railway network after its construction in the 1880s,

---

[5] The pogroms occurred in October. Mariia S. Zhak was born in 1901 and says that the pogroms were the first real clear memory from her early childhood. Interview by author, 3 June 1995. On pogroms in Russia between 1903 and 1906, see John D. Klier and Shlomo Lambroza, *Pogroms: Anti-Jewish Violence in Modern Russian History* (Cambridge: Cambridge University Press, 1992); and Charters Wynn, *Workers, Strikes and Pogrom: The Donbas-Dnieper Bend in Late Imperial Russia, 1870–1905* (Princeton, NJ: Princeton University Press, 1992).

providing another major source of employment.[6] In 1941 there were seven districts in Rostov: Stalinskii, Zheleznodorozhnii, Andreevskii, Kirovskii, Leninskii, Proletarskii, and Oktiabrskii.

In the late 19th century Rostov was the fifth-largest city within the boundaries of present-day Russia; by the turn of the century, it had nearly 140 factories employing an estimated 14,500 workers, most of whom inhabited tenements near their factories and endured difficult living and working conditions. The city became a center of working-class agitation in 1902, when Vladimir Lenin highlighted a railway strike in Rostov as a key turning point for the country because it was the first major strike to raise political as well as economic demands.[7] By the eve of World War I Rostov was one of the empire's largest and most vibrant cities with a population of nearly 230,000 in 1915, making it the eighth-largest urban center in the Russian Empire.[8] W. W. Krysko was born in Rostov near the end of the first decade of the 20th century, and he remembers it as an "expanding metropolis" and "an exceptionally vibrant place in which to live, work, and grow up."[9] The city, Krysko writes, was "fast losing the appearance and atmosphere of an outpost of empire by reason of a spate of building and reconstruction which had completely transformed Rostov" in a decade. "Most of the old town," he elaborates, "had disappeared in the building boom, along with the customs and traditions of an earlier era."

Rostov in the early 20th century was caught between the forces of tradition and modernity, with the latter clearly winning out. Industry and commerce in the town flourished, Krysko notes, with new buildings "continually going up along the main street, Sadovaya"; at the same time, however, "camel caravans laden with tea from China and Mongolia would come into the city, winding their way wearily along the streets after the long journey across the steppes." Krysko also remembers that the town had a reputation for lawlessness because "as a port it attracted many nefarious characters." When someone said he was a native of Rostov-on-Don a fellow Russian would invariably reply "Ah! *Rostovsky zhulik!*" [Rostov thief]," associating the city with crime, which, as we will see, remained a major problem during reconstruction as well. Krysko recalls a joke that a taxi driver in Riga told him:

---

[6] Rostov was the administrative center of the North Caucasus Railroad Department. See J. N. Westwood, *A History of Russian Railways* (London: G. Allen and Unwin, 1964).

[7] See Wynn, *Workers, Strikes and Pogrom*, 167n3; V. I. Lenin, *Collected Works* (Moscow: Progress Publishers, 1964), 6: 278–83; and Henry Reichman, "The Rostov General Strike of 1902," *Russian History* 9: 1 (1982): 1. For the number of factories and workers, see "Rostov Region" in *Kommersant: Russia's First Independent Media Holding Online* at www.kommersant.com/tree.asp?rubric=5&node=408&doc_id=-64 (accessed April 2007).

[8] Holquist, *Making War, Forging Revolution*, 9.

[9] W. W. Krysko, *Witness to the Birth of Political Anti-Judaism* (New York: Vantage Press, 1999), 1.

A man just like you left Rostov many years ago. He returned for a visit and coming out of the railway station with his luggage, put his bags on the ground and threw up his hands in delight on seeing the city again. "Rostov my home town, how beautiful you have become! The new houses, the lovely trees, the wonderful gardens! I don't recognize you at all." Lowering his hands to pick up his bags he was amazed to find they had been stolen. "Ah, my Rostov," he said sadly, "now I recognize you."[10]

Rostov in the early 20th century was growing rapidly, which included both positive and negative consequences.

Rostov had a very heterogeneous population, as Krysko attests, recalling that along with Russians there were Jews, Greeks, Tartars, Armenians, Georgians, "tribal minorities from the Caucasus, and a large band of Don Cossacks, which altogether made a very rich ethnic mix."[11] In 1780 an Armenian commercial suburb, Nakhichevan', sprang up next to the city, and the two merged in 1928, giving Rostov a significant Armenian minority. In the 19th century a number of Jews settled in the city, when it was still part of the Pale of Settlement, the area of the Russian Empire where Jews were allowed to openly live. However, in 1888 Tsar Alexander III incorporated Rostov and the nearby city of Taganrog along the Sea of Azov as part of the military district of the Don Territory,[12] as a result of which many Jews were expelled from the region, though some remained, especially in urban areas like Rostov (their status, however, was tenuous at best under tsars Alexander III and Nicholas II). While Rostov-on-Don was ethnically mixed, the Don Territory of which it became a part was defined mostly by the Cossacks, frontiersmen who, fleeing serfdom, settled the area beginning in the 15th century.[13] The estimated population of the Don Territory in 1897 was 2,585,920, roughly half of whom were Cossacks. In 1906 the estimated population for the territory as a whole was 3,125,400, which reached nearly four million in 1914, by which time the Cossacks comprised only 39 percent of the population as a whole.[14] In the city of Rostov, which was located in the far south of the Don Territory, the propor-

---

[10] Krysko, *Witness*, 1–2.

[11] Ibid., 1.

[12] The Don Territory bordered Kuban Territory and Stavropol Province to the south, Astrakhan and Saratov provinces to the east, Voronezh Province to the northwest, and Kharkov and Ekaterinoslav provinces to the west.

[13] Cherkassk (now Starocherkassk), the capital of the Don Cossacks until 1805, sits on an island several kilometers upstream from Rostov-on-Don. Novocherkassk, the Cossack capital thereafter, is also situated near Rostov. On the Don Cossacks, see Shane O'Rourke, *Warriors and Peasants: The Don Cossacks in Late Imperial Russia* (New York: St. Martin's Press, 2000).

[14] Holquist, *Making War, Forging Revolution*, 8.

tion of Don Cossacks was smaller than for the territory as a whole throughout this period. The 1897 figure for the entire Don Territory includes about 27,000 Armenians, most of whom resided in Nakhichevan', and about 16,000 Jews, a significant portion of whom lived in Rostov, so the ethnic composition of the city itself did not reflect that of the surrounding territory.[15]

Krysko had a turbulent childhood, witnessing at a young age in Rostov World War I (1914–17), two revolutions (1917), and civil war (1918–21). As a child he followed these events partly through the changing posters in the city's streets. During World War I, tsarist authorities decorated Rostov with "brightly colored posters" showing a Don Cossack on horseback with the words "KUSMA KRYUTSHKOFF POBEDITEL (The Victorious Kusma Kryutshkoff), which everyone understood, even illiterates like me."[16] During the Civil War Rostov changed hands numerous times; the White Army forces of General Aleksei Kaledin pushed the city's Bolshevik party administration out of the city in December 1917, but the Reds returned triumphantly in late February 1918.[17] Krysko recollects the communists' posters in the streets of Rostov, including one depicting a fat man wearing a gold watch across his huge belly while seated on the backs of poor peasants and workers. "This sort of propaganda touched the primitive feelings of the people even more than the earlier patriotic posters," he relays, adding that communist posters' "direct messages with their well-drawn, uncluttered graphics appealed to all classes of society, even well-to-do folk."[18] Peace in the east came with the signing of the Treaty of Brest-Litovsk in March, and in early April German troops marched into Rostov in accordance with the pact, bringing with them, according to Krysko, a sense of law and order, which the city desperately needed amid chaotic times. The first dead man the youngster saw was a German soldier hanged by his own commander for robbing civilians.[19] After Germany sued for peace with the Western allies in November, their troops withdrew and the city became engulfed by the civil war. Krysko recalls that, after losing a battle to the Reds, a White Army force of Kuban Cossacks retreated through the city and senselessly massacred people for no apparent

---

[15] "Territory of the Don Cossacks," *LoveToKnow 1911 Online Encyclopedia,* © 2003, 2004 LoveToKnow, http://56.1911encyclopedia.org/D/DO/DON_COSSACKS_TERRITORY_OF_THE. htm (accessed April 2007).

[16] Krysko, *Witness,* 33. "What I failed to realize," he adds, "was that the posters were designed to arouse my patriotic feelings."

[17] See Peter Kenez, *Civil War in South Russia, 1919–1920: The Defeat of the Whites* (Berkeley: University of California Press, 1977).

[18] Krysko, *Witness,* 54. He also remembers posters making fun of church figures and highlighting corruption in the church.

[19] Ibid., 52.

reason. "It was an appalling scene for me to have witnessed at such an early age."[20]

Krysko's account conveys the uncertainties of this period in Rostov, when, he states, for a brief time even British troops occupied it on behalf of the Whites.[21] He remembers that they brought a strange contraption onto the city's streets: an early type of tank.[22] "In Rostov," Krysko writes, "it was never known from one day to another who, if anyone, was going to be in charge." He and his friends would listen in the streets for the words used by those with guns to find out who was ruling the city for the day: *tovarishchi* (comrades) meant it was the Reds; *rebiata* (mates) meant it was the Whites; and *patsani* (boys) meant it was Ukrainian bandits.[23] Krysko recounts numerous instances of attacks against Jews in Rostov, which obviously becomes an important issue during World War II as well. In the Odessa area, an anarchist group led by a bandit, Nestor Makhno (dubbed the "Makhnovtsi"), "became the scourge and terror of the Jewish population" throughout the region.[24] They made their way to Rostov, taking advantage of the chaotic situation and vacuum of power in the city. While in Rostov, the Makhnovtsi engaged in what they called "cleaning up operations," which meant rounding up as "many Jews or Jewish-looking people as they could find" and publicly hanging them in a gruesome manner:

> They made a number of loops in a rope and each loop was thrown loosely around a man's neck. The rope was then suspended between posts. As the loops tightened, the victims began struggling and trying to save themselves by clinging to the next man on the rope but this only prolonged their agony. The Makhnovtsi sat back and enjoyed the spectacle while they drank and laughed.[25]

Fortunately the group's stay in Rostov was brief, but then another bandit group, the "wolves," moved into the city. They "felt it a duty to rid Russia of its Jewish population," Krysko adds, but they mainly concentrated on robbing the city's wealthier inhabitants.

---

[20] Ibid., 55.

[21] For the account of an American pilot serving in the British Royal Air Force in southern Russia in 1919, see Marion Aten and Arthur Orrmont, *Last Train Over Rostov Bridge* (New York: Messner, 1961).

[22] Krysko, *Witness*, 59.

[23] Ibid., 60–61. "Only after they had received our news would my parents and their friends venture out of doors," he adds, "feeling a little less uneasy about how to act and speak in that day's political climate."

[24] Ibid., 50, 57.

[25] Ibid., 61–62. The Makhnovtsi called this brutal technique "drying the herrings"; they would make bets as to how long it would take the last victim to die.

The Whites also stirred up anti-Semitism, associating the Bolsheviks with a Jewish conspiracy—a common tactic and stubborn association, as we will see—because some of the party's leaders were Jews. "The Whites had their own propaganda posters, their own catch phrases and their own songs," he states, "all of which equated Judaism with the Bolsheviks and blamed all of Russia's misfortunes on the Jews." Several of the Whites' songs, he says, actually incited the murder of Jews, including "Kill the Jews! Save Russia! They have already sold Russia!" Another song proclaimed: "Bravely we go into battle; For Russia and our Faith; And we will kill all Jews; Such vermin!"[26] Krysko remembers a circus skit in Rostov in early 1920, near the end of the Whites' occupation of the city. They placed a chair in the middle of the ring to symbolize a throne with a clown dressed as a tsar seated on it. A group of "peasants" entered from one side and a group of "workers" from the other and "removed" the tsar. But while the workers and peasants argued over who would occupy the empty seat of power, a clown dressed as a rabbi crept from behind it, hit them all on the head, and sat himself on the "throne." Krysko, who was ten or eleven at the time, remembers being amused and not consciously aware of the anti-Semitic aspects of the skit until he thought about it years later.[27] Mariia Zhak, 16 years old at the time of the revolutions in 1917, was not politically active at the time, but, as a Jew, she supported the Reds more than the Whites because of the latter's vicious (and well-known) anti-Semitism. Looking back on the era from the mid-1990s, she states that she and many others saw the Reds as the "lesser of two evils."[28] The Reds, of course, prevailed, with Commander S. M. Budenny marching triumphantly into Rostov in January 1920, thereby earning (eventually) a main thoroughfare in his name.

The fighting ended, but the horrors did not subside. Krysko vividly remembers the famine that began in the summer of 1920 when thousands of "the starving from the Volga," as his father called them, began streaming into Rostov. "When people from other regions also started moving in," he adds, "it became difficult to see how all these starving millions were going to be fed."[29] Epidemics of cholera and typhoid soon broke out in the severely overcrowded city where so many were weak from starvation. By autumn "conditions in Rostov had deteriorated rapidly" and "food stocks had disappeared altogether from the shops." Money lost all value as prices soared to "astronomical heights" and a "flourishing black market" based on barter devel-

---

[26] Ibid., 62 and 68.

[27] Ibid., 68–69. He also recalls people saying that "the Revolution had been founded on 'Jewish tongues and Latvian bayonets.'"

[28] Interview by author, 3 June 1995.

[29] Krysko, *Witness*, 87. For a gripping account of the famine on the Volga, see Orlando Figes, *Peasant Russia, Civil War: The Volga Countryside in Revolution, 1917–1921* (Oxford: Clarendon Press, 1989).

oped, which, as we will see, also happened during World War II. Krysko attributes the famine to the devastation of many crops due to the fighting, the fact that other fields lay fallow because there were not enough laborers in the countryside, the fact that both armies seized grain almost at will during the war, and, finally, because the retreating, defeated Whites scorched fields out of vengeance and bitterness. He also says that during the worst of the inflationary spiral "one simple doughnut suddenly cost four million rubles."[30] One had to be careful what kind of meat one bought at the market: "a butcher was arrested after some children's bones had been found on his premises." Krysko claims that the authorities publicly executed him without a trial. The author recalls one gruesome episode when his father traded some tools for a *kholodets*, "a jellied meat dish made usually made from veal with chopped pigs' ears to make it crunchy." While eating it his father found the tiny fingernail of a child sticking to a small bone. "We were horrified," he says, "but nevertheless finished the meal as there was no point now in rejecting the nourishment."[31]

Despite the problems in the city, "hordes of starving people" descended upon Rostov. "Those who had struggled" to get there, he conveys, "were nearly dead by the time they reached [the city], mere skeletons, longing for their lives to end." Krysko recounts pitched battles in Bataisk, a village near Rostov, as starving people sought to seize the food supplies of wealthy peasants, or *kulaks*, who, he says, were hoarding food. Both sides were armed because of the abundance of weapons and ammunition left behind by the various armies that came and went during the Civil War. Krysko saw *many* dead bodies in Rostov in 1920–21; the victims of disease, he elaborates, looked different from the victims of starvation, both of which died in large numbers along the roadside. The elderly and very young were most susceptible, and Krysko lost his grandfather and two grandmothers during the famine. When spring came and the snow began to melt in 1921, thousands of corpses and skeletons appeared in the fields around Rostov, dumped there because no grave diggers could be found. Groups of homeless children (*bezprizornye*) roamed the city stealing and robbing to survive, which became a major problem again in the 1940s as we will see.[32]

During the civil war, Cossacks tended to oppose the communist forces that eventually formed the Soviet state, although the Don Cossacks were less

---

[30] Krysko, *Witness*, 91–92.

[31] Ibid., 93.

[32] Ibid., 94 and 98. He left Rostov with his mother, a German citizen, and brother in 1921, because the new rights given women allowed his mother to "divorce" his father and repatriate to Germany. The family was reunited a couple of years later when his father escaped to Germany.

committed to the White cause than their brethren from the Kuban.[33] One of
the leaders of the Whites, General A. I. Denikin, made the lower Don his base
of operations against the new communist government led by Lenin and the
Bolsheviks. Thus the Reds viewed Cossacks as a pro-tsarist counterrevolutionary element that should be exterminated, despite the fact that some
Cossacks supported the Bolsheviks. This led to a brutal policy of "de-
Cossackization" by the Reds, who executed thousands in early 1920 before
rebellions forced them to moderate their policies.[34] Soviet attitudes toward
the Cossacks did not soften with time. K. S. Karol asserts that Cossacks subsequently suffered disproportionately during the purges of the late 1930s due
to their history of opposition to Bolshevik rule.[35] One could argue that the
region's strong Cossack influence perhaps made Rostov a more fertile breed-
ing ground for anti-Soviet sentiment during and after World War II than
other areas of the country. Yet we should not exaggerate this point since the
Cossack population in the region had been decimated by the eve of World
War II, while Rostov-on-Don itself had always been more Russian than Cossack and was a very ethnically-mixed city. Moreover, opinions expressed by
Rostovians during the war and postwar years do not differ greatly from those
noted elsewhere in the country in that and earlier periods.[36]

After the civil war and the imposition of Soviet control in the region,
Rostov-on-Don became a key industrial city in southern Russia. It also served
as the administrative center for Rostov oblast (or province), which, since its
formation in 1937, has been a major agricultural producer and supplier of
coal, making the region's role in the national economy crucial.[37] The most
important enterprise in Rostov before and after the war is *Rostsel'mash*, an
enormous producer of farm machinery constructed during the First Five-Year

---

[33] A classic account of the civil war years among the Don Cossacks is Mikhail Sholokhov's *Quiet Flows the Don*, trans. Robert Daglish, ed. Brian Murphy (New York: Carroll and Graf Publishers, 1996). On the Cossacks' pro-tsarist tendencies, see also Valentina Bogdan, *Mimikriia v SSSR: Vospominaniia inzhenera 1935–1942 gody* (Frankfurt:
Polyglott-Druck, 1981), 45.

[34] Holquist, *Making War, Forging Revolution*, 166–202. Shane O'Rourke notes that, for
the Soviet regime, "there was a specific hostility towards the Cossacks for their role in
the Civil War," and that "the long campaigns against the Cossacks during the Civil
War entrenched a particular hostility to the Cossacks by the new Soviet state"
(*Warriors and Peasants*, 13–14).

[35] Karol, *Solik*, 6.

[36] See, for example, Sheila Fitzpatrick, *Stalin's Peasants: Resistance and Survival in the
Russian Village after Collectivization* (Oxford: Oxford University Press, 1994), and *Everyday Stalinism*; Davies, *Popular Opinion in Stalin's Russia*; Lesley Rimmel, "Another Kind
of Fear: The Kirov Murder and the End of Bread Rationing in Leningrad," *Slavic
Review* 56: 3 (1997): 481–99; and Zubkova, *Obshchestvo i reformy*.

[37] Rostov-on-Don was administrative center for the Azov-Black Sea *krai* (territory)
until 1937, when the territory was broken up and Rostov oblast was formed.

Plan (1928–32). Thousands of young people came to Rostov from all over the USSR in the 1930s to work at *Rostsel'mash*. On the eve of World War II the plant employed 17,000 workers and produced over half of the Soviet Union's agricultural equipment. *Krasnyi Aksai*, a major producer of agricultural equipment initially built in pre-Soviet days and rebuilt in the 1920s, employed a workforce of 5,000 in 1940, while Factory No. 168, Rostov's most prominent machine-tools plant transferred to military production during the war, also employed several thousand workers. The major light industry plants included the Mikoyan Shoe Factory, Factory No. 359 (*Emal'posud*), an enamel goods and kitchenware manufacturer converted to military production during the war, the cigarette factory Don State Tobacco Plant (*Donskaia Gosudarstvennaia Tabachnaia Fabrika*),[38] the beer factory Daybreak (*Zaria*), a champagne factory, meat-packing plant, several bread factories, and three leather goods' plants, *Kozhazavodi* Nos. 1–3.

As a vibrant and expanding Soviet urban center, Rostov had a diverse population made up of more than just factory workers. There were service and clerical workers, "white-collar" employees (office workers, typists, and lower-level administrators), members of the intelligentsia, as well as a relatively small number of nomenclatura or high party officials. Also, as noted, the city's population was not homogenous; ethnic and gender differences were significant (though a disproportionate number of those in leadership circles were ethnic Russian and male). The city's Jewish population increased in the Soviet period after the abolishment of the Pale of Settlement. Peter Seraphim offers a "rough approximation based on 1926 data," putting the number of Jews in the city at 40,000, or a little over 13 percent of the overall population of around 528,000.[39] During occupation the Germans estimated that until November 1941 there had been about 50,000 Jews in Rostov.[40] There was, as noted, a significant Armenian presence in the city as well; Nakhichevan' had a population of around 20,000 Armenians by 1914 (although, by that time, 60 percent of Nakhichevan''s population was non-Armenian). Separate Armenian schools operated until their closure in 1940.[41]

As elsewhere in the Soviet Union, the late 1930s was a time of tremendous upheaval due to the purges, which took a devastating toll in the Don region. Roy Medvedev indicates that the NKVD arrested thousands of party members and non-party engineers and economic managers in the Rostov

---

[38] Formerly the Asmolov Tobacco Factory; hereafter DGTF.

[39] Peter-Heinz Seraphim, *Das Judentum im osteuropäishcen Raum* (Essen: Essener Verlagsanstalt, 1939), 716–18, cited in Raul Hilberg, *The Destruction of the European Jews*, 3rd ed. (New Haven: Yale University Press, 2003), 1: 296.

[40] See Arad et al., *The Einsatzgruppen Reports*, 358.

[41] "Armiane na Donu," http://www.melkonchaltr.narod.ru/chaltr.htm (accessed April 2007).

region and replaced them with inexperienced workers.[42] The repression of the late 1930s hit the area and the Cossack population hard.[43] Of course, Cossacks were not the only victims of the purges in Rostov, which decimated the local party leadership. The Rostov branch of the secret police (NKVD) arrested a band of "counterrevolutionary Trotskyites" in autumn 1936, and in January 1937 Moscow removed the regional party leader of the previous five years, B. P. Sheboldaev, due to a "lack of vigilance" in uncovering the evil deeds of the Trotskyites in his midst. The alleged Trotskyites included G. F. Ovchinnikov, chairman of the city soviet, N. P. Glebov-Avilov, director of Rostsel'mash, L. D. Gogoberidze, secretary of the party committee at Rostsel'mash, and numerous others. Sheboldaev admitted fault and so was not immediately purged. By the end of the year, however, he too had been arrested and shot. Moscow dispatched central leader A. A. Andreev to read the pronouncement removing Sheboldaev from power in January 1937. Andreev noted that the lack of vigilance shown by Sheboldaev is particularly troubling given that the Don region "is inhabited by Cossacks and therefore demands special attention, special attention on the part of the political leadership, and this should have put you in a state of ultra-Bolshevik vigilance, but this was not so."[44]

Rank-and-file members also fell victim; arrests were so widespread that some enterprises in Rostov lost their entire party organization. In October 1937 the Central Committee sent Mikhail A. Suslov, an up-and-coming party leader who would later emerge as a key figure and member of the Politburo, to Rostov to help sort out the problems there. Medvedev states that, whereas many blame Suslov for the harshness of the purges in Rostov, there is little evidence to elucidate his role. The party leadership in Rostov had already been destroyed before Suslov's arrival, Medvedev points out, but the

---

[42] Roy Medvedev, *All Stalin's Men*, trans. Harold Shukman (New York: Blackwell, 1984), 67.

[43] Aleksandr Solzhenitsyn claims that Rostov's secret police had a particularly nasty reputation for torturing prisoners during the purges, but cautions that there is no proof to support this oft-heard claim. Solzhenitsyn, *Gulag Archipelago*, 2 vols., trans. Thomas P. Whitney (New York: Harper and Row, 1974), 103. Victor Kravchenko describes a form of torture in Rostov which involved hitting people in the stomach repeatedly with a sandbag. Kravchenko, *I Chose Justice* (London: Scribner's, 1951), 252–54, cited in Robert Conquest, *The Great Terror: Stalin's Purge of the 1930s* (New York: Collier Books, 1968), 136. As noted above, K. S. Karol asserts that the purges were worse in the lower Don because of the region's Cossack influence and support for the Whites during the civil war, although he presents no evidence to support this view. Karol, *Solik*, 6.

[44] For documents pertaining to Sheboldaev's case and the turnover of leadership in Rostov, see J. Arch Getty and Oleg Naumov, *The Road to Terror: Stalin and the Self-Destruction of the Bolsheviks, 1932–39* (New Haven: Yale University Press, 1999), 331–52, esp. 339.

repression also continued while he was there.[45] Suslov was in Rostov in June 1938 when the local paper reported that "a Rightist-Trotskyite counterrevolutionary organization" had once again infested the top echelons of power in the oblast.[46] Among them was the man who had recently replaced Sheboldaev as obkom First Secretary, E. G. Evdokimov, although his arrest was not announced publicly. Evdokimov had worked his way up through the NKVD apparatus and was a protégée of its (soon-to-fall), head, N. I. Ezhov.[47] It seems likely that Suslov played a role in the change of leadership that led to the rise of Boris A. Dvinskii, who remained in charge for seven years. Suslov himself later claimed that, far from destroying the Rostov Party organization, he rebuilt it by readmitting two thousand members who had been wrongfully accused of being spies, traitors, Trotskyists, etc., and by recruiting some three thousand new members.[48]

In her 1981 memoir intended for an émigré audience in Europe, Valentina Bogdan, an engineer at a macaroni factory in Rostov in the late 1930s, says that Sheboldaev and Evdokimov were victims of "a wave of arrests" at the time. In each case, shortly after they were arrested their friends and colleagues were as well, including, she notes, the director of Rostsel'mash and "many specialists in the factory." A small park near Bogdan's apartment was named after Sheboldaev, but following his arrest they changed the name. Nonetheless, she overheard children calling it "traitor Sheboldaev park." Despite the lack of an official announcement regarding Evdokimov's arrest, Bogdan asserts that the news spread quickly. At the macaroni factory she overheard a cleaning woman and security guard saying that he had been arrested, and his wife, who was also a party member, had hanged herself. Bogdan does not express great concern about her own fate during the purges, but she did worry about her husband Sergei. As a professor of physics at Rostov State University he was part of a high-risk group. The local NKVD did

---

[45] Roi Medvedev and Dmitrii Ermakov, *"Seryi Kardinal" M. A. Suslov: Politicheskii portret* (Moscow: Izd-vo "Respublika," 1992), 33.

[46] *Molot*, 9 June 1938, cited in Medvedev and Ermakov, *"Seryi Kardinal,"* 33.

[47] On the lack of a public announcement of his arrest, see Bogdan, *Mimikriia v SSSR*, 125. According to Abdurkhman Avtorkhanov, Evdokimov complained against "arbitrary arrests" at a meeting of the Central Committee in Moscow in 1937; soon thereafter he was arrested himself. Alexander Uralov [Abdurkhman Avtorkhanov], *The Reign of Stalin*, trans. from French by L. J. Smith (Westport, CT: Hyperion Press, 1975), 147. He does not, however, cite a source for this information.

[48] Dvinskii remained First Secretary of the Rostov obkom, as we will see, until 1944. On Suslov's role during the purges in Rostov, see Serge Petroff, *The Red Eminence: A Biography of Mikhail A. Suslov* (Clifton, NJ: Kingston Press, 1988), 42–43. In 1939 Suslov was transferred from Rostov to Stavropol province, where, as Mikhail S. Gorbachev recalls in his memoir, "people link his name with the end of the brutal Stalinist repressions of the 1930s" (*Memoirs*, 17).

arrest some of his colleagues in the physics department, which made Valentina and Sergei *very* uneasy. They were so worried about Sergei's impending arrest that they decided to have Valentina's mother come take their young daughter because they did not want her to witness it. However, although the Rostov NKVD arrested a number of their acquaintances, they did not arrest Sergei or Valentina. She recalls that they purged Rostov's branch of the NKVD, and afterward the arrests subsided.[49]

Aleksandr Solzhenitsyn grew up in Rostov and was a student at Rostov State's Department of Mathematics and Physics where Sergei Bogdan taught. Solzhenitsyn remembers that, as a Komsomol member and "true believer," he was not too concerned about the purges as they unfolded. Looking back on 1937 from the vantage point of 1972, Solzhenitsyn explains that, at the time, he did not realize that the arrests being made were unjust, nor that NKVD officials were torturing people to obtain confessions. He would like to say that he saw it all clearly then, "but," he admits, "it isn't true."

> After all, the Black Marias [the NKVD's cars] were going through the streets at night, and we were the same young people who were parading with banners during the day. How could we know anything about those arrests and why should we think about them? All the provincial leaders had been removed, but as far as we were concerned it didn't matter. Two or three professors had been arrested, but after all they hadn't been our dancing partners, and it might even be easier to pass our exams as a result. Twenty-year-olds, we marched in the ranks of those born the year the Revolution took place, and because we were the same age as the Revolution, the brightest of futures lay ahead.

Solzhenitsyn believed at the time that "the struggle against the internal enemy was a crucial battlefront, and to share in it was an honorable task," obviously accepting the official line on the purges.[50] While his account cannot be taken as widely representative, the image of the naïve, gullible populace depicted therein suggests that people in Soviet society *did* believe the arrests were justified and did *not* exhibit constant fear during the purges, whereas Bogdan's account shows that many in the intelligentsia and higher party circles *were* afraid.[51]

The worst of the purges finally ended—locally and nationally—in early 1939, amid growing international tensions. British Prime Minister Neville

---

[49] Bogdan, *Mimikriia*, 125, 126, 128, and 188.

[50] Solzhenitsyn, *Gulag Archipelago*, 161.

[51] On this point, see Robert Thurston, *Life and Terror in Stalin's Russia, 1934–1941* (New Haven: Yale University Press, 1996); and Thurston, "Fear and Belief in the USSR's 'Great Terror,'" *Slavic Review* 45: 2 (1986): 213–34.

Chamberlain's policy of "appeasing" Hitler fell apart with the Nazi conquest of Czechoslovakia in March, prompting Britain and France to guarantee the defense of Polish sovereignty. In the months that followed, Soviet diplomacy took a sharp turn. Leder recollects that she and her friends in Moscow "were shocked" when, in August, Nazi and Soviet foreign ministers Joachim von Ribbentrop and Vyacheslav Molotov signed the "Soviet-German Friendship and Non-Aggression Pact." She remembers the pictures splashed all over the newspapers and that "all criticism of Nazi Germany vanished from the press." Films and plays with anti-fascist themes were suddenly closed.[52] Leder and her friends opposed this dramatic change in course by the Soviet leadership. Karol, who was 15 years old in 1939, lived in Łódź, Poland, and vividly recalls the invasion of his country at the beginning of September that sparked World War II and sent him fleeing to Soviet Russia. Since the signing of the German-Soviet Pact eight days earlier the threat of an invasion, he tells us, "had been in the air," but it still came as a bit of a surprise. He also recollects his dismay on hearing in November 1939 that the USSR had invaded Finland.[53] Both Leder and Karol came to Rostov for the first time in late summer 1940, Leder to visit her newlywed husband's parents, Karol to settle in the city his family had fled in 1921.[54] Leder describes Rostov as "livelier than Moscow [with] more going on outdoors." The population of Rostov, she notes, "had a large proportion of Don Cossacks, black-haired, black-eyed, wiry men and women."[55] Karol fondly remembers the first months he spent in a Rostov high school, where he befriended a number of Cossacks. He excelled as a student, and, as a true believer in Soviet socialism, joined the Komsomol in Rostov in early 1941. He remembers thinking mainly about his plans to study at a university in the fall; looking back on it in the early 1980s, he writes, "I realize that no one was really expecting this war that was imminent."[56]

---

[52] Leder, *My Life in Stalinist Russia*, 161. Bogdan likewise says that the pact was a "very big surprise" to her. "Yesterday," she writes, "Ribbentropp was a wild dog, and today Molotov vowed eternal friendship with him" (*Mimikriia*, 239). On people's shock on hearing about the Soviet-Nazi Non-Aggression Pact, see Davies, *Popular Opinion in Stalin's Russia*, 93–98.

[53] Karol, *Solik*, 18 and 28. Leder recalls the fierce resistance to Soviet troops put up by the Finns (*My Life in Stalinist Russia*, 162).

[54] Karol was escaping from a camp for Polish (mostly Jewish) refugees in Western Siberia.

[55] She was amazed at the amount of fruit still available at Rostov's central market in August (Leder, *My Life in Stalinist Russia*, 178).

[56] Karol, *Solik*, 73.

The Great Patriotic War of the Fatherland

On 22 June 1941, German troops invaded the Soviet Union. Karol recounts that only ten days earlier Soviet leaders had assured everyone that the Germans would respect their mutual treaty and refrain from any aggression.[57] He heard Molotov's announcement about the invasion over a radio loudspeaker in the streets of Rostov, noting that people dispersed afterward in silence "without offering each other a single word of hope." He laments that Stalin did not have the country better prepared, but also recalls that when Stalin addressed the Soviet people in early July his speech "raised the morale of a whole country, and mine in particular." Karol calls the speech a "masterpiece," a turning point for a country looking for guidance out of a terrible crisis.[58] As Nazi forces advanced, party leaders in Rostov and elsewhere began mobilizing troops, while Rostov, Karol reports, emptied surreptitiously and without much official control over the process. Local authorities evacuated factory personnel and machinery, but at a very slow pace. "The people in the town," he writes, were "visibly sad, [but didn't] talk openly about their fears—defeatist talk is forbidden and wouldn't help them one bit." People mainly discussed difficulties in the distribution of food, he adds. Karol was in Rostov until autumn and remembers that a thriving market economy—based to a large degree on barter—sprang up almost overnight, "creating an outlet for a great many repressed entrepreneurial talents."[59] People bought up the

---

[57] John Erickson makes the same point. See *The Road to Stalingrad* (London: Harper and Row, 1975), 92, cited in Catherine Merridale, *Ivan's War: Live and Death in the Red Army, 1939–1945* (New York: Metropolitan Books, 2006), 82–83.

[58] Karol, *Solik*, 74–76. Of course, not everyone saw the speech in the same light. Valentina Bogdan remembers that Stalin began the speech by addressing everyone as "brothers and sisters," to which her father, a Kuban Cossack, said disgustedly, "devil take you 'brother,'" then referred to Stalin as Satan (Bogdan, *Mimikriia*, 293). On the powerful impact of the speech, see also Alexander Werth, *Russia at War* (New York: Dutton, 1964), 165. For positive *and* negative reactions to the speech, see Merridale, *Ivan's War*, 96–100.

[59] Elena Skrjabina, 35 years old in 1942, fled the blockade in Leningrad with her two sons toward the Caucasus Mountains (they eventually settled in Piatigorsk). She kept a diary during and after the war, and on 29 April 1942, she wrote about passing through Rostov and the surrounding Don region on the train: "Peasants have begun to appear at the stations exchanging various articles of food for clothing and other things. Money has lost all its value. Wherever the train stops, a whole market opens up immediately. The women of our car unpack their baggage and are happy to receive food in exchange. Eggs, milk, butter, and other fresh country products are more valuable than jewels. It is difficult to convey by words the happiness of the occupants of the car who are no longer menaced by starvation." Skrjabina, *Siege and Survival: The Odyssey of a Leningrader*, trans. Norman Luxenburg (Carbondale: Southern Illinois University Press, 1971), 109.

items of those in a hurry to leave at a low price and resold them at an incredible mark-up to those who remained, while the authorities, struggling as they were to provide the population with basic needs, ignored such dealings. "Looking after Number One [became] the general rule."[60]

Mary Leder returned to Rostov during the first months of the conflict. Her husband Abram left for the front soon after the war began, and as German forces approached Moscow, Mary decided to move to Rostov with her infant daughter to be with her in-laws, thinking it would be safer there. She left for Rostov the second week in August and arrived in a very different city from the one she had visited the previous year. "Gone were the lively crowds in the streets and the parks" because people were eager to get home before dark and the blackouts.[61] "The absence of men in the streets was noticeable," she adds. The Germans were not yet bombing Rostov regularly, but they did drop incendiary bombs on the city from time to time. Reconnoitering planes flew over frequently, and there were air-raid alerts almost every night. Mary received a letter from her husband advising her *not* to go to Rostov only after she had already arrived. Abram's letter, she relays, "recommended that I stay away from Rostov because of the Don Cossacks' well-known anti-Soviet and anti-Semitic sentiments. As he put it, 'I don't much like the population there.'" Mary's experiences in Rostov confirmed her husband's concerns. Once while walking along Engels Street, the city's main thoroughfare, she struck up a conversation with a young Cossack woman. They discussed mundane problems like the difficulty of attaining food, the frequent air raids, etc. Then the young Cossack woman said, "It will be over soon. The Germans will be here before long. They'll take care of the Communists and the Jews." Leder reasons that either the young woman did not realize that she was Jewish or ("more likely") that she did not care. "From the day I arrived in Rostov," she writes, "I sensed the antagonism of the population and knew that if the Germans captured the city, we'd [Jews] be in great trouble." The episode "intensified" her fears, Leder recounts; "an ordinary woman, gloating over the approach of the Germans and not afraid to show how she felt. She must have been pretty sure that her time was at hand."[62] After the incident Leder left Rostov and returned to Moscow. She tried to convince her in-laws to leave too, but they refused.

Valentina Bogdan remembers a conversation early in the war with a young Jewish woman at the macaroni factory. She told Bogdan rumors she had heard from the refugees in Rostov's central market: "They say that the Germans are especially cruel toward Jews," the young woman said. "Well,"

---

[60] Karol, *Solik*, 90–91.

[61] Leder, *My Life in Stalinist Russia*, 192. Karol likewise notes that, with nightfall, Rostov plunged into total darkness and silence because people were afraid to leave their homes in case of air raid alerts (*Solik*, 91).

[62] Leder, *My Life in Stalinist Russia*, 192 and 194.

Bogdan replied, "judging from the press reports, they are cruel to everyone," illustrating her case by referencing a recent newspaper story on Nazi atrocities in the Ukrainian city Zhitomir: "it did not say that only Jews were killed," she asserted. "It is unbelievable that the Germans killed only Jews," Bogdan reasoned, adding that she could not even imagine anyone carrying out acts of cruelty against innocent people simply because of their race. In spring 1942, Valentina's brother Aleksandr, a Red Army soldier, unexpectedly dropped by for a brief stay. He warned his sister to evacuate Rostov because it was likely to fall soon and the Germans, as he had seen on a newsreel, were *very* cruel toward the civilian populations of cities they captured, killing thousands for no reason. "They simply kill people for no reason?" Valentina asked incredulously. "That is simply impossible to believe. Why would they want to incite the population to resist?... Aren't the Germans cultured people?" Alex assured her that "to fall under German control is extremely dangerous," but Valentina remained unconvinced: "That's all just Soviet agitation," she insisted. "It's Bolshevik propaganda to compel Soviet citizens to fight for them." She also instructed her brother, much to his shock and distaste, not to fight hard or risk his life because, as she saw it, "the Bolsheviks will lose the war." People did not want to fight for communism and were surrendering by the thousands, she claimed. Alexander responded in horror: "You're telling me to give our motherland to the enemy without a fight, and you're a Cossack!" Valentina answered that their motherland had already been in the hands of enemies for 23 years—the communists, who had carried out far worse atrocities (i.e., collectivization and famine) than the Germans possibly could.[63] This conversation between brother and sister—both Cossacks of course—illustrates the variant views of this diverse group—much like Sholokhov's novel of the Civil War.[64]

As the war raged the front several times moved to and through Rostov, a significant railway center leading to the oil-rich Caucasus. The largest city in the Russian Republic seized by Nazi forces, Rostov was devastated by major battles in November 1941, July 1942, and February 1943, as well as by periodic bombardment in between and after. The Germans took and held Rostov for about ten days in November 1941, and even in that brief stay they made a significant impact. The Nazis saw the USSR as *Lebensraum* (living space) for the superior German people, and believed that the Slavs were *Untermenschen* (subhuman), suitable mainly as a source of hard labor. In January 1942, Molotov released a long statement on behalf of the Soviet government, part of which was later read at the Nuremburg trials in 1946. "In Rostov-on-Don, later liberated by the Red Army," it declares, "the Germans ransacked all

---

[63] Bogdan, *Mimikriia*, 281, 282, 302–04. In response to his sister's vehement anti-Soviet tirade, Aleksandr reportedly said, "after such statements they would shoot you on the spot," meaning, of course, Soviet authorities.

[64] Sholokhov, *Quiet Flows the Don*.

shops; stripped passers-by in the streets of their clothing, footwear, watches, and valuables; pillaged houses wholesale, and senselessly destroyed everything they found difficult to carry away." In one infamous episode described by Molotov, a 15-year-old boy reportedly was playing in a courtyard with his pet pigeons when German soldiers passing by began to chase the birds. The boy protested, so the Germans shot him and, according to the Soviet statement, stamped on the boy's face with their boots, deforming it beyond recognition. The statement notes:

> The Nazi blood-thirstiness towards the citizens of Rostov has become well known. During their ten days' stay in Rostov the Germans not only wreaked vengeance on individuals and families, but in their blood-lust they annihilated hundreds of inhabitants, especially in the working-class districts of the city. Near the premises of the Railway Board, German machine-gunners shot forty-eight people in broad daylight. Sixty people were shot by the Hitlerite assassins on the pavements of the main street of Rostov. Two hundred people were murdered in the Armenian cemetery. Even after being driven from Rostov by our troops, German generals and officers publicly boasted that they would return to Rostov purposely to vent bloody retribution on the inhabitants, who had actively helped to drive their mortal enemy from their native city.[65]

German forces did return to Rostov, retaking the city in late July 1942, and the second fall of Rostov marked the end of a year of spontaneous de-Stalinization, a breakdown of state control due to the war, and the Red Army's battlefield losses. The press blamed Soviet troops and officers alike for fleeing in panic before the German onslaught. Stalin responded by reasserting a degree of terror and control, issuing his "Not a step back" order, which called for military police to shoot Soviet troops retreating without permission.[66] Throughout the vast territory they occupied, the Germans required the population to register with them, stamping an insignia from the German

---

[65] For Molotov's full statement, see www.biblio.org/pha/policy/1942/420106b.html (accessed 2 August 2004). For the excerpts used at Nuremburg, see *The Trial of Major German War Criminals Sitting at Nuremberg, Germany, 14th February to 26th February, 1946. Fifty-Ninth Day: Thursday, 14th February 1946* (Part 14 of 15), 35–40.

[66] Nina Tumarkin, *The Living and the Dead: The Rise and Fall of the Cult of World War II in Russia* (New York: Basic Books, 1994), 71. On this order (No. 270), see also Merridale, *Ivan's War*, 112–13; Elena Kozhina, *Through the Burning Steppe: A Memoir of Wartime Russia, 1942–1943* (New York: Riverhead Books, 2000), 39; Karol, *Solik*, 148; and John Barber and Mark Harrison, *The Soviet Home Front, 1941–1945: A Social and Economic History of the USSR in World War II* (New York: Longman, 1991), 31. For a good description of the disorderly retreat on the southern front, see Karol, *Solik*, 150–67.

Commandant in their passport; anyone caught on the street without this insignia could be arrested or even executed. In Rostov the occupying forces also began publishing a newspaper, *The Voice of Rostov* (*Golos Rostova*), and recruited sympathizers from among the remaining population. Nazi forces had orders to execute Jews, communist leaders, partisans, and active party members at all levels.[67] Special units of the Gestapo, *Einsatzgruppen*, carried out Adolph Hitler's "final solution" with efficient brutality in the occupied Soviet territories, eliminating the city's Jewish population. Otto Ohlendorf, commander of *Einsatzgruppen* D, which operated in Rostov and surrounding regions, explained at Nuremburg that their first priority in a newly-occupied area was the "Jewish question." They nominated a Jewish Council of Elders and charged them with registering all Jews and assembling them at a central marketplace at an appointed time for "resettlement," presumably for their own protection. They loaded the victims onto trucks and drove them to a designated site out of town with either a natural ravine or a gutter dug by Jewish prisoners; hundreds of thousands of Jews were shot and buried in these mass graves throughout the occupied territory.[68]

The macabre events in Rostov in 1942 fit the pattern described by Ohlendorf. On August 1 the Nazis installed a Jewish Council, which posted an announcement signed by the "Jewish elder" Lourié, assuring Jews that remained in the city (approximately 15,000) that they could live calmly and that "the German command would guard their safety."[69] On August 9 another announcement signed by Lourié explained that Jews would be resettled outside of town for protection from "irresponsible acts of enraged elements." They should gather at designated spots in two days and bring only valuables, clothing, and the keys to their apartments, which would be protected in their absence. Several knew the real meaning of the summons and committed suicide. One 82-year-old woman refused to abide by the order until German troops threatened to arrest her two non-Jewish caretakers. On August 10–11 Nazi forces executed thousands at a ravine (the Snake's Gulch) on the outskirts of Rostov, including about 300 prisoners of war (POWs) from the Red Army. Most of the victims were Jews, however, including Mary Leder's in-laws. A neighbor later informed Abram that Soviet authorities arrested his father for illegal trade earlier in the year; he was then presumably killed by

---

[67] Arad et al., *Einsatzgruppen Reports*, viii.

[68] For a discussion of Ohlendorf's testimony, see John Mendelsohn, ed., *The Holocaust #18: Punishing the Perpetrators of the Holocaust. The Ohlendorf and Weizsaecker Cases* (New York: Garland, 1982), 7.

[69] On the establishment of a Jewish Council, see Arad et al., *Einsatzgruppen Reports*, 358. On the announcement, see Ilya Ehrenburg and Vasily Grossman, *The Black Book: The Ruthless Murder of Jews by German-Fascist Invaders Throughout the Temporarily-Occupied Regions of The Soviet Union and in the Death Camps of Poland during the War of 1941–1945* (New York: Holocaust Publications, 1981), 258.

the Germans when they returned. Abram's mother reported to the assigned gathering place on the appointed morning and was never seen or heard from again.[70] The Germans employed one of their infamous gas vans in Rostov. The vehicle's exhaust was piped into the air tight compartment in back, which could hold 30 or so occupants, most of whom died in 10–15 minutes. Their bodies were unloaded in the Snake's Gulch along with those who had been shot. There were also reports of Jews being told to report for a "vaccination" against cholera, when in fact they were injected with a deadly poison.[71] Some, including prominent psychiatrist Sabina Spielrein and her two daughters, were allegedly herded into Rostov's synagogue and killed there.[72] On the day after the massacre, Ilya Ehrenburg informs, *The Voice of Rostov* proclaimed, "the air has been cleaned." Thousands more were killed in the subsequent months of occupation, including Jews, Armenians, partisans, and just about anybody else who got in the way.[73]

Fortunately most of the Jews who remained in Rostov following mobilization for the Red Army, like Mary Leder and Mariia, Veniamin, and Sergei Zhak, fled the city before the Germans took it. We can only speculate about the decision of the roughly 15,000 who stayed. As Abram Leder wondered with regard to his parents after the war, "Why didn't they leave the city when the others left?" They had stayed in Rostov despite their son's desperate urgings for them to evacuate. Mary recounts her father-in-law's "skepticism" regarding news reports of Nazi atrocities, stating that "many others" shared his doubts "about the reliability of anything they read in the Soviet press" (obviously including Valentina Bogdan and her father), which shows that the regime's propaganda machine was not wholly successful.[74] Basing his conclusion on the German occupation of Rostov during the First World War, the elder Leder asserted "that the Germans were civilized people. He believed that the press reports on Nazi atrocities against the civilian population were the usual lies of Soviet propaganda," his sense of denial, Mary adds, "aided by the press's silence about the Nazis' efforts to single out the Jews."[75] Spielrein, whose two brothers, father, and husband all perished in the purges of the late 1930s, may have shared such sentiments. Russian psychoanalyst

---

[70] See Leder, *My Life in Stalinist Russia,* 240–41.

[71] See, for example, TsDNI f. 13, op. 4, d. 50, l. 3.

[72] See Linda Munk's review of Ronald Hayman, *A Life of Jung* (New York: W. W. Norton, 2002), in *University of Toronto Quarterly* 72: 3 (Summer 2003): 757–61.

[73] For an account of the fate of some of the Jews in Rostov, see Ehrenburg and Grossman, *Black Book,* 258–61. Ehrenburg estimates that between 15,000–16,000 Jews were killed in Rostov during occupation. The marker on the memorial at Snake's Gulch states that there were 26,000 "Soviet" victims; a number of non-Jews were killed as well.

[74] Leder, *My Life in Stalinist Russia,* 241.

[75] Ibid., 193.

Alexander Etkind writes that Spielrein made the "free will decision to stay in Rostov." He speculates further that "probably she didn't believe in a word of the Bolsheviks and thought that all information on Nazi massacres was just one more piece of propaganda."[76] Zvi Gitelman notes that the "Soviet media had draped a blanket of silence over Nazi atrocities" aimed at Jews, and that, "together with older people's memories of the Germans of World War I as 'decent people,' this may have left many Soviet Jews unprepared for the mass murder campaigns conducted by [the] *Einsatzgruppen*."[77] In this instance, unfortunately, skepticism of the Soviet press proved fatal for Rostov's Jews who stayed behind.

Reports of the battles for Rostov and life in the city during the first year-and-a-half of the war are scarce. Elena Skrjabina and her two sons, evacuees from Leningrad resettled in Piatigorsk in the North Caucasus in 1942, fled with German forces as they retreated through Rostov in early 1943. In her mid-30s at the time, Skrjabina described the scene in a diary entry for January 28, 1943, during the final battle for the city (about two weeks before the Red Army retook Rostov):

> While driving past the fields just before coming to Rostov we noticed masses of smashed artillery pieces, bodies of horses, crippled tanks. Everybody is longing for only one thing: to get past Rostov as quickly as possible. We were delayed in Rostov, since the [German soldiers they were with] were waiting for someone or something. The city has suffered great damage; everywhere there are heaps of rubble of what must have been large and attractive buildings. Finally we drove out of the [city's center]. Everybody breathed more easily.

In the outskirts of Rostov, she continues, their column of vehicles halted due to a terrible traffic jam of people fleeing the city. As night fell, she and her sons found themselves caught up in the battle for Rostov. Skrjabina writes:

> The bombing of Rostov [by Soviet planes] began: the deafening whistle of bombs, the roar of planes, the crashing of smashed buildings. It was a painful picture. We were all silent, our eyes tensely following the diving airplanes. It was depressing not to be able to move further and to get out of this endless line of cars. It seemed certain that the planes would notice the column and drop a few bombs. Then there

---

[76] Alexander Etkind, "The Reception of Psychoanalysis in Russia until *Perestroika*," online at http://psychoanalyse.narod.ru/english/ruetkind.htm (accessed May 2007).

[77] Zvi Gitelman, "Soviet Reactions to the Holocaust, 1945–1991," in *The Holocaust in the Soviet Union: Studies and Sources on the Destruction of the Jews in the Nazi-Occupied Territories of the USSR, 1941–1945*, ed. Lucjan Dobroszycki and Jeffrey S. Gurock (New York: M. E. Sharpe, 1993), 5–6.

would be nothing left of the entire transport. Indeed, there was no-where to hide—and the bombing was growing more intense. The sky was flaming. The explosions were deafening.[78]

Eventually their column of vehicles moved on and they left Rostov behind. Skrjabina's account relays the utter devastation wrought on the city by the fighting.

In the roughly six months that they controlled Rostov, the Germans ran the city as if they intended to stay. They disseminated pro-Nazi, anti-Soviet and anti-Semitic propaganda.[79] They obliged residents to turn in Jews, parti-sans, and communists or risk death themselves, and, as throughout occupied territory, they threatened to execute 100 Rostovians for every German officer killed by partisans. They terrorized women, as Karol's former schoolmate and future wife Klava recalled. She only went out when absolutely necessary and then disguised as an old woman, which, she realized, did not afford her much protection. "Some of them even raped grandmothers," she told Karol.[80] She also noted that during occupation "certain women decided to take advantage of the times, and presented a sorry spectacle of debauchery and venality" with the Germans. Nazi leaders turned the city's main theater, which was built in the shape of a tractor, into their headquarters and an officer's club. They operated factories and schools, distributed apartments—no doubt many belonging to their Jewish victims—to their own troops and supporters, and billeted troops among the local population. The Germans introduced a new currency in the territories they occupied, but, as noted, a market economy thrived based largely on barter.[81] There were reports after the war that some

---

[78] Elena Skrjabina, *After Leningrad: From the Caucasus to the Rhine (9 August 1942–25 March 1945): A Diary of Survival During World War II* (Carbondale: Southern Illinois University Press, 1978), 74–76. She says that she suggested they all run into an adjacent field, but that the driver of the truck they were in "morosely" told them to "stay seated quietly" (76).

[79] I have already noted the local paper *Voice of Rostov*; in addition, Skrjabina notes that she and her acquaintances feared retribution from the Red Army as it approached Piatigorsk in early 1943, and that her friend Varia was "in even greater danger than we are, for she was working in the propaganda section [of the occupying German Army] and the Communists will never forgive her incendiary articles." Skrjabina ran a café in the city during occupation, and she writes that a German Officer named Sulzbach, a friend who visited the café often, promised to take her and her sons with him when they fled, which he did (Skrjabina, *After Leningrad*, 56–57).

[80] Karol, *Solik*, 287.

[81] Skrjabina recalls that as Soviet forces were set to retake Piatigorsk in January 1943, her friend Iurii shouted: "The Germans are abandoning the city. There is complete an-archy. If you have any occupation money, burn it. The Reds might come today and it might be dangerous to have that money." She talked him out of doing so, however,

locals opened cafes to cater to the occupying forces.[82] Food was difficult to obtain for the city's population, and an outbreak of typhus took a heavy toll on the population, including one of Karol's high school friends, Clarissa, who died of typhus during the occupation in 1942.[83]

Beginning in fall 1942, Nazi forces rounded up young people, mostly women aged 15 to 20 or so, in Rostov and the surrounding environs for hard labor in Germany. In the Donbas region north of Rostov the occupiers initially portrayed their campaign to raise workers for Germany as a great opportunity, and thus the first wave of young Russians who went to work there often did so voluntarily. However, word quickly spread that life for the conscripts in Germany was difficult, and thereafter the Germans forcibly conscripted young people.[84] Karol notes that Klava hid "in her cellar to avoid 'voluntary work' in Germany, but she knew that, among the women of Rostov, volunteers were not in short supply."[85] Skrjabina's diary entry for December 11, 1942 notes that the Nazis "have begun taking people for work in Germany." She states that at first the Germans raised workers on a voluntary basis, "but the number of volunteers was not too large," so they decided to forcibly round up workers, especially among young people. "It is said that entire trains of workers are being sent [to Germany] from the Ukraine and from Rostov." Some of her acquaintances, she notes, had already departed.

> Before leaving, one of my Leningrad friends told us how beautifully her future life in Germany had been described to her—a nice, secure, comfortable life in a small German city, good pay, easy work, and good rations. This woman, one of the evacuees who had endured all the hardships connected with the war and was living in very impoverished circumstances under the occupation, looked on this as a chance to go to paradise.[86]

According to an internal party source, for Rostov oblast as a whole, 37,185 people were taken to Germany, though it is not clear how many were from the city itself.[87] Many perished in German labor camps, but, as we will see, quite a few returned after the war to face official suspicions of their loyalty.

---

and they used the money to help them escape with the German forces (*After Leningrad*, 56).

[82] See, for example, TsDNI f. 13, op. 4, d. 29, l. 39.

[83] Karol, *Solik*, 8.

[84] Hiroaki Kuromiya, *Freedom and Terror in the Donbas: A Ukrainian-Russian Borderland, 1870s–1990s* (New York: Cambridge University Press, 1998), 272–73 and 299–300.

[85] Karol, *Solik*, 287.

[86] Skrjabina adds, though, that in Germany the woman could "easily again have to undergo all the hardships, including bombing," all over again (*After Leningrad*, 52–53).

[87] GARO f. 3737, op. 6, d. 40, l. 3.

ॐ ॐ

Rostov-on-Don was a very vibrant city in the 19th and 20th centuries with a great deal of ethnic diversity and economic development and opportunities. As a port city it gained a reputation for lawlessness and crime, which it *definitely* carried over into the Soviet period. Its importance as a major railway center beginning in the late 19th century spurred further economic development as the city grew into one of the largest urban centers in southern Russia. Tradition gave way to modernity, and in the years prior to the First World War Rostov underwent a construction boom that redrew the face of the city. The region's history during the brutal Civil War era reflects much of what would reoccur over 20 years later with the breakdown of central authority during the Great Patriotic War for the Fatherland. The construction of Rostsel'mash during Stalin's industrialization drive in the late 1920s and early 1930s further increased the city's industrial base and its significance to the national economy. As part of a national trend, peasants migrated from the surrounding countryside (and from other parts of the country) to work at Rostsel'mash and the city's other factories. The purges of the late 1930s were, unfortunately, also part of a national trend, and they brought great tragedy to Rostov's inhabitants, including a high turnover rate among the local party branch's top leaders. Shortly thereafter the war brought still more tragedy, as well as incalculable physical, material, and no doubt psychological damage to the city and its residents. The demographic impact of the conflict was apparent because of the "few men in the streets" during the war. Even after demobilization there were far fewer men than women of marriageable age, and thus there were many single women, including numerous single mothers, in Rostov as throughout the USSR. Occupation, moreover, brought even more demographic flux, with the Germans rounding up thousands of young people to send as laborers to Germany. To paraphrase Karol's friend Kolia, everything eventually was rebuilt "from scratch" in the USSR, including their "own Rostov." The chapters that follow document this process, starting with a look at varying perceptions of the harsh living conditions endured by the Soviet people during "reconstruction."

Chapter Two

"I will have to hang myself now—life has become simply impossible": Living Conditions during "Reconstruction"

Mariia S. Zhak, 44 years old at the time, returned to Rostov from evacuation with her husband and young son in October 1945 after a four-year absence. A major fire had destroyed the tram park and there was no transportation, so they walked from the train station to a relative's apartment near the city's center. "As we went along Engels Street," she recalled, "the sight of destruction and burned out buildings in our home (*rodnoi*) town was so distressing that I cried nearly the whole way."[1] An estimated three-quarters of the housing had been destroyed or severely damaged in a city full of single mothers, demobilized troops, orphans, wounded war veterans, and displaced people, as the war took a devastating toll in material and demographic terms. As noted, in the Soviet Union as a whole, as many as 26.6 million people perished and the war destroyed cities and villages throughout the country.[2] Survivors returning from evacuation or the front found an entirely different landscape than the one they had left behind. Instead of the improvements they expected and wanted, Soviet citizens faced famine and a continuation of the wartime economy for over two years. Fear of crime plagued society during these years as well. The situation eventually did improve and people did put the pieces back together again, but not without tremendous challenges, difficulties, and problems. Zhak and others remembered the words, "We will rebuild you our beloved Rostov!" painted on the wall of a burned out downtown building. "Indeed," she said, "we did, but that was one of the hardest times in my life."[3]

This chapter examines varying perceptions and representations of material conditions during "reconstruction" by analyzing several different source bases (or levels of discourse): the local party press; internal/closed party materials, including informant reports and lists of questions posed by workers and

---

[1] Mariia S. Zhak, unpublished memoir.

[2] Andreev, *Naselenie Sovetskogo Soiuza,* 73.

[3] Interview by author, 3 June 1995. Mariia Zhak was born in 1901. Svetlana S. Semenova also remembers the sign painted on the wall (*My vozrodim tebia rodnoi Rostov*). Interview by author, 16 April 1995.

others at open meetings with party representatives; and interviews and memoir accounts. The postwar years were *very* difficult throughout war-torn Eurasia. Most of Japan's major cities, including the capital Tokyo and the economic center Osaka, were scorched, and much of the country's urban populace lived in temporary shelters and dugouts at the end of the war. Approximately two million Japanese lost their lives in the conflict, a majority of whom were young men, creating a gender imbalance in society.[4] In Europe several major cities were severely damaged, among them Berlin (and numerous other German cities), Rotterdam, Warsaw, and many more.[5] After the war the threat of famine haunted the devastated countries of Eurasia. In April 1946, US President Harry Truman asked Americans to reduce their intake of food in order to stave off the starvation of millions in the "greatest threat of mass starvation in the history of mankind."[6] At Truman's behest former President Herbert Hoover, who had played such a pivotal role in Red Cross famine relief efforts in the USSR in the early 1920s, traveled to more than 25 countries. Afterward Hoover said, "I have seen with my own eyes the grimmest specter of famine in all the history of the world," calling aid relief "part of the moral and spiritual reconstruction of the world. Hunger," he added, "hangs over the homes of more than 800,000,000 people—over one-third of the people of the earth."[7]

Given this bleak scenario, rationing of key items remained in effect for years after the war in some countries. Britain, which was in a comparatively favorable position with regard to food supplies, maintained rationing of many items until the early 1950s, and the regulation of consumption became a

---

[4] See Dower, *Embracing Defeat*; Carola Hein, "Rebuilding Japanese Cities after 1945," in *Rebuilding Urban Japan After 1945*, ed. Carola Hein, Jeffry M. Diefendorf, and Ishida Yorifusa (New York: Palgrave Macmillan, 2003), 2–3. She adds that it was not until the beginning of the Korean War in 1950 that the Japanese economy really started to recover; the direct US occupation ended in 1952, and in 1955 the government officially declared the reconstruction period over because production had returned to prewar levels, which is the same measuring stick used by the Soviet Union—albeit much earlier—to announce the end of "reconstruction." Hein also states that the US occupying authorities saw the hardship of the population as "proper punishment" for its aggression against its neighbors and the US during World War II.

[5] See Diefendorf, *Rebuilding Europe's Bombed Cities*.

[6] Europe was the primary focus of US concerns, but on March 12, 1946, Secretary of State James Byrnes warned in a memorandum to President Harry S. Truman that the nations of Asia were "facing as severe if not more severe [threat of widespread starvation] than those of Europe." See the Joint Project of the Hoover and Truman Presidential Libraries at www.trumanlibrary.org/hoover/world.htm (accessed February 2007).

[7] The Hoover and Truman Presidential Libraries (Entry no. 47, "Hoover Address"), www.trumanlibrary.org/hoover/world.htm (accessed February 2007).

major element of the relationship between the state and British society.[8] Poland introduced rationing in mid-1945, which dramatically lowered food expenditures, although only, of course, when goods were available to cover the cards. With improvements in food production and distribution, the government phased out ration cards following the bitterly cold winter of 1947, although the population still faced difficult material conditions as the Polish Communist Party consolidated its power.[9] Of course, the terms "material conditions," "living standard," and "standard of living" are vague,[10] and obviously the difficulties endured by the Soviet people at this time varied, although most people certainly suffered some degree of hardship. Because of the centrality of these issues to the everyday lives of workers and others, I focus here on sanitary conditions; the severe shortage of housing; the mobilization of young people for work in factories with the promise of shelter and improved material conditions; the crime problem; bread supply difficulties, which, of course, were especially acute during the 1946–48 famine; and factory cafeterias that, if functioning properly, were a key component to workers' livelihood.[11] While concentrating on these issues, I am not excluding other factors that affect the population's standard of living, many of which I will return to in subsequent chapters, such as the impact of the illegal market, the city's inadequate system of transportation, corruption, etc. I focus on the aspects of material conditions defined above because of the frequency with which these topics were raised in public and internal party sources.

By the time the fighting finally ended in May 1945, Rostov, like much of occupied Soviet territory, lay in ruins. Studies of the period show the devastating human and material impact of the war on the USSR as a whole—"people lived in holes in the ground"—as well as the demographic and economic

---

[8] Ina Zweiniger-Bargielowska, *Austerity in Britain: Rationing, Controls, and Consumption, 1939–1955* (Oxford: Oxford University Press, 2000), 1. She adds that "this development was not gender neutral," since women were more impacted by the purchase of rationed goods.

[9] Kenney, *Rebuilding Poland*, 87. In May 1945, workers in Poland received a mere 30 percent of the goods they were entitled to through rationing.

[10] The Pension Board defines "standard of living" as "the degree of prosperity in a nation, as measured by income levels, quality of housing and food, medical care, educational opportunities, transportation, communications, and other measures.... On an individual level, the standard of living is a measure of the quality of life in such areas as housing, food, education, clothing, transportation, and employment opportunities." See http://www.pbucc.org/pension/tools/glossary.php (accessed April 2007).

[11] On the importance of cafeterias in another "lean year," 1932, see Jeffrey Rossman, *Worker Resistance Under Stalin: Class and Revolution on the Shop Floor* (Cambridge, MA: Harvard University Press, 2005).

changes underway afterward.[12] Several works depict the harsh material conditions and indicate that the population was on the move, with peasants migrating to cities to enter training schools and work in factories. Many demobilized soldiers from rural areas settled in cities as well.[13] The war accelerated trends underway for over a decade such as urban migration, women's entrance into the workforce, and huge investments by the state in heavy industry (over-and-above consumer goods). As in the 1930s people endured a lack of housing, endless shortages of the most basic goods, rationing, and famine—such hardships were not unprecedented for Soviet citizens.[14] During the industrialization drive of the 1930s, the shortage of and extreme demand for workers gave them a great deal of leverage in dealing with factory managers, who were willing to overlook serious transgressions of "labor discipline."[15] There was also popular discontent with low real wages and harsh material conditions and thus a discrepancy between the party's claims and people's perceptions of Soviet reality.[16] The war, its impact unprecedented and profound, compounded society's problems, and there was a "women's

----

[12] Alec Nove, *An Economic History of the USSR* (New York: Penguin Books, 1969), 287. Nove adds that "it is hardly possible to compute the losses suffered by the economy and the population of the Soviet Union. Many towns lay in ruins," he continues, "and thousands of villages were smashed." On the material impact of the war, see N. A. Voznesensky, *The Economy of the USSR during World War II* (Washington, DC: Public Affairs Press, 1948). See also Susan J. Linz, ed., *The Impact of World War II on the Soviet Union* (Totowa, NJ: Rowman and Allanheld, 1985); Eugene Zaleski, *Stalinist Planning for Economic Growth, 1933–1952* (Chapel Hill: University of North Carolina Press, 1980). On the economic and demographic changes afterward, see Edward Bubis and Blair A. Ruble, "The Impact of World War II on Leningrad," in Linz, *Impact of World War II*, 189–206. See also I. M. Volkov, *Trudovoi podvig Sovetskogo krest'ianstva v poslevoennye gody: Kolkhozy SSSR v 1946–1950 godakh* (Moscow: Mysly, 1972); "Postanovlenie Soveta Ministrov SSSR: O poriadke provedeniia organizovannogo nabora rabochikh," in *Resheniia partii i pravitel'stva po khoziaistvennym voprosam, 1917–1967 gody*, ed. K. U. Chernenko and M. S. Smirtiukov (Moscow: Izd-vo Politicheskoi literatury, 1967–88), 117–25; S. L. Seniavskii and M. I. Khlusov, "Industrial'nye kadry SSSR v 1946–1955 godakh," *Voprosy istorii* 10: 4 (1965): 15–37; A. V. Smirnov, "Rabochie kadry tiazhelogo mashinostroeniia SSSR v 1946–1958 godakh," *Istoricheskie zapiski* 71: 3 (1964): 17–62.

[13] One source puts Rostov's population at 550,000 before the war; 170–180,000 in February 1943; 273,000 by the first of January 1944; 358,000 by the first of January 1945; and 420,000 by the first of January 1946. TsDNI f. 13, op. 4, d. 260, l. 59. A secondary source puts Rostov's population in 1939 at 510,000. Skrjabina, *After Leningrad*, 22.

[14] On the 1930s, see Fitzpatrick, *Everyday Stalinism*, 42–45 (shortages), 46–50 and 144–55 (housing), and 41–42 and 150–51 (famine).

[15] See Filtzer, *Soviet Workers and Stalinist Industrialization*, 62, 118–19, 212, 219–20, 221, and 230.

[16] Davies, *Popular Opinion*, chap. 1.

crime wave" during the postwar famine.[17] According to incomplete figures, in the fall of 1946 in the country as a whole 53,369 people were prosecuted for stealing bread, about 50 percent of whom were women with young children.[18] Rostov is in the southern part of the region most impacted by the famine, in which an estimated one–two million people perished.[19] The regime blamed the lack of grain on drought in Ukraine and southern Russia (including Rostov oblast) and excessive rains in Central Asia at harvest time. However, the USSR continued during this time to export grain abroad, which, as we will see, caused consternation for many people.[20]

The sliding scale of ration distribution reflected the class and gender differences of Soviet society, wherein most workers, especially single mothers, endured low real wages. As of December 1943, "first category" rations for local party leaders and skilled workers in heavy industry were 650 grams of bread per day, 100 grams higher than those of "second category" recipients, comprised of mid-level bureaucrats and some industrial workers; "third category" rations for lower-level employees and unskilled workers, the majority of the work force and disproportionately female, were 200 grams of bread less a day than the "first category" and with significant reductions in monthly rations on other items as well.[21] Real wages for workers in the official economy, moreover, were extremely low between 1943 and 1948.[22] The piece-rate wage

---

[17] V. F. Zima, *Golod v SSSR 1946–1947 godov: Proiskhozhdenie i posledstviia* (Moscow: Rossiiskaia akademiia nauk, 1996), 99. See also Zubkova, *Russia After the War*, 49.

[18] Zubkova, *Russia After the War*, 49; Zima, *Golod v SSSR*, 116.

[19] Michael Ellman, "The 1947 Soviet Famine and the Entitlement Approach to Famines," *Cambridge Journal of Economics* 24: 5 (2000): 603; Zima, *Golod v SSSR*, 5. On the famine, see Nicholas Ganson, "Famine of Victors: The Soviet Hunger of 1946–1947 in Historical and Global Perspective" (Ph.D. diss., University of North Carolina-Chapel Hill, 2006).

[20] According to a May 1946 memo drafted for President Truman by former President Hoover, the Soviet Union had previously agreed to provide about 700,000 tons of grain to Finland, Czechoslovakia, France and Poland. The Hoover and Truman Presidential Libraries (Entry no. 46, "Hoover Notes of Meeting with Truman"), www.trumanlibrary.org/hoover/world.htm (accessed 28 February 2007).

[21] First and second categories received monthly rations of two kilograms of groats, 2.2. kilograms of meat and fish, 800 grams of fat, and 500 grams of sugar per month. "Third Category" recipients got 1.5 kilograms of groats, 1.2 kilograms of meat and fish, 400 grams of fat, and 300 grams of sugar a month. Dependents were allotted 300 grams of bread per day, 1 kilogram of groats, 600 grams of meat and fish, 300 grams of fat, and 250 grams of sugar monthly. This information compiled from Lazar Volin, *Survey of Soviet Russian Agriculture* (Washington, DC: U. S. Department of Agriculture, 1951), 175, and from GARO f. 3737, op. 4, d. 1389, l. 9.

[22] Real wages rose and fell throughout the Stalinist period. See Lewis Siegelbaum, Sarah Davies, and others, who note a sharp drop in real wages between 1928 and 1934 (coinciding with the First Five-Year Plan), followed by a relative leveling off between

system contributed to this problem, while the process of determining rates and norms—and thus, eventually, wages—was *extremely* complex and "arbitrary."[23] But this form of payment also meant that power outages, lack of material, equipment failure, or anything that shut down production lowered wages, as did the constant pressure to increase production quotas. Most workers received only enough for bare subsistence (if that), and wages definitely did not correspond to the labor market, where the need for workers was dire. This situation did, however, give workers some room for negotiation in achieving the best possible living conditions. For the regime, the mobilization of labor through occupational training schools (*fabrichno-zavodskoe obuchenie*, hereafter FZOs) was vitally important.[24] The factory was central to an employee's life with ration cards, housing space, even plots of land for gardens distributed through the workplace. Food and other items were sometimes distributed to workers at their place of employment, but goods were usually sold outside the factories. The system led to competition among factory managers as to who could best provide for workers' needs—factories that had housing space to offer in particular were at an advantage in attracting workers, but such space was limited in a war-ravaged city. Also, most factories had cafeterias that were crucial to workers' overall "survival strategy" in the postwar years because they "guaranteed" access to at least one good meal as long as workers could afford it.[25]

1934–38, and then three "exceptionally lean years" prior to the war. See Siegelbaum, *Stakhanovism and the Politics of Productivity in the USSR, 1935-1941* (Cambridge: Cambridge University Press, 1988), 214–23; Davies, *Popular Opinion in Stalin's Russia*, 24; Janet Chapman, *Real Wages in Soviet Russia Since 1928* (Cambridge, MA: Harvard University Press, 1963), 196.

[23] See Donald Filtzer, *Soviet Workers and Stalinist Industrialization: The Formation of Modern Soviet Production Relations, 1928–1941* (New York: M. E. Sharpe, 1986), chap. 8; and Lewis Siegelbaum, "Soviet Norm Determination in Theory and Practice, 1917–1941, *Soviet Studies* 36: 1 (1984): 45–68. In the 1930s Stalin had proclaimed that the equalization of wages had nothing in common with Marxism, encouraging wage differentiation as a way of rewarding the "best workers."

[24] The regime created FZOs in 1940 as part of a system of *de facto* labor conscription for teenagers. FZO students, who were overwhelmingly from the countryside, were 16–17 years old and were recruited for six-month training sessions before being sent into the factories to work. See Filtzer, *Soviet Workers and Late Stalinism*, 34–39.

[25] As we will see, workers reacted negatively to a significant price increase on these meals at the beginning of the famine in September 1946.

The Public Party Record on Living Conditions

Local press coverage reveals that material conditions in Rostov were *very* harsh in this period, as was true throughout much of the USSR at this time.[26] There were, for example, serious sanitation problems in the city in the immediate aftermath of occupation; an April 1943 editorial in *Molot* called on people to "clean the streets of filth and trash" that "create the danger of extremely infectious diseases developing. We must admit," it added, "that there are great insufficiencies with regard to the cleanliness of our city." The report noted that of almost 500 housing complexes inspected, only 27 percent had been adequately cleaned of trash.[27] A subsequent piece compared a housing manager who mobilized residents to clean the courtyards on their block with several others who forgot the importance of sanitation. "The majority of courtyards and streets in Leninskii district," for example, "are very dirty, while ice and heaps of rubbish pile up on the street," none of which seemed to bother the district housing department or other responsible parties. Several housing managers "do nothing."[28] Ten days later V. Zarin reminded *Molot*'s readers of the problem. "On Engels Street, a little bit below Budennovskii Prospect," he wrote, "a wide, dark puddle crosses the path. Little streams of water flow from the courtyard of Housing Complex No. 60, completely covering the asphalt, while dumpsters and stairwells are crammed full with rubbish." One housing manager was removed from his job for not dealing with the situation, and two others were due to stand trial for their inaction.[29]

The devastation of the city's housing was apparent to all, as apartments, which were not plentiful before the war, were in severely short supply afterward.[30] A book published on the fifth anniversary of Rostov's liberation

---

[26] See Donald Filtzer, "Standard of Living versus Quality of Life: Struggling with the Urban Environment in Russia during the Early Years of Post-War Reconstruction," in Fürst, *Late Stalinist Russia*, 81–102.

[27] *Molot*, "Ochistit' gorod ot otbrosov i musora," 3 April 1943, p. 2.

[28] *Molot*, "Delo vsei obshchestvennosti," 4 April 1943, p. 1.

[29] V. Zarin, "Kogda zabyvaiut o chistote," *Molot*, 14 April 1943, p. 2. Zarin further noted that sanitation inspectors fined housing managers that did an inadequate job cleaning up. For another report a week later see *Molot*, "V Obkom VKP(b)," 21 April 1943, p. 1. It stated that "in the majority of cases trash and filth from the courtyards is not taken to the dumps, but straight to the street or, most often, to burned out and destroyed buildings, with no regard for even the most basic rule of sanitation. Unsanitary conditions prevail also in and around marketplaces, bazaars, and factory complexes." For subsequent coverage of this issue, see also *Molot*, "Zima ne gorami," 21 August 1943, p. 4.

[30] Filtzer reports that in 1940 the total urban housing stock for the country as a whole was 270 square meters, which provided the average urban resident with 5.1 square meters of living space. In 1945 wartime destruction had reduced the stock to 200 million square meters (*Soviet Workers and Late Stalinism*, 92).

stated that more than 75 percent of the city's housing was rendered unlivable. Of 2.6 million square meters of housing space in the city before the war, 29 percent was destroyed and another 48 percent severely damaged.[1] So where did people live? In October 1943, *Molot* printed a city soviet decree forbidding the construction of huts on the left bank of the Don River and on Green Island, located just north of the city's center. It called for the destruction of "voluntarily built housing structures" and required people to get permission before setting up makeshift living quarters in bombed out buildings.[2] In the final years of the war many residents illegally occupied apartments belonging to soldiers at the front or evacuees. The Central Committee passed a special decree calling on the police to evict those illegally occupying apartments, but a February 1944 editorial complained that "some organizations in Rostov do not fulfill this order." As an example it mentioned an employee in the oblast police department who took over an apartment to which he had no legal claim. The chief of police for that precinct, however, refused to evict him because "he did not want to ruin relations with the Oblast Police Department." *Molot* cited similar cases, including that of a man who already owned a large apartment and illegally seized another one. Attempts to evict him failed because "appropriate organs did not help us deal with those illegally seizing apartments," which, as we will see, is code for corruption, a prominent problem among housing administrators.[3]

Molot took up the topic again in May 1944, 15 months after occupation and a year before the end of the war, describing lines of people waiting every day in legal offices and housing administrations with disputed claims to apartments. With the return of evacuees "the number of law suits over housing grows and grows," while responsible authorities often delayed dealing with them. The family of engineer M. D. Davydovich occupied Apt. 14 in one building for many years prior to the war. When they returned from evacuation, however, the family's "joy of being home was immediately soured when they found someone living in their apartment." That someone was Comrade Shishkin, director of Rostov's Medical Institute, who, although he "already had an apartment," refused to relinquish Apt. 14, setting the legal process in motion. The courts sided with the Davydovich family, but with the help of a complicated appeals process and documents signed by a different judge under mysterious circumstances (he "signed orders extending Shishkin's stay *in private* instead of in an open courtroom"), Shishkin continued to delay

---

[1] *Piat' let spustia* (Rostov-on-Don: Rostov State University, 1948), 6, 8. These numbers coincide with those in an internal party report, presumably the author's source. TsDNI f. 13, op. 4, d. 2, l. 424.

[2] *Molot*, "Ob uporiadochenii dela zastroiki vosstanovleniia g. Rostova-na-Donu," 9 October 1943, p. 4.

[3] A. Tarasov, "Eshche raz o samozakhvatchikakh kvartir," *Molot*, 6 February 1944, p. 3. I cover corruption in housing and other sectors of the economy in chap. 8.

moving out of the disputed apartment. The Davydovich family, meanwhile, "lives in very difficult conditions without adequate shelter." The author listed other examples, noting that the courts' rulings sometimes were ignored and that those who illegally seized apartments continued to live in them.[1] The obvious implication of documents being signed outside of the courtroom is that it involved a payoff.

In addition to addressing the city's sanitation and housing woes, the local party press also played a key role in the mobilization of youth for training in the FZOs and/or for work at Rostsel'mash. A 1944 call for youth to attend training schools observed that the previous year more than 4,000 young people were trained for Rostov's factories, construction work, transportation and communications systems, etc. This piece informed that local leaders were obligated to mobilize 4,700 youth in a month, including more than 3,000 young people from the countryside. "We must teach and instill in young people a sense of workers' feats and of the heroism of the working class."[2] Trainees were to be provided with living space, clothes, shoes, sheets, and food—some very significant promises at that time. A number of the trainees were mobilized for work at Rostsel'mash, which, like other major plants, had an FZO attached to it. Amid hunger three years later in February 1947, *Molot* published an open letter from young Rostovians to all members of the city's youth organization (*Komsomol*) entitled "Youth—to Rostsel'mash!" It pointed out that a recent plenum of the Central Committee had called for dramatic increases in agricultural production, which required farm machinery. "Tractors," the piece stated, "are as necessary now as tanks were during the war." The adjusted five-year plan required Rostsel'mash to produce 3,300 combines, 10,000 tractor plows, and a million rubles worth of spare parts for farm machinery by 1950. Written during the peak of the famine the letter opined, "We understand very well that the struggle for combines is the struggle for bread, for the further development of our beloved Fatherland, and for the improvement of material conditions for Soviet people." The letter called for all Komsomol members and non-party youth to come voluntarily to work at the plant.[3]

Mobilization of labor was a recurring theme in these public party texts. During the recruitment efforts for Rostsel'mash described above, *Molot*

---

[1] G. Iakushchenko, "Dela kvartirnye," *Molot*, 16 May 1944, p. 3 (my emphasis).

[2] *Molot*, "Delo gosudarstvennoi vazhnosti," 3 September 1944, p. 2. See also *Molot*, "Nakanune prizyva gorodskoi i sel'skoi molodezhi v remeslennye, zheleznodorozhnye uchilishcha i shkoly FZO," 2 September 1944, p. 1. "These young boys and girls should feel, in short, from the first day the great care shown to them by our party and government."

[3] *Molot*, "Molodezh'—na Rostsel'mash!" 11 May 1947, p. 1. "We are certain," the authors concluded, "that the young men and women of Rostov will follow our example and come to build combines!"

printed an account of two young workers who volunteered to work at the plant. One of them, former dockworker Aleksei Pustoshkin, recalled a meeting when the party secretary of his organization said, "Who wants to build combines?" "I do!" Aleksei answered, "and me too" said the young communist Mark S. Piliugin. The plant's personnel office asked where in Rostsel'-mash they would like to work and both responded enthusiastically "wherever we're needed." The two mastered their new jobs so quickly that by October, on the eve of the 30th anniversary of the revolution, they were teaching youth at the plant's FZO. Aleksei, in particular, influenced one young man who "often disrupted labor discipline, patiently explaining [to him] the meaning of their labor and that they were working for the common good and the entire collective of the factory." According to this account, the young man became more attentive, while Aleksei and Mark both established new factory production records as Stakhanovites.[4] In another report, *Molot* acknowledged that the plants that provided the best housing, cafeterias, and conditions for production were the ones that lured the most workers. Not understanding this basic fact, factory leaders at the food-processing plant Smychka and the Mikoyan Shoe Factory did not adequately provide for the daily needs of employees and thus failed to mobilize workers. Rostsel'mash, moreover, suffered from frequent interruptions in production, which reflected poorly on workers' wages. Thus, this editorial declared, "it is no surprise" that in 1944 the plant most in need of new workers signed on 1,118 workers but then lost 768.[5]

Along with enthusiastic editorials, *Molot* discussed many problems with the mobilization of youth for FZOs and for work at Rostsel'mash. Not long after the call went out to mobilize youth for FZOs in the autumn of 1944, there were a number of reports that this was being done unsatisfactorily. As noted, the mobilization decree required the training schools to provide housing, food, clothing, and other items, a front-page editorial stating that "factories should create the best possible conditions for the new trainees and provide them with everything they need." However, a check-up revealed that several places did a poor job preparing for the youth, as a result of which they had not successfully mobilized their quota. At Krasnyi Aksai, Rostsel'mash, and several other places dormitories for trainees were in horrible condition.[6] Another editorial admitted that while youth were eager to go to the FZOs and train for jobs in industry, the mobilization of young workers unfortunately was being carried out very poorly in several areas of the city and oblast. Those in charge did inadequate agitational work, this account lamented, while many of the schools failed to provide trainees with adequate living conditions. The lofty promises made in the earlier reports, in short, were not

---

[4] F. Vlasenko, "Po putevke gorkoma," *Molot*, 11 November 1947, p. 2.

[5] *Molot*, "Zakrepit' kadry na proizvodstva," 24 December 1944, p. 1.

[6] *Molot*, "Trudovye rezervy nashei Otchizny," 12 September 1944, p. 1.

upheld. Consequently, whereas the city as a whole should have mobilized 450 youth, only 160 were actually recruited. In Stalinskii district (where Rostsel'-mash is located) the situation was particularly bad: instead of the required 90 they mobilized only 7.[7] Thus the enthusiastic account of the recruits who rose through the ranks to become instructors at the training schools and helped mold a new generation of workers was not the full story. Also, the admission of the earlier piece that some of the trainees displayed "discipline problems" seems all the more significant given that so few were actually mobilized.

Yet another problem featured prominently in the party press was crime, if only to show that local leaders were aware of and dealing with this pervasive problem that reflected poorly on living conditions. The paper usually treated this issue in a small section on the last page. An announcement in mid-March 1943 warned that criminals were disguising themselves in military uniforms and illegally carrying out searches. It noted that one group had already been arrested for this, but cautioned that there may be others.[8] In the spring of 1944 the paper reported on the "bandit activities of a gang of criminals" from Rostov. Four men stopped a produce truck on a road outside Rostov-on-Don, killed the driver with a machine gun, painted the truck and changed its serial number, then drove around Rostov oblast and robbed collective farms.[9] Without elaborating an account in late 1944 assured readers that because of "measures" taken by the NKVD and oblast procurator's office, "street crime in Rostov has sharply declined." However, it further noted that criminals killed a woman and stole her clothes, and that three robbers posed as returning Red Army troops with letters for a friend's family.[10] The paper printed an interview with the head of the oblast police who said that while there had been "isolated instances" of street crime, all cases had been solved and the guilty parties caught. He also addressed "rumors circulating in town" about an organized band of criminals called "black cat" (*chernaia koshka*). "From day to day," he noted, "all sorts of stories about the many crimes of this gang

---

[7] *Molot*, "Naverstat' upushchennoe vremia," 20 October 1944, p. 2.

[8] *Molot*, "Proisshestviia," 12 March 1943, p. 2. The piece informed that searches could only be carried out by officials of the police, NKVD, and assistants to the procurator with a special order. In April 1943 the paper announced the arrest of another group of bandits carrying out these illegal searches, with five people sentenced from seven to ten years. *Molot*, "Proisshestviia," 1 April 1943, p. 2. The problem remained that fall, however, when *Molot* published another warning. See *Molot*, "Ot komandatury goroda," 21 November 1943, p. 4.

[9] *Molot*, "Bandity," 8 April 1944, p. 4. The article does not clarify how long they operated before getting caught and does not list their sentences.

[10] *Molot*, "V oblastnoi prokurature i NKVD," 19 November 1944, p. 4. The article does not clarify exactly what "measures" were being taken, an issue we return to below. Thieves often stopped residents and stole their clothing. See also, for example, *Molot*, "Arest prestupnikov," 19 November 1946, p. 4.

make their rounds, some of them told by people who were supposedly victimized by 'black cat.'" These were all just legends, he assured, and those spreading them were doing a major disservice to the public by creating unnecessary panic.[11]

The numerous accounts of crime in this five-year period always reported that the culprits had been arrested and usually listed their sentences (often death for gang leaders) or noted that they were due to stand trial soon.[12] For example, in late 1945 the paper announced the upcoming trial of a criminal group with ten bandits,[13] and about a month later it described how a group of four traveled the road between Novocherkassk and Rostov-on-Don in a stolen car, robbing people along the way.[14] In June 1946 the light bulbs from street lamps began to disappear, especially along Socialist Street near the city's center. The culprits, two residents of Rostov who set out with their ladder when darkness fell, were caught and sentenced.[15] Later that year *Molot* reported on the arrest of several small gangs and a thief who went door to door promising to deliver cheap produce to those who paid up front.[16] In December two men were arrested for robbing someone in the street, and authorities apprehended

---

[11] *Molot*, 13 June 1946, p. 1. On the distinct meaning of the term "panic" and the legal connotations it carried in the Soviet context, see Timothy Johnston, "Subversive Tales? War Rumours in the Soviet Union, 1945–1947," in Fürst, *Late Stalinist Russia*, 62–78.

[12] Instances of corruption are reported much the same way, as we will see in chap. 8, but I deal with street crime separately here. For other reports of crime, see *Molot*, "V gorodskom otdele militsii," 6 August 1943, p. 4; *Molot*, "V upravlenii NKVD," 18 February 1944, p. 4; *Molot*, "V gorodskom otdele militsii," 21 July 21 1944, p. 4; *Molot*, "Bandity," 8 December 1944, p. 4; *Molot*, "Proisshestviia," 5 October 1945, p. 4; *Molot*, "Sud nad banditami," 11 November 1945, p. 4; *Molot*, "Proisshestviia," 13 November 1945, p. 4; *Molot*, "Bandity prigovoreny k rasstrelu," 18 November 1945, p. 4; *Molot*, "Proisshestviia," 16 December 1945, p. 4; *Molot*, "Proisshestviia," 18 December 1945, p. 4; *Molot*, "Proisshestviia," 17 September 1946, p. 4; *Molot*, "Proisshestviia," 18 September 1946, p. 4. *Molot*, "Aferist," 30 October 1946, p. 4; *Molot*, "Arest na meste prestupleniia," 24 December 1946, p. 4; *Molot*, "Bandity prigovoreny k rasstrelu," *Molot*, 19 April 1947, p. 4; "Proisshestviia," *Molot*, June 3, 1947, p. 4; "Proisshestviia," 13 June 1947, p. 4; *Molot*, "Proisshestviia," 14 June 1947, p. 4; *Molot*, "Grabiteli," 27 December 1947, p. 4.

[13] *Molot*, "Bor'ba s prestupnost'iu i khuliganstvom," 26 December 1945, p. 4. See also *Molot*, "Grabiteli surovo nakazany," 28 December 1945, p. 4; *Molot*, "Proisshestviia," 29 December 1945, p. 4; *Molot*, "Pokazatel'nyi protsess nad banditami," 18 January 1946, p. 4.

[14] *Molot*, "Sud nad grabiteliami," 24 January 1946, p. 1.

[15] *Molot*, "Nochnye montery," 2 June 1946, p. 4.

[16] *Molot*, "V gorodskoi prokurature," 20 November 1946, p. 4. One of the groups consisted of six criminals, another of three, and the third of four. *Molot*, "Aferist," 11 October 1946, p. 4. The thief in question collected several thousand rubles.

a gang of 17 that had carried out robberies for years.[17] One announcement noted that a "bandit" under arrest for murder and robbery would stand trial in the workers' club at Rostsel'mash.[18] In the spring of 1947 the paper cited several pending cases as well, including three separate gangs of criminals consisting of from three to four people each.[19] In one case a night watchman at a warehouse turned out to be part of a criminal gang; he let his cohorts tie him up and pretended he had been attacked and the warehouse robbed.[20] In February 1948, *Molot* reported the arrest of a thief who professed to be a repairman and stole a valuable clock from an elderly woman's apartment.[21] Three days later several men were held for stealing a watch from a young woman on the street.[22]

Frequent bread supply problems also kept *Molot* reporters busy. In the midst of a prolonged bread crisis in May 1943 the paper announced that I. F. Palamarchuk, director of the city's grain department, "is guilty of tolerating a terribly wasteful stoppage of train cars destined for the workers of Rostov," for which he would stand trial.[23] In June it reported that, whereas the bread industry fulfilled its plan for April by only 85 percent, it fulfilled May's plan by 112 percent, the assumption behind the numbers being that the situation would be improving.[24] Periodic difficulties continued, however, and famine struck in 1946. Despite promises to end rationing in 1946, *Pravda* in September announced that rationing would continue into the next year and that prices

---

[17] *Molot*, "Proisshestviia," 14 December 1946, p. 4; *Molot*, "Proisshestviia," 20 December 1946, p. 4. See also *Molot*, "Grabitel'," 21 December 1946, p. 4.

[18] *Molot*, "Pokazatel'nyi protsess nad banditom," 22 December 1946, p. 4.

[19] *Molot*, "V gorodskoi prokurature," 16 March 1947, p. 4.

[20] *Molot*, "Ograblenie magazinov," 17 May 1947, p.4. For other instances when night guards proved to be criminals, see also *Molot*, "Raskhititeli," 18 August 1944, p. 4. For more on the theft of grain, see also *Molot*, "V oblastnoi prokurature," 22 July 1943, p. 4.

[21] *Molot*, "Monter," 8 February 1948, p. 4.

[22] *Molot*, "Proisshestviia," 11 February 1948, p. 4. There were also reports of "hooliganism," or disrupting the peace, often by fighting. *Molot*, "Molodye khuligany," 31 May 1944, p. 4; *Molot*, "Khuligany budut surovo nakazany," 18 July 1945, p. 4. On "hooliganism" in the pre-war Soviet Union, see Eric Naiman, *Sex in Public: The Incarnation of Early Soviet Ideology* (Princeton, NJ: Princeton University Press, 1997); Anne Gorsuch, *Youth in Revolutionary Russia: Enthusiasts, Bohemians, Delinquents* (Bloomington: Indiana University Press, 2000).

[23] *Molot*, 8 May 1943, p. 2. We will see that there is a great deal more to this story.

[24] *Molot*, "Na soveshchanii v Obkome," 18 June 1943, p. 2. Showing how prominent the problem is at the time, there is another report in the same issue on a party conference to deal with "problems in the supply of bread to the population." *Molot*, "Neotlozhnye zadachi khlebopekarnoi promyshlennosti," 18 June 1943, p. 2. Also, the following January there were more reports of problems in bread supply. *Molot*, "Pis'mo v redaktsiiu," 14 January 1944, p. 4.

on rationed goods would increase. The price of rye bread increased from one ruble to 3 rubles and 40 kopeks, and the price of wheat bread from 3 rubles and 80 kopeks to 11 rubles and 25 kopeks. The price of pasta, potatoes, meat (the availability of which was limited anyway), butter, cheese, sugar, milk, and eggs all rose sharply, as did the price of other items such as vodka, cigarettes, clothing, and soap.[25] *Pravda* explained that this measure was due to drought and the lack of state grain reserves stemming from the war, and stated that the price increases were necessary to prepare conditions for the abolition of rationing in 1947.[26] After the cessation of rationing in December 1947 periodic problems in bread supply continued, including a bread crisis in 1948.[27] In July *Molot* noted that lines of 60 to 80 people were forming around several bread stores on Saturday and Sunday. "It is well known," the article stated, "that the sale of bread in Rostov has not been interrupted for months" (an implicit admission that there were problems earlier). "Supply is more than enough to satisfy the population's demand." So why did lines form? Investigation revealed that speculators had infiltrated the stores where the bread lines formed and bought up the bread for resale on the city's flourishing illegal market.[28]

Another article reported numerous problems in the city's cafeteria trust, as a result of which many cafeterias in Rostov served workers poorly and were in terrible sanitary condition. "The problem," it stated, "is that people in the trust have not taken the necessary initiative or shown persistence in the struggle to improve their service." It ended by noting that all cases of workplace pilfering should be punished, suggesting perhaps a more telling reason cafeteria service was so poor.[29] A letter from the Managing Director of the Oblast Trade Department, V. Anisimov, declared the sanitation in cafeterias intolerable and assailed those in charge for having "made peace" (*mirilis'*) with this situation.[30] *Molot* occasionally exposed such problems in the workers' "own voice," such as a 1944 account of a factory meeting at Rostsel'mash.

---

[25] See Filtzer, *Soviet Workers and Late Stalinism*, 49; Zaleski, *Stalinist Planning for Economic Growth*, 688–96; and Irving B. Kravis and Joseph Mintzes, "Soviet Union: Trends in Prices, Rations, and Wages," *Monthly Labor Review* 34: 2 (1947): 33.

[26] *Pravda*, "V Sovete Ministrov SSSR," 16 September 1946, p. 1.

[27] Ellman states that the famine caused excess deaths in the USSR between (July) 1946 and 1948, but that the "peak of the famine was in February–August 1947" ("The 1947 Soviet Famine," 612).

[28] *Molot*, "Bespereboino vesti torgovliu khlebom," 6 July 1948, p. 3. On the illegal market, see chap. 6.

[29] *Molot*, "Zavodskaia stolovaia," 4 August 1943, p. 1. See also *Molot*, "Tsennaia initsiativa sovetskikh patriotov," 27 February 1944, p. 1.

[30] *Molot*, "Bol'shevistkii dolg rabotnikov torgovli i obshchestvennogo pitaniia," 20 February 1944, p. 3. He cited a number of deficiencies, including cheating customers, pilfering by employees, and the illegal sale of goods.

At the meeting workers "could comment on any issue," the author assured, and they reportedly assailed the cafeteria manager for serving poor quality food and keeping the kitchen in an unsanitary condition. The factory director, Comrade Kozlov, also fell under criticism for "blaming problems on those around him and forgetting that the primary responsibility of the plant's leadership is to fulfill the everyday needs of workers."[31] A "Letter to the Editor" by a group of communication workers expressed relief when their collective received a cafeteria.[32] "However," they informed, "our hopes of improvements in food supply were not realized." The cafeteria "systematically fails to provide lunch" because by noon "either they are already out of food or there is no fuel to cook with." Cafeteria employees, they added, were rude and cheated customers, and when faced with the "justifiable objections" of workers forced to go without lunch, a cook asked sarcastically, "What, you expect us to wait for you?" This account pitted different segments of the working class against each other while leaving one wondering about the cafeteria's supply of food and fuel: either it was *severely* under-stocked or material was being "diverted" to the market—a common practice among those in the food industry as we will see—or both.

The press portrayed the material hardship endured during "reconstruction," if only because it could not deny the obvious and needed to project an image that the regime was aware of and dealing with the problem. Public pronouncements described the city's horrendous sanitary conditions, the lack of housing and illegal seizure of apartments (even by highly placed officials), the mobilization of workers with (unfulfilled) material promises, the prominence of street crime, bread supply problems, and the poor work of factory cafeterias. Articles on the enthusiasm of workers mobilized to work in FZOs or at Rostsel'mash contradicted accounts that this work was carried out inadequately. In addition, the public party narrative explained material difficulties as a consequence of the war and the incompetence of individual leaders. It celebrated the arrest of "bandit crime gangs"—and in all of the cases announced arrests had already been made—assuring readers that the problem was being solved. The occasional public trial of "bandits" underscored the party's effort to show it was dealing with crime. Such reports, however, also implicitly conveyed a sense of lawlessness and breakdown of order. The press dismissed tales of the "black cat" gang as "rumors" but announced the arrests and trials of numerous sizable criminal gangs, some of which carried out elaborate crimes and operated for long periods of time. Crime reports also indicated wide availability of weapons and military uniforms and hinted at "panic" over the issue. Public assurances of the healthy supply of bread likewise pointed by inference to periodic crises, while the regime's public stance on the price increase for rations in the autumn of 1946 emphasized the war

---

[31] *Molot*, "Za strozhaishii rezhim ekonomii," 28 April 1944, p. 3.

[32] *Molot*, "Pis'mo v redaktsiiu," 14 January 1944, p. 4.

and drought as the primary causes. Finally, cafeterias were unsanitary and, despite the fact that many people relied on them to provide at least one meal a day, reportedly sometimes left workers "without lunch."

Living Conditions in the Internal Party Record

People in the Soviet Union endured dire poverty between 1943 and 1948, especially, as internal party sources further elucidate, single mothers and young workers.[33] A speaker at a plenum during the war declared, "We talk of help to the families of soldiers but don't even give bread to their children."[34] Several months after the war a district secretary acknowledged that "many families lost their main provider [read: *man* of the house], many children lost their parents, and many families now live in destitution."[35] A report on living conditions for workers at the Porcelain Goods Factory (*Emal'posuda*) concluded that the mostly female work force lived under "extremely difficult economic circumstances," especially single mothers with several children.[36] In February 1946, Gorkom Secretary Grigor'ian candidly asserted to his comrades at a closed gathering, "You yourselves see that material conditions are poor, that there's not enough food, [and] that we're doing an inadequate job providing for our children."[37] Elsewhere a komsomol leader complained that young workers endured unbearable living conditions in factory dormitories, an issue that also made its way into the press. The workers' dormitory at Rostsel'mash, for example, was filthy and overcrowded, with people sleeping two–three to a cot and covering themselves with mattresses to stay warm. Residents, according to this speaker, thought their dormitory was no different than a prison. Discussing still another worker dormitory, he noted that there was no electricity and added, "it's embarrassing to say so here, but the young men and women there do not even have separate toilet facilities."[38] A gorkom report from February 1944 stated that "daily living conditions in many workers' dorms in the city are unsatisfactory." In one dorm 24 people slept in a room only 25 square meters in space, and the dirty, cold, damp conditions there contributed to constant illness among workers.[39]

---

[33] Ellman notes that "[a]n important category of victims of this famine was large families where the father had been killed in the war and, hence, was no longer able to provide for his children" ("The 1947 Soviet Famine," 616).

[34] TsDNI f. 13, op. 4, d. 14, l. 99.

[35] TsDNI f. 13, op. 4, d. 144, l. 197.

[36] TsDNI f. 13, op. 4, d. 232, l. 6. This is also Military Factory No. 359.

[37] TsDNI f. 13, op. 4, d. 252, l. 33.

[38] TsDNI f. 13, op. 4, d. 144, l. 136. For conditions at Rostsel'mash's worker dormitories, see also l. 38.

[39] TsDNI f. 13, op. 4, dl. 68, l. 133.

Sanitation was a grave concern for the USSR as a whole and, as we have seen, a major topic of discussion in the public record. Party leaders also dealt with this problem extensively in closed meetings. Speaking at the Seventh City Party Conference in February 1943, Comrade Iakovlev of the Rostov Health Department told delegates that the clean up of streets and courtyards was hampered by the lack of water, a point made by others at the conference too.[40] Clearly the problem was not just the inaction or incompetence of individual housing managers as portrayed in public party texts. Comrade Tkachenko complained, for instance, that people mobilized for the city's cleanup often did not show up for work.[41] Gorkom Second Secretary Comrade Pastushenko noted as well that "there is very little transportation available for carrying trash out of the city." He proposed mobilizing the population to load up wheelbarrows and carts and to bury the trash in bomb craters and the basements of destroyed buildings. In a disturbing note, Pastushenko added that there were still corpses of Red Army and enemy soldiers in bombed-out buildings in the city and that they posed obvious health hazards.[42] In April leaders in health organizations reported 41 cases of typhus in Andreevskii district alone, as well as other serious diseases.[43] The situation had worsened by late 1944, when 210 cases of typhus were recorded in the final quarter of the year compared to only 19 in the final quarter of 1943. A major contributing factor, according to this gorkom account, was the lack of soap for the population.[44] Problems remained after the war as well, a gorkom protocol reporting 25 cases of typhus in the final quarter of 1945.[45] At a party plenum in March 1946, Comrade Korshunov of the Rostov obkom bemoaned that "right now the city's center is one huge trash pile," adding that the situation was worse than immediately after occupation.[46] There were several internal reports about the city's poor sanitary conditions in this five-year period.[47]

The lack of housing was also taken up by party leaders in closed sessions, their discussions revealing the complexities involved with an issue so central

---

[40] TsDNI f. 13, op. 4, d. 29, l. 38. See also TsDNI f. 13, op. 4, d. 29, l. 12; TsDNI f. 13, op. 4, d. 29, l. 24.

[41] TsDNI f. 13, op. 4, d. 29, l. 13. Two-thirds (400 of 600) of those mobilized to clean the city's streets and bridges did not show up. It is not clear, but this may be in reference to "voluntary" collective workdays on Saturdays (*subbotniki*).

[42] TsDNI f. 13, op. 4, d. 29, ll. 24–25.

[43] GARO f. 3955, op. 1, d. 1, l. 35.

[44] TsDNI f. 13, op. 4, d. 145, l. 40.

[45] TsDNI f. 13, op. 4, d. 291, ll. 36–37.

[46] TsDNI f. 13, op. 4, d. 213, l. 119. See also l. 206. See also TsDNI f. 13, op. 4, d. 218, l. 87.

[47] For more on sanitary conditions, see also GARO f. 3955, op. 1, d. 1, l. 26; TsDNI f. 13, op. 4, d. 213, l. 206; TsDNI f. 13, op. 4, d. 218, l. 87; TsDNI f. 13, op. 4, d. 292, l. 84; TsDNI f. 13, op. 4, d. 293, l. 105.

to people's everyday lives. As we have seen, hundreds of thousands of people returned to a city with roughly three-quarters of its housing destroyed or severely damaged. At a party plenum in July 1944, Comrade Andreev said that 216,800 people (out of a population of about 300,000) had been moved from bombed-out buildings and mud huts (*zemlianki*) into apartments, lamenting only that many remained in inadequate shelter.[48] At another meeting gorkom secretary Krasikova pointed out that fifteen young workers lived at a factory because they had nowhere to reside, and there were reports of workers living in the storage facilities at Rostsel'mash and Krasnyi Aksai.[49] *Molot* reported a case in which Comrade Shishkin, director of Rostov's Medical Institute, refused to relinquish a dwelling to its prewar owners of many years, the Davydovich family, after their return from evacuation.[50] The public account noted that the Medical Institute's director "already had an apartment," whereas an internal party document reveals the nature of that dwelling—Shishkin had lived in the morgue for two years.[51] This example, which seemed clear-cut in the party press, with Shishkin obviously in the wrong, illustrates the profound complexities involved in the issue of housing facing most of the country. The public account of this dispute *strongly* hinted that Shishkin had paid a bribe to an unidentified judge, but there is no mention of such suspicions in the closed party material about this case, which emphasized the destitute living conditions endured by the Medical Institute's director prior to his occupation of the Davydoviches' apartment.

These sources, moreover, reveal a penchant for quantification—a common characteristic of internal party texts as we will see. One gorkom report in January 1946 stated that they gave out 2,185 apartments in 1945, but noted that 5,476 families in Rostov still needed apartments.[52] Of those, 1,312 were demobilized troops with families, and 2,253 the families of soldiers who perished or were still serving.[53] In June the gorkom recorded that in the eight months since demobilization began, 895 families of demobilized troops had received apartments, but 1,292 still needed adequate housing. Among those was a sergeant's family who for several months had been living "under the open skies."[54] A subsequent report noted as well that, due to "formal bureaucratic" work by party representatives, "countless families of demobilized troops, fallen soldiers, disabled veterans, and others are without housing and

---

[48] TsDNI f. 13, op. 4, d. 64, l. 75.

[49] TsDNI f. 13, op. 4, d. 150, l. 80; TsDNI f. 13, op. 4, d. 302, l. 17.

[50] This information is cited above. G. Iakushchenko, "Dela kvartirnye," *Molot*, 16 May 1944, p. 3.

[51] TsDNI f. 13, op. 4, d. 426, l. 18.

[52] TsDNI f. 13, op. 4, d. 217, l. 31.

[53] TsDNI f. 13, op. 4, d. 280, l. 1.

[54] TsDNI f. 13, op. 4, d. 283, l. 132.

live on the streets, in entranceways, and in corridors." In just two districts, according to this internal report, 103 families were without housing, 56 of them
families of soldiers or demobilized troops and nine of them families of
wounded war veterans.[55] This internal material hardly takes into account the
lack of housing due to war-time devastation; the unspoken assumption of
these texts is that either the state would rebuild housing and construct new
housing rapidly to provide for everyone—which contradicted the regime's
emphasis on heavy industry during "reconstruction"—or that existing apartment space would be further and further divided into communal apartments
(*kommunalki*) until everyone had a "corner" (*ugol*) to themselves. Also, "'formal bureaucratic' work by party representatives," a phrase encountered in
several of these documents, alludes to corruption; as we will see, housing administrators sometimes accepted bribes to distribute apartments.[56]

Another recurring theme in these sources is the illegal seizures of apartments, which the media also discussed. Boris Dvinskii, first secretary of the
Rostov obkom, signed a decree in February 1943, stating that "several individuals took advantage of the lack of inhabitants in the city to seize apartments and pilfer the property of evacuated citizens." The document obligated
those illegally occupying the apartments of evacuated citizens to leave by
March 10, 1943, but it did not clarify where such residents—many of them
displaced by the destruction of their own apartment buildings—should go.[57]
Oblast Procurator Comrade Polozkov raised the issue in interesting terms at
the Seventh City Party Conference in early 1943. "People began to reason to
themselves," he explained, "'Why live in a workers' section of town when I
can live on Engels Street,' and with that began arbitrary rule." Polozkov
added, "I know of literally hundreds of cases of apartments being illegally
occupied."[58] In September 1943, a gorkom check-up revealed that throughout
the city 1,345 apartments were illegally seized; city leaders complained that
district housing bureaus were not doing enough to deal with the problem.[59]
At a closed party gathering Comrade Il'in of Kirovskii district told delegates

---

[55] TsDNI f. 13, op. 4, d. 220, l. 302. For more reports on the lack of housing, see also,
TsDNI f. 13, op. 4, d. 29, l. 37; TsDNI f. 13, op. 4, d. 130, ll. 75, 92–93; TsDNI f. 13, op. 4,
d. 131, l. 31; TsDNI f. 13, op. 4, d. 144, l. 139; TsDNI f. 13, op. 4, d. 150, l. 94 ob; TsDNI f.
13, op. 4, d. 233, ll. 92–92 ob.; TsDNI f. 13, op. 4, d. 283, l. 143.

[56] On corruption in the city's housing administrations, see, for example, TsDNI f. 13,
op. 4, d. 146, l. 62; TsDNI f. 13, op. 4, d. 291, l. 73; and TsDNI f. 13, op. 4, d. 220, l. 304.
Chap. 8 deals with corruption.

[57] GARO f. 3737, op. 8, d. 34ᵃ, l. 14. This decree was not published in *Molot* and there is
no indication that it was made public.

[58] TsDNI f. 13, op. 4, d. 29, l. 39.

[59] TsDNI f. 13, op. 4, d. 23, l. 49. This is separate from the problem of apartments being
distributed by the Germans during occupation to collaborators, a topic we will explore
in chap. 5.

of a recent conversation with an employee at the prison about an apartment on Donskoi Street. "He came to me for an official document confirming his right to live there, but because he already has an apartment in another district I refused to give him the requested papers." The prison assistant supposedly told Il'in he did not care about the papers and, indeed, continued to illegally reside in the apartment without official documentation. "We must give apartments to those *comrades* returning from evacuation," Il'in concluded, "and also to those who were burned out."[60] This statement clearly implies that party members had an advantage in this process. By February 1944 the official stance was softening, and those who repaired empty apartments that had been damaged in the war were allowed to stay in them.[61]

The mobilization of workers was another frequent topic of conversation behind closed doors, party leaders often complaining that it was being carried out poorly, as was also reported in the press. Internal accounts, however, are much more detailed and specific. The gorkom in mid-1944 discussed a report on Krasnyi Aksai's FZO, which prepared only 118 new workers, or 66 percent of its plan. Also, the factory had only 724 workers instead of the required 1,000.[62] At an oblast conference to discuss the mobilization of labor, Comrade Kozhetiakin said that at Rostsel'mash mobilized workers received the worse jobs, partly explaining the plant's high turnover rate. This contrasts sharply with the *Molot* report of the two workers voluntarily mobilized for work at the plant who were eager to take on any job. Kozhetiakin described how one woman with a mobilization notice for work at Rostsel'mash hid it in her pocket when she came in and pretended to be a volunteer. Consequently she was able to negotiate a better spot and receive better pay compared to other mobilized workers. "Those who are not mobilized," he said, "can talk their way into better positions, while those who are mobilized are practically under arrest [*tam vrode arestanta*]."[63] Competition for workers figured into these discussions of mobilization as well, one account lamenting that factories took on deserters from elsewhere.[64] Some factory directors clearly resented the preference given Rostsel'mash in the demand for labor power. At a party plenum in October 1945, the director of Krasnyi Aksai complained "we still need a great deal of help shoring up the workforce [too]," stating that the plant needs 1,300 people for a full complement of workers (at the time it had around 800). "They should send demobilized troops from our [Proletarksii] district to work

---

[60] TsDNI f. 13, op. 4, d. 29, l. 35 (my emphasis). For more closed party discussion of the illegal seizure of apartments, see also TsDNI f. 13, op. 4, d. 29, ll. 13, 15; GARO f. 3737, op. 8, d. 34a, ll. 28–29, 34.

[61] See GARO f. 3737, op. 8, d. 34a, l. 35.

[62] TsDNI f. 13, op. 4, d. 101, l. 6. For more on the poor mobilization of workers and trainees for the FZOs, see also TsDNI f. 13, op. 4, d. 45, ll. 77–78, 93, 95.

[63] GARO f. 13, op. 4, d. 1397, ll. 10–11.

[64] GARO f. 3737, op. 4, d. 1391, l. 38.

at our plant, but for some reason they do not." He said that Krasnyi Aksai sent propagandists door to door in the district recruiting workers among demobilized troops and repatriated citizens, but that several times they mobilized workers who were then sent to Rostsel'mash.[65]

As reported in *Molot*, factories had a difficult time luring and keeping workers if they could not provide adequate living conditions, an issue discussed at length in internal documents. Decrees ordering the mobilization of thousands of youth, all of whom were to be provided housing, food, clothing, etc., were impossible to implement. In late 1943 the city soviet issued a decree that, despite the sore need for workers, none was allowed to return until housing could be arranged for them ahead of time. While not all held to this law, it clearly would have restricted efforts to recruit new workers.[66] In January 1944 the director of Military Factory No. 359, Comrade Beriuza, wrote to Soviet deputy Kiparenko regarding a decree ordering the mobilization of 500 workers for the factory. Beriuza noted that there was only space for about 100 children in the factory's day care—the implication being that many of those mobilized would be single mothers—and requested that recruitment be carried out among people already living in Rostov-on-Don because the plant could not provide housing to anyone.[67] A separate report noted the difficulty keeping mobilized workers, especially those from the countryside because of the "failure of factory managers to provide even the most basic, necessary living conditions for them," a common theme in these sources just as in the party press.[68]

We noted that efforts to mobilize workers for Rostsel'mash and the city's FZOs received a lot of press coverage, both positive and negative. Internal party sources exposed the hyperbole of enthusiastic public accounts. One gorkom protocol complained that at Rostsel'mash, shop foremen did not assign trainees from the factory's FZOs to the correct jobs, giving them the

---

[65] TsDNI f. 13, op. 4, d. 144, ll. 21–22. V. K. Morkovin shows in his unpublished dissertation that the transfer of workers from Krasnyi Askai to Rostsel'mash greatly hindered production efforts at the former. In the first quarter of 1947, for example, the workforce at Krasnyi Askai was only 86 percent of the plan, but the director was nonetheless required to send 300 workers to Rostsel'mash. As a result, Krasnyi Aksai did not fulfill its monthly production plans again until August. V. K. Morkovin, "Rabochie Dona v poslevoennom periode, 1946–1950" (Kandidatskaia dissertatsiia, Rostov State University, 1972), 50.

[66] GARO f. 3737, op. 8, d. 34a, l. 38.

[67] GARO f. 3737, op. 4, d. 1391, l. 31.

[68] TsDNI f. 13, op. 4, d. 64, ll. 16–17. For reports on the inadequate job mobilized workers and trainees for FZOs and providing for them, see also TsDNI f. 13, op. 4, d. 146, l. 54; TsDNI f. 13, op. 4, d. 219, ll. 212–13; TsDNI f. 13, op. 4, d. 292, ll. 90–91; GARO f. 3737, op. 4, d. 1391, ll. 6–7; GARO f. 3737, op. 4, d. 1392, l. 44; GARO f. 3737, op. 4, d. 1394, ll. 11–12; GARO f. 3950, op. 1, d. 2, l. 47; GARO f. 3955, op. 1, d. 11, l. 51.

worst possible positions, as a result of which many of them did not show up for work.[69] According to a separate gorkom account, 290 people were "chosen" from among other factories to work at Rostsel'mash in the summer of 1945, but even after "individual discussions" the majority refused; only six agreed, but a subsequent check-up revealed that even they did not go to work at the plant.[70] Similar difficulties remained two years later when a report lamented people's refusal to work there. A gorkom protocol informed that instead of the required 2,330 only 994 new workers (42 percent) were mobilized for the plant.[71] Elsewhere an obkom secretary explained that in the first seven months of 1947, the plant lost 1,306 workers, most of whom abandoned their jobs without permission, and took on a mere 442 new volunteers.[72] The fact that so many workers left their jobs *without permission* reveals the impossibility of enforcing labor laws penalizing such behavior and shows that workers themselves evidently did not pay much attention to these statutes.[73] Commentators often attributed such problems to the poor conditions provided by the plant. A speaker at a party plenum claimed that the poor conditions of production and thus low pay at the plant contributed to the death of one of its workers, a wounded war veteran.[74] A separate gorkom report about Military Plant No. 359 clarified that the failure to build housing made it difficult for factories to attract the necessary workforce.[75]

---

[69] TsDNI f. 13, op. 4, d. 146, l. 54. The report noted that 39 of the 109 young workers trained in the factory's FZOs did not work in their specialty. Of the last 415 trainees to work at the plant, 118 had abandoned their jobs, whereas another 72 never showed up for work. Filtzer shows that nationwide the turnover rate among FZO trainees was significantly higher than for other workers (*Soviet Workers and Late Stalinism*, 38–39).

[70] TsDNI f. 13, op. 4, d. 172, l. 141.

[71] TsDNI f. 13, op. 4, d. 294, l. 89. See also TsDNI f. 13, op. 4, d. 292, l. 90, which noted that for the first quarter of 1947 only 41 workers had gone to Rostsel'mash instead of the required 400.

[72] TsDNI f. 13, op. 4, d. 302, l. 25. For more reports on workers refusing to go to Rostsel'mash, see also TsDNI f. 13, op. 4, d. 297, ll. 21, 33–34, 42; TsDNI f. 13, op. 4, d. 299, ll. 53, 78, 120.

[73] A December 1941 law made it illegal to quite work in a defense plant, and laws in April and May 1943 extended this to transportation workers. The remainder of the workforce was still governed by the Labor Law of 26 June 1940, in which the penalty for quitting work was a relatively mild two to four months in jail. Absenteeism in all industries still came under the June 1940 law as well, and the penalty remained "up to" six months corrective labor at your place of employment with "up to" 25 percent loss of pay. For an excellent discussion of these laws, see Filtzer, *Soviet Workers and Late Stalinism*, chap. 5.

[74] TsDNI f. 13, op. 4, d. 300, ll. 51–53. For similar reports on other industries, see also TsDNI f. 13, op. 4, d. 63, ll. 17–18.

[75] TsDNI f. 13, op. 4, d. 147, l. 148.

Internal material also highlighted some serious problems at the FZOs not noted in the press, including a link to Rostov's crime problem. In early 1945 Police Chief Kozlov informed delegates at the city party conference that FZO trainees accounted for a large percentage of the city's crimes, especially hooliganism and robbery. Arrests, he said, were made "almost every day."[76] In 1947 the head of the NKVD's department of struggle with child negligence complained to leaders in Rostov that FZOs often mobilized youth who "have fallen under the influence of the streets."[77] Youth "in need of a special regime of support," he explained, should be sent not to the FZO training schools but to the "labor education colonies" under the NKVD's jurisdiction. These accounts have little in common with press reports on enthusiastic voluntarism. Talk of crime often filled conference halls and party reports in this five-year period, as in the party press, but these sources noted the lack of police as a large part of the problem, an issue not discussed publicly. A district secretary at the Seventh City Party Conference in February 1943 told delegates that "in one instance a group disguised as soldiers burst into an apartment and robbed it. We are currently taking the appropriate measures, but we don't have enough people on the force."[78] The public announcement of disguised soldiers robbing people did not come for several weeks—only *after* suspects had reportedly been apprehended. Comrade Tkachenko of Zheleznodorozhnyi district similarly proclaimed, "we have gangs that run into apartments and rob them, but with only ten policemen for the whole district we cannot pacify the situation."[79] Several other speakers noted the lack of police, an acute problem in the early post-occupation period that obviously compounded the city's crime problem but was overlooked in press reports of crime.[80]

As noted, in November 1944 *Molot* reported that "street crime in Rostov has sharply declined," but a mere two months later Comrade Kozlov, the city's police chief, "admitted" at a party conference "that the crime rate [in the city] is still very high." The main reason, he added, "is that we [police] work poorly," taking on the brunt of the blame. Women, youth, and "even wounded war veterans," Kozlov noted, carried out a "significant number" of the city's petty crimes. Women under age 18, for example, committed 23 percent of all thefts in 1944. Most women caught stealing, he added in passing, had not been involved in crime before.[81] Petty crime in Rostov increased sig-

---

[76] TsDNI f. 13, op. 4, d. 131, l. 47. Kozlov added that 23 people from FZO No. 11 were arrested, 18 from FZO No. 16, and 7 from FZO No. 7.

[77] GARO f. 3737, op. 4, d. 1394, l. 16.

[78] TsDNI f. 13, op. 4, d. 29, l. 34.

[79] TsDNI f. 13, op. 4, d. 29, l. 13.

[80] For more comments at the conference on the inadequate number of police, see also TsDNI f. 13, op. 4, d. 29, ll. 12, 35–36.

[81] TsDNI f. 13, op. 4, d. 131, ll. 44, 47.

nificantly during the famine, a gorkom protocol citing 576 thefts and robberies in the final quarter of 1946, 483 (84 percent) of which were reportedly
solved. In the first quarter of 1947, this account further noted, 600 crimes were
committed and 456 (76 percent) solved.[82] The famine was underway by the
time of a December 1946 meeting, in which a district party secretary conceded, "in our city right now the situation with street crime is worrisome."[83]
Crime was a major issue of discussion during election campaigns in Rostov in
1946 and 1947; in one closed account a party propagandist noted that voters'
"fear of being robbed and returning home without clothes kept them from
coming" to campaign meetings held after dark.[84] The mere fact that robbers
literally stole the clothes off of people's backs because they seldom had anything else of value says a great deal about the material conditions endured by
the population at this time.

Beginning with the February 1943 conference, internal party documents
also relayed serious discussions over Rostov's periodic bread supply problems.[85] We saw that amid a bread crisis in May *Molot* announced the upcoming trial of Palamarchuk, director of the city's grain department, for allegedly
holding up the transport of grain. Yet internal party documents exposed a
complicated history behind that brief public announcement. The day before
Molot's notice, leaders of the bread industry discussed the whereabouts of
several missing train cars with 320 tons of grain supposedly headed to
Rostov. "Somewhere along the way," gorkom secretary A. I. Shevchenko
stated in opening remarks, "these train cars disappeared and are now no-
where to be found. This means," he informed those present, "that this grain
we counted on to get us out of the difficult bread crisis is not on the way."[86]
Shevchenko, the highest-ranking official at the meeting, further proclaimed,
"We can no longer tolerate the outrageous situation we have at the current
time when we are unable to provide bread to the workers of Rostov." He
ended on a threatening note: "Those who do not fulfill their tasks will be
looked upon by the gorkom of the party as saboteurs and will be dealt with
accordingly."[87] A second speaker made clear that this was not the first time
Rostov encountered such problems. "Here we have again the same situation

---

[82] TsDNI f. 13, op. 4, d. 293, l. 95. For more on crime, see also TsDNI f. 13, op. 4, d. 337,
l. 55.

[83] TsDNI f. 13, op. 4, d. 221[a], l. 172.

[84] TsDNI f. 13, op. 4, d. 221a, l. 170. Chap. 7 looks at the elections.

[85] TsDNI f. 13, op. 4, d. 29, ll. 24–25.

[86] TsDNI f. 13, op. 4, d. 29, l. 1. Shevchenko said, "We don't know where these
mythological train cars of grain are located."

[87] TsDNI f. 13, op. 4, d. 29, l. 2.

that we had recently," he said, "we warn, we warn, but the disruption in the bread supply to the population continues and continues."[88]

Those in charge of the city's bread production and distribution pinned the blame on others and did not even mention Palamarchuk, whose trial was noted in *Molot*. There were several "guilty" parties in this drama, including Vointenko who organized the grain shipment. "You cannot say I failed to supply Rostov with bread," he began, explaining that the grain was either seized by the Germans or mistakenly sent elsewhere. "Perhaps we are partially to blame," he admitted, "in that we do not travel around and check up on shipments, but even today I was unable to ride here due to the lack of transportation."[89] The director of Mill No. 3, moreover, reneged on a promise to prepare rye for bread production. "You ask, you bow to people, but nothing comes of it," Vointenko noted sourly. He concluded by calling for the creation of a special commission to determine what happened to the missing train cars of grain.[90] The director of Mill No. 3 complained that there was no storage space, no transportation, and not enough workers to unload grain.[91] The head of the city's bread distribution trust expressed his preparedness to take blame, "but you all clearly understand our situation—there is no work force and no transportation." He said that several times Voitenko had informed him that a shipment of grain was expected. He organized workers to unload it, but the shipment never showed up.[92] As in the case of the city's poor sanitary conditions, there was clearly more to this problem than the incompetence of a few individuals, though *Molot* only reported on the arrest of a lower-level figure.

Leaders discussed problems in the city's bread supply many times throughout this five-year period; the next major development was the onset of famine in autumn 1946.[93] In conjunction with the price increases an-

---

[88] TsDNI f. 13, op. 4, d. 29, l. 1.

[89] Vointenko wondered aloud what happened to 46 tons of wheat he sent to *Krupzavod* for processing. As we will see in chap. 6, the director of Krupzavod, a plant that processed grain into cereal primarily for the Red Army, was running a scheme at this time whereby he and co-workers stole many tons of grain and sold it on the illegal market. *Molot* reported on the crime in August 1943, but made no connection between this scam and the earlier bread crises.

[90] TsDNI f. 13, op. 4, d. 29, l. 5.

[91] TsDNI f. 13, op. 4, d. 29, l. 9.

[92] TsDNI f. 13, op. 4, d. 29, l. 8. For reports on subsequent bread supply problems in June 1943, see TsDNI f. 13, op. 4, d. 16, l. 25; TsDNI f. 13, op. 4, d. 28, l. 2.

[93] TsDNI f. 13, op. 4, d. 56, l. 104 (October 1943); TsDNI f. 13, op. 4, d. 68, l. 34 (January 1944); TsDNI f. 13, op. 4, d. 70, l. 64 (May 1944); TsDNI f. 13, op. 4, d. 149, l. 25 (September–October 1945); TsDNI f. 13, op. 4, d. 149, l. 145 (December 1945); TsDNI f. 13, op. 4, d. 299, l. 64 (December 1947).

nounced in *Pravda* in mid-September, the Central Committee issued an order "not for publication" that prompted some tough talk in closed party circles. The decree noted that the price hikes would demand "sacrifice" (which was not included in the public announcement), without which "we will not be able to rebuild our devastated economy." To offset the price hikes somewhat the measure lowered prices in commercial stores and raised the wages of the lowest-paid workers by several hundred rubles a month.[94] At a party meeting in Rostov to discuss the order one speaker cautioned, "we must correctly explain these measures and repulse whiners and skeptics while instilling faith in a bright, happy future." A subsequent speaker seconded these thoughts: "There will be whiners who will complicate matters, and we must rebuff backward attitudes." Rostov Obkom First Secretary Aleksandriuk told those present to "explain" the decree to the population in terms of "the common good," reminding them of sacrifices made during the revolution, Civil War, and Great Fatherland War while supporting the decision with the promise of a better future.[95] The emphasis on "explanatory work" exposed a condescending approach, the use of a hard hand against "whiners" encouraged. These (male) local party leaders, moreover, couched their "explanation" of this dramatic drop in living standards in terms (the past and the future) that obscured the severity of the present situation. They clearly expected opposition, categorizing it at the outset as "backward."[96] At the end of September the regime issued a subsequent decree paring down the list of ration recipients by eliminating children and non-working adult dependents from the lists. This removed 27.5 million people from the rationing system nationally, a measure so harsh that even provincial party leaders complained to central leaders about the measure.[97] The procurator of Rostov oblast cited opposition to the fact that, in the oblast as a whole, 5,486 children and over 40,000 adult dependents had lost ration entitlements.[98]

Internal documents evince that party leaders knew the party's public narrative was untrue, or at least that it was greatly exaggerated. During "reconstruction," Rostov's population—families of soldiers, single mothers, disabled veterans, young workers, war orphans, and others—endured extremely harsh

---

[94] In 1944 the regime began operating commercial stores selling goods without ration cards, but at very high prices. On these aspects of the measure, see RGASPI f. 17, op. 3, d. 1061, ll. 8–16.

[95] TsDNI f. 13, op. 4, d. 221a, ll. 156–59.

[96] A gorkom report during the March 1948 bread crisis likewise noted that "enemy elements" whipped up "panic" and that some stores illegally resumed rationing. TsDNI f. 13, op. 4, d. 415, ll. 205 and 242.

[97] See Zima, *Golod v SSSR*, 173–75; and Filtzer, *Soviet Workers and Late Stalinism*, 52–62.

[98] GARF f. 8131, op. 37, d. 3200, l. 1–1 ob. Cited in Filtzer, *Soviet Workers and Late Stalinism*, 61.

material conditions, and the party could do very little to alleviate their suffering. The terrible sanitary conditions discussed in *Molot* were due to more than just the inaction of individual housing managers: the lack of water, transportation, and workers also contributed to the problem. In addition, these sources revealed that families lived in mud huts, burned out buildings, corridors, workplaces (including the morgue), or in some instances "under the open skies." There were "workers' sections" in the city but the best apartments were located in the center (where most party leaders lived). As also reported in the paper, people in positions of power illegally seized apartments, though at times there were extenuating circumstances, while the distribution of housing in the war-torn city favored party members, a detail not mentioned in the local party press. Mobilization efforts, moreover, were carried out poorly and promises to trainees went unfulfilled; FZOs were so desperate for young workers that they took on troublemakers "under the influence of the streets." Criminal gang activity in the city was facilitated by the lack of police, but crime was not solely the work of "gangs of bandits," as emphasized in the party press, but also of individuals acting out of desperation (especially at the height of the famine). There were many first-time offenders, including women and youth, and, despite *Molot*'s emphasis on criminal cases that had been solved, internal party material shows that—as one would expect—some crimes went unsolved. Finally, these sources include candid discussions of the frequent bread supply problems plaguing Rostov, revealing *far* greater detail and complexity than press reports of this issue. Those in charge of supplying the city with bread passed the blame for persistent difficulties, while even local leaders felt that the elimination of rations for children and non-working adults was harsh. Party leaders, moreover, clearly anticipated worker opposition to the regime's measures in autumn 1946 in response to the drought and poor harvest.

Popular Perceptions of Living Conditions

The recorded statements and questions of workers and others, supplemented by material from memoirs and interviews, offer us a view of the population's concerns and opinions. Women have a strong voice in these sources, which focus sharply on material difficulties. Workers and others often aped the party press or "spoke Bolshevik,"[99] such as one young worker at Rostsel'mash who in 1946 reportedly avowed, "the government clothed me and fed me when I was at the FZO, so I decided to repay that debt by over fulfilling my production quota by May first."[100] A year later a demobilized soldier and worker at another plant also allegedly declared, "We are the owners of the country and Soviet power brings happiness to our lives. On the thirtieth anni-

---

[99] On "speaking Bolshevik," see Kotkin, *Magnetic Mountain*, chap. 5.

[100] TsDNI f. 13, op. 4, d. 415, ll. 116, 133.

versary of the October Revolution we will all go to the demonstration, but now we must work hard and fulfill our yearly plan ahead of schedule."[101] Positive comments always precede criticisms in these formulaic accounts, and the reports invariably note that these opinions reflect the "healthy attitudes" of the "vast majority" of the population. The regime propagated an ideology to win support among the population for the party's policies (to "manufacture consent"), so we should not be surprised to see workers and others "speaking Bolshevik" for whatever reason and whether sincere or not. The reports then proceed to list the negative comments, which tend to be more numerous than the positive statements listed. In any case, statements supporting the regime do *not* disprove the existence of underlying class tensions in Soviet society.

While acknowledging supportive comments by workers and others, my focus is on acts of protest and negative commentaries in part because they are less tainted by the function of power. People were critical of the Soviet regime *despite* the possibility of career advancement offered by "speaking Bolshevik," not *because of* it, and they protested despite the threat of repression. In this material people expressed concern over living standards repeatedly, such as the seven students who asked to be released from the FZO for railway workers due to "difficult material conditions" resulting from the price hikes on rationed items and the reduced norms in September 1946.[102] A revealing query appeared in local and central reports: "Why are disabled veterans begging for money in the streets?"[103] One of the local reports included a follow-up question not in the central record: "Why didn't the government provide for them?"[104] Summing up the main problem for most, someone in July 1945 asked, "Why do we eat so poorly?"[105] A mother in 1946 inquired whether

---

[101] TsDNI f. 13, op. 4, d. 337, l. 34. During the holiday bond drive the following year another worker reportedly announced: "Life in our country will be even brighter and more beautiful and the bond drive, another sure step along the path to communism, will speed us along toward the dawning of our beloved motherland." TsDNI f. 13, op. 4, d. 414, l. 42. For more supportive comments on a wide variety of occasions, see also TsDNI f. 13, op. 4, d. 414, ll. 2, 42; TsDNI f. 13, op. 4, d. 415, ll. 77, 89–90, 93. I will discuss the importance of holiday celebrations as part of the myth of reconstruction in the next chapter.

[102] TsDNI f. 13, op. 4, d. 232, ll. 9, 23. This report also states that 55 women workers in the city's garment factories quit for the same reason.

[103] This question appears in two local sources, TsDNI f. 13, op. 4, d. 30, l. 152; TsDNI f. 13, op. 4, d. 92, l. 284. It was also passed on to the center. See RGASPI f. 17, op. 88, d. 331, l. 10. For similar comments, see also RGASPI f. 17, op. 88, d. 332, l. 8. In another local source, someone asked, "When will unemployed people and beggars stop gathering in the streets?" (TsDNI f. 13, op. 4, d. 233, l. 48).

[104] TsDNI f. 13, op. 4, d. 30, l. 152.

[105] TsDNI f. 13, op. 4, d. 180, l. 44. This comment, of course, is recorded well *before* the famine.

children would be given shoes and clothing so they could attend school.[106] In a preface to a list of questions posed by workers at public meetings in 1947, a district party secretary noted: "workers and civil servants exhibit particular interest toward improvements in material conditions and matters of daily life."[107] Difficulties remained at the end of this five-year period as well. "Where," a housewife inquired in 1947, "are wives supposed to get potatoes, onions, groats, and butter?"[108] These questions highlight the difficult economic conditions endured by the population and show the party's failure to supply the most basic needs.

K. S. Karol remembered that real wages in the official economy were ridiculously low, the average worker earning between 300–500 rubles a month, enough to buy merely a few kilos of bread at the market. While studying at Rostov State University Karol worked as a factory administrator in a metallurgical plant, but even if he and his wife pooled their salaries they could have purchased only 750 grams of butter at market prices. He also recalled the importance of cafeterias for workers' survival, relaying official figures for 1944 that the USSR allotted 27 percent of available foodstuffs to canteens in which over 40 million meals a day were produced.[109] However, the measure raising prices on rationed items in autumn 1946 also impacted the price of meals in factory cafeterias, which became too costly for many workers. Interviewees certainly recalled the harsh living conditions. Sergei Zhak observed that most people were "equally poor" and that he himself went around in "hand-me-down rags from my father." Like many people he owned one nice set of clothes that he wore on special occasions such as his graduation in 1947.[110] Nina Nikitichna K. and several other people remembered that a large number of homeless children roamed the streets, especially in the period just after occupation.[111] Svetlana Semenova said that she could not start school at age seven in 1943 because she had no clothes. "We lived in extremely difficult conditions," she added.[112] Aleksandra Ermolenko remembered that to stay warm during the war and after they burned furniture, books, anything they could; her family gave her the task of "taking" coal from train cars at the train station.[113]

---

[106] TsDNI f. 13, op. 4, d. 335, l. 27.

[107] TsDNI f. 13, op. 4, d. 233, l. 48.

[108] TsDNI f. 13, op. 4, d. 415, l. 140.

[109] Karol, *Solik*, 324.

[110] Interview by author, 7 March 1995.

[111] Interviews by author with Nina Nikitichna K., 17 March 1995; Svetlana Chernysheva, 3 March 1995; Svetlana Semenova, 16 April 1995.

[112] Interview by author, 16 April 1995.

[113] Interview by author, 16 April 1995. She adds that it was explained to her in such a way that it would not seem like stealing.

People asked and commented on housing, sometimes in a sharp tone. "When," a resident of Leninskii district stated, "will our housing bureau begin repairing apartments instead of just collecting rent money?"[114] In an unpublished memoir written in the early 1990s, Mariia Zhak reveals the tremendous complexity of housing-related issues. Even before her family's return to Rostov from evacuation in October 1945, they knew that their apartment had been occupied. A family of six had moved there supposedly from a bombed-out building, saying they heard a rumor that the Zhaks had drowned during evacuation. Zhak's husband, however, discovered that the family's building had not been bombed, just abandoned. In the dispute that followed, the courts ruled in favor of the Zhaks but delayed the eviction of the other family until adequate housing could be found for them. "We agreed to live in the large bedroom while they stayed in a smaller, adjacent room," Zhak noted, and eventually the other family found housing and moved out, but the whole process "took a long while." The bottom line for *many* people in formerly occupied territory was simply that there was not enough housing to go around, although, as our sources also show, existing housing was distributed advantageously to those with party connections.[115] Svetlana P. Chernysheva returned with her family to Rostov in November 1943 to find their apartment building in the city's center destroyed, but because her father was a highly placed official in the railroad department they were quickly granted another apartment near the center of town.[116] Nina Nikitichna K., a party member since 1939 who returned from evacuation ten days after occupation to work at Rostsel'mash, was likewise promptly granted a new apartment.[117] In contrast, Svetlana Semenova said that she and her family of "simple working people" lived on the outskirts of Rostov, where city services were especially poor and transportation a major problem, whereas "only rich people lived in the center of town."[118] Semenova clearly perceived the prevailing class bias in the distribution of housing, which, as revealed by internal party sources, was in fact handed out selectively.

Archival sources divulge workers' perspective on the poor mobilization of labor for Rostsel'mash and on crime. "The following conversation," accord-

---

[114] TsDNI f. 13, op. 4, d. 180, l. 44. For other questions about the situation in housing, see also TsDNI f. 13, op. 4, d. 221a, l. 178.

[115] Mariia S. Zhak, unpublished memoir. Zhak added that little of their furniture remained. One of her greatest losses was the family's library, including some rare books and several original publications of Pushkin, all of which were gone when they returned. "I suppose if they kept someone warm at that difficult time," she writes, "then it was worth it." She remembered years later seeing several of her former possessions in a neighbor's apartment.

[116] Interview by author, 3 March 1995.

[117] Interview by author, 17 March 1995.

[118] Interview by author, 16 April 1995.

ing to one report, "is openly heard among workers in plants throughout the city: 'We will not go to Sel'mash, and if we're not needed in our current positions fire us!'"[119] Another account from October 1945 relayed workers' response after discussions with party representatives about working at the plant. "As a rule," it stated, "workers said they did not want to work at Rostsel'mash because the city's transportation was deficient and because the plant did not adequately feed workers."[120] Significantly, this report coincided with the fire that destroyed many of the city's streetcars and greatly worsened its transportation system. This evidence suggests again that workers negotiated for the best possible conditions at work. Also, at least some workers clearly were not afraid of being "fired"; some seemed to welcome it. This was because the tight labor market gave them room to maneuver and, as we will see, because people knew they could make a better living working full-time on the city's illegal market. In these documents, moreover, workers pose specific questions about crime, which came up often at public meetings, usually wanting to know why more was not done to solve the problem.[121] Someone asked: "Why are workers sentenced more harshly for workplace theft than are thieves and robbers?"[122] One worker identified as a rank-and-file party member wanted to know what was going to be done about the fact that "prostitutes walk the streets in Rostov?" City leaders did not notice the problem, he added, nor had *Molot* taken up the issue.[123]

The crime of the period is etched in people's memories. Mariia Zhak recalled that there were countless criminal gangs during the war and after.[124] Sergei Zhak said that crime was rampant until Marshall Zhukov dispatched army brigades to round up and execute criminals, a "not very democratic but yet very effective way of dealing with the problem," he added.[125] There is no way to determine whether these were the "measures" taken against crime by the NKVD and oblast procurator's office reported in the 1944 *Molot* article described above.[126] Several people remembered hearing of the criminal gang "Black Cat."[127] Oleg Pianiatsev, 12 years old at war's end, said tales of the

---

[119] TsDNI f. 13, op. 4, d. 415, l. 83.

[120] TsDNI f. 13, op. 4, d. 181, l. 123.

[121] For questions at public meetings on crime, see TsDNI f. 13, op. 4, d. 221a, ll. 177–78; TsDNI f. 13, op. 4, d. 233, l. 93; TsDNI f. 13, op. 4, d. 259, l. 124.

[122] TsDNI f. 13, op. 4, d. 313, l. 18.

[123] TsDNI f. 13, op. 4, d. 415, l. 82. *Molot* did not report on prostitution during this five-year period.

[124] Interview by author, 6 March 1995.

[125] Interview by author, 7 March 1995

[126] *Molot*, "V oblastnoi prokurature i NKVD," 19 November 1944, p. 4.

[127] See interviews by author with Svetlana P. Chernysheva, 3 March 1995; V. I. Akimenko, 20 May 1995; Sergei V. Zhak, 7 March 1995; Mariia S. Zhak, 6 March 1995.

"black cat" gang were probably just legends, "although there was an awful lot of talk about it." He remembered that street crime was a huge problem, saying that in either 1946 or 1947 he found a young woman's body in Gor'kii Park. "This was not an uncommon discovery at that time."[128] Genadii Ermolenko maintained that there definitely were organized criminal gangs like "Black Cat." He spoke with some of their victims and recalled the public trial of one such group consisting of 20 people that was called either "White Rose" or "Red Rose." "Such groups existed," he asserted, "and were dealt with harshly when caught." Ermolenko also remembered widespread looting in Rostov-on-Don when the Red Army retook the city in February 1943. "People emptied stores, warehouses, apartments, anything in sight."[129] V. I. Akimenko, 18 when he came to Rostov to study art in 1946, said that he clutched his bread ration cards because he was afraid someone would steal them.[130] Svetlana Semenova said that once when her aunt returned home from work at 10:00 p.m. in either 1946 or 1947 robbers attacked her in the street and stole her purse and clothes. "She begged them to let her keep her documents," Semenova recalled, "and oddly enough they did." The police caught the muggers and sent them to jail and her aunt got her money and clothes back.[131]

Along with crime, bread and food supply was also a major concern for the city's inhabitants. Workers posed a lot of questions about this problem and proffered different "explanations" than those promoted in party sources. At a factory meeting in 1944 a worker identified as having "a lot of children" asked, "Why don't dependents regularly receive bread?"[132] Two years later and several months before leaders *decreased* rations for dependents a worker inquired when bread rations for children and housewives would be increased.[133] Several workers objected publicly to the higher prices for rationed goods in September 1946, which, among other problems, dramatically increased the cost of meals in factory cafeterias beyond what many workers could afford.[134] Tailor Kovalev, for example, deplored at one meeting that half of his salary already went for bread, while one worker told a party representative, "I will have to hang myself now, there is no other choice; life has

---

[128] Interview by author, 17 April 1995.

[129] Interview by author, 16 April 1995.

[130] Interview by author, 20 May 1995.

[131] Interview by author, 16 April 1995.

[132] RGASPI f. 17, op. 88, d. 331, l. 40.

[133] RGASPI f. 17, op. 88, d. 331, l. 41; TsDNI f. 13, op. 4, d. 259, l. 124.

[134] Filtzer notes this problem for the country as a whole, pointing out that as a result of the price hikes the number of workers taking meals at factories fell dramatically (*Soviet Workers and Late Stalinism*, 64–65). In Rostov there were reports of mini-hunger strikes of a sort, workers protesting the increased prices on rationed lunches by refusing to eat in factory cafeterias. See, for example, TsDNI f. 13, op. 4, d. 232, l. 26.

become simply impossible."[135] In a particularly symbolic statement, two mother heroines at the fish-processing plant purposely slowed their rate of production.[136] Also, as noted above, the USSR exported grain despite famine conditions, which did not escape the population's attention. At a lecture in August 1947 someone asked why the commercial sale of bread had not yet begun and added, "Does the export of grain reflect on the end of rationing here at home?"[137] At the Mikoyan Shoe Factory a worker straightforwardly inquired, "Are we going to help the new democratic countries [of Eastern Europe] this year and, if so, will we have enough grain to end rationing?"[138] At another meeting in September someone pointedly asked, "Why do we sell bread abroad when the supply for our own population is so poor?"[139] One woman who lived with her two children in a worker's dorm complained publicly in November 1947, "They want us to work, and we are not against working. We even overfulfill our [production quotas], but life is difficult and our children are hungry and bloated from malnutrition."[140]

Several reports described individualized public protests by workers over the lack of bread, including leaving work and slowdowns in production. Rostov's procurator informed Moscow that the price increases and the paring down of the list of ration recipients had provoked illegal quitting among workers and an "amoral phenomenon"—people were refusing to work.[141] During the 1948 crisis two loading-dock workers at the Kalinin Paper Mill quit work, one saying to the factory manager, "You aren't worried about supplying workers with bread, so everyone should quit and then you would start to think about our problems." A construction worker told his boss, "we will not work for 300 grams of bread and if they don't give us enough bread I will not come to work tomorrow." Two saw operators at a Military Plant left work "due to the difficulties with bread," returning only after "being persuaded."[142] A woman whose husband reportedly left with the Germans asked "sharply" at one meeting, "Are we going to get bread or are we supposed to work hungry?"[143] These texts also convey complaints about bread lines. Confronted by a plant director for being three hours late, two women workers

---

[135] TsDNI f. 13, op. 4, d. 232, l. 24. For similar comments, see also ll. 39, 55.

[136] TsDNI f. 13,op. 4, d. 232, ll. 63–64. One of the women was a *stakhanovitsa*, a worker who consistently over fulfills work norms.

[137] TsDNI f. 13, op. 4, d. 233, l. 3.

[138] TsDNI f. 13, op. 4, d. 233, l. 60.

[139] TsDNI f. 13, op. 4, d. 233, l. 71.

[140] TsDNI f. 13, op. 4, d. 233, l. 68.

[141] GARF f. 8131, op. 37, d. 3200, l. 1–1ob. Cited in Filtzer, *Soviet Workers and Late Stalinism*, 61.

[142] TsDNI f. 13, op. 4, d. 415, l. 146.

[143] TsDNI f. 13, op. 4, d. 415, l. 142.

declared in their defense, "We stood in line for bread all night and just now got it, and we have three kids to feed." The author of this report added that school attendance was low because children stood in bread lines all day, and several accounts noted that workers who lived alone complained most vehemently because there was no one to stand in line for them while they were at work.[144] A shop foreman at DGTF complained that it is impossible to get any sleep because workers have to stand in line all night to get bread.[145] An engineer and rank-and-file party member proclaimed, "I think whoever is in charge of bread distribution is specifically trying to upset the population," while another account concluded that the supply crisis fostered a lack of faith in the party not just among the population at large, "but even among several secretaries of party organizations."[146]

Workers' voices recorded in *svodki* reflect the views asserted in public meetings, albeit in a starker tone. In response to the cut in rations someone in the women's dressing room at the cigarette factory DGTF reportedly said, "What a low point Stalin has reached to begin taking away our bread." A construction worker was overheard objecting to her friends, "they've told us about the five-year plan, promised improvements in living standards for workers, and in reality they decrease our bread rations down to the last crumb." Two women workers at DGTF complained that life was becoming simply impossible.[147] Workers were often overheard objecting to the Soviet government's export of grain. At the Kalinin Paper Mill, for instance, a saw operator commented to a co-worker, "We gave bread to other countries and now we ourselves have nothing to eat." An engineer at the train station repeated this opinion, while a lathe operator and metal worker at Rostsel'mash lamented "our working class is without bread again because we send it abroad."[148] These comments confirm what the lists of questions posed at public meetings strongly hint at (but the other source bases examined above completely ignore)—the export of grain abroad was seen by many as a major factor leading to famine, and thus as contrary to the population's interests.[149] The criticisms further show that some people were well informed about the causes of the grain shortage beyond what the regime revealed publicly.

---

[144] TsDNI f. 13, op. 4, d. 415, l. 160. For more reports of single people suffering from the crisis, see also TsDNI f. 13, op. 4, d. 415, ll. 159, 205.

[145] TsDNI f. 13, op. 4, d. 415, l. 159.

[146] TsDNI f. 13, op. 4, d. 415, l. 147; and TsDNI f. 13, op. 4, d. 415, l. 164. For similar comments, see also ll. 148–49.

[147] TsDNI f. 13, op. 4, d. 232, l. 3. For similar comments, see also ll. 4, 6, 27–28, 33, 39, 44, 51, 63–64.

[148] TsDNI f. 13, op. 4, d. 232, ll. 47–48.

[149] For similar comments nationally, see Zubkova, *Russia After the War*, 43–46.

Several people recalled that fish from the river Don saved the population from total starvation in the immediate aftermath of occupation.[150] The abundance of fish is confirmed by documented evidence as well. In May 1943 Obkom Secretary Dvinskii sent a telegram to the Central Committee informing them that the oblast fish industry fulfilled its six-month plan by 212 percent. He added that it could have been even better except there was no salt to store the fish with. One can assume that the good fishing was due to the disruption of the city's fishing industry during the war and occupation, allowing a fish population explosion.[151] Remembering the postwar famine no one recalled a victim they knew who died from starvation. Svetlana Chernysheva said "there was little food and almost all people lived poorly. However, no one died of hunger," she added, not even during the famine.[152] Mariia Zhak also could not remember anyone who perished from hunger, while V. I. Akimenko confided that he was constantly hungry and weak from malnutrition during the famine, which Genadii Ermolenko called a year of "frightening hunger," maintaining "it was very difficult at times just to get a piece of bread."[153] Ekaterina Karotskova volunteered, "there was practically nothing to eat" at the time. She remembered so-called "Stalin chocolate" made from the shells of sunflower seeds left over after pressing oil, the name revealing a sense of critical irony.[154] Not surprisingly, therefore, the material difficulties and hunger they endured during "reconstruction" figured prominently in most interviewees' memories.

These sources give us a glimpse at popular views on material conditions in Soviet Russia during "reconstruction." Women have a strong voice in these sources, which point to the existence of beggars, homeless children, and, allegedly, prostitutes in the streets of Rostov. Like the previous sources examined, this material suggests that party members received preference in the distribution of housing, one of the most important (and scarce) items in the city. Reflecting Oblast Procurator Polozkov's comment behind closed doors that during the war workers seized apartments downtown out of envy, one respondent expressed the belief that the "richest" denizens resided in the city's center, whereas "simple" workers had to live in the outskirts. The failure to mobilize workers for Rostsel'mash, furthermore, resulted from the poor conditions provided to prospective employees by that plant, since the workplace played such a pivotal role in the lives and daily affairs of workers. One might surmise from this material that workers not only picked which plants

---

[150] Interviews by author with Vadim P. Iakovlev, 15 March 1995; Genadii Ermolenko, 16 April 1995; Svetlana Semenova, 16 April 1995.

[151] RGASPI f. 17, op. 122, d. 27, l. 42. Ermolenko also noted the unfortunate lack of salt at the time. Interview by author, 16 April 1995.

[152] Interview by author, 3 March 1995.

[153] Interviews by author, (Akimenko) 20 May 1995 and (Ermolenko) 16 April 1995.

[154] Interview by author, 5 March 1995.

they wanted to work at, exhibiting flexibility in the job market (albeit within limits), but also that they knew from talking among themselves which factories provided the best overall deal. Comments on crime, moreover, indicate dissatisfaction with the party's struggle against it, while a number of workers publicly protested the lack of bread in word and/or deed during frequent crises, some of them citing the export of grain as a factor in the postwar famine. Interviewees, meanwhile, revealed their own "apartment litigation" and recalled the prominence of crime—some of them through personal experience—and of stories about gangs like "Black Cat," though there was no consensus as to whether such tales were true. Finally, respondents drew a picture of hunger and harsh poverty during the war and postwar years, as we saw in the other sources as well.

అ అ

The varied material examined here paints a harsh picture of living conditions in Soviet Russia during "reconstruction." The party press blamed shortcomings in the city's sanitation, housing, mobilization of workers, crime, bread supply, and factory cafeterias on the individuals in charge, while closed party discussions showed that these problems were far more complex. People expressed doubts about the party's public claims and criticisms of its policies throughout this five-year period, but especially during the famine (1946–48). While the party publicly depicted the food shortages as a result of war and drought, many workers blamed the export of grain abroad, an issue not mentioned in press reports. The regulation of consumption through rationing was a key element of the relationship between state and society and the bottom line is that, for the regime, feeding, clothing, and housing the population was *not* the highest priority. Stalinist planning in the postwar period (as before) invested disproportionately in heavy industry, perhaps because of the developing Cold War and the perceived need to maintain military readiness in case of another conflict. This compounded the material hardship of the population, but workers did at least have some room to maneuver in order to negotiate the best possible living conditions because of competition among factory managers for limited labor power. The country suffered a crime wave during "reconstruction," press coverage of which stops short of acknowledging poverty as a causal factor, even though this is a fundamental premise of Marxist sociological thought.[155] Instead the press focused on "criminal individuals" and "criminal gangs" and the punishments for them, while internal material shows that many common people took up theft out of necessity and also that the population was very fearful of street crime.

Conflicting perceptions of material conditions and the hardship of everyday life comprise one of the clearest expressions of the class divide underly-

---

[155] As Merridale points out, crime was, of course, also made easier during this period by the movement of people and the availability of guns (*Ivan's War*, 366).

ing the USSR's socioeconomic structure during "reconstruction." Workers' criticisms of the regime for exporting grain amid the famine, for instance, are a stark illustration of the perceptive gap of Soviet "reality" separating the powers-that-be and the population at large (especially workers in this urban setting). Such criticisms, I contend, are an articulation of a separate class consciousness, an expression of a shared identity and interests vis-à-vis the outlooks and interests of the ruling party and those carrying out its policies, the nomenklatura. The grain was shipped according to commitments made by the Soviet government well before the onset of the famine. Presumably Stalin did not suspend the grain shipments despite his own country's lack of food because he wanted to keep the famine secret, preferring not to look weak and vulnerable to his wartime allies. In addition, aside from the exported grain the regime did not release emergency reserves that would have alleviated the worst of the famine—choosing instead, as we have seen, to see out the crisis by curtailing consumption—because it feared a possible calamity in the event of another bad harvest.[156] Also, in the months prior to the famine Stalin refused to provide *additional* requested grain shipments to the United Nations' Relief and Rehabilitation Administration (UNRRA), which caused some consternation between the Soviet regime and the US government. Hoover recorded that in a May 1946 meeting Truman expressed his dissatisfaction with Stalin for refusing to contribute more grain to the UNRRA. Hoover penned a memo to Stalin on Truman's behalf, stating, "I hope you will reconsider whether Russia can make further contributions beyond those already assured," which "approximate about 700,000 tons." Hoover requested that the USSR provide an additional 500,000 tons "prior to the end of August."[157] Perhaps Stalin was weary of contributing more of the country's dwindling grain reserves prior to the fall harvest. If Stalin had agreed to send more aid, the Soviet famine would have been much worse, provided of course that he continued to conceal the severity of the situation. On the other hand, the Ukraine received UNRRA aid, otherwise, again, the overall impact of the famine could have been *much* worse. It remains to be seen how the regime portrayed (and mythologized) the process of "reconstruction" amid such horrible material conditions prevailing in the country.

---

[156] On this point, see Ganson, "Famine of Victors," 164.

[157] The recipients of the 700,000 tons of Soviet aid were identified as Finland, Czechoslovakia, Poland, and France. The additional aid, if it had been provided, would have gone to Finland, Poland, Czechoslovakia, and Yugoslavia. See www.trumanlibrary.org/hoover/world.htm (accessed 28 February 2007).

Chapter Three

"When will that 'near future' finally arrive?": The Myth of "Reconstruction" and the "Politics of Productivity"

K. S. Karol, who returned to Rostov in 1943 and stayed there until 1946, recalls that amid official promises of a happy future and a quick "reconstruction" of the city, he and his friends expected immediate demobilization after victory so troops could return home and begin rebuilding the economy, leading soon to improved living standards for the population. They interpreted a phrase from Stalin's speech on May 24, 1945 ("our government has made a rather large number of mistakes") as a hint of self-criticism for the Nazi-Soviet Non-Aggression Pact of 1939, hoping it presaged a period of postwar openness.[1] Their hoped-for immediate material improvements and anticipated political thaw, however, did not materialize, and the exploitative Stalinist system of production that took shape before the war prevailed. The regime promoted a myth of "reconstruction" in part to conceal its systemic deficiencies, as well as to motivate workers to increase production. The myth linked the rebuilding effort with the war, calling on the population to endure tremendous sacrifice and hardship amid promises of a much happier future. The myth of "reconstruction," moreover, was inseparably tied to the myth of the war, like flip sides of the same coin.[2] Victory in May 1945 marked a clear dividing line in the heroic tale of reconstruction. During the war the focus was on the front, whereas afterward rebuilding became the primary task. Postwar reconstruction, described as "peacetime economic development" by Stalin in

---

[1] Karol, *Solik*, 41–46. None of Karol's circle of friends foresaw the division of Europe with Soviet occupation of the east and increasingly cold relations with the allies. Karol left for his native Poland in 1946 but imagines that the regime's tough line toward POWs, which I discuss in chap. 5, must have "very badly shaken" the morale of his small circle of friends back in Rostov.

[2] I discuss the myth of the war in chap. 7. As we will see, the myth of the war promoted by the Soviet regime is that the USSR achieved victory due to the Soviet peoples' unity behind the ingenious leadership of the great Stalin and due to the superior socialist economic system. On the power of the myth of the war, see Amir Weiner, "The Making of a Dominant Myth: The Second World War and the Construction of Political Identities within the Soviet Polity," *The Russian Review* 55: 4 (October 1996): 638–60.

his speech announcing victory, was an extension of the war myth into the postwar period. In Rostov, Rostsel'mash, the city's main industrial enterprise almost completely destroyed in the war, was a focal point for both praise and criticism (along with a number of other important factories) as the tale of "reconstruction" unfolded.

This chapter looks beneath the myth of "reconstruction" at the "politics of productivity," examining the exploitative nature of productive relations through the unrealized hopes of Soviet citizens for a better life.[3] Throughout Eurasia reconstruction in the 1940s and 1950s reflected the particular political conditions of the postwar period and was, as one scholar notes with regard to Japan, "related intimately to issues of victory and defeat, as well as to national and local pride," thus carrying "strong symbolic meaning."[4] It was, moreover, "a task of enormous complexity, fraught with potential for conflict."[5] In Britain (and elsewhere) a myth of the home front prevailed that was characterized by universal sacrifice, egalitarianism, and common purpose, a myth that the government extended into the postwar years to facilitate recovery.[6] Amir Weiner highlights "the politics of myth" for the USSR, in which a Marxist "metanarrative provided the Soviet polity with historical meaning by situating it in the context of a perceived human destiny." Certain myths, such as those of the Civil War, the industrialization drive, and the Great Fatherland War, legitimized the Marxist metanarrative and related it to concrete historical situations. "These mythical representations were often referred to as historical turning points and constituted frameworks for meaning that ordained them with a structure for understanding and accepting change."[7] With its promises of a bright, happy future emerging from the ruins of war, "reconstruction" constituted the type of myth Weiner describes, and my goal is to look at everyday life beyond the myth by focusing on the sphere of production and its contested politics.

In his criticism of capitalism, Marx argued that owners derived profit from wages by not paying workers the full value of their production, extracting "surplus value" from their labor. In the Soviet Union such exploitation of workers allegedly ended with the Bolshevik Revolution; the 1936 Stalin Constitution declared that "the exploitation of classes" had been eliminated in the country. Instead of allowing a market driven by the profit motive to control

---

[3] Siegelbaum, *Stakhanovism and the Politics of Productivity.* "If productivity is defined as output per fixed unit of working time," Siegelbaum maintains, "then the struggles over the means of raising output and ways of deflecting or minimizing the burdens associated with this effort were its politics" (7).

[4] Hein, "Rebuilding Japanese Cities," in Hein, Diefendorf, and Yorifusa, *Rebuilding Urban Japan After 1945,* 3.

[5] Diefendorf, *Rebuilding Europe's Bombed Cities,* 1.

[6] Zweiniger-Bargielowska, *Austerity in Britain,* 2.

[7] Weiner, "Making of a Dominant Myth," 639.

economic decision making, the central government determined investment outlays, rates of growth, and production quotas for all branches of the economy on the basis of short- and long-term plans.[8] In Stalinist lore this system was, of course, in the best interests of the people, especially the proletariat. The party and state "belonged to the working people" as did the factories they labored in, the fields they farmed, and all other forms of "collective property" in Soviet "socialist democracy." Workers theoretically labored for themselves, for the betterment of society as a whole, rather than for the profit of a few wealthy capitalists. The state used such rhetoric to mobilize an exhausted population and get the economy functioning again during "reconstruction." Yet theory proved to be far removed from practice, as the "politics of productivity" took on a decidedly exploitative form, and for most people in the USSR daily reality was unfortunately much harsher than the mythic tale of "reconstruction" relayed.

The hope for immediate improvements after victory failed to materialize, in part because of the nature of Stalinist production. The Soviet regime expropriated workers' "surplus value" from before the onset of industrialization (and even more so during), while workers often found themselves at odds with the state in the realm of production. Stalinist industrialization was inherently exploitative, and industrialization de-politicized workers, who were preoccupied with personal survival amid difficult material circumstances. During the industrialization drive of the 1930s, workers endured widespread shortages of goods, production speed-ups, and many other problems without collective protest, but workers were on relatively equal terms with the regime. The state, moreover, never completely controlled labor in the 1930s or 1940s because of individualized worker resistance to party policies.[9] Relations between state and society in the industrial sphere were highly complex, as revealed by the Stakhanovite movement, which began in 1935 and promoted heroic shock workers who produced far above their production norms as role models.[10] Raising labor productivity in the 1930s was "a nearly constant aim of the Soviet leadership" that assumed various forms, including Stakhanovism and "socialist competition," which pitted producers against each other in

---

[8] For details of the Soviet economic planning system, see Zaleski, *Stalinist Planning for Economic Growth*; Filtzer, *Soviet Workers and Stalinist Industrialization*, chap. 8; and Siegelbaum, "Soviet Norm Determination."

[9] Filtzer, *Soviet Workers and Stalinist Industrialization*; and idem, *Soviet Workers and Late Stalinism*. Filtzer shows that workers resisted their terms of work, but only in individual ways like frequently changing jobs. On the inherently exploitative nature of Soviet industrialization, see also Solomon M. Schwarz, *Labor in the Soviet Union* (New York: Praeger, 1952).

[10] Siegelbaum, *Stakhanovism and the Politics of Productivity*, xi–xii. Since profit is not the driving force for increasing productivity, he notes, "it is the state that must introduce or at least choose mechanisms that will achieve this end" (8).

public challenges, a strategy introduced during the First Five-Year Plan (1928–32). Bonuses were paid to those with the highest rates of production. Workers responded in a variety of ways, and the party was concerned over "labor discipline" in the period leading up to a June 1940 Labor Law, which forbade tardiness, unexcused absences, and desertion from factory jobs.[11] In addition, in the 1930s periodic government bond drives, a form of taxation in which people were expected to enthusiastically give the equivalent of one month's salary back to the regime, met with grumbles on the part of some Soviet citizens.[12] The "politics of productivity" between workers and managers played out during "reconstruction" amid severe economic difficulties and against a backdrop of jubilation and high hopes in the wake of victory.

The Fourth Five-Year Plan (1946–50) called for Rostov to rebuild and "exceed considerably the prewar level of economic development" by 1950.[13] Central leaders designated Rostov one of fifteen priority cities in the Russian Republic for reconstruction because of its importance in industry and transportation, which meant that it received a large share of resources (and a great deal of scrutiny). Rostsel'mash and many other factories were reduced to rubble as both sides engaged in scorch and burn tactics to ensure that nothing useful fell into enemy hands. Workers returning to the bombed-out premises of their factories remember bringing their own tools to begin the rebuilding process.[14] In 1941 and 1942 Soviet authorities evacuated some of the machinery from Rostsel'mash and other enterprises to Central Asia and elsewhere, and after the war they decided not to return the evacuated equipment. Instead, they retooled devastated factories with new technology, partly with equipment taken from Germany. Reconstruction began immediately after the city's liberation in February 1943, with Rostsel'mash and a few other major factories given priority because of their importance to the national economy. The main source of growth for the Soviet economy during the five-year period was to be an increase in labor productivity achieved through improvements in the technological base of industry. There is debate as to whether the

---

[11] The law made these offenses punishable by short-term (six-month) "correctional labor" sentences. Z. K. Zvezdin, L. S. Rogachevskaia, and D. A. Baevskii, eds., *Politicheskii i trudovoi pod"em rabochego klassa SSSR (1928–1929 gg.): Sbornik dokumentov* (Moscow: Gosudarstvennoe izdatel'stvo, 1956), 258. Siegelbaum argues that Stakhanovism peaked in the late 1930s and subsided in importance thereafter. Citing a labor journal from the time, he further notes that socialist competition was turned into "sham proclamations without the participation of the masses," and notes that this movement was marred by "deficiencies and distortions" (*Stakhanovism and the Politics of Productivity*, 53).

[12] Davies, *Popular Opinion in Stalin's Russia*, 35–37.

[13] Cited in Zaleski, *Stalinist Planning for Economic Growth*, 347.

[14] See, for example, N. N. Shchemalaev et al., *Rostsel'mash* (Rostov-on-Don: Rostov State University, 1968); interview by author with Nina Nikitichna K., 17 March 1995.

plan was achieved, but there is little doubt that the progress made during the postwar years was considerable.[15] In order to increase production the regime continued campaigns from the 1930s, such as Stakhanovism and socialist competition, which was linked to two holidays central to Soviet political culture, May Day and the anniversary of the Bolshevik Revolution (November 7). Government bond drives were likewise linked to holidays and, as we will see, elicited harsh comments from some people as they had in the 1930s.

"Reconstruction" and the "Politics of Productivity" in the Press

With the return of Soviet power in February 1943, the party's public narrative began to weave an heroic tale of "reconstruction" while at the same time reporting extensively on the many problems encountered during the process, a common form of two-sided reporting for the Soviet press as we will see. Four days after liberation local leaders held an open town meeting amid the ruins in the chilly February air on Engels Street, sending a letter to Stalin signed by Obkom First Secretary Boris Dvinskii. The letter appeared on the front page of *Molot*:

> Dear Iosif Vissarionovich!
> We know our duty. For all Soviet peoples, for our Soviet government, [and] for you we are obligated to all stand as one at our posts, roll up our sleeves, and get down to work. We will avenge the enemy, rebuild ruined enterprises, and return our city to normal. We will do everything to help the Red Army smash the enemy to oblivion. All for the Front, All for Victory![16]

This proclamation expressed the myth of "reconstruction" — the master narrative of a population working as one with great heroism and sacrifice, overcoming all difficulties to rebuild their beloved city and make it even better than before the war. Like many myths, this one was based in part on truth — the city was rebuilt and undoubtedly there was a great deal of heroism and sacrifice on the part of Soviet people and a genuine love by Rostovians for their native city. But when those aspects are blown out of proportion the whole picture is distorted, as was the case for many of the public tales of "reconstruction" during and after the war. Borrowing a phrase from Stalin, *Molot* declared three days after victory that while triumph was grand, "now the great task standing before us is the period of peaceful development. We must concentrate all our strength and attention on the complete reconstruction of all branches of the economy and raise production to a new level."[17] Thus pub-

---

[15] Zaleski, *Stalinist Planning for Economic Growth*, 400–01.

[16] *Molot*, 19 February 1943, p. 1. See also TsDNI f. 13, op. 4, d. 28, l. 1.

[17] Untitled editorial, *Molot*, 12 May 1945, p. 1.

lic party rhetoric linked reconstruction with the dire need to raise productivity, promoting the collective goal of "peaceful development."

Not surprisingly, *Molot* celebrated the early achievements of "reconstruction." In the first week of March 1943 the paper noted that the Rostov Post Office sent 36,000 letters out of the city and delivered more than 10,000 letters in Rostov. It added as well that medical clinics were once again providing free care to citizens and that movie theaters were set to open soon. Workers from the Mikoyan Shoe Factory, according to this account, brought their own material and instruments to make boots for the Red Army, while through their own initiative workers at the Oktiabr'skaia revoliutsiia (October Revolution) plant, which made building materials, brought it into production.[18] Another report chronicles the revival of Rostov's theater life, and in April the paper announced that the famed Gor'kii Theater, built in the shape of a tractor, would begin having performances while it remained under reconstruction.[19] The factories Krasnyi Don and Krasnyi Moriak, both of which made equipment for and repaired damaged ships, were the topic of discussion at the beginning of Rostov's navigational season. The director of Krasnyi Don wrote that, despite serious damage to the factory wrought by the Germans, "thanks to the self-confidence of our workers, engineers, and technicians, we were able to organize our work and get several shops operating right away." Brigades worked with great enthusiasm, he noted, "overcoming all difficulties, which are not few in number."[20] The director and party secretary of Krasnyi Moriak published a letter stating that "people came to their native [*rodnoi*] factory on the day after liberation, working with passion and with a drive to do as much as possible right away." No one went home until the factory bell rang for the first time in liberated Rostov, "the signal for the beginning of joyous labor, for the rebirth of a life of freedom."[21]

Holiday celebrations, an essential element of Soviet political culture, were linked to production. The war engendered new holidays, especially victory day but also Rostov's liberation, which was observed locally, but neither of these was recognized as an official holiday with time off from work. I will

---

[18] *Molot*, "36 tysiach pisem," "Meditsinskaia pomoshch' naseleniiu," "Otkryvaiutsia kinoteatry," and "Na vozrozhdennom zavode," 9 March 1943, p. 2.

[19] *Molot*, "Pervye spektakli," 10 March 1943, p. 2, and *Molot*, "U artistov teatra imena Gor'kogo," 23 April 1943, p. 2.

[20] *Molot*, "Navstrechu navigatsii 1943 goda," 11 March 1943, p. 2. Several brigades, he added, took on the obligation to fulfill their yearly plans ahead of schedule, a task they fulfilled "with honor."

[21] Iu. Gerkovich and A. Lebedev, "Pervyi gudok," *Molot*, 13 March 1943, p. 2. The paper also reported that eight banks were now operating, encouraging citizens to put their money into savings, and that amid "tremendous demand for books" a total of seven libraries had already reopened in Rostov. *Molot*, "Novye vkladchiki sberkass" and "Ogromnyi spros na knigi," 11 March 1943, p. 1.

deal with these holidays separately as part of the myth of the war; here I concentrate on the traditional celebrations, May Day and the anniversary of the
1917 Revolution in November. In the aftermath of occupation in 1943 city
leaders made preparations for May Day festivities. In early April the paper
announced that the traditional relay race would be held "as always"—emphasizing continuity and the brevity of occupation—from the train station to Karl
Marx Square.[22] A year later *Molot* gave an account of life in the city on the eve
of May Day. "The city has taken on a holiday face with squares, streets, and
countless buildings sporting bright posters and slogans, including 'I swear we
will win,' 'You gave life back to us,' and 'In the name of the Motherland.'"
The text of the Soviet Union's new national anthem was painted on one wall
in Lenin Square. Factories held holiday parties, and the official celebration
opened in Gor'kii Park with films and the traditional relay race, culminating
with the mass march to Theater Square.[23] *Molot* depicted a similar scene on
May Day 1945. "Lenin Square is decorated with the portraits of the government and party leaders, war heroes and heroes of labor." The paper reported
large crowds at the central telegraph station, where people had come to send
holiday greetings to loved ones all over the country, another sign of life returning to "normal."[24]

May Day spawned countless tributes to Stalin and Soviet power, and the
holiday was linked to socialist competition in an effort to increase worker
productivity. Veniamin Zhak published a holiday poem in the paper entitled
"May in Rostov":

> The squares are warmed by light, by a downpour of redness, songs
> and flowers, and by the smile of our chief looking down from
> portraits.
> Rostov in the spring holidays, flags fly from every balcony, the
> streets are dressed in red, and all around are wondrous tributes of
> our glorious triumphant path: freshly resurrected buildings awaken-
> ing to city life. Amid the warm breath of the five-year plan, the will of
> decisive labor marches on. Here is the delegation from Rostsel'mash,
> the first combines and ploughs, long since known as our friends and
> loved ones! Sing, Sel'mash, and let your heart beat stronger. All of
> Rostov stands at military readiness: Workers from Mikoyan, Len-

---

[22] *Molot*, "Podgotovka k pervomaiskoi estrafete" and "Ob"iavleniia," 4 April 1943, p.
2. The paper felt obliged to print a warning from the city soviet that all posters would
have to be approved by district propaganda departments before they could be displayed: "Distributing or posting fliers without prior approval is forbidden."

[23] *Molot*, "Pered prazdnikom: Rostov v pervomaiskie dni," 30 April 1944, p. 3. The
paper claimed there were more than 1,000 participants.

[24] *Molot*, "Mai v Rostove," 2 May 1945, p. 1.

zavod, and DGTF. All hearts are filled with joy in a peaceful, spring-like city![25]

As we will see, Zhak did not necessarily mean these words (or at least not the reference to Stalin), but this type of tribute was typical in the press during this era of the Stalin cult.[26] Also, May Day was tied to the realm of production through socialist competitions; in the weeks prior to the holiday brigades from various factories, individual workers within plants, etc. challenged each other publicly or took on the task of fulfilling production norms ahead of schedule. In late March 1943, for example, workers at Krasnyi Don announced their intention "to exert all their strength to repair ships and prepare the navy for use." One work brigade, this account noted, "achieved new Stakhanovite production norms in preparation for May First."[27] In April 1943, *Molot* reported further on preparations, noting that workers at the Leather Factory "successfully carry out socialist competition for the upcoming holiday," and that "with every day the productivity of labor grows as more and more items are produced."[28]

Reporting on the anniversary of the Bolshevik Revolution also offered a standard account, a front-page lay out complete with large photos and two sections under the title "October celebrations in Rostov." *Molot* described the city's military parade, stating the names of the current oblast leadership who sat atop the tribunal in Theater Square to greet soldiers and workers as they marched by. The paper also reported on the work brigades of various factories, noting in 1946 that "huge portraits of party and military leaders" led the way in the workers' march. Thousands marched holding posters with official slogans like, "Fight for the fulfillment and over fulfillment of the new five-year plan, for the material and cultural improvement of the masses!" Winners of socialist competitions and those who had already fulfilled their production plans for the year led each brigade. Students marched by the podium of local leaders in Theater Square singing the following song: "Stalin, our glorious general; with songs of struggle and triumph, our people follow Stalin's lead." "Stalin's name," the report added, "is in the heart of every demonstrator. The workers' thoughts are of him, our beloved chief, friend, and teacher who leads the country from one great victory to another!"[29] The

---

[25] *Molot*, "Mai v Rostove," 3 May 1947, p. 3. For more tributes on the holiday, see also *Molot*, "Vchera v stolitse Dona," 3 May 1947, p. 3.

[26] I will return to the Stalin cult in chap. 8.

[27] *Molot*, "Dosrochnyi remont sudov," 31 March 1943, p. 2.

[28] *Molot*, "Na raionnom partiinom sobranii," 4 April 1943, p. 2. *Molot* noted as well that women workers at the Rostov train station actively took part in socialist competition. A. Krasikova, "Sovetskie zhenshchiny novymi podvigami v tylu i na fronte pribliziat chas nashei polnoi pobedy nad vragom," *Molot*, 8 March 1945, p. 3.

[29] *Molot*, "Oktiabr'skie torzhestva v Rostove," 8 November 1946, pp. 1–2.

report on the 30th anniversary noted that "the Soviet Army eagerly defends the gains of the October Revolution with the highest military technology in the world." The 30th anniversary had special meaning for workers at Rostsel'-mash because as a gift to Stalin the plant unveiled the one-thousandth post-war combine, "inspiring all workers with the desire to achieve new feats of labor."[30] Thus press reports directly linked holiday celebrations to the realm of production while using them to promote the Stalin cult.

As it had in the 1930s, the regime held a number of bond drives during the war and after, including one in June 1943. Soon *Molot* was filled with en-thusiastic reports on the campaign's successful fulfillment. An account of a meeting at DGTF, for example, told of an elderly woman worker who, "pre-maturely gray because the Germans shot her daughter and grandson," gave more than her monthly salary for the cause. "Everyone at the meeting," the author assured, "met the announcement of the new war bond drive with joy."[31] A follow-up three days later announced the successful completion of the drive, Rostovians having contributed 19,244,900 rubles, thereby fulfilling "their obligation to the motherland" and exhibiting "the highest level of patri-otism."[32] Subsequent bond drives received similar press coverage, including a campaign for a postwar reconstruction bond announced in May 1946. A re-port in *Molot* entitled "Not one worker refused to sign the new bond drive" celebrated the "resounding success" of yet another campaign. At DGTF one worker who had been there almost 50 years reportedly said, "I am so glad that the war is over and we can now quickly rebuild our country. But, of course, the government needs money for this, so I eagerly sign on to the bond drive and hope that all will do the same." Her "enthusiastic" statement was an implicit admission that, despite the unanimity of opinion suggested by the title, not all workers necessarily agreed with her point of view. This article in-formed that many promised more than a month's salary (at a time when the average worker's monthly wage was between 300 and 500 rubles), as a result of which the factory fulfilled its obligation for the bond drive by 141 percent, giving the government 345,750 rubles.[33]

Rostsel'mash, which received millions of rubles for rebuilding as a prior-ity factory, was the topic of countless tributes and tirades in this five-year pe-riod. Well-known local writer and former Rostsel'mash worker Vladimir Fomenko memorialized its devastated condition after occupation with a

---

[30] Ibid. As for previous years, this report also highlighted the winners of the holiday socialist competition, who marched at the head of their factory brigades with portraits of Lenin and Stalin.

[31] *Molot,* "Mesiachnyi zarabotok—vzaimy gosudarstvu," 5 June 1943, p. 2.

[32] *Molot,* "Vsenarodnaia podderzhka novogo zaima," 8 June 1943, p. 1. This issue also reported the successful completion of the war bond drive by Don Cossacks, the signifi-cance of which I elaborate on in chap. 5.

[33] G. Dal', "Kollektiv DGTF zakonchil podpisky," *Molot,* 4 May 1946, p. 2.

poem in *Molot*: "Rostsel'mash! One would not even know you now, pride of Rostov, pride of the country" with your "black, charred walls, blown up pipes and scraps of metal whimpering in the wind."[34] In factory lore the reconstruction of Rostsel'mash, as with the city's other plants, began immediately after liberation, when workers themselves returned to their jobs with their own tools for work.[35] Much of the *Molot* material about the plant in this period celebrated the factory's achievements in production, such as this poem welcoming the one-thousandth postwar combine: "In 1945 we marched to Berlin! Threshing machines rang out again amid fresh ruins at Sel'mash. Factory shops rose as if from the native soil. Motors began to sing their prewar song. High walls arose anew, and new shops bloomed amid the ashes. While on the conveyor, with pride, the one-thousandth combine took form!"[36] As we will see, the public praise for Rostsel'mash's achievements contradicted countless internal reports bemoaning the plant's many shortcomings, including, as already noted, its inability to create decent living standards for employees and thereby mobilize more workers.

For Rostov as a whole the myth of "reconstruction" was immortalized in verse and promoted in special publications. In 1947 *Molot* regaled "our city": "The Germans burned it to the ground, but from the ruins we are raising our city again toward the sky. Every hour we raise the walls higher with our own hands, with every stone dear to us. Our Rostov will be eternally courageous and happy."[37] A year earlier the city's publishing house released a collection of essays entitled *The Rebirth of the Soviet Don*,[38] a canonization of the myth of "reconstruction." While not all the information was positive, the overall tone of the publication was celebratory. For example, A. G. Goncharov, an official in the city's railroad department, described "one of a thousand episodes" of tremendous heroism. Amid the fighting near Rostov in early 1943, the city's railway workers set to work repairing vitally important lines that the Germans had destroyed upon retreat. Suddenly they fell under a German aerial attack, "but work was not suspended." Even the death of the brigade leader did not cease their efforts.[39] The authors were leading figures in the realm of

---

[34] Vladimir Fomenko, "Korichnevaia chuma," quoted in Shchemalaev et al., *Rostsel'-mash*, 86–87.

[35] See, for example, Shchemalaev et al., *Rostsel'mash*, chap. 3.

[36] Anatolii Sofonov, "Tysiacha kombainov na Rostsel'mashe," *Molot*, 3 November 1947, p. 1. See also Shchemalaev et al., *Rostsel'mash*, 97.

[37] Aleksandr Olenich-Gnenenko, "Nash gorod," *Molot*, 18 January 1947, p. 2.

[38] A. G. Goncharov, A. G. Kobilev, A. I. Korolev et al., *Vozrozhdenie Sovetskogo Dona, 1943 — February 14 — 1946* (Rostov-on-Don: Rostov State University 1946).

[39] A. G. Goncharov, "Zheleznodorozhnyi transport," in *Vozrozhdenie Sovetskogo Dona*, 25. The account claimed that the next in line stepped in to fill the brigade leader's place and ended by noting that "soon workers were unloading train cars that arrived in Rostov via the repaired lines."

the economy they were reporting on, so there was clearly a vested interest in showing a job well done. On the other hand, they did not shy away from or deny shortcomings. A. I. Korolev, for instance, bemoaned that "the tempo of reconstruction work in light industry in particular lags way behind the demands of the population and the government."[40] The formulaic essays began with the successes in a specific branch of the economy, then noted the shortcomings, and ended with a call for workers to step up their effort.[41]

While weaving a mythic tale of reconstruction, the press also dealt with and attempted to explain problems in production—addressing the "politics of productivity" from the perspective of those in power—including the familiar topics of poor "labor discipline" and a shortage of workers. The press exhibited a tough stance toward workers who abandoned their jobs or otherwise broke labor laws. For example, a 1943 account of railway workers, the topic of a number of heroic tales, conceded that a minority of them "display a lack of discipline and irresponsibility in their work."[42] Another editorial called on factory directors to "piously watch over discipline," lamenting that "some factory directors underestimate the importance of labor discipline," tolerating tardiness and pilfering by workers.[43] In August 1944, a few months before an amnesty was declared for workers who had abandoned jobs in military production, the paper noted that "recently a number of people have been brought to justice for deserting military plants, as well those who helped protect and hide them." An NKVD tribunal gave three deserters sentences of six–eight years, and two people who helped them were sentenced to three–five years.[44] Although authorities only caught and prosecuted a small percentage of cases, these accounts single out a few illustrative examples to show a tough

---

[40] A. I. Korolev, "Stroitel'nye materialy i legkaia promyshlennost'," in *Vozrozhdenie Sovetskogo Dona*, 22.

[41] In one of the essays, for example, obkom secretary A. G. Kobilev stated that while Rostov's workers had accomplished a great deal, "we want every worker to produce more today than he did yesterday" and "exhibit great will power, strength, and ability in the further development of the economy." A. G. Kobilev, "Promyshlennost'," in *Vozrozhdenie Sovetskogo Dona*, 16–17.

[42] "Ukaz Prezidiuma Verkhovnogo Soveta SSSR: O vvedenii voennogo polozheniia na vsekh zheleznykh dorogakh," *Molot*, 16 April 1943, p. 1. The report noted that railway workers could be punished for lax discipline by being sent to a "penal battalion" at the front, a punishment that would obviously only apply to men.

[43] *Molot*, "Sviato bliusti distsiplinu, sobliudat' organizovannost' i poriadok," 23 May 1943, p. 1.

[44] *Molot*, "V Oblastnoi prokurature i Voennom tribunale voisk NKVD," 12 August 1944, p. 4. The report noted that several more cases were under consideration as well.

stance against poor labor discipline, which, as we know, local party leaders perceived as a *major* problem in the realm of production at this time.[45]

Molot reported on countless other shortcomings plaguing production and "reconstruction." An issue that came up often was the lack of building supplies. The paper pointed out, for example, that rebuilding the city would require 116 million bricks, warning that the city's construction industry would have to achieve a great deal more than it had to reach that goal.[46] According to another editorial, the Central Committee complained to the obkom about "insufficient work" in the production of building materials.[47] The city's transportation system was the topic of numerous reports noting that delays kept people from getting to work and thus decreased productivity. *Molot* described the scene at Tolstoi Square on a "typical" morning at 7:00. A crowd of workers and office employees gradually gathered to wait for a streetcar but "after more than two hours none had arrived." Finally one was spotted, but it passed them on the way back for mechanical work. The city's transport, the author added, was utterly disorganized, prompting "justified complaints from workers."[48] Another account described the problem of overcrowding on the streetcars. "Often one hears someone yell: 'get off me I can't breathe.' 'You'll have to try for a little longer, till I get off,' someone responds." At many stops "a distinctive bloody battle arises just to get on the streetcar as the crowd besieges the cars." Young people often caught rides on top of the streetcars, a dangerous practice that the police ignored.[49] A commentary entitled "Streetcar tragedy" included a cartoon depicting people hanging out of a streetcar and a policeman calmly looking on above the caption "Neutral observer." These were but a few of the daily problems plaguing workers and affecting the "politics of productivity" during "reconstruction." Other common topics in *Molot* included major shortcomings in the city's water administration, communications, and the poor job by the city's factories in collecting scrap metal.[50]

---

[45] Filtzer shows that the numbers convicted of "labor desertion" from military plants were but a fraction of recorded offences (*Soviet Workers and Late Stalinism*, 167, 176).

[46] *Molot*, "Nazrevshie voprosy stroitel'stva," 14 November 1944, p. 2. By comparison the piece noted that in 1936–37 the city used close to 63 million bricks for construction projects. See also *Molot*, "K novomu pod"emu, tovarishchi stroiteli!," 20 February 1945, p. 1.

[47] *Molot*, "Stroitel'nye materialy nam nuzhni," 14 July 1945, p. 1.

[48] *Molot*, "Eshche raz o rostovskom tramvae," 27 July 1945, p. 4.

[49] *Molot*, "Eshche raz o tramvainykh delakh," 25 March 1945, p. 3. See also *Molot*, "Marshrut No. 10," 16 April 1944, p. 3; and *Molot*, "Navesti poriadok v tramvainom treste," 15 January 1947, p. 3.

[50] On the poor work of the city's water administration, see *Molot*, "Iskliuchitel'no plokho rabotaet vodoprovod," 14 July 1945, p. 1. On the poor work of the city's communications system, see *Molot*, "Eshche raz o rabote sviazi," 23 April 1944, p. 3; and

Finally, while public accounts often celebrated feats in production by measuring output in terms of the five-year plan, stories in *Molot* also criticized factory directors and others for falsifying numbers. An editorial in late 1943 berated the leaders of trade organizations for signing "very strange contracts" to supply factories with large numbers of necessary items. Such contracts usually became "empty promises on paper," however, because they were not upheld, while the failure to provide the necessary goods and materials stifled production.[51] A 1944 article reported on the "insidious practice" by many of the city's factory directors and accountants, who commonly produced some easy-to-make items well above the required quota, then used those exaggerated figures to cover shortfalls in the production of other items.[52] The brochure released on the third anniversary of Rostov's liberation was the topic of an editorial in *Molot* entitled "Clearly confused," claiming it relied on incorrect figures. The author, S. P. Afanas'ev, one of the officials in charge of meeting the goals of the Fourth Five-Year Plan for Rostov oblast, wrote that "the publication was released for one reason—to mobilize the broad masses of workers for further struggle in the total reconstruction of our economy." However, he continued, much of the information in several of the articles is inaccurate. The essay in the brochure celebrating the reconstruction of industry, for example, made a number of blatant mistakes, and "unfortunately, the reality is somewhat different." Afanas'ev noted in conclusion that "there are many such examples of inaccuracies, and the authors of this brochure did not pay close enough attention to the details."[53] Statistics, so important to Soviet narratives of production, were clearly susceptible to manipulation.

The myth of "reconstruction" propagated in the party press and the "politics of productivity" were closely intertwined. Intended to increase production, press reports trumpeting the city's "reconstruction" emphasized worker initiative, a collective labor effort, and individual worker heroism. Reporting on holidays, socialist competition, bond drives, and mobilization efforts, the paper sought to instill patriotic pride and a sense of civic duty in readers, the

---

Molot, 12 May 1944, p. 4. On the poor job collecting scrap metal, see *Molot*, "O metallome i bespechykh zagotoviteliakh," 13 June 1944, p. 2. In June 1944 *Molot* reported that, instead of the 1,500 tons of scrap metal Rostsel'mash was supposed to collect, it gathered a mere 576 tons. At Krasnyi Askai nearly 400 tons of scrap metal just lay there without anyone touching it, and numerous plants in the city had not prepared any scrap metal at all. "We must no longer tolerate," the editorial concluded, "irresponsibility on the part of specific leaders toward this very important governmental affair."

[51] *Molot*, "Proizvodstvo tovarov shirpotreba tempom voennogo vremeni," 3 November 1943, p. 3.

[52] *Molot*, "Za strozhaishii rezhim ekonomii," 28 April 1944, p. 3. The piece specified that such creative accounting took place at Rostsel'mash and Krasnyi Aksai, but noted that it was common elsewhere as well.

[53] S. P. Afanas'ev, "Iavnaia putanitsa," *Molot*, 29 March 1946, p. 3.

Soviet working class playing the central role in these narratives. Rostsel'mash, the economic centerpiece of the city, was crucial to the tale of "reconstruction," which was inseparably linked to the war cause and to the realm of production from the outset. Poems celebrating the rebuilding effort conveyed a sense of verticality, with a new life blooming amid the ashes and city walls "reaching higher" "toward the sky," language that gives the impression of longing, of constantly "looking up" and striving for a better future just beyond one's reach. These sources also depicted problems in the city's "reconstruction." Displaying a tough face to workers with "poor labor discipline," for example, the press revealed desertion from the workplace and showed that, as we noted previously, workers had considerable leverage. Taking advantage of their lack of numbers (rather than, for example, collective protest), workers negotiated with factory managers, determining where they wound up and under what conditions. Editorials berating factory managers for not being tough on tardy workers, moreover, contradicted articles on the horrendous state of public transport that showed why many workers were late. Should a worker be held accountable for tardiness if the streetcars run so poorly? Along with the severe shortage of workers, this helps explain why factory managers were reportedly lenient toward workers with "disciplinary" problems despite the draconian legislation. Finally, *Molot* hinted at the "statistical fiction" of Soviet accounting, which cast doubt on production as measured and reported by those in power.

"Reconstruction" and the "Politics of Productivity" Behind Closed Doors

Internal party sources echo the public myth of "reconstruction" while likewise dealing with problems in production, poor "labor discipline," etc.; these documents, however, tend to be more forthcoming about the difficulties faced during "reconstruction." Hidden discussions of holidays perhaps most clearly expressed the official myth of the era by repeating familiar language of production. An April 1943 memo from one district claimed that agitators instilled a "deep understanding" in workers of the need for a "decisive battle to rapidly rebuild our economy." At open meetings party activists read Stalin's report on the 25th anniversary of the Bolshevik Revolution, issued the previous November while Rostov oblast was occupied, which "inspired them to sign up for the May 1st socialist competition."[54] Gorkom instructions to district party secretaries in 1944 called on them to involve workers in the holiday competition as well and collect gifts for soldiers at the front. It promoted the slogan "All for the front! All for victory!"[55] Two years later holiday rhetoric focused on the "postwar peacetime development of the economy" and the five-year plan. Agitators were instructed to "call on workers to successfully

---

[54] TsDNI f. 13, op. 4, d. 53, l. 22.
[55] TsDNI f. 13, op. 4, d. 69, ll. 76–77.

complete the plan, more quickly rebuild the city, and further develop the country's economic and cultural life."[56] There were several such reports on the propagandistic purpose of May Day, all of them including references to Stalin's holiday speeches, which were discussed at factory meetings.[57] Accounts of the anniversary of the Bolshevik Revolution did not vary greatly from the standard set by May Day. At a party conference on aid to the families of soldiers in November 1943, Comrade Tabakova, an assistant manager at Rostsel'mash, described efforts by the factory's party organization to give gifts on the anniversary to the wives of Red Army troops. "Certainly we could not provide presents to everyone in need," she stated, but the plant was able to supply meat and other items to the neediest workers.[58] While repeating public rhetoric, these accounts of official Soviet holidays emphasize the link between propaganda and production and reveal once again the dire living standards of "needy" citizens.

As with the public narrative, Rostsel'mash occupied a central place in party leaders' closed discussion of the "politics of productivity." At the Seventh City Party Conference in late February 1943, Stalinskii district secretary Comrade Galafeev gave an account of the city's most important plant. "Rostsel'mash was 60–70 percent destroyed," he stated, "but part of it has already resumed operation. The factory is casting spoons for the army, repairing motor vehicles and taking orders for coil." There were 500 workers on hand, and the casting section, lumber section, construction and mechanical sections were left intact. In a major boon for the plant some excellent German and French equipment was left behind by the occupants, some of which could be used in place of equipment evacuated to Tashkent.[59] In October 1945 the factory's director, Comrade Titarenko, reiterated the plant's severe shortage of workers at a party gathering. Answering for his factory's poor performance numbers of late, Titarenko said that after the return of Soviet power people went to work in the city's small factories, especially food-processing plants "because of the difficulties with supplies," and thus there were few workers to help rebuild Rostsel'mash. Moreover, after the government's late 1944 amnesty of workers if they *returned* to work others, interpreting it as a sign of tolerance for desertion, actually *left* the plant. Those who left had not yet been replaced with an influx of new workers, the director expounded, and thus much of the plant's equipment stood idle.[60] At a party plenum that same month Titarenko added that the plant was poorly supplied with cement and

---

[56] TsDNI f. 13, op. 4, d. 218, l. 54. As before, they were also instructed to develop socialist competition for the holiday.

[57] For more internal party reports on May Day, see TsDNI f. 13, op. 4, d. 16, ll. 18–19; TsDNI f. 13, op. 4, d. 51, ll. 47, 62, 69; TsDNI f. 13, op. 4, d. 54, l. 28.

[58] TsDNI f. 13, op. 4, d. 28, l. 35.

[59] TsDNI f. 13, op. 4, d. 29, ll. 18–19.

[60] TsDNI f. 13, op. 4, d. 178, ll. 6–9.

other necessary items for reconstruction and noted that the transition from military to civilian production after the war caused further difficulties.[61]

Countless documents show that all was not well in the city's industrial jewel. Little had been done to repair the ceilings of several factory shops, as a result of which they could not operate during winter.[62] At the October 1945 party plenum Gorkom Secretary Stepanov berated Titarenko and the secretary of the plant's party organization for "not raising Rostsel'mash" despite the assistance of the entire city. The factory director did not feel these shortcomings were his own fault, Stepanov declared, but others put the blame squarely on Titarenko's shoulders. "If you two continue to work as before in a bureaucratic style [po-chinovnich'i]," he scolded, "and do not show tremendous effort in improving conditions for workers, the city's help will not be enough." Labor discipline at Rostsel'mash, he concluded, was worse than at any other plant in the city.[63] Problems persisted in January 1947, when a gorkom report lamented the plant's failure to fulfill its plan the previous year primarily because of "the poor organization of labor and low labor discipline stemming from unsatisfactory daily material conditions for those at the factory."[64] At a party plenum later in the year, an obkom secretary elaborated: "there is no discipline [at the plant]; workers leave a half-hour early and arrive a half-hour late." A random check-up revealed the absence of 30 out of 158 workers in one shop, but "no one asks" about such issues nor does anything about the situation.[65]

Rostsel'mash was not the only problem spot: a number of plants failed to fulfill production plans throughout this five-year period. At closed meetings and in confidential reports, industry leaders often discussed their goal of raising worker productivity, their language indicating a conceptualization of Soviet society in "us" and "them" terms. For instance, they often mulled over ways to bring "lagging" (otstaiushchie) workers into line and, as in public, roused workers to increase production for the holidays. An early 1945 gorkom report pointed out the importance of propaganda work in raising the productivity of labor. "We can do a number of things," the report elaborated, "to have workers who are lagging behind tighten their belts [po podtiagivaniiu]," recommending "the severe criticism of careless workers." As an ex-

---

[61] TsDNI f. 13, op. 4, d. 144, ll. 26–27.

[62] TsDNI f. 13, op. 4, d. 151, l. 73.

[63] TsDNI f. 13, op. 4, d. 144, l. 60. Another speaker at the plenum said the city was plagued by "exceptionally low labor discipline and labor productivity" and singled out Rostsel'mash for particular criticism (l. 36).

[64] TsDNI f. 13, op. 4, d. 230, l. 19. For more on production problems at Rostsel'mash, see also TsDNI f. 13, op. 4, d. 83, ll. 34–35. For more reports on problems with labor discipline in this five-year period, see also TsDNI f. 13, op. 4, d. 21, l. 74; TsDNI f. 13, op. 4, d. 220, l. 205; TsDNI f. 13, op. 4, d. 293, l. 102.

[65] TsDNI f. 13, op. 4, d. 287, l. 142.

ample it cited one worker at DGTF who did not fulfill her production quota until party agitators "paid attention to her." Specifically, they "judged her behavior at a workers' brigade meeting, wrote about her in the wall newspaper, and explained to her in individual discussion that the order of a factory director is like the order of a commander at the front." As a result of this "attention" she "became more serious" and caught up with other workers, now consistently overfulfilling her quotas.[66] In November 1946 the central government passed a decree calling for increased labor productivity, and the following February the city soviet checked up on its implementation. "This decree," it noted, "is not just another temporary campaign" but rather "a program for further developing the economy." Although little had been done so far, according to this account, oblast leaders were obligated to fulfill the yearly plan by the November 7 holiday and decrease the costs of production by at least seven percent. Also, the central decree called for "strengthening labor discipline and raising workers' awareness in the struggle against workplace pilfering."[67] Thus public and internal party materials overlap with an emphasis on worker productivity and an overt connection between holidays and the realm of production.

Internal reports often harp on the *many* difficulties encountered in "reconstruction," usually in much sharper terms than in the media and also with a familiar penchant for quantification. For example, one report observed that the construction industry fulfilled the 1944 plan for the reconstruction of housing for workers of Military Plant No. 359 by only 65 percent and the plan for the first half of 1945 by an abysmal 20 percent. Two of the main reasons for this poor performance were the lack of labor power, with only 45 percent of the necessary workforce on hand, and the severe shortage of building materials.[68] As in the party press, padded statistics play an important role in these narratives. A gorkom report from April 1947 pointed out that several factories did not fill their plans for the first quarter of the year (the city as a whole fulfilled it by only 95 percent). The report stated that a total of 38 plants in the city fell short of their goals.[69] There were similar reports on the city's poor production numbers later in the year.[70] The Lenin Ship-Building Plant was singled out in a report in August 1948 which stated that the plant did not fulfill quotas because of the "low level of mass political work" among the

---

[66] TsDNI f. 13, op. 4, d. 180, l. 20.

[67] GARO f. 3907, op. 1, d. 5, ll. 18, 20. Workplace pilfering, as I show in chap. 6, was very pervasive at this time.

[68] TsDNI f. 13, op. 4, d. 147, l. 148.

[69] TsDNI f. 13, op. 4, d. 293, l. 101. The report specifically mentioned the Lenin Shipbuilding Plant and Krupzavod No. 1.

[70] See, for example, TsDNI f. 13, op. 4, d. 292, l. 76; TsDNI f. 13, op. 4, d. 298, l. 85 and TsDNI f. 13, op. 4, d. 299, l. 63; TsDNI f. 13, op. 4, d. 375, l. 129; GARO f. 3907, op. 1, d. 5, ll. 3–5.

work force. The plant's party secretary, Comrade Khanturin, however, refused to realize this and deal with the problem, blaming instead "the lack of
necessary spare parts" and frequent "interruptions in production due to
power outages." Khanturin focused as well on the "bad mood" of the majority of skilled workers at the plant stemming from the constant interruptions in
production, which adversely affected their wages. He alleged that once when
the electricity shut down a group of workers left at 9:00 A. M. and went to the
train station to get drunk.[71]

Closed party documents constantly highlight shortages of material, electricity, and/or labor power. At one party plenum a district representative
complained that a lack of building material slowed the city's reconstruction.
"It's as if oblast leaders expect us to magically come up with necessary materials out of thin air," he stated, and thus they do not provide the supplies
needed.[72] Plants frequently experienced interruptions in production due to a
lack of energy and/or water. Mikoyan Shoe Factory, among others, reported
breaks in production time due to these problems (which, of course, reflected
negatively on workers' wages).[73] A 1943 report on Leather Factory No. 3
noted that the loss in production time was as high as 75 percent, which would
have greatly lowered wages for workers in the plant (see table 3). A separate
report on the factory saw the acute shortage of labor as another stumbling
block in production. "There are shops with unused equipment," the account
claimed, "because of a lack of labor." In the "sterilizing department," for example, there should have been 180 workers but there were only 40.[74] One
reason for the city's poor transport, electrical, and water services was the lack
of workers in these fields. An internal report stated that there were 140 electrical workers in the city before the war, but as of late 1943 there were only 92,
most of them unskilled.[75] At a party plenum in early 1944 obkom first secretary Dvinskii admonished the head of the city's water department, Comrade
Karasev, for its poor service to the city's population and industry. Karasev responded that the shortcomings were due to a lack of energy and labor
power.[76] These issues were raised again and again throughout this five-year
period.[77]

---

[71] TsDNI f. 13, op. 4, d. 416, ll. 134–35.

[72] TsDNI f. 13, op. 4, 3. 143, l. 135.

[73] TsDNI f. 13, op. 4, d. 47, l. 25.

[74] TsDNI f. 13, op. 4, d. 47, l. 25.

[75] TsDNI f. 13, op. 4, d. 56, l. 111. A separate report stated that before occupation there
were 2,897 transportation workers in the city, but at the end of 1943 there were only
258. TsDNI f. 13, op. 4, d. 55, ll. 71–72. On the lack of transportation workers, see also
TsDNI f. 13, op. 4, d. 218, l. 40.

[76] TsDNI f. 13, op. 4, d. 63, ll. 31–35.

[77] See, for example, TsDNI f. 13, op. 4, d. 29, ll. 24–24; TsDNI f. 13, op. 4, d. 55, ll. 29, 31,
33, 66; TsDNI f. 13, op. 4, d. 56, ll. 56, 87–88, 93, 203; TsDNI f. 13, op. 4, d. 101, l. 3;

1943	Table 3: Production Time Lost at Leather Factory No. 3 Because of Power Outages and Lack of Water.	
1943	HOURS of non-PRODUCTION	PERCENT of TOTAL PRODUCTION TIME
July	533.5	72%
August	515	69.2%
September	425.9	59.2%
October	444.9	59.2%
November	325	48.2%
December	560.9	75%
Total	2,804.2	64%
Source: TsDNI f. 13, op. 4, d. 78, ll. 64–65.		

Behind closed doors industry leaders discussed the difficulties in mobilizing workers, as well as changes in the workforce and the lack of enthusiasm for "socialist competition." At a meeting in late 1944 Gorkom Second Secretary Comrade Pastushenko said that in the city as a whole there were 31,836 workers, about 30 percent of the prewar level of 101,334. "Moreover," he noted, "a very large percentage of the workers at the plants are new, Soviet women and youth who took the place of their fathers and sons, husbands and brothers defending the motherland. The majority of them did not previously work in factories," Pastushenko concluded, and "need to learn greater labor discipline."[78] A year later obkom secretary Kobilev likewise highlighted the changing face of Rostov's working class at a meeting of labor union activists. Their efforts, he said, "are exceptionally important in Rostov right now because the working class is being formed like never before."[79] The turnover rate at many factories, moreover, was high throughout this five-year period, peaking in 1947. A year earlier at Rostsel'mash the workforce fluctuated be-

TsDNI f. 13, op. 4, d. 143, ll. 222, 236–37, 240; TsDNI f. 13, op. 4, d. 151, ll. 28, 52; TsDNI f. 13, op. 4, d. 270, ll. 6, 17; TsDNI f. 13, op. 4, d. 273, l. 3; TsDNI f. 13, op. 4, d. 276, ll. 1, 4, 9, 17; TsDNI f. 13, op. 4, d. 221a, l. 23; GARO f. 3737, op. 4, d. 1397, l. 10; GARO f. 3950, op. 1, d. 2, l. 132.

[78] TsDNI f. 13, op. 4, d. 65, l. 53. According to Pastushenko, an indication of the inexperience and poor discipline of workers was the extremely high turnover rate for workers at most of the city's plants.

[79] TsDNI f. 13, op. 4, d. 150, l. 70.

tween 87 and 97 percent full as the factory took on 1,221 new workers but lost 948 for various reasons.[80] Problems were noted in the city's service industry as well; one report described the lack of barbers in the town and the lack of trainees for the position.[81] In 1947, which was, again, the worst year of turnover in labor, the city's plants took on 19,163 new workers but lost 13,398, roughly 70 percent.[82] Workers, furthermore, responded unenthusiastically to "socialist competition," in sharp contrast to public accounts. Only 481 of 862 employees at the Mikoyan Shoe Factory participated in the May Day 1944 competition, while at the fish-processing plant "socialist competition between brigades is unsatisfactorily organized and poorly developed."[83] Contradicting press reports, a gorkom protocol lamented that socialist competition was being carried out "in a lackluster and perfunctory manner" in the city.[84]

There was, however, heated competition for the most advantageous jobs; several reports noted that demobilized troops held out for the best possible positions, hoping, no doubt, to utilize the social capital that came with fighting for the victor. A gorkom protocol in December 1945, more than four months after the beginning of demobilization, noted that in Andreevskii district alone 370 demobilized troops had not yet taken jobs. "Many of them," it stated, "agree to work only in trade organizations or cafeterias even if they did not work in such jobs before, or they demand leadership positions with higher rations."[85] Jobs in the food industry were favored because they gave access to scarce goods. A document from Kirovskii district similarly informed that 981 demobilized soldiers were still unemployed. "It is necessary to note that most of the demobilized troops do not want to work at their previous jobs, saying they have a right to leadership positions."[86] Another district

---

[80] TsDNI f. 13, op. 4, d. 230, l. 20.

[81] GARO f. 3955, op. 1, d. 1, l. 79. For reports on the lack of qualified medical personnel, see TsDNI f. 13, op. 4, d. 46, ll. 11, 13.

[82] TsDNI f. 13, op. 4, d. 375, l. 123. The city's construction industry, obviously an important part of "reconstruction," took on 1,235 new workers but lost 1,531, a net loss of 296 workers (l. 136). On labor turnover and 1947 as the worst year for it, see Filtzer, *Soviet Workers and Late Stalinism*, chap. 5.

[83] On the Mikoyan Shoe Factory, see TsDNI f. 13, op. 4, d. 72, l. 53. On the fish-processing plant, see TsDNI f. 13, op. 4, d. 21, l. 74.

[84] TsDNI f. 13, op. 4, d. 298, l. 85. For more on the inadequate job of carrying out socialist competition, see also TsDNI f. 13, op. 4, d. 219, l. 77; TsDNI f. 13, op. 4, d. 375, l. 129.

[85] On the sense of entitlement among Red Army veterans, see Mark Edele, "Soviet Veterans as an Entitlement Group, 1945–1955," *Slavic Review* 65: 1 (2006): 111–37; idem, "More than Just Stalinists: The Political Sentiments of Victors 1945–1953," in Fürst, *Late Stalinism*; and idem, "A 'Generation of Victors'? Soviet Second World War Veterans from Demobilization to Organization 1941–1956" (Ph.D. diss., University of Chicago, 2004).

[86] TsDNI f. 13, op. 4, d. 172, l. 141.

report admitted "demobilized troops often delay their job placement by refusing countless positions and demanding either leadership positions or jobs
in trade organizations." Few if any agreed to work at Rostsel'mash, it added,
and "as a rule" demobilized troops assigned to work at Krasnyi Aksai did not
show up, including one party member and saw operator who refused to work
there, saying he wanted "a more appropriate position."[87] In Leninskii district,
a worker and 15-year party veteran refused his former position as a brigade
leader at the railway station, saying it "does not interest or satisfy him." At
first he refused to work because he did not have an apartment, but when
given one "he found other reasons, always trying to get on where the work is
easy and the pay more."[88] Such reports, plentiful in the years following demobilization, show that troops returning from the war believed they had leverage within the "politics of productivity," which suggests that society's interaction with the state was a two-way street.

Demobilized troops, furthermore, held considerable sway over (and were
perceived as a threat by) factory directors who stayed in occupied territory.
As we will see, many did so and a significant percentage of them even
worked for the Germans. Although gradually replaced in the years after victory and demobilization, the skills of these factory directors were in high demand while the war still raged and immediately afterward, so many of them
retained their positions temporarily. Not surprisingly, countless internal
party reports revealed an uneasy relationship between factory directors, especially those who were in occupied territory, and demobilized troops, precisely
because the latter held so much leverage in postwar Soviet society. In a July
1946 letter to the gorkom a military officer from Stalinskii district complained
that a number of factory directors refused to hire war veterans, while one of
the reports cited above noted that several times factory directors fired demobilized troops without authorization.[89] The Leninskii district party secretary
informed the gorkom that several factory directors were not only irresponsible toward the mobilization of demobilized troops, but even showed a "lack
of political comprehension" of this important matter. The directors of Rostov's fish-processing plant and Leather Factory No. 3, for instance, "systematically refuse" to replace workers who stayed in occupied territory with
demobilized troops, saying the newcomers would not master their new jobs

---

[87] TsDNI, f. 13, op. 4, d. 172, l. 142. For a similar report on Proletarskii district, see also
l. 143. I show in chap. 6 that many of the demobilized troops who refused to "work" in
the official economy chose instead to engage in illegal trade.

[88] TsDNI f. 13, op. 4, d. 171, l. 72. Another gorkom protocol cited the lack of housing
for demobilized troops and their families as a reason they could not be mobilized for
work. TsDNI f. 13, op. 4, d. 205, l. 28.

[89] TsDNI f. 13, op. 4, d. 283, ll. 153–54; TsDNI f. 13, op. 4, d. 172, l. 142.

quickly enough, which would interrupt production.[90] As late as March 1947 a number of factory directors continued to show a "formal-bureaucratic relationship toward demobilized troops" in their plants.[91] Obkom First Secretary Aleksandriuk explained at a party conference that factory directors preferred underlings who stayed in occupied territory—especially if they themselves were under German rule—because such employees were pliant, whereas demobilized troops were not.[92]

"Labor discipline" was another common topic in these documents, party leaders complaining that factory managers were too lenient toward disobedient workers, charges which, as we saw, also made their way into the press. Shortly after occupation the gorkom required district leaders to investigate labor discipline in the city's factories. The results of their check-up in April 1943 revealed that "labor discipline is in poor shape in many factories throughout the oblast" and that "several leaders of industry ignore the problem of strengthening labor discipline," not taking necessary measures against absences or people abandoning their jobs. At DGTF, for example, a group of ten workers did not show up for work, but the factory director did not pursue a legal case against them. Leaders at the same plant fired one worker for missing work but then took her back within a month. There were similar problems at other factories, including Garment Factory No. 12, where ten workers left work early but were not punished.[93] At the Mikoyan Shoe Factory time cards were in such a mess it was impossible to tell if anyone was absent from work or not. During one random check 283 of 430 workers were there, a mere 66 percent. Of those missing 130 had "legitimate excuses" (17 did not), but while 83 of them were supposedly absent because of volunteer duties at the hospital, "the factory's personnel department could not confirm that any of them were actually at the hospital." The text of a letter one worker sent to the factory director was cited as an example of the chaotic state of labor discipline:

> Dear Nikolai Fedoseevich! I am very sorry, but a car came for me and my family at 4:00 to take us to a village. If I can't return right away, will you please find someone to work for me until fall.... I will try to return and prove your trust in me by helping out in your work![94]

---

[90] TsDNI f. 13, op. 4, d. 171, l. 71. For more on factory directors not wanting to take on demobilized troops, see also TsDNI f. 13, op. 4, d. 205, l. 23.

[91] TsDNI f. 13, op. 4, d. 292, l. 70.

[92] TsDNI f. 13, op. 4, d. 214, l. 83.

[93] TsDNI f. 13, op. 4, d. 47, l. 4. It is unclear from this account whether they walked out under protest, which, as we will see, was a common reaction against unpopular policies. A worker at Bread Factory No. 1 returned to the plant after serving a year-long sentence for pilfering. TsDNI f. 13, op. 4, d. 408, ll. 113–14.

[94] TsDNI f. 13, op. 4, d. 47, ll. 2–6. For more on disciplinary problems at the Mikoyan Shoe Factory, see also TsDNI f. 13, op. 4, d. 47, l. 25; TsDNI f. 13, op. 4, d. 72, l. 54.

This early report on labor discipline during "reconstruction" shows that workers broke labor laws with impunity and that, faced with a lack of labor power, factory directors tolerated major transgressions.

Internal party material highlighted problems at several key plants, including the Mikoyan Shoe Factory, where reportedly in late 1944 "the situation with labor discipline has not yet reached a suitably high level." Most absences or desertions, moreover, involved trainees from the FZOs, a familiar problem as we know, showing "that mass political work among young workers is inadequately developed."[95] An investigation of several food-industry plants revealed little or no "political-educational work among new workers," as a result of which "there are numerous cases of workplace pilfering and poor labor discipline."[96] At Krasnyi Aksai out of a workforce of roughly 750 in 1944, 201 had abandoned their jobs, of whom 146 had been mobilized through FZOs.[97] Two years later a report bemoaned that on some days as many as 200 workers laid out of work at Krasnyi Aksai.[98] During the war desertion from military plants became such a problem (despite laws criminalizing it) that in December 1944 the Supreme Soviet passed an amnesty for those who voluntarily returned to work. The results of the amnesty, however, were not encouraging: as of February 1945 only nine workers (out of several hundred) had obliged.[99] Also, as we have noted, behavior in the training schools was problematic, one report citing "very low labor discipline among the trainees, with only 70 percent attendance."[100]

---

[95] TsDNI f. 13, op. 4, d. 102, l. 7. In the first quarter of the year there were 38 cases of layouts and desertions from work, in the second quarter 76 cases, and in the third quarter 73.

[96] TsDNI f. 13, op. 4, d. 23, l. 45. The director of the Macaroni Factory, the report further noted, left the "serious transgression of worker Prokof'ev unpunished" (it does not clarify what this transgression was). A late 1944 investigation of labor discipline in one district concluded it was "not on a very high level," citing "numerous instances of serious transgressions." TsDNI f. 13, op. 4, d. 102, l. 76.

[97] TsDNI f. 13, op. 4, d. 102, l. 76. In the final two quarters of the year the number of workers at the plant actually decreased from 763 to 628. There were also 84 layouts and 28 cases of tardiness reported, but, this account cautioned, "not all cases are accounted for in these numbers."

[98] TsDNI f. 13, op. 4, d. 287, l. 46.

[99] TsDNI f. 13, op. 4, d. 176, ll. 5, 9. A subsequent gorkom protocol on Military Factory No. 359 declared that "the situation with labor discipline at the plant is very bad." TsDNI f. 13, op. 4, d. 147, l. 148. This report informed that in April 4 people deserted the plant and in May 22 more did so as well. For more internal party reports on poor labor discipline and desertions from work, see also TsDNI f. 13, op. 4, d. 65, l. 98; TsDNI f. 13, op. 4, d. 149, ll. 65–66; TsDNI f. 13, op. 4, d. 375, l. 129; GARO f. 3737, op. 4, d. 1390, l. 3.

[100] TsDNI f. 13, op. 4, d. 146, l. 54. At a party plenum gorkom secretary Comrade Bogachev said that the director of Rostsel'mash, Comrade Titarenko, had done

The mythical nature of Soviet accounting is yet another point of comparison between public and internal party material on "reconstruction." According to several closed reports, many plants fudged the books to show that they fulfilled their production plans, the realm of numbers allowing for creativity in accounting. At a party plenum in July 1945 obkom secretary Comrade Chusovskii examined the production numbers of Rostsel'mash and other plants closely, revealing an interesting bookkeeping trick. Rostsel'mash fulfilled its plan for the first quarter of the year by 113 percent, "about all one could wish for it seems," according to Chusovskii. "But," he continued, "if one looks deeper one sees a number of serious deficiencies in the plant," and it could have produced far more than it did with better organization of equipment and labor. Later a district secretary at the meeting exposed a common tactic by factory directors and their accountants. As noted in the press as well, to inflate production numbers industry leaders often concentrated on items of secondary importance, overfulfilling the plan for such items at the expense of more important but more time-consuming products. Proletarskii Molot, for instance, fulfilled its overall production plan for June by 117 percent, but its plan for nails, the main item produced by the plant, by a mere 28 percent.[101] At a party gathering several months later Gorkom Secretary Comrade Nazamaev announced that the city's bread industry had fulfilled its plan by well over 100 percent the first half of the year. "But what is hiding behind these numbers?" he rhetorically asked. Four of five of the city's main bread factories produced bread at well above the established cost of production. Industry leaders, Nazamaev lectured, should concentrate on keeping production costs low instead of forcing the tempo of production at higher operating costs.[102]

Internal party sources resemble pubic party texts to a significant degree but expose more about the problems and difficulties encountered during "reconstruction." This material described the "remaking" of the Soviet working class during the war, as party leaders lamented that an inexperienced workforce still needed to be "molded" into shape. As we saw in the previous chapter regarding the level of living standards provided by employers, workers were in a strong position in the "politics of productivity" and had room for negotiation. Demobilized troops had the most leverage, and they occasionally clashed with factory directors who had stayed in occupied territory. In con-

nothing to improve conditions in the plant's dormitories, especially for FZO trainees, which contributed to disciplinary problems. TsDNI f. 13, op. 4, d. 144, l. 38. For more accounts of poor labor discipline at the FZO training schools, see also TsDNI f. 13, op. 4, d. 130, l. 59; and GARO f. 3737, op. 4, d. 1394, l. 16.

[101] TsDNI f. 13, op. 4, d. 151, ll. 35, 52.

[102] TsDNI f. 13, op. 4, d. 193, l. 23. A report on the city's non-alcoholic beverage industry noted that it fulfilled the plan for 1947 by a mere 54 percent but that the factory director and main accountant hid this fact with false production reports, the two of them pocketing the extra rubles they received. GARO f. 3907, op. 1, d. 5, ll. 3–5.

trast to the press, internal reports exposed a lack of enthusiasm for "socialist competition" during the holidays. Rostsel'mash, the city's industrial show-place, was plagued by a number of serious problems typical of other plants, such as a shortage of workers, inadequate materials and supplies, frequent in-terruptions in production due to the lack of electricity, water, etc. "Labor dis-cipline," defined broadly as absenteeism, desertion, and pilfering, remained a serious concern for industry leaders. Workers worried about survival pre-ferred positions with access to food, which suggests the prominence of work-place pilfering, and even the threat of punishment could not keep them tied to jobs they did not want. The amnesty, moreover, brought very few people back to work and actually led to further desertions. These narratives proffer the "inexperience" of the workforce and their "lack of political training"—or, in a word, "backwardness"—as the primary cause for problems in "labor dis-cipline," indicating an "us" and "them" mentality on the part of party leaders charged with organizing production. Finally, as in the press numbers were very important in the party's hidden material, the regime preoccupied with raising productivity and lowering production costs, quantifying everything in the process.

Popular Reactions to "Reconstruction" and the "Politics of Productivity"

The questions and commentaries of workers and others, along with memoir accounts and interviews with those who remember this difficult time, offer another interesting perspective on Soviet "reconstruction" and the "politics of productivity." Karol poignantly captured the high hopes of the era. On Vic-tory Day he recalled a populace "intoxicated by triumph"; his friend Kolia kept saying over and over again, "Now we really are going to be happy."[103] Karol relayed the hopes and aspirations he and friends in Rostov held at the time. "It is difficult to hold any certainties on the future of this Soviet Russia," he cautioned, but

> Suppose it were to become more bearable to live in after victory? Perhaps it would learn to govern itself differently, allowing its citizens to decide on their own affairs and to discuss matters openly. Kolya hoped for the arrival of a Soviet Union without suffering, Klava for a society in which everyone was well educated, Chourik and Galia for a USSR less dependent on hierarchy, more egalita-rian.... All of these aspirations seemed to me to be legitimate in this hour of victory.

---

[103] Karol, *Solik*, 342. He also remembers that amid the victory celebration a grey-haired woman sang a famous aria from *Eugene Onegin*: "What does tomorrow have in store for us?"

During the following months "we dreamed together of the advent of a fraternal and more just world." Soviet citizens, Karol explained, seemed "convinced that barely perceptible signs presage[d] a thaw." Indicating the power of ideology, he noted that the prevailing propaganda "restricted our vision," as "everything combined to maintain us in this false perspective, from our university syllabus to our repertoire of films." Karol also described "the arrogance of demobilized soldiers who, because they have fought in the war, believe that they can get away with anything."[104] His friend Chourik, for instance, a disabled war veteran studying to be a history teacher, "thinks everything is permitted." At times he even criticized Stalin, barely appreciating "the point beyond which it is unsafe to go in the USSR." "What is strange," Karol added, "is that the number of these 'invulnerable characters' has increased prodigiously."[105] Several interviewees echoed the myth of "reconstruction," showing the persistence of the ideas propagated by the regime. For example, Nina Nikitichna K, a party member since 1939 and a worker at Rostsel'mash who returned shortly after occupation, remembered people rebuilding the factory with "colossal enthusiasm." She said Rostsel'mash had no problem finding workers because everyone in the city was proud of it and wanted to work there.[106] She and other interviewees emphasized the sacrifice and enthusiasm of people at the time, claiming that "Rostov was rebuilt quickly" and that the city became "even more beautiful than before the war," phraseology promoted by those in power.[107]

Lists of questions posed by workers at party meetings clearly indicate their high expectations and hopes for an end to rationing after the war, as workers tended to interpret the party's myth of "reconstruction" in terms of its (unrealized) promises for improved living standards. As early as June 1945, workers were already asking, "When and how will rationing end?" a

---

[104] Karol, *Solik*, 303, 316, 344–45, 347. Karol, who passed his university exams with flying colors, recalls "it is no mystery to anyone that, at the university, preference is shown to students who have fought in the war, and that they are given an easy ride by their examiners in acknowledgement of their services to the country." In contrast, at the same time his wife Klava had to face "a panel of hostile examiners who have probably been ordered to fail the majority of women students" (348).

[105] Karol, *Solik*, 303. He writes that in time Chourik's fiancée will make of him "a good history teacher who will teach the official syllabus and consign his private thoughts to his study drawers" (362).

[106] Interview by author, 17 March 1995. This claim, totally contradicted by a wealth of archival evidence from the time, illustrates Merridale's point that the narrative of memory is at least partly constructed by other dominant narratives, be they state-controlled or constructed over time by peers (Merridale, *Night of Stone*, 325).

[107] For example, interviews with Svetlana Chernysheva, 3 March 1995; Sergei Zhak, 15 March 1995; Svetlana Semenova, 16 April 1995; Oleg Pianiatsev, 17 April 1995; S. I Emel'ianenko, 23 May 1995.

question repeated numerous times over the next two-and-a-half years.[108] In August someone asked, "Why wasn't rationing ended and why didn't life improve after the war?"[109] As we saw, rationing continued through the worst of the famine, ending in late December 1947. Earlier that autumn the government announced a strong harvest, a relief to people on the tail end of a very difficult year. In an October meeting workers at Mill No. 1 expressed impatience with regard to rationing: "We waited for the non-rationed sale of bread in May, June, July, August, September, when is it finally going to happen?" People specifically linked their questions and comments to Stalin's promise in February 1946 that it would end "in the near future." In the fall of 1947 one worker asked, "When will Stalin fulfill his promise to end rationing?" A young woman at a garment factory stated, "I and all the other women in our shop wonder about one thing. Comrade Stalin in one of his speeches before the Soviet people said that in the near future rationing would end. Now tell us, when will that 'near future' finally arrive?"[110] Someone else allegedly asked, "How can you explain the fact that rationing hasn't ended although this year's harvest is higher than before the war?"[111] In November 1947 a communist party member at the Railroad Institute asked, "when will they supply workers better? To live like this," he added, "is very difficult." The report noted that two other communists at the Institute expressed similar opinions.[112] Of course, an end to rationing under famine conditions would have been disastrous, and the rationing system itself was *not* the main problem, but rather the cuts in ration entitlements and the chronic shortage of goods. Nonetheless, it is clear that many workers *perceived* rationing as *the* problem and anxiously awaited its cessation, as if that alone would lead to a dramatic rise in their living standards. Thus public pressure for an end to rationing intensified in the late summer and autumn of 1947, as workers held the regime and Stalin personally accountable for promises made a year-and-a-half earlier.

Workers occasionally linked their criticisms of the regime to official holidays, which they also associated with expectations for improved living standards. There were a few reports of workers refusing to attend holiday demon-

---

[108] TsDNI f. 13, op. 4, d. 180, l. 44. This report is from a railway workers' meeting in Zheleznodorozhnii district.

[109] TsDNI f. 13, op. 4, d. 259, l. 124.

[110] TsDNI f. 13, op. 4, d. 233, ll. 2, 21. For similar questions, see also ll. 48–49, 59, 76–77, 87, 93–94, 98, and TsDNI f. 13, op. 4, d. 313, l. 18.

[111] TsDNI f. 13, op. 4, d. 313, l. 18.

[112] TsDN f. 13, op. 4, d. 233, l. 67. "I am an engineer," he continued, "they pay me only 600 rubles [a month] and 600 grams of bread." For similar comments, see also l. 3, and RGASPI f. 17, op. 88, d. 332, l. 8.

strations, one woman staying home because of "poor food supply."[113] Another worker asked at a party meeting, "Why is there no bread for the holiday?"[114] With all the hoopla surrounding Soviet holidays, it is not surprising that many workers expected an end to rationing for the 30th anniversary of the Bolshevik Revolution in 1947. As early as August workers in Rostov's water treatment plant were asking whether bread would be added to their rations for the holiday, and the end of rationing was the talk of the town as November 7 neared. In September a worker at DGTF publicly expressed her hope that Soviet leaders would end rationing for the holiday "because life with ration cards is very difficult." An October report on a workers' meeting stated that "half of them did not believe food supplies and services to the population would get better, but the other half felt that after the holiday things will improve." A woman worker at Rostsel'mash declared, "Everything will be different when the thirtieth anniversary is here!" while, according to an agitator's report, "workers are waiting for the holiday with great excitement, waiting with the deep-rooted belief that things will probably dramatically improve."[115] Rationing did not end and living standards did not get better with the holiday, however, and, significantly, Molotov instead of Stalin addressed the Soviet people on the anniversary. Stalin's absence from the podium did not escape people's attention, one worker wondering aloud, "Why didn't Comrade Stalin give a statement during the thirtieth anniversary of the October Revolution?"[116] We can only guess at an answer to this question, but it seems feasible that, still not in a position to end rationing and fulfill his promise of February 1946, Stalin decided not to appear at all before a population that had built up high expectations for the holiday.

After the 30th anniversary of the revolution an interesting conversation among workers in one plant "became known" to an informant, who dutifully recorded it, while interviewees 50 years later relayed varying recollections of Soviet holidays. The informant overheard workers suggesting that Stalin's second-in-command lied to the Soviet people in his holiday address: "Perhaps Molotov's claim that the USSR has more grain than last year is a result of the current international situation and is in fact untrue," they stated, "especially since they didn't end rationing for the thirtieth anniversary of October." The workers feared that the misinformation presaged war with the West. Aside

---

[113] TsDNI f. 13, op. 4, d. 233, l. 67. While the war still raged there was some question whether holiday festivities in November would even be held because of the harsh weather and lack of warm clothing for the population. Someone asked at a party meeting, "Will we have a demonstration for the anniversary of the October Revolution this year?" RGASPI f. 17, op. 88, d. 331, l. 90. Zubkova shows that for this reason holiday demonstrations were not held in the north.

[114] TsDNI f. 13, op. 4, d. 233, l. 67.

[115] TsDNI f. 13, op. 4, d. 313, ll. 2, 68–69, 86–87.

[116] TsDNI f. 13, op. 4, d. 313, l. 98.

from revealing skepticism toward Molotov's claims, the comment also reflected a common anxiety about the possibility of war as tensions with the West mounted with the developing Cold War.[117] For their part, several interviewees, such as Sergei Zhak, Svetlana Chernysheva, and Nina Nikitichna K., recalled the holidays as a time of genuine pride in their country's achievements.[118] Oleg A. Pianiatsev remembered the excitement surrounding the unveiling of the 1,000th postwar combine from Rostsel'mash during the 30th anniversary of the Bolshevik Revolution.[119] S. I. Emel'ianenko, a coal miner and worker during these years, recalled the "collective energy" of holiday demonstrations, which he always attended with pleasure and enthusiasm. He remembered the strong bond between veterans and the inspiration he felt when gathering with friends on the holidays to sing. "However," Emel'ianenko added, "not everyone came voluntarily" because some co-workers did not want to attend the demonstrations.[120] Genadii Ermolenko worked at Krupzavod for much of this five-year period, and he never attended the holiday demonstrations. He recalled that "propaganda was, of course, very heavy" during holidays, but that he and his cohort of friends always enjoyed themselves. "We celebrated not because of the propaganda but because we were young and we had nothing better to do." In general, Ermolenko said, "I understood that we lived like slaves; we worked and worked and they paid us nothing."[121] Despite the glowing May Day tribute to Stalin printed in *Molot* and noted above, poet and writer Veniamin Zhak, according to his wife Mariia, hated Stalin but felt obligated to write such lines.[122]

As noted the regime often linked government bond drives to holidays, and, in sharp contrast with the celebratory press coverage of these campaigns, archival sources recorded numerous negative comments by workers and others about the bond drives. In 1944 a teacher objected aloud to a party representative "soon you'll be taking money from the dead." He was immediately led out of the meeting, the report stated, and the collection proceeded and was completed on time.[123] A report on the loan campaign for May Day 1947—amid the peak of the famine—noted that, along with great patriotism and a high political consciousness, there were "isolated instances of an unhealthy attitude among workers who did not fully understand the meaning of

---

[117] TsDNI f. 13, op. 4, d. 233, l. 20. See also l. 27. On the prevalence of rumors of war during this period, see Johnston, "Subversive Tales?" in Fürst, *Late Stalinist Russia*, 64–66.

[118] Interviews by author, 3 March 1995, 15 March 1995, and 17 March 95.

[119] Interviews by author, 17 April 1995.

[120] Interview by author, 23 May 1995. Emel'ianenko advised them to "grab some sausage and come help him drink his bottles of vodka."

[121] Interviews by author, 16 April 1995.

[122] Interviews by author, 6 March 1995.

[123] TsDNI f. 13, op.4, d. 72, l. 219.

the new bond drive." Following a meeting about the bond drive a group of construction workers stood up and left, refusing to sign, and "it was necessary to carry out explanatory work with them," the report noted. In Kirovskii district a dockworker proclaimed, "Enough! We earn little and work like oxen without even bread to eat. Comrade Stalin promised to end rationing, we are waiting, but rationing is still here."[124] A driver and union leader at Military Factory No. 306 refused to give his full salary because, he said, "I live poorly myself." Four other workers refused outright to contribute, and two rank-and-file party members were expelled for not donating enough.[125] The bond drive that autumn was met with similar skepticism. At a technical school for future mechanics three students refused to sign due to "material difficulties." They agreed to participate in the campaign only after the secretary of the party bureau "explained to them the political meaning of the bond drive and about measures being taken to improve living conditions." When told to sign on to the bond drive, one woman attacked an agitator with a shovel, "cursed district leaders (in uncensored words) and insulted Comrade Stalin and Soviet power." The Leninskii district procurator, this account ended hauntingly, "is taking the necessary actions to deal with this incident."[126]

There were numerous reports of public statements against these campaigns by workers in this five-year period, while an unpublished letter to *Pravda* reveals an interesting perspective as well. One worker refused to donate even half of her monthly wages, and when party representatives tried to "explain to her" the need to increase the contribution she declared, "Don't even try to talk me in to anything more or I won't sign at all. I don't care what kind of government we have as long as I can earn a piece of bread."[127] During the December 1947 monetary reform the government exchanged the state loan money only at a three-to-one rate, a significant loss for many. In the very next bond drive in 1948 a worker proclaimed "again they're taking money from us! They've cheated (lied to) me long enough. They should give me back the money they've taken during all these bond drives."[128] Countless complaints were recorded about the government bond drives, contradicting the enthusiastic picture depicted in press reports.[129] Workers also penned letters to *Pravda* expressing their discontent with these campaigns. A letter from a dockworker in Rostov said he and co-workers gladly signed the bond drive

---

[124] TsDNI f. 13, op. 4, d. 234, l. 2.

[125] TsDNI f. 13, op. 4, d. 234, l. 24. For more critical comments on the bond drive, see also TsDNI f. 13, op. 4, d. 234, ll. 29, 36; TsDNI f. 13, op. 4, d. 296, ll. 30, 43.

[126] TsDNI f. 13, op. 4, d. 414, ll. 9–10.

[127] TsDNI f. 13, op. 4, d. 414, l. 11.

[128] TsDNI f. 13, op. 4, d. 415, l. 83. I discuss the monetary reform and workers' discontent with the exchange rate of the bond money in chap. 6.

[129] For more reports on negative comments about the bond drives, see also TsDNI f. 13, op. 4, d. 233, l. 94; TsDNI f. 13, op. 4, d. 414, ll. 41, 45.

for sums ranging from 200 to 700 rubles (the average worker's pay was 300 to 500 rubles a month). But the party representative, who the letter identified by name, said they could not return to work until they signed up for 1,000 rubles. As a result 70 people missed work on May 5, and a total of 80 more missed work over the next two days. This was difficult for the dockworkers to endure, the author noted, particularly those with large families. A worker and former partisan with six children, for instance, cried from humiliation when forced to sign on for 1,000 rubles. "One wonders," the letter continued, "why the rules of the Stalin Constitution are broken so easily, since the bond drive is supposed to be voluntary and since we all agreed to sign anyway (but at our own sum)."[130] This unpublished letter shows that some workers felt pressured into contributing more than they wanted to in these patriotic campaigns *and* that they evoked Stalinist rule of law in their defense.[131]

Lastly, these sources give us some insight into workers' perspective on the "politics of productivity" and their position therein. First and foremost workers' commentaries highlight the inadequate compensation they received for their labor. *Svodki* recorded many complaints by workers about low wages and also occasionally about the late payment of their wages. Amid the famine in late 1946 a construction worker told a co-worker, "We don't even get paid enough to eat normally."[132] The following year a railway worker stated a strong opinion with regard to the holiday socialist competition: "It's all just propaganda so that we will work better," she said, "but they don't even pay us decent wages. If I had figured this out sooner I would not have contributed to the bond drive." In the same report another worker allegedly complained, "I would love to be a Stakhanovite and earn a lot, but because of interruptions in production I can't even make enough to buy bread with." It added that at two plants workers did not receive their wages for the first half of June 1947,

---

[130] RGASPI f. 17,op. 122, d. 325, l. 168. An account from Moscow is particularly telling. I. M. Tarasenko, an employee of the Moscow Bean Processing Plant, wrote to *Pravda* that he refused to sign the bond drive, and the following day at 11:00 Comrade Makagon of the plant's party organization called him in for a discussion. "A policeman who I did not recognize was already waiting," he wrote. The policeman explained to Tarasenko that if he did not agree to sign the bond drive, "he would write up an eviction order and kick me out of the city within twenty-four hours." Under such intimidation he reluctantly signed for what was a large sum for him "given my economic circumstances," and when he returned to his factory shop he told all his co-workers what had happened and they were very upset. "Did they act correctly?" Tarasenko asked of the party representative and policeman. "I still have not been able to calm down after this threat," he added. RGASPI f. 17,op. 122, d. 325, l. 165. For similar complaints, see also ll. 138–39.

[131] On the population's use of Soviet law to defend its positions against the regime in the 1930s, see Davies, *Popular Opinion in Stalin's Russia*, chap. 6.

[132] TsDNI f. 13, op. 4, d. 233, l. 68. See also TsDNI f. 13, op. 4, d. 415, l. 73.

"which caused concern and a bad mood."[133] The district party secretary who wrote the report at the end of 1946 noted that discussions and lectures were held with workers to emphasize the temporary nature of the difficulties brought by the war and the need for them to increase productivity.[134] "Only the successful fulfillment of the country's plan for 1947," the author concluded, "will allow for the improvement of workers' material daily lives." This summation of the workers' (critical) opinions reflects a fundamental disconnect between those in power and the workers in whose interests they claimed to rule: in internal reports party leaders focused overwhelmingly on low production numbers and "poor labor discipline," whereas in their commentaries workers emphasized the poor pay they received for their labor— two very different perspectives on the "politics of productivity."

Worker discontent with their inadequate (and sometimes delayed) wages took a variety of forms, including work slowdowns or stoppages, highly symbolic acts of resistance.[135] As noted, workers occasionally walked off the job when faced with interruptions in production, a frequent problem that further reduced their already low wages.[136] In June 1943, four workers left the Mikoyan Shoe Factory for that reason, and a woman railway worker proclaimed to her boss "fire me if you want because I can't live on my wages anyway. Let them arrest me but I'm not coming back to work."[137] Three years later the reduction in rations in late September 1946 led to protests at Lenzavod, where 19 workers refused to come to work one day and several workers "purposely reduced their labor productivity when given the new ration card with the reduced amount." One of the workers initially refused to work at all, agreeing to return only after plant managers "had a discussion with him."[138] A central report in October 1946 lamented "numerous worker walkouts in local industry" in several oblasts, including Rostov.[139] Periodic work stoppages continued throughout this five-year period. Coinciding with the announced completion of Rostov's "reconstruction" in August 1948, workers at Military Fac-

---

[133] TsDNI f. 13, op. 4, d. 415, l. 47.

[134] TsDNI f. 13, op. 4, d. 233, l. 68.

[135] Jeffrey Rossman defines "resistance" as signifying "individual and collective efforts by workers to alter, undermine, or abolish policies or practices implemented by local, regional, and/or central authorities, and to compel the same to fulfill what were popularly perceived to be their obligations to the industrial labor force" (*Worker Resistance Under Stalin*, 6).

[136] TsDNI f. 13, op. 4, d. 47, l. 6.

[137] TsDNI f. 13, op. 4, d. 47, l. 25 and TsDNI f. 13, op. 4, d. 415, l. 47.

[138] TsDNI f. 13, op. 4, d. 232, ll. 3–4.

[139] RTsDIDNI f. 17, op. 122, d. 188, ll. 21, 26. "Leaving work" often meant going to work in the illegal economy, which I discuss in chap. 6, and obviously a number of workers felt compelled to do so as the lowered rations decreased what were already extremely low living standards.

tory No. 10, which makes naval vessels, stopped work to protest "systematic delays in the payment of wages." Having not yet received the previous month's wages, 26 workers refused to work until they finally got paid. The work stoppage lasted two hours, and the quick settlement of this problem *in the workers' favor* again points to the considerable leverage they held. This report noted that the delayed payment of wages existed in other plants as well, adding "about 30 percent of lumber mill workers complain and work poorly because they have not received wages to buy bread with."[140] Seldom faced with acts of collective protest by workers, local leaders no doubt responded so quickly to the demands at Military Factory No. 10 for fear their protest might spread.

Karol observed the "politics of productivity" during his stint after the war as a factory administrator in a metallurgical plant in Rostov. The factory director's "managerial authority," he notes, "rests on his right to hand out bonuses to the 'best' workers and to penalize the 'slackers,'" but in actuality the "bonuses" paid for higher production rates were almost meaningless given prices on the illegal market. "The promise of a bonus of twenty rubles—half the price of a bowl of borsch [at the market]—cannot encourage anyone to exert themselves." He noted that at the factory there was wide differentiation in pay and "a great deal of arbitrariness" in the calculation of wages. "It is the useless nature of these calculations that most astonishes me," Karol wrote, wondering, "Is there any rhyme or reason at this time of labor shortage in maintaining a whole cohort of productivity inspectors and chasing after the phantom of socialist competition at work?" Karol left Rostov in 1946, and although he remembered his friends and life in the city fondly, he took with him a negative impression of Soviet power:

> The mistrust I feel towards the USSR is nourished by my everyday experience in the rather favorable circumstances of my life in Rostov. For let us speak the truth: Stalin writes letters of thanks in honeyed tones to the peasants for their donations, knowing full well that their savings have been extorted from them, in the same way that the state extorts from us our "voluntary" subscriptions for a state loan [in the bond drives].... For seven years the leaders of this country have done their best to convince me, at every opportunity, that they don't give a damn for their own people.[141]

Once a "true believer" in Soviet power, Karol left in a totally different frame of mind.

---

[140] TsDNI f. 13, op. 4, d. 416, ll. 139–40. Filtzer shows that there was a wave a wildcat strikes nationwide in the first four months of 1948 due to the late payment of wages (*Soviet Workers and Late Stalinism*, 84–88).

[141] Karol, *Solik*, 295, 321, 374.

In these sources, workers and others expressed a variety of opinions on a number of issues facing them, much of it in the language of the regime but challenging the basic precepts of the official myth of "reconstruction." Some protested low real wages, unpopular party policies, and the delayed payment of wages with small-scale collective acts of protest, showing their room for maneuverability in the "politics of productivity." In sharp contrast with descriptions in the party press workers often stated their opposition to government bond drives. The unpublished letter to *Pravda* indicated that "explanatory work" sometimes included intimidation or pressure, conveying the strong resentment of at least some workers at the tactics used by party representatives during these campaigns. Workers had high expectations for improved living standards after the war, especially for the end of rationing, a hope many tied to the 30th anniversary of the Bolshevik Revolution. Significantly, Stalin did not address the nation on the holiday and rationing continued until the end of the year, prompting some to wonder about the validity of Molotov's speech, the availability of grain, and the possibility of war. Workers complained vehemently about low wages and the poor conditions for production. The regime occasionally responded to workers' objections, showing the considerable leverage workers had in a tight labor market. The recollections of interviewees, meanwhile, reflect a wide variance of opinion, confirming that support and enthusiasm for the regime was genuine. The earnest patriotism of "true believers" existed alongside more sanguine reminiscences of "slavery" for Soviet workers and the insincerity of public tributes like the May Day poem by Veniamin Zhak. Karol's account fills in our picture of the population's expectations for a postwar thaw; the boldness of demobilized troops, who enjoyed a strong sense of entitlement; the emptiness of production rituals like "socialist competition"; and, finally, the arbitrariness of Soviet accounting.

A variety of sources shed light on the myth of "reconstruction" and the underlying "politics of productivity" characterizing an exploitative Stalinist regime of production. The party press wove a mythical tale of heroism and sacrifice, intending to inspire the population through its reporting of holidays, socialist competition, bond drives, and mobilization efforts. At the same time, *Molot* reported a number of problems and difficulties, contradicting its own mythic tale of "reconstruction." Internal party material revealed that the lack of workers, shortage of building materials, electrical power, and other difficulties compounded efforts to rebuild the city and improve living standards for the population. Moreover, if the industrialization of the 1930s resulted in the "making" of the Soviet working class, the working class portrayed in these texts was now being "remade" due to the war, with women and young people filling in at the factories.[142] As in the previous decade "labor discipline" remained difficult to uphold during and after the war. Workers abandoned jobs, especially during the height of the famine in 1947, and negotiated for the best possible positions in an extremely tight labor market. Workers' comments indicate considerable opposition to bond drives and campaigns to boost productivity, and people pinned their expectations for improvements in daily life to official holidays, especially the 30th anniversary of the Bolshevik Revolution in 1947, when such high hopes went unfulfilled. It was, not coincidentally, one of the few times Stalin failed to address the country on a major holiday and anniversary, which, again, suggests a degree of responsiveness from the top leadership to the mood and sentiments of the population.

The Soviet state's centrally-planned wages, furthermore, clearly did *not* compensate workers for the full value of their labor, at least when measured in prices at the market, which, as I will show, was the dominant sector of the economy. Thus the "myth of reconstruction" masked a fundamentally exploitative system of production, as is apparent in the class dialogue that emerges in the texts examined here. Whereas party materials quantified and emphasized increasing "labor productivity," fulfilling "production quotas," and lowering "production costs," workers focused on low real wages. Industry leaders conceptualized production in "us" and "them" terms, worrying about "labor discipline" at the same time they promoted propaganda about workers "owning their factories" and "working for themselves." Workers' statements (and acts) of discontent, meanwhile, negated the public narrative of happy laborers selflessly building a new tomorrow. Emboldened by the war experience, workers, especially demobilized troops, had high expectations for improved living standards after victory. People picked up important survival skills in the 1930s, and during "reconstruction" a "remade" working class used the system to its benefit, negotiating the best possible conditions (defined in part by access to goods for pilfering) in a tight labor market. In addition, even small-scale acts of collective protest required some organization, a frightening precedent for industry leaders. The party was aware of the population's high expectations and relatively strong position in the labor market, and responded *leniently*—at least in practice—to acts of insubordination because the problem was so ubiquitous. For most workers official wages made it difficult to maintain a family, despite the fact that, as we will see in the next chapter, the regime constantly extolled the virtues of the family unit and described society itself in terms of a "family."

---

[142] On the "making" of the Soviet working class, see Siegelbaum and Suny, "Class Backwards? In Search of the Soviet Working Class," in *Making Workers Soviet*, 1–26.

Chapter Four

"When will we be able to feed our children?":
Gender, National Identity, and Soviet "Family Rhetoric"

In 1941 German troops killed ten-year-old Z. S. Smirtova's mother in a village near Rostov, forcing her to move to the city to live with her grandmother, who died near the end of the war. In an orphanage after victory, Smirtova could not locate her father, a Red Army officer. She assumed he was dead until they found each other, quite by accident, in 1948, when she was seventeen.[1] Many other families in Rostov, the Soviet Union as a whole, and other combatant nations had similar stories to tell, as four years of war left enormous dislocation and personal suffering in their wake.[2] Not only was the USSR's economy and infrastructure shattered by the war, so too were many of its families, the most basic and fundamental unit of society. Death, displacement, and the chaotic condition of war and occupation impacted millions. Along with rebuilding their country, people in the USSR needed to rebuild their lives; almost everyone lost relatives and loved ones (sometimes several) during the brutal conflict. Reconstructing the family, both literally and symbolically, was essential to reconstructing the country itself. Of course, the term "family" is imbued with political and ideological meanings and understood differently in different cultural contexts; it is a construct, a juridical concept defined linguistically and legally, but, at the same time, *lived* by people at a social level in their everyday lives. "Family," to borrow Joan Scott's definition of "gender," is a socially constructed process and characteristic fundamental in *all* social relationships, including those involving class.[3] In the USSR, as elsewhere in postwar Eurasia, the state saw the family unit as a crucial building block in the process of reconstruction, concentrating on women's role therein as a key lynchpin for society while depicting the "Soviet family" rhe-

---

[1] GARO f. 3950, op. 1, d. 162, l. 118.

[2] As Mark Mazower notes, "War and wartime displacement broke up innumerable families across the continent." Mazower, *Dark Continent: Europe's Twentieth Century* (New York: Vintage Books, 1999), 221.

[3] See Joan Scott, "Gender: A Useful Category of Historical Analysis," *American Historical Review* 91 (1986): 1053–75.

torically as a unifying concept in national terms—i.e., familial unity over-and-above national differences.

This chapter looks at the regime's use of "family rhetoric," a term I use to refer to social discourse on family,[4] showing varying perspectives on familial matters, including the issues of gender and national identity that are central to *all* societies.[5] Several scholars examining interwar and postwar Eurasia highlight the centrality of gender to social reform and family policy.[6]

---

[4] Examples are terms describing the Soviet Union itself. The official title given World War II was the *Velikaia Otechestvennaia Voina* (Great Fatherland War), which is often translated as the "Great Patriotic War," but I translate *otechestvennaia* as "Fatherland" because it comes from the root word *otets*, meaning "father." In addition, people frequently described the country as their "Motherland" (*Rodina*), a word that is *always* capitalized in public texts examined here, so I will capitalize it as well because it adds to the significance of the word, which stands out among those around it for no particular grammatical reason. On the importance of the imagery of Motherland during the war and the word *rodina*, see Lisa Kirschenbaum, "'Our City, Our Hearth, Our Families': Local Loyalties and Private Life in Soviet World War II Propaganda," *Slavic Review* 59: 4 (Winter 2000): 825–47. Lynn Hunt detects the discourse of *family romance*, "the collective, unconscious images of the familial order that underlie revolutionary politics," during the upheavals of late 18th-century France. Hunt, *The Family Romance of the French Revolution* (Berkeley: University of California Press, 1992), xiii. I agree with Martha Fineman, who writes with regard to contemporary American society that the political use of "family rhetoric" "serves as a powerful ideological symbol with political implications." Fineman, "Masking Dependency: The Political Role of Family Rhetoric," in *The Subject of Care: Feminist Perspectives on Dependency*, ed. Eva Feder Kittay and Ellen K. Feder (Lanham, MD: Rowman and Littlefield Publishers, 2002), 216.

[5] "Gender" refers to the social processes by which cultural meanings come to be associated with sexual difference. These social sexual differences, in turn, form the basis for social exclusions and inclusions and constitute inequalities in power, authority, rights, and privileges. While sexual difference is the basis for gender discourses, which are constructed through a range of institutions (such as the family, the state, and unions) and policies, gender is a socially constructed process and characteristic that is fundamental in all social relationships. Thus, the term "gender" refers to both historically and socially constituted relationships and to a tool of analysis used to understand how social relationships and cultural categories are constituted. See Scott, "Gender."

[6] Dutton, "Overlooked Source of Social Reform," 376; Nancy M. Wingfield and Maria Bucur, *Gender and War in Twentieth-Century Eastern Europe* (Bloomington: Indiana University Press, 2006). Gisela Bock and Pat Thane note that "much recent writing about the history of women, of the women's movement and about welfare states has stressed the degree to which modern welfare reforms are about women." Pat Thane and Gisela Bock, eds., *Maternity and Gender Politics: Women and the Rise of the European Welfare States, 1880s-1950s* (New York: Routledge, 1991), 1. See, for example, Miranda Pollard, *Reign of Virtue: Mobilizing Gender in Vichy France* (Chicago: University of Chicago Press, 1998); Elinor A. Accampo, Rach G. Fuchs, and Mary Lynn Stewart, *Gender and the Politics of Social Reform in France, 1870–1914* (Baltimore: Johns Hopkins University Press, 1995); Seth Koven and Sonya Michel, eds., *Mothers of a New World: Maternalist*

Depopulation and the devastation of World War I led European countries to pursue pronatalist policies in the interwar period, culminating in the creation of welfare states after World War II.[7] The 1939 Family Law Code in France, for example, sought to increase the population by greatly raising government spending for rural family welfare.[8] France's defeat to Germany in 1940, moreover, "politicized family" to a new degree, and mobilizing women was crucial to Vichy's mission.[9] A heavy dose of paternalism underscored Vichy's mission, which relied on very specific conceptions of gender: men as producers and women as reproducers.[10] After the war Western European governments tried to convince women to withdraw from the workforce and return to the domestic realm, giving employment priority to returning servicemen while also encouraging the production of babies.[11] In postwar Britain women's un-

---

Politics and the Origins of Welfare States (New York: Routledge, 1993); Linda Gordon, ed., *Women, the State, and Welfare* (Madison: University of Wisconsin Press, 1990); Joan Acker, "Class, Gender, and the Relations of Distribution," *Signs* 13: 3 (Spring 1988): 473–97; Amy Gutman, ed., *Democracy and the Welfare State* (Princeton, NJ: Princeton University Press, 1988); A. A. Sasoon, ed., *Women and the State: The Shifting Boundaries of Public and Private* (London: Hutchinson Education, 1987); J. Dale and P. Foster, eds., *Feminists and State Welfare* (London: Routledge, 1986).

[7] See Dutton, "Overlooked Source of Social Reform," 375–412; Pollard, *Reign of Virtue*, 7; Bock and Thane, *Maternity and Gender Politics*, 15–21; and Mazower, *Dark Continent*, 76–87.

[8] Dutton, "Overlooked Source of Social Reform," 402–03 and 408. The 1939 Code, he explains, focused on rural areas since most industrial workers were covered by existing legislation regarding family allowances. The Vichy regime and the post-liberation government strengthened the trend of heavy state interventionism in family welfare, leading to the Provisional Government's Decree in October 1945 that laid the foundation of France's postwar welfare state. France and Great Britain created an "emulation effect," as Mazower calls it, in the formation of welfare states throughout Western and Eastern Europe" (Mazower, *Dark Continent*, 208).

[9] Pollard, *Reign of Virtue*, 5. She describes women as "as much an immensely powerful symbolic category as an actual constituency of sexed citizens." Pollard further asserts that the Vichy regime, whose slogan was *Travail, Famille, Patrie* (Work, Family, Fatherland), embraced the idea of national regeneration through support for large families, both in its policies and its propaganda, a tendency she defines as "familialism."

[10] Ibid., 6, 195–96. Discontent among the French public with the Vichy regime had become widespread by 1943, she concludes, due in large part to its failure to fulfill promises to raise family living standards.

[11] See Mazower, *Dark Continent*, 208–09. Giselda Bock and Pat Thane show that throughout Western Europe, the "indirect impact" of welfare measures was to strengthen women's dependency on men and "hence also to reinforce the gender gap" in terms of poverty. Women increasingly worked in the European welfare states as social workers, which, Bock and Thane assert, "reinforced the gender division of labor" because they are seen as "within the caring sphere." Thane and Bock, introduction to *Maternity and Gender Politics*, 2, 4.

paid work in the domestic sphere constrained their abilities as wage earners and imposed a double burden on them.[12] The assumption that those who bear children will also rear them results in an unequal division of domestic and "*caring* work," which stems from women's inferior position in the labor market and their economic dependence on men.[13]

We will examine the relevance of these issues for the "reconstruction" of Soviet society, where the demographic impact of the war was strongest. Seventy-six percent of wartime losses (roughly 20 of the 26.6 million) were men born between 1901 and 1931, so women greatly outnumbered men after the conflict.[14] According to incomplete data, in the country as a whole in 1940 there were about 100.3 million women and 92.3 million men, the difference due to the purges and women's longer life expectancy. In 1946 women outnumbered men 96.2 million to 74.4 million, the greatest difference among those 20 to 44 years old. In 1940 there were 37.6 million women and 34.8 million men between the ages of 20 and 44; in 1946 while there was a roughly equal number of women there were ten million fewer men in that age range.[15] This gender imbalance had several consequences. As in the 1930s, when the imbalance was less pronounced, absconding husbands and neglected children were among society's worst "family problems."[16] Also, women entered the workforce in high numbers during the war—the number of women in the

---

[12] Sandra Fredman, *Women and the Law* (Oxford: Oxford University Press, 1997), xi, 103, and 138. Fredman further argues that the presumption among (mostly male) lawmakers that women's role in society should be primarily *reproductive* underlies legislation (or the lack thereof) undermining pay and employment opportunities for women due to the common British principle of a "family wage" for *men*. She adds that this is coupled with the "assumption that women are less productive than men" in the economic realm. I agree with her that "gender is an important and at times determinative feature in patterns of domination, and needs to be studied, not to the exclusion of other features of domination [i.e., class—JWJ], but in conjunction with them" (2).

[13] Jane Lewis, "Models of Equality for Women: The Case of State Support for Children in Twentieth-Century Britain," in Thane and Bock, *Maternity and Gender Politics*, 74–75. Examining state support for children in 20th-century Britain, Lewis finds that the 1945 Family Allowances Act allowing payment of a monthly stipend directly to mothers did "not address inequalities in the division of paid and unpaid work [between men and women] and indeed may be argued to encourage the assumption that *caring* for children is 'women's work.'" Subsequent legislation also made similar mistakes, she asserts (88). I emphasize "caring" in these quotes because of the importance of that word in Soviet rhetoric, as I show below.

[14] Andreev, *Naselenie Sovetskogo Soiuza*, 77. Sheila Fitzpatrick indicates that in the countryside there was a four to one ratio of women to men after the war. Fitzpatrick, "Postwar Soviet Society: The 'Return to Normalcy,' 1945–1953," in Linz, *Impact of World War II*, 131.

[15] See Andreev, *Naselenie Sovetskogo Soiuza*, 73; Zubkova, *Russia After the War*, 21.

[16] Fitzpatrick, *Everyday Stalinism*, chap. 6.

USSR employed in official economic activity increased from 39 to 56 percent between 1940 and 1945—and many of them remained in their jobs afterward.[17] Yet, despite their higher numbers in society as a whole and their increased role in industrial production, the party failed at repeated attempts to increase the proportion of women in its ranks, while the mostly male leaders drawing up production plans looked upon women as potential laborers *and* mothers of laborers.[18] The "double burden" of employment and domestic work weighed upon women as well.[19]

Like gender, national identity was obviously an important issue throughout Eurasia during and after the war, especially with regard to anti-Semitism in Europe. Unfortunately anti-Semitism did not disappear with the end of the Holocaust and the liberation of the concentration camps in 1945; to the contrary, it intensified across the continent immediately after the war ended as Jewish survivors returned home to find their property inhabited by others and their goods plundered.[20] Anti-Semitic sentiments remained strong, for example, in Poland (though not *just* Poland), home to Europe's largest prewar Jewish population and its largest concentration camp during the war. Jews made a promising scapegoat for economic and political problems in the postwar years, especially in Łódź, one of the strongest centers of Polish anti-Semitism.[21] A pogrom in Kielce in July 1946 led to the murder of 42 Jewish residents, and there was a "pogrom atmosphere" in Łódź during this time as well.[22] There was clearly a strong current of anti-Semitism lurking beneath the surface of the popular stereotype of a "Judeo-commune" syndrome—the view of an alleged "special affinity between Jews and communism" that

---

[17] Morkovin, "Rabochie Dona v poslevoennyi period," 56.

[18] See Mary Buckley, *Women and Ideology in the Soviet Union* (Ann Arbor: University of Michigan Press, 1989), 3; and Gail Warshofsky Lapidus, *Women in Soviet Society: Equality, Development, and Social Change* (Berkeley: University of California Press, 1978), 338.

[19] On the "double burden," see Buckley, *Women and Ideology*, 3; and Barbara Jancar, *Women under Communism* (Baltimore: Johns Hopkins University Press, 1978), 41–46. Buckley notes that from early in the Soviet era women were channeled into traditionally female sectors, tending "to concentrate in unskilled and low-paid jobs." See Buckley, *Women and Ideology*, 2–3. T. H. Rigby and others have shown that the overwhelming majority of party leaders were men (Rigby, *Communist Party Membership*, 361).

[20] Mazower, *Dark Continent*, 209, 215–16. This was certainly true of Rostov's Jewish population, as we saw in chap. 2 with the example of the Zhak family, who returned to find their apartment inhabited and many of their belongings gone.

[21] Kenney, *Rebuilding Poland*, 110. He notes two strikes by workers in Łódź in June 1945 opposing the appointment of Jewish factory directors. The first of the strikes lasted two-and-a-half days with only one demand by workers: "'we don't want a Jew director.'" Kenney adds that "the protest was apparently successful in changing the director to workers' satisfaction," and states that a similar conflict nearly led to a third strike in another factory as well (111).

[22] Ibid., 114.

many Poles (and others) held in the postwar years as the communists gained political control over the country. Quite apart from being in control or linked to those in power, however, the dominant Jewish experience in post-World War II Poland was that of fear.[23] Whereas popular views held Jews to be in league with the communist security police despised by most Poles, in fact those same security police often targeted Jews with anti-Semitic attitudes and measures.[24] Anti-Semitism, in short, was alive and well in postwar Poland and throughout postwar Europe, including the Soviet Union, which experienced a resurgence of anti-Semitism after the war.

As noted, anti-Semitism reared its ugly head with a vengeance in the lower Don during the Civil War as the Whites promoted it and bandit groups randomly killed Jews for sport. During World War II, the Red Army had strict regulations against making anti-Semitic comments, "but among themselves," Catherine Merridale notes, "the soldiers—and even many officers—were liberal with their racist gibes." The stereotypical image of Jews as cowards emerged during the war; despite the fact that thousands of Jews served in the Red Army, some veterans claimed that "Jews did not fight" but "sat around in warm offices or anywhere that money might be found lying about."[25] Amir Weiner reports that in the Vinnytsia region in Ukraine, local Jews complained in an unpublished letter to *Pravda* that First Obkom Secretary Mikhail Stakhurskii "is 'deeply convinced' that, to a man, all Jews were in Tashkent and not one of them has fought!" Yet, the letter continues, every Jew of draft age "was at the front and fought fairly well for the Motherland, no worse than other nationalities." A year later the *Izvestiia* correspondent in Vinnytsia repeated these allegations against Stakhurskii, noting that "decorated *frontoviki* who returned to their former jobs were not reinstated on the order of comrade Stakhurskii only because they are Jews."[26] The official emphasis on a "single

---

[23] Jan T. Gross, "A Tangled Web: Confronting Stereotypes Concerning Relations between Poles, Germans, Jews, Communists," in Deák et al., *Politics of Retribution*, 105. Gross examines the files of the Central Committee of Jews in Poland, part of a Jewish-run organization intended to protect Jews remaining in the country, an "umbrella organization put together by representatives of all prewar Jewish political parties." On popular anti-Semitism in Poland, see also Jan T. Gross, *Neighbors: The Destruction of the Jewish Community in Jedwabne, Poland* (Princeton, NJ: Princeton University Press, 2001); and his *Fear: Anti-Semitism in Poland After Auschwitz. An Essay in Historical Interpretation* (Princeton, NJ: Princeton University Press, 2006).

[24] Among the anti-Semitic incidents documented by Gross was a play performed by a Polish sports club in, "of all places," Auschwitz, the content of which reportedly made "fun of the Jews in various sketches and songs." The source reporting this incident stresses that "the main part in these anti-Jewish gimmicks was played by the commander of the Security Police" (Gross, "A Tangled Web," 109).

[25] Merridale, *Ivan's War*, 289, 296. She states that Jews "were christened 'Tashkent partisans' after the city where so many had found refuge."

[26] Weiner, "Making of a Dominant Myth," 641.

Soviet family" of equal sufferers, moreover, denied the disproportionate suffering of Jews at the hands of the Nazis in occupied Soviet territory.[27] The Stalinist regime integrated "the unique Jewish tragedy into the universal narrative of Soviet suffering and the denial of Jews' contribution at the front."[28] At the core of this problem of official denial was "an imagined hierarchy of suffering" with Russians as the central victim, and they did not want to share their "victimhood." Of course, the Soviet regime did not approve of the mass killings of Jews, but "neither was it eager to accord them a special place in the myth of the war."[29] However, as we will see, there was ambiguity in the official treatment of these issues and "no consistent Soviet 'party line' on the Holocaust."[30]

There was likewise no consistency over time in family legislation, which changed greatly during the Soviet period in accord with shifting attitudes and the needs of the state. Early Soviet legal codes made women equal before the law, secularized marriage, facilitated divorce, legalized abortion, tacitly recognized consensual relationships outside of wedlock, and rendered the term "illegitimate offspring" meaningless. Like its Eurasian counterparts the Soviet regime promoted pronatalist policies during the 1930s. A new code in 1936 passed more demanding divorce laws, greatly restricted abortion, and introduced financial incentives to have children, as Stalinist lawmakers began to encourage family stability.[31] The Family Law of 1944 continued this trend, tightening divorce policy and requiring that registered marriages be con-

---

[27] Tumarkin, *Living and the Dead*; Merridale, *Ivan's War*, 289. See also Judith Miller, *One, by One, by One: Facing the Holocaust* (New York: Simon and Schuster, 1990).

[28] Weiner, "Making of a Dominant Myth," 641. Tanja Penter notes that the regime suppressed the "Jewish memory discourse about the Holocaust," promoted "an official narrative touting the suffering of all nations during the war," and ignored the question of anti-Semitic attitudes in the postwar trials of alleged collaborators—"even the term *anti-Semitism* failed to be mentioned in a single trial." Penter, "Collaboration on Trial: New Source Material on Soviet Postwar Trials against Collaborators," *Slavic Review* 64: 4 (Winter 2005): 785 (emphasis in the original). She adds that "despite the immense number of Jews murdered, Soviet accounts in general ignored, played down, or universalized the Holocaust. The number of Jewish victims was generally minimized in Soviet accounts and included as a rather small part in the death of twenty million Soviet citizens."

[29] Merridale, *Ivan's War*, 293.

[30] Zvi Gitelman makes this point. See Gitelman, "Soviet Reactions to the Holocaust," 7, 3.

[31] See Wendy Goldman, *Women, the State and Revolution: Soviet Family Policy and Social Life, 1917–1936* (New York: Cambridge University Press, 1993); idem, *Women at the Gates: Gender and Industry in Stalin's Russia* (Cambridge: Cambridge University Press, 2002); W. E. Butler, *Soviet Law* (London: Butterworths, 1988), 203–07.

firmed by a stamp in one's passport.[32] The law eliminated alimony payments, promised government support to single mothers, and increased the "childless tax" on bachelors, single women, and couples without children to 6 percent of their income (compared to 1 percent for those with one child and 0.5 percent for those with two or more). This legislation also introduced decorations for motherhood, from the second-class Motherhood Medal granted those with five children to the title of Heroine Mother given those with ten.[33] The 1944 Family Legislation underlines the symbolic significance of families and their material well-being for party leaders, who wanted to cultivate a Soviet "baby boom." Trying economic conditions, however, impeded population growth. Everyday experience and the ruling ideology shape perceptions of "family rhetoric" (as either acceptance of or reaction against that ideology), and I examine these perceptions among party leaders and workers during "reconstruction."

"Family Rhetoric" in the Local Press

In this five-year period hundreds of thousands of evacuees and demobilized troops returned to Rostov, many with family members missing or killed, while thousands of single mothers, demobilized troops, wounded war veterans, orphans, and national minorities also called the city home. In the official parlance of the time survivors were all part of "one Soviet family," a depiction that writes national, gender, and class differences out of the picture. Several days after the Red Army retook Rostov, returning party leaders organized a mass meeting, declaring "Before the entire native (*rodnoi*) Soviet people, we must all, as if one, remain at our posts and seriously get down to work!"[34] *Molot* published a letter that they composed to Stalin.[35] This early proclamation set the tone for the party's use of family rhetoric emphasizing

---

[32] See Mie Nakachi, "Population, Politics and Reproduction: Late Stalinism and Its Legacy," in Fürst, *Late Stalinist Russia*; and David Hoffman, "Mothers in the Motherland: Stalinist Pronatalism in Its Pan-European Context," *Journal of Social History* 34: 1 (2000): 35–54.

[33] See Buckley, *Women and Ideology*, 134–35. The title "Mother Heroine" came with a certificate from the Presidium of the Supreme Soviet of the USSR. See also TsDNI f. 13, op. 4, d. 86, l. 25.

[34] TsDNI f. 13, op. 4, d. 28, l. 1. *Rodnoi* is an important word in Soviet family rhetoric that is difficult to translate precisely. It comes from the root word *rod*, which the *Oxford Russian-English Dictionary* translates as "family, kin." The word for "Motherland," *Rodina*, comes from the same root, as does the verb *rodit'*, "to give birth." When used as an adjective, *rodnoi* is translated as "own, native, or home," in non-adjective form as "relations, relatives, or family." Because of the impreciseness of the word, I choose to use the Russian term here.

[35] See *Molot*, 20 February 1943, p. 1.

collective unity with a focus on production. A 1945 editorial stated that "workers feel like soldiers in one friendly family."[36] An electoral bulletin the following year maintained the theme of oneness, claiming that voters would meet the elections as a "single, united family."[37] One could cite many such examples, but the focus here is on the two main issues undercutting such rhetoric of social unity—gender and national identity, crucial areas of social interaction directly impacted by the regime's policies. As noted, in examining Soviet society I do not see gender and national identity as somehow competing with class for analytical supremacy—every relationship of class is at the same time a relationship of gender and of national identity. In fact, the complex interrelationship between these overlapping and intertwining divisions within human societies makes it paramount to study gender and national identity when focusing on class (and vice versa).

Women were key actors in the Soviet regime's imagined "family" and the unfolding drama of "reconstruction," as is apparent in the countless gendered representations in *Molot*. In November 1944, the paper reported on a Russian woman with a "large family" who, representing the "Motherland" itself, sacrificed a great deal for the cause. Author L. Rutskaia informed that Mariia Andreevna Fedorova, mother of 11, "is divided into equal parts for each of her children or, more accurately, she belongs completely to each one of them" (just as the country presumably belongs equally to each of its citizens). Thumbing through a family photo album, Mariia Fedorova remembered the last time the family was together, May Day 1941, "but soon the war began and my little ones flew from the nest. I remember how hard it was for me," she recalled, "but then I thought, 'I mustn't be like that, I'm not alone, many others have left their mothers as well.'" A simple Russian peasant woman, her sons grew up under Soviet power to become engineers, doctors, and technicians. Every line of their letters home, Rutskaia informed, "is filled with honor and loyalty to the Fatherland, bitter hatred for the enemy, and tender love for their mother." Mariia Fedorova lost nine sons in the war; a daughter and one son survived.[38] In this narrative, she stands in for the Motherland, dissolving her tremendous individual loss among "other mothers," i.e., society as a whole. Fedorova's "sons," understood collectively as Red Army troops, represent society's "children," specifically the male generation of the revolution, those "raised" by Soviet power, upwardly mobile, devoted, faithful sons willing to sacrifice their lives for their country. In this case the

---

[36] A. Krasikova, "Sovetskie zhenshchiny novymi podvigami v tylu i na fronte pribliziat chas nashei polnoi pobedy nad vragom," *Molot*, 8 March 1945, p. 3.

[37] TsDNI f. 13, op. 4, d. 259, l. 89. The electoral bulletin, although from an archival source, is clearly an example of the party's public record since the intention was to disseminate it widely. For more on the Soviet Union as "one family," see also an article on the elections, A. Kutsko, "Vsei sem'ei," *Molot*, 22 December 1947, p. 2.

[38] L. Rutskaia, "Bol'shaia Sem'ia," *Molot*, 5 November 1944, p. 2.

Fedorov sons were fighting for their mother and their Motherland simultaneously, the implicit message being that, albeit a terrible sacrifice, they died for Mariia Fedorova herself and their deaths were worth the survival and "freedom" of the "Motherland." Thus masculinity—in the sense of *being manly*—was equated with the willingness to die for the cause. The two remaining children, moreover, offered hope for the future.

Women were central to the "Soviet family" in the narrative of "reconstruction," moreover, as both mothers and workers—producers *and* reproducers—in contrast to the tendency of other states to separate those two roles. During the war, the party press penned a tale of women's "liberation" and female heroism on the home front, its language revealing a subtle but significant gendered difference in the use of the word "care" (*zabota*). A *Molot* editorial on the eve of International Women's Day in 1943 explained that "Soviet power creates conditions for unfettered creative work and a happy motherhood," thereby "achieving full and actual equal rights for women in all realms of life."[39] The electoral pamphlet asserted that women helped secure victory by heroically filling in for men in production and claimed that "women in no other country enjoy equal rights in all spheres, political, social, and daily family life, as they do in our country."[40] Women, moreover, contributed to victory by exhibiting "motherly care." *Molot* asserted: "Soviet women overwhelm wounded troops with care and attention while giving motherly care to the families of soldiers."[41] Women "cared" for injured soldiers, making their days in the hospital "cozier" (*uiutnee*).[42] *Molot* excerpted two letters from soldiers to women's collectives thanking them for their "warm care and tender attention" and noting that "for us they are now *rodnye* sisters and mothers." Motherly care was "warm, tender, and cozy," words that underscored women's role in the domestic realm, while shared wartime experiences created strong "familial" bonds between people. A poem beneath the picture of Valia Kamaeva, a nurse who cared for troops on the battlefield, proclaimed her a "faithful daughter of the people," so young and, although "supposedly a weak woman, strong enough to carry out manly [*muzhestvennyi*] labor without tiring."[43] Such language masculinizes "supposedly weak" women and points to their dual role in Soviet society, emphasizing the do-

---

[39] *Molot,* "O mezhdunarodnom kommunisticheskom zhenskom dne," 7 March 1943, p. 1.

[40] TsDNI f. 13, op. 4, d. 259, l. 89. See also party discussions on the preparations for International Women's Day 1944, TsDNI f. 13, op. 4, d. 68, l. 143.

[41] *Molot,* "O mezhdunarodnom kommunisticheskom zhenskom dne," 7 March 1943, p. 1.

[42] *Molot,* "Blagodarnost' voinov," 1 April 1943, p. 2. For similar accounts, see also *Molot,* "Zabota o rodnom gorode," 28 March 1943, p. 2.; *Molot,* "Patriotki," 7 April 1943, p. 1.

[43] Vera Inber, "Voennaia medsestra," *Molot,* 1 July 1943, p. 2.

mestic realm and "motherhood" while at the same time accentuating women's "liberation" and role in production.

International Women's Day (March 8) presented the regime with an opportunity to tout its "liberated" views on women. A *Molot* tribute to the "women of our city" in 1945, for example, noted that on that day "the oath of Soviet women's faithfulness and love for the Motherland rings particularly loud as they prepare for new outstanding achievements in the name of victory." Author A. Krasikova, gorkom secretary in charge of agitation and propaganda, stated that "courage [*muzhestvo*],[44] heroism, and daring are the qualities of the Soviet women supporting the Red Army for the honor and independence of our Motherland." During the battle for Rostov and the "gloomy days of occupation the women of our city proved themselves to be true patriots, worthy daughters of the great masses." One "modest Russian woman," for instance, carried wounded troops from the field of battle and even killed an enemy machine gunner herself. Two women hid 15 wounded Red Army troops in their apartment during occupation, "nursing them back to life with great care." Also, Krasikova noted, more than 40,000 housewives went to work in the city's factories. Half of the workers at the train station were women, including the director. Due to the constant care given them and their children at the city's plants, these women "have become close to their factories like relatives" and "have played a huge role in the countless victories of the Red Army," Krasikova concluded. Photographs highlighted "Rostov's great female pilot" Klavdiia Byba and three women coal miners.[45] This piece celebrated women who did heroic *manlike* things or *men's* jobs, i.e., coal miners, a pilot, railway workers, rather than those (the vast majority of Soviet women) who endured the everyday drudgery of low-paying jobs and economic hardship.

The party, meanwhile, assumed the "fatherly" role of provider, declaring "care for the families of soldiers" (which, of course, meant mostly women and children) to be its highest duty. *Izvestiia* published a decree obligating district party organizations to identify soldiers' families and make them aware of their rights to receive government assistance, including child care, tax breaks, and other advantages (*l'goty*).[46] The Central Committee promoted as a slogan

---

[44] The Russian word *muzhestvo* comes from the root word for man, *muzhchina,* and has a strong masculine connotation.

[45] A. Krasikova, "Sovetskie zhenshchiny novymi podvigami v tylu i na fronte pribliziat chas nashei polnoi pobedy nad vragom," *Molot,* 8 March 1945, p. 3. The article also quotes Stalin: "The exemplary labor achievements of Soviet women and our glorious youth will forever live in history, as they carry the country on their shoulders with their work in factories and in the fields."

[46] TsDNI f. 13, op. 4, d. 21, l. 49. The government measure was published in *Izvestiia,* "Vsenarodnaia zabota o sem'iakh frontovnikov," 17 March 1943, p. 1. The measure

for the 25th anniversary of the Red Army in February 1943: "Care for the families of those at the front is half of the care for the Red Army itself."[47] Following this lead, *Molot* proclaimed, "There is no more important task than caring for the families of those who are defending our Motherland."[48] *Molot* also highlighted the "care" given by the local party branch to children and wounded troops. One article assured readers that "the party and government display great care for orphans of the Fatherland War," and another declared to children who lost their parents, "You are not an orphan, little one!"[49] The latter editorial added, "We must cuddle every orphan of the Great Fatherland War with the warmth of motherly and fatherly care!" Orphanage No. 3, a "special" home reserved for the children of soldiers, was the topic of an enthusiastic report describing the first day of 12-year-old Iura Zhelnin, who after only a few hours was "well-fed, washed up, and dressed in a clean, new suit with brown shoes." Every employee of the orphanage, according to the author, "displays fatherly care and attention, motherly tenderness and love to all the children."[50] Another piece pointed out that "young boys and girls" training for work at FZOs "should feel, in short, from the first day the great care shown to them by our party and government."[51] The party's paternalism is apparent in frequent talk of providing for and protecting the population, as well as in its claim to be a surrogate father "taking care" of orphans and the families of soldiers.

In the family rhetoric of "reconstruction," moreover, all nationalities were absorbed in a broader "Soviet" construct that rhetorically melted another dividing line in society. Again, however, the reality on the ground belied the rhetorical picture of unity drawn by the public record, with Russians clearly in the prominent role throughout the Soviet Union and Jews subject to discrimination solely for being Jewish. Stalin confirmed ethnic Russians' favored position within the single-family construct when, shortly after the war, he publicly toasted "Russians" for their decisive role in the war and added that they were the "leading force of the Soviet Union among all the peoples of our

---

was discussed at meetings with workers. See, for example, TsDNI f. 13, op. 4, d. 21, l. 49 ob.

[47] GARO f. 3737, op. 4, d. 1392, l. 18.

[48] *Molot*, "Okruzhit' zabotoi sem'i voinov," 9 April 1943, p. 1.

[49] *Molot*, "Okruzhim zabotoi i liubov'iu sirot Otechestvennoi Voiny," 6 April 1943, p. 2; and *Molot*, "Zabota o detiakh—vsenarodnoe delo," 14 May 1943, p. 1.

[50] *Molot*, "V spetsial'nom detskom dome," 1 December 1943, p. 4. Iura hesitated at first, but then read on a banner, "Welcome to your new home, sweet children," and rushed upstairs to meet his comrades.

[51] *Molot*, "Nakanune prizyva gorodskoi i sel'skoi molodezhi v remeslennye, zhelezno-dorozhnye uchilishcha i shkoly FZO," 2 September 1944, p. 1. As we saw in chap. 2, the promises to FZO recruits were *not* fulfilled.

country."[52] If all of the nationalities of the Soviet Union comprised a single family, the Russians were evidently the elders or big brothers. Stalin's toast was all the more significant given that, during the war, entire nationalities had been exiled on his order for allegedly collaborating with the Germans.[53] Echoing Stalin's words two years later, in March 1947 a party agitator gave a public lecture in Rostov's Stalinskii district, which includes the Armenian suburb Nakhichevan, entitled, "The great Russian people—the leading nationality and force of the USSR."[54] Sometimes (as we saw with the failure to report that Jews were targeted for repression by the Nazis) silence speaks volumes, and one way Soviet officialdom dealt with differences in national identity was simply by ignoring them. Denial of national differences (and discrimination) in the press was the converse of the "single family unity" rhetoric—if all nationalities are part of one big family, then there is no need to cover them separately or differentiate on grounds of national identity. A thorough review of *Molot* between February 1943 and August 1948 revealed hardly a mention of Rostov's sizeable Armenian population with one notable exception. In March 1945, A. K. Bostandzhian, himself Armenian, wrote that a group of actors producing Armenian-language plays had "found no support from the oblast department of art." Bostandzhian did not elaborate on reasons for the lack of support, nor was there further mention of the matter or of Armenian affairs in general in the press.[55]

In Rostov-on-Don and throughout occupied Soviet territory, as we have seen, Jews suffered disproportionately at the hands of the Nazi forces. As we also noted, Soviet press accounts of German atrocities did *not* report the fact that the Nazis singled out Jews.[56] It was, however, openly acknowledged that Jews suffered more than most at the hands of the Nazis—a fact that would have been apparent to a majority of people anyway—immediately after Rostov's liberation in February 1943. At a public speech in 1944, Comrade Fedunov, leader of the partisans in Rostov during German occupation, said that in August 1942 the Germans "began the extermination of the Jewish population."[57] Also, less than a month after liberation *Molot* remembered one of Rostov's music teachers, Veniamin Isaakovich Sorkin. The tribute identifies him as a Jew whose "small, limp figure" belied the talents of a tremendous musician. Sorkin, author M. Nikulin informed, fell victim to the Nazis, "fascist barbarians who shot all Jews," but "his fate will not be forgotten" by the

---

[52] *Pravda*, 25 May 1945, p. 1.

[53] We examine this topic in the next chapter.

[54] TsDNI f. 13, op. 4, d. 253, ll. 21–22.

[55] A. K. Bostandzhian, "Ob Armianskom teatre," *Molot*, 21 March 1945, p. 2.

[56] See, for example, Leder, *My Life in Stalinist Russia*, 193.

[57] TsDNI f. 13, op. 4, d. 116, l. 114.

many who loved him.[58] This piece contradicts the master narrative of "equal sufferers" that developed later, and a comprehensive reading of *Molot* and other public sources between 1943 and 1948 found no subsequent admissions of specifically *Jewish* suffering. Thus, while as a rule national differences were blurred in the party's public texts, these rare exceptions suggest a desire early on to confirm those differences, as well as some ambiguity in the official line on the "national question."[59] The pieces by Bostandzhian and Nikulin indicate an atmosphere of uncertainty about aspects of the regime's "national" policy.

Public party texts on the "Soviet family" write gender, national, and class differences out of the narrative of "reconstruction," their depiction of society stressing unity and the collective identity of a "family." Women in the "Soviet family" were, like Mariia Fedorova, called upon to make the ultimate sacrifice—to give their sons, nine in her case, to the war effort. In the tale penned by the regime, that price had to be paid to secure the "freedom" of the "Motherland," and clearly it was well worth it. In the regime's narrative, moreover, a gendered distinction in the use of the word "care" conceals a dual role for women—the domestic realm ("tender, motherly" care) *and* the realm of production. At the same time, the language in the party press subtly masculinizes women who displayed great (manly) "courage," even killing German soldiers, an association with the troops at the front. Through it all, women maintain their "modesty" in these depictions, not asking for acknowledgment or recognition of their acts and sacrifices. Party material intended for public consumption, furthermore, portrays paternal care as the domain of the (male-dominated) party, which promised to provide for the families of soldiers, women, and orphans, an emotionally-charged image of the war's impact on Soviet society. The constructs "fatherland" and "Motherland," moreover, dissolve national and ethnic differences, begging the questions *whose* "fatherland" and *whose* "Motherland"?[60] At the same time, there are clear rifts and inconsistencies regarding aspects of the official stance on the "national question." Albeit for mere fleeting moments, expressions of national identity—both Armenian and Jewish—are apparent in the party's public record, espe-

---

[58] *Molot*, "Muzykant," 11 March 1943, p. 2.

[59] This, of course, adds credence to the contention by Gidelman noted above that there was always ambiguity in the Soviet stance on the Holocaust and no official "party line" regarding the event, although it should be noted that he is dealing mostly with Soviet scholarly material for a specialized audience and *not* material in the Soviet press. See Gitelman, "Soviet Reactions to the Holocaust," 3.

[60] Merridale makes this point very well, pointing out that motherland for early Soviet generations "was a troublesome idea with no defined boundaries or single meaning. It may have been a single village or a region, but it was also the entire space, a multinational empire in all but name, in which "we" Soviets lived. Ethnic diversity, in Soviet culture, was more likely to generate confusion than pride" (*Ivan's War*, 380–81).

cially early in this five-year period while the war still raged. Presumably the official tale of "equal sufferers" at the hands of the Nazis was not set in stone when, shortly after Rostov's liberation, *Molot* depicted the fate of Sorkin, the Jewish musician who perished during occupation along with "all Jews."

"Family Rhetoric" in Internal Party Discussions

The party's closed record during "reconstruction" is embedded with discussions about "family," indicating some deep fissures within the supposedly unified Soviet society. For example, the inverse of the "soldiers' family" was the "traitors' family," the parents, spouses, and children of those perceived as supportive of the Germans, an image that clearly contradicts the single unified family construct. While *Izvestiia* published the decree mentioned above that required district party organizations to make soldiers' families aware of their rights, a subsequent unpublished ruling ordered district party organizations in formerly occupied areas to reregister everyone receiving government aid. It instructed them to "thoroughly check all documents" and to withhold assistance from those with questionable loyalties.[61] Several months later, a gorkom report cited cases of people "illegally using government aid," including one woman with two small children whose husband and eldest son had voluntarily left with the Germans.[62] A district secretary compared one family, whose father "actively helped the Germans" during occupation, to another that evacuated, lost a son in the war, and returned in early 1943 to help rebuild the city. Arguing that the latter family had a greater claim to a disputed apartment, the author added that this was but one of many cases in which loyal families were struggling to get their apartments back from the families of traitors.[63] The party also did not tolerate members with non-loyal relatives. In January 1945, for example, the gorkom expelled L. N. Zakharova because her father and brother had fought for the Germans, a detail she failed to mention on her application for party candidacy.[64] The problem of "collaboration" shows that official "family rhetoric" emphasizing collective unity concealed some deep divisions within the "Soviet family."

These sources likewise expose significant gender differences in Soviet society. Like the local party press, though often more straightforwardly, party discussions behind closed doors described women as subjects to be exploited for production *and* reproduction. At the Seventh City Party Conference in

---

[61] GARO f. R-3737, op. 8, f. 34a, l. 22.

[62] TsDNI f. 13, op. 4, d. 21, l. 154.

[63] TsDNI f. 13, op. 4, d. 233, l. 92.

[64] TsDNI f. 13, op. 4, d. 145, l. 79. Technically she would have been expelled for falsifying information on her application, but obviously she would never have been allowed into the party had she admitted that close members of her family supported the Germans and even fought for them. I examine collaboration in the next chapter.

October 1943, Comrade Andreev of the Rostov Soviet observed that the pool of potential workers was made up "primarily of women," and thus that difficulties "mobilizing" labor power stemmed from a lack of day care. "Because the [1936] law banning abortions has already shown its beneficial effects," he said, "we need to worry now about creating day care centers so women coming to work won't have to leave their children to the mercy of fate."[65] A gorkom decree on the preparation for International Women's Day in March 1944 pointed out that the holiday was not just a "joyous celebration for all," but also a chance to "fully mobilize all reserves of female labor" (read: housewives and speculators) and "rally working women to increase production," sentiments that came across less blatantly in the party's public record.[66] Three years later the tune of party leaders remained the same. "Summon Soviet women to increase the productivity of their labor," the gorkom instructed district party leaders prior to the holiday, "and to fill and over fulfill production plans."[67] Gorkom secretary Pastushenko expressed a common concern when he lamented that the majority of women workers were undisciplined, by which he meant inexperienced and difficult to control.[68]

Meanwhile, internal documents show that few women joined the party and/or occupied positions of leadership. At the Seventh City Party Conference, Comrade Tokareva pointed out that only 57 women delegates were present compared to 276 men. This proved, she said, "that our work among women is still insufficient, which is especially important to correct now that women are the main source of labor power."[69] Later at the conference Tokareva raised these concerns again, maintaining that "the political role of women has increased dramatically during the war, but we don't seem to have taken that into stock and bring few women into the party."[70] She is, in short, calling for a fairer gendered representation within the halls of power, but, alas, to no avail. At the Eighth City Party Conference a year-and-a-half later, the situation had not improved much, with only 73 women present and 373 men.[71] As

---

[65] TsDNI f. 13, op. 4, d. 1, l. 72.

[66] TsDNI f. 13, op. 4, d. 68, l. 143. This link between holidays and increasing production was noted in the previous chapter as well.

[67] TsDNI f. 13, op. 4, d. 292, l. 17. The celebration of the third anniversary of Rostov's liberation in February 1946 led to a similar call to "mobilize" women workers and "improve worker discipline" among those that have already been mobilized. See TsDNI f. 13, op. 4, d. 217, l. 62.

[68] TsDNI f. 13, op. 4, d. 65, l. 54. For other references to problems with women's "labor discipline," see also TsDNI f. 13, op. 4, d. 4, l. 89; TsDNI f. 13, op. 4, d. 69, l. 14; TsDNI f. 13, op. 4, d. 149, l. 45; TsDNI f. 13, op. 4, d. 231, l. 38.

[69] TsDNI f. 13, op. 4, d. 1, l. 31.

[70] TsDNI f. 13, op. 4, d. 1, l. 265.

[71] TsDNI f. 13, op. 4, d. 132, l. 2. The delegate reading these statistics repeated verbatim the statement Tokareva had made in 1943: "our work among women is still insuf-

of January 1945, 153 of 489 secretaries of party cells were women.[72] A year later an internal party report stated that, "despite a series of measures by the gorkom and obkom," women comprise only 16 percent of new party members in 1945.[73] The low numbers of women in the party meant, of course, that few women were in positions of leadership. A February 1947 gorkom report noted that 53 percent of the 8,021 employees in the city's trade organizations were women, but they occupied only 4 of the top 55 positions in those organizations.[74] Nor had the numbers improved at the end of this five-year period, when, in April 1948, Rostov held its Ninth City Party Conference with a little less than ten percent of the delegates women. Comrade Khripkova, a district party secretary, argued that this reflected a "not very serious attitude" among local leaders toward women. Few women, she complained, worked in district party organizations, "although the majority who come there with complaints are women with children, and I think that a woman is better able to talk to and understand women and children."[75] Her commentary called into question the paternal role assumed for itself by the party in its "family rhetoric."

Women were underrepresented in the party and in positions of leadership because they endured the "double burden" (i.e., dual role) of work and/or study coupled with child care and housework.[76] Near the end of her speech at the Ninth City Party Conference, Khripkova queried, "Why is it that positions that should belong to women are filled by men?"[77] She included orphanage director and gynecologist on her list of jobs that should belong predominantly to women but did not. Other sources suggest an answer to Khripkova's rhetorical query: women were expected to carry out laborious and time-consuming domestic chores that greatly limited their time. A few women party members brought this problem to light. At a discussion of Stalin's *Short Course*, for example, Comrade Inkina declared, "Women have a number of different domestic chores to attend to," and thus have less time to read than men. Women, however, "should also study, work, and know as much as men," so Inkina proposed that female party members be allowed to

---

ficient, which is especially important to correct now that women are the main basis of labor power."

[72] TsDNI f. 13, op. 4, d. 91, l. 1.

[73] TsDNI f. 13, op. 4, d. 217, l. 16.

[74] TsDNI f. 13, op. 4, d. 309, l. 9; TsDNI f. 13, op. 4, d. 330, l. 136. On this problem for the 1930s, see Goldman, *Women at the Gates*, 174–75.

[75] TsDNI f. 13, op. 4, d. 375, l. 257.

[76] Of course, even if such structural problems as the double burden could have been resolved, gender discrimination would have still complicated their path to career advancement.

[77] TsDNI f. 13, op. 4, d. 375, ll. 257–58. For more references to the lack of women in the party and in positions of leadership, see also TsDNI f. 13, op. 4, d. 45, l. 78; TsDNI f. 13, op. 4, d. 354, l. 18.

stay home on Mondays in order to read theoretical texts, a wish that was not granted.[78] At a meeting of rank-and-file party members at Rostov's Medical Institute, Timofeeva declared, "it's difficult for women to study and have a family, but the party bureau doesn't take that into consideration."[79] Public pronouncements of female heroism and manly achievements notwithstanding, for many women "liberation" amounted to an overwhelming workload. Their domestic role continued while their numbers in industry increased markedly, making party membership impractical for many women, no doubt especially single mothers. The party did not acknowledge the "double burden" for women and thus failed to deal with the problem, which largely explains the failure of efforts to increase female membership.

Those in power, moreover, implicitly *promoted* the double burden by pressuring women from the home into the workforce. These texts expose a negative view toward "housewives," also known in official jargon as "non-working adult dependents," who were seen primarily as potential laborers to be "mobilized." Party leaders associated "housewives" with "speculators," that is, as segments of the population that "do not work." In 1945 at a closed meeting on problems mobilizing people for factory employment, Comrade Zaitsev described the activities of one party member's spouse. "A magnificent wife," he began, "she used her husband's assigned car to speculate food at the market."[80] Another party member was fired from his job and censured because he allowed his wife to illegally sell goods at the market.[81] These and other women, according to a speaker at one party plenum, needed to be brought into the industrial work force. District party organizations, he explained, should "talk with housewives" and put them to work rebuilding the city.[82] Once in the city's factories, however, women faced pay and rationing scales weighted against them; a wage comparison from the first quarter of 1945 shows that women were on the low end (see table 4), a discrepancy that widened after demobilization. Also, as we saw, rationing mostly favored male skilled workers in the first category, who received roughly one-and-a-half times more than the disproportionately female third category.[83] As we have seen, in response to the drought, the regime raised ration prices on bread and other food items on September 16, 1946, and 11 days later it eliminated rations for "non-working adult dependents." This would have forced still more women into the work force (or into crime, prostitution, or speculation) to get food.

---

[78] TsDNI f. 13, op. 4, d. 107, l. 6. See also TsDNI f. 13, op. 4, d. 186, ll. 109–10.

[79] TsDNI f. 13, op. 4, d. 231, l. 38.

[80] GARO f. 3737, op. 4, d. 1397, l. 3.

[81] TsDNI f. 13, op. 4, d. 293, l. 147. Speculation is the topic of chap. 6.

[82] TsDNI f. 13, op. 4, d. 85, l. 54.

[83] See chap. 2.

There were, furthermore, a lot of single mothers due to the lack of marriageable-age men after the war. Taking advantage of this situation (and the elimination of alimony payments in the 1944 legislation), some men abandoned their families (a practice noted by Fitzpatrick for the 1930s as well), despite pressures (especially for party members) against such behavior.[84] In 1947 the gorkom heard the case of S. P. Rykunov, a member of the party for 15 years and employee of the city police department who hid from his wife and four small children and lived with "a certain Rudukhina."

Table 4: Women in Industry in Rostov, 1945		
FACTORY	PERCENTAGE OF WOMEN WORKERS	AVERAGE SALARY OF WORKFORCE
Lenzavod	Majority male	858 rubles per month
Rostsel'mash	47.5%	750 rubles per month
Factory No. 359	58%	615 rubles per month
Proletarskii Molot	66%	580 rubles per month
Rabochii	60%	400 rubles per month
DGTF	64.5%	193 rubles per month
Bread Factory No. 1	82%	100 rubles per month
Garment Factory No. 4	89%	100 rubles per month
Sources: TsDNI f. 13, op. 4, d. 101, l. 25; TsDNI f. 13, op. 4, d. 193, l. 4; TsDNI f. 13, op. 4, d. 198, ll. 20, 42.		

After his wife found him, Rykunov decided to live with his lover, abandoning his family in "difficult material circumstances."[85] In May 1948 the gorkom heard about the "morally corrupted life" of A. M. Aseev, a demobilized soldier and party member since 1941. During the war Aseev kept a list of 30 lovers in cities throughout the country, justifying it on the grounds that "in war it is no sin to live with different women." After demobilization he re-

---

[84] On the 1930s, see Fitzpatrick, *Everyday Stalinism*, 143–47.

[85] TsDNI f. 13, op. 4, d. 294, l. 10.

turned not to his wife and two small children in Rostov but to one of his lovers. Even when he finally went to live with his family he continued to have affairs, for which Aseev was expelled from the party.[86] There were numerous other such cases, including a man who did not live with either of his *two* wives, another who abandoned his wife the day their child was born, and yet another who caught syphilis from one of his lovers.[87] Showing social and political pressures to conform to accepted "family" life, several of these accounts noted that members who admitted their mistake and returned to their families were allowed to stay in the party.

Another prominent theme in party discussions behind closed doors is the inability of the local party apparatus to fulfill the "single most important task" of providing "care" to the families of soldiers, wounded war veterans, and orphans. A gorkom secretary bemoaned that "instead of the necessary care, party bureaucrats give soldiers' families empty promises."[88] Amid the aforementioned bread crisis with the missing grain cars in May 1943, a speaker at one closed party meeting asserted, "The population has been without bread for five days, and the families of soldiers come to us and complain, 'Why did you give us ration cards? When you didn't give us cards, at least we knew that we wouldn't get any bread. Now we have cards but no bread.'"[89] One district soviet in the city stated that nothing was being done for wounded war troops, while investigators from Moscow concluded that Rostov's leaders "pay very little attention to disabled veterans," failing to provide for their material needs or to adequately train them for new professions.[90] In January 1945, obkom Secretary Kobilev reported that only 300 of the city's 4,000 disabled veterans were being trained for work that will "make them into men and provide for their children."[91] Nor were the party's efforts to "take care of

---

[86] TsDNI f. 13, op. 4, d. 393, l. 159.

[87] TsDNI f. 13, op. 4, d. 393, ll. 189, 199; TsDNI f. 13, op. 4, d. 394, l. 164. For more cases of men leaving their spouses for other women, see also TsDNI f. 13, op. 4, d. 252, l. 26; TsDNI f. 13, op. 4, d. 394, ll. 99, 101; TsDNI f. 13, op. 4, d. 395, l. 150.

[88] TsDNI f. 13, op. 4, d. 104, l. 5. For more sources on the difficult material conditions of soldiers' families and "formal, bureaucratic, impersonal" treatment of them, see also TsDNI f. 13, op. 4, d. 21, ll. 49–49 ob., 154; TsDNI f. 13, op. 4, d. 144, l. 112; TsDNI f. 13, op. 4, d. 130, l. 74; TsDNI f. 13, op. 4, d. 150, l. 81.

[89] TsDNI f. 13, op. 4, d. 29, l. 3.

[90] GARO f. 3955, op. 1, d. 1, ll. 74–75; RGASPI f. 17, op. 122, d. 71, l. 195.

[91] TsDNI f. 13, op. 4, d. 130, l. 75. For more reports on the inadequate "care" for wounded war veterans, see also GARO f. 3950, op. 1, d. 2, l. 16. As Beate Fieseler states, "The new order eliminated the previous health-related understanding of invalidity in favor of a purely production-oriented approach. Invalidity status was no longer granted on the basis of just bodily injuries, but judged according to the claimants' complete or partial inability to work." Beate Fieseler, "The Bitter Legacy of the 'Great Patriotic War': Red Army Disabled Soldiers under Late Stalinism," in Fürst, *Late*

the little ones" satisfactory. We dealt with the problem of crime in chapter 2, and, in accordance with what we found, Police Chief Kozlov divulged that "many kids wind up roaming the city's streets committing crimes." In the first half of 1943 children committed 37 percent of Rostov's thefts and the police discovered "serious criminal gangs of children."[92] The problem remained a year later when a gorkom report lamented that "despite repeated measures," homeless and neglected children "continue to gather on the streets, in public places, and in the train station."[93] A separate local report in late 1944 accounted for only 2,462 of the city's known 4,483 war orphans in homes, with guardians, or at training schools.[94]

Conditions were not much better for those in orphanages, the gorkom disclosing in 1943 that, due to the poor work of the director, the situation in Orphanage No. 1 was "exceptionally difficult." Most of the children were "emaciated," and an outbreak of typhus infected half of the 75 residents. "Rooms were in an unsanitary state, the courtyard was filthy, and the home lacked sheets and clothing."[95] Another account warned that "the situation in the [city's children's] hospitals is serious because they are overloaded, there is no food and fuel, and no dressings for serious wounds."[96] Problems remained in the city's orphanages four years later (and two years after victory) in 1947.[97] Internal party accounts starkly contrasted the *Molot* article on conditions in "special" Orphanage No. 3.[98] A check-up by Moscow authorities in the fall of 1945 uncovered "major deficiencies" in the treatment of orphans in Rostov, including the failure to provide them with adequate food and "impersonal" treatment of them by local bureaucrats.[99] Serious problems also plagued daycare centers, schools, and hospitals. A report in the fall of 1943 bemoaned that 95 of one district's 135 children in day care, all of them sons

---

Stalinist Russia, 47. See also Chris Burton, "Medical Welfare During Late Stalinism. A Study of Doctors and the Soviet Health System, 1945–1953" (Ph.D. diss., University of Chicago, 2000), 268–69.

[92] TsDNI f. 13, op. 4, d. 2, l. 309.

[93] GARO f. 3737, op. 4, d. 1392, l. 80. For other reports on child crime, see also TsDNI f. 13, op. 4, d. 69, l. 144; TsDNI f. 13, op. 4, d. 130, l. 74.

[94] TsDNI f. 13, op. 4, d. 203, l. 35.

[95] TsDNI f. 13, op. 4, d. 20, l. 46. A subsequent report on the city's orphanages said the children are inadequately fed and "do not look good." TsDNI f. 13,op. 4, d. 44, ll. 11–12.

[96] TsDNI f. 13, op. 4, d. 29, l. 38.

[97] See TsDNI f. 13, op. 4, d. 291, ll. 193–94. This report notes that more than 300 orphans still needed to be placed in homes, and that unsanitary conditions in the homes were contributing to the outbreak of serious illnesses.

[98] A follow-up to the report discussed above noted that the situation in Orphanage No. 1 did not improve. GARO f. 3950, op. 1, d. 2, ll. 76–77.

[99] GARO f. 3737, op. 8, d. 34, l. 1.

and daughters of soldiers, were in "severe need" of warm clothing and winter shoes.[100] A number of internal party sources indicated that children in the city could not attend school due to a lack of shoes and clothing.[101] A 1946 survey noted that only 71 percent of the prewar capacity of childcare centers had been reached, creating a "stressful" situation for families. The same report noted that children were not adequately fed in daycare.[102] At a closed party meeting, Comrade Skladnaia of the city's bread trust stated, "our women workers don't have daycare for their children, so they come to work with a heavy heart, worrying about their kids."[103] One report described an "extremely unfavorable situation" in the city's primary children's clinic. Over a ten-month period, 58 of 224 patients died as a "result of criminally negligent treatment by the clinic's leadership."[104]

Finally, national identity, an issue obscured in public texts, is prominent in discussions behind closed doors. In this material, Jewish identity is linked to religious practice, which is assumed to be a bad thing. For example, the party expelled the Jewish director of a furniture factory because he reportedly fulfilled an order from a Jewish religious group.[105] At a party gathering one speaker complained that the director of a bakery had used flour to make *matsa* for a Jewish religious group.[106] One party member admitted giving money to a group for a memorial to be built to Jewish victims of Nazism, which included his own father, on the ravine outside of town.[107] A report at the end of this five-year period bemoaned that there were "two Armenian religious groups" and "a Jewish religious group" (*obshchina*) practicing in the city.[108] On the other hand, some Jewish party members tried to hide their identity, changing their names and falsely claiming to be Russian, for which

---

[100] GARO f. 3955, op. 1, d. 1, l. 140.

[101] See, for example, TsDNI f. 13, op. 4, d. 130, l. 74; TsDNI f. 13, op. 4, d. 131, l. 31; TsDNI f. 13, op. 4, d. 145, l. 125; TsDNI f. 13, op. 4, d. 157, l. 46; TsDNI f. 13, op. 4, d. 260, l. 38.

[102] TsDNI f. 13, op. 4, d. 260, l. 38. For other reports on the lack of day care and on poor food in day cares and schools, see also TsDNI f. 13, op. 4, d. 1, l. 72; GARO f. 3737, op. 4, d. 1391, l. 31; GARO f. 3955, op. 1, d. 1, l. 155.

[103] TsDNI f. 13, op. 4, d. 193, l. 6.

[104] TsDNI f. 13, op. 4, d. 68, ll. 15–16. In another interesting use of language, the clinic's main doctor was accused of nepotism, "familiness" or "family relations" (*semeistvennost'*), because she hired two nieces as assistants and illegally put another relative on the payroll as a "sanitary worker."

[105] TsDNI f. 13, op. 4, d. 149, ll. 48–49.

[106] TsDNI f. 13, op. 4, d. 221a, l. 115.

[107] TsDNI f. 13, op. 4, d. 375, l. 407.

[108] TsDNI f. 13, op. 4, d. 427, l. 22. The term *obshchina* as used in this sense implies the operation of churches or temples.

they were excluded from the party.[109] Clearly these members considered it beneficial to have "Russian" stamped on their party cards and internal passports instead of "Jewish," no doubt due to the widespread (and accurate) perception that the Soviet state discriminated against Jews. Internal reports also document anti-Semitic acts, including the case of one citizen who allegedly "cursed the NKVD and the Jewish people."[110] In November 1947 someone painted swastikas on the wall of a training school, and during the December 1947 elections two voters drew swastikas on their ballots.[111] Evidently not everyone agreed with official "family rhetoric" on the "friendship" and "mutual trust" of all nationalities under Soviet rule.

Correspondence between Jewish soldiers at the front and party representatives in Rostov reveals an unspoken assumption of disproportionate Jewish victimization, a fact acknowledged by one article but mostly ignored by the party press. During the war stories circulated that the Nazis were wiping out Soviet Jews, and as a result Jewish soldiers in the Red Army inquired about loved ones they had not heard from in a while.[112] In May 1944, the gorkom answered an inquiry by Red Army Commander Guberman as to the whereabouts of his family, informing him that the Germans had killed his mother and aunt during occupation.[113] Another Red Army soldier discovered that his wife died after the Germans gave her a "vaccination" against cholera.[114] Many Jewish soldiers at the front received such letters, usually with the phrase "the terrible fate of being victimized by the blood-thirsty Hitlerist bandits befell your relatives (*rodnye*)," and always with a call to avenge the Germans. One young man found out that his mother, father, fiancée, and her two children were all killed.[115] Another notice declared, "What those scoundrels did in Rostov is unspeakable. They murdered and executed hundreds of thousands, tortured women, children, and elderly, made hundreds of children into orphans."[116] Significantly, the local government's correspondence with Jewish soldiers inquiring about their families' whereabouts *never* openly acknowledged that Jews were specifically targeted; as in the party press, Jewish victimization dissolves into a broader "Soviet" experience, negating a separate

---

[109] See, for example, TsDNI f. 13, op. 4, d. 297, l. 64; TsDNI f. 13, op. 4, d. 393, l. 151.

[110] TsDNI f. 13, op. 4, d. 205, l. 83.

[111] TsDNI f. 13, op. 4, d. 233, l. 21; TsDNI f. 13, op. 4, d. 335, l. 172.

[112] Most of the soldiers writing to local authorities in Rostov point out that repeated attempts to contact relatives in the city have gone unanswered. TsDNI f. 13, op. 4, d. 50, ll. 1–13.

[113] TsDNI f. 13, op. 4, d. 50, l. 11. According to neighbors, Guberman's sister and niece had been evacuated, but their location was unknown.

[114] TsDNI f. 13, op. 4, d. 50, l. 3.

[115] TsDNI f. 13, op. 4, d. 50, l. 13.

[116] TsDNI f. 13, op. 4, d. 50, l. 4.

Jewish identity and disproportionate Jewish suffering. Yet, at the same time, the mere fact that these are responses to inquiries by *Jewish* soldiers indicates an implied or assumed realization of disproportionate Jewish victimization—a realization inherent in the correspondence itself.

The language in these internal documents contradicts the official "family rhetoric" of collective unity and paternal party "care" trumpeted in the local press. Along with recognition of national difference there was also a clear divide between "loyal" and "traitorous" families in the minds of party leaders. There is, moreover, an inconsistency in Moscow's call to weed out unworthy recipients of government aid by "thoroughly checking" all documents and subsequent complaints of "red tape," especially given the often severe understaffing of local party bureaus.[117] Party leaders, most of whom were male, exhibited a paternalistic attitude toward a population in need of "care" and women workers in need of "discipline." One of these texts directly linked "providing" for one's family to "manhood," the insinuation being that disabled veterans were not "men" unless they could do so. This is interesting given that there were *a lot* of single mothers in Rostov as well. For them, official pro-family propaganda notwithstanding, wage and rationing policies (crafted primarily by men) were disadvantageous. Local party leaders pushed women into factories by "mobilizing" (read: pressuring) them. Meanwhile, men (especially party members) were pressured to maintain "acceptable" family lives; as in the 1930s, abandoned wives clearly had the support and sympathy of party representatives over-and-above their cheating (party member) husbands.[118] On the other hand, the elimination of alimony payments encouraged men to abandon their families, or at least made it more economically feasible for them to do so in a demographic environment where they would have been in great demand.[119] The "other women" in these dramas were invariably portrayed in a negative, threatening light. Finally, by its own admission the local party organization failed in its "single most important task" of "taking care" of the families of soldiers, orphans, and wounded war veterans, an admission made less explicitly in the party's public record.

"Family Rhetoric" and Popular Opinion

The record of society at large is accessible through a variety of sources, which taken together offer an impressionistic view of popular opinions on family matters, including gender and national identity. Regarding the city's gender imbalance, Karol's friend Kolia estimated in 1944 that there were 20 or 30 women for every one man. Although the estimate is an exaggeration, since

---

[117] I show the severity of understaffing for party bureaus in chap. 8.

[118] Fitzpatrick, *Everyday Stalinism*, 145.

[119] See Nakachi, "Population, Politics and Reproduction," in Fürst, *Late Stalinist Russia*, 31–32.

this was prior to demobilization it may not have been too far off the mark. Promoting his plan to become a public works engineer, Kolia told Karol, "we shall avoid flirtatious dissipation by each choosing a proper, serious girl, preferably one with accommodations in the center of town, not too far from the Institute of Public Works."[120] Leder notes the many "visible signs" of the war's impact, especially "war invalids hobbling around on crutches, often drunk and belligerent, [and] a shortage of men of marriageable age." Archival evidence reveals a vague understanding of "family" and family legislation along with a keen awareness of the regime's failure to provide adequate "care" — in a material sense — to "the Soviet family." List of questions to party representatives at open meetings, for example, often revealed confusion over what constitutes a "family" in official terms, especially in this period of demographic upheaval. The 1944 Family Legislation in particular sparked a lot of inquiries. One woman wanted to know if her illegitimate child, born while her husband was away in the Red Army, qualified for assistance, while others asked what responsibilities the fathers of such children shouldered.[121] A number of people inquired about the families of traitors, or how women with children by a German soldier would be treated.[122]

Marriage and divorce laws were brought up often as well. A train station employee inquired, "if a couple [informally] divorced before the war, do they need to officially do so now?"[123] One man whose wife lived with a German soldier wanted to know if that constituted legal grounds for divorce, and several people asked why they were now required to have marriage stamps in their passports.[124] Tax laws caused confusion, a stepfather of three wondering whether he should pay the childless tax since he had no children of his own. Someone else asked, "If a woman is not able to have children, do she and her husband still have to pay the higher tax for childless families?"[125] Questions also highlighted the "morally corrupt behavior" of men discussed in the party's hidden record. "Why," a woman worker at one meeting asked, "do a few of the leaders of the Red Army marry in every city without bearing any

---

[120] Karol, *Solik*, 272.

[121] RGASPI f. 17, op. 88, d. 331, l. 84; RGASPI f. 17, op. 88, d. 331, l. 19. A question about illegitimate children also appeared in a local source, TsDNI f. 13, op. 4, d. 92, l. 427.

[122] TsDNI f. 13, op. 4, d. 92, l. 284. For similar questions, see also RGASPI f. 17, op. 88, d. 331, ll. 20, 26; TsDNI f. 13, op. 4, d. 92, l. 427.

[123] RGASPI f. 17, op. 88, d. 331, l. 84. For more such questions, see also RGASPI f. 17, op. 88, d. 426, l. 125.

[124] RGASPI f. 17, op. 88, d. 426, l. 143; RGASPI f. 17, op. 88, d. 331, ll. 41–42. For more questions on marriage stamps in passports, see also ll. 19, 25.

[125] RGASPI f. 17, op. 88, d. 331, l. 26. For similar questions, see also ll. 20, 25, 84.

responsibility for their actions?"[126] "What will be done," a woman at another meeting asked, "to a man who abandons his family of five children and a wife, an excellent industrial worker, and marries a younger woman?" Several people inquired why the government changed alimony laws, and one woman asked, "won't the elimination of alimony payments lead to sexual promiscuity?"[127] These questions expose women's concerns over family (and, by implication, financial) stability, implying that state action on their behalf is either lacking or counterproductive, as in the elimination of alimony payments.

People openly criticized the regime's policies, expressing doubts about claims of women's rights while pointing to the tremendous workload and material hardship they endured. The "liberation" of women proclaimed so loudly in party propaganda was evidently not readily apparent to all; someone asked, "What are the equal rights of women reflected in?"[128] The election campaign in early 1946 gave rise to similar queries, someone wanting to know if there were women leaders in capitalist countries, and another citizen doubtfully asking, "surely there are not countries that deny women the right to vote?"[129] Someone else asked, "Can housewives be elected as deputies to the Supreme Soviet?"[130] In a further indication of the many chores women were responsible for, one female voter complained about being expected to attend lectures and discussions. "Who," she protested, "is going to run around the stores and stand in line, fix dinner, wash clothes, take care of the kids?"[131] Other women criticized local party leaders for their overzealous "mobilization" efforts that illegally forced mothers with small children into the workforce.[132] Single mothers in particular posed sharp questions. In the fall of 1944 someone asked, "How do you explain the fact that the government has not given much assistance to single mothers?"[133] Two women workers at a bakery told an agitator that organizations for the families of slain soldiers did not pay any attention to them. Noting that their husbands died in the war and they had large families, they asked why their factory did not help provide childcare. [134] Several years later a number of women workers at that

---

[126] TsDNI f. 13, op. 4, d. 92, l. 284. For other comments on men guilty of bigamy, see also RGASPI f. 17, op. 88, d. 426, l. 143.

[127] RGASPI f. 17, op. 88, d. 426, l. 143. For similar inquiries, see also RGASPI f. 17, op. 88, d. 331, ll. 19, 21.

[128] RGASPI f. 17, op. 88, d. 426, l. 1. *V chem vyrazhaetsia ravnopravie zhenshchin?*

[129] TsDNI f. 13, op. 4, d. 259, ll. 24–25. France granted women the right to vote only in 1945, and Japan did so in 1946.

[130] TsDNI f. 13, op. 4, d. 259, l. 24.

[131] TsDNI f. 13, op. 4, d. 415, l. 140.

[132] RGASPI f. 17, op. 88, d. 331, l. 24.

[133] RGASPI f. 17, op. 88, d. 331, l. 41.

[134] TsDNI f. 13, op. 4, d. 233, ll. 77, 95.

same factory complained that since their husbands had perished in the war, there was no one to help them make ends meet.[135] Casting serious doubt on the party's pro-family public rhetoric, a woman cafeteria worker asked, "When will we be able to feed our children?"[136] Workers (especially women) seem keenly aware of the local party organization's admitted (in closed gatherings) failure to "take care" of the population.

Svodki reveal opinions and views at odds with official policies along with a keen awareness of the wide discrepancy between official pro-family rhetoric and state policies that hurt families. These comments echo the complaints over harsh living standards relayed in chapter 2, but here the focus is the impact of state policy *on families*, as workers with large families realized that the party's measures during the famine represented a severe blow to their interests. According to one report, several workers at the beer factory expressed discontent with the price increases on rationed goods, including Moiseenko, a loading-dock worker, who said, "The price hikes mostly affect those of us with large families, whereas those with small families actually gain from the wage increases." His co-worker Men'shikov declared, "I have five mouths to feed, and the 100-ruble wage hike won't even help me buy bread," adding, "in my opinion this is all a fraud." A lathe operator complained that she and her child would not be able to survive, and a cafeteria worker stated that she would have to die so that the other five people in her family might survive. Similar sentiments were encountered elsewhere as well, especially following the decrease in rations for dependents in September. Afterward a young woman worker at DGTF declared, "I have eight people in my family and even before we didn't have enough bread; now we'll really suffer." In the story on International Women's Day described above, the author mentioned that 50 percent of the employees at the Rostov Train station were women. One of them was overheard complaining to a co-worker, "I have four children, and I don't know what I'll feed them with." A metalworker at Lenzavod reportedly said, "I guess we'll have to strangle our children," while someone elsewhere complained that pregnant women would no longer receive rations. A dispatcher at the main train station lamented that the changes would be tough for the families of those, like herself, who receive "miserly wages," and shoemaker Korovtenko retorted that he had five small children and that the 100-ruble increase in his salary would not make up for the higher bread prices.[137]

These sources give a voice to the workers of this "worker's state," and it is not a happy one—the regime's policies directly contradicted its own "family rhetoric," and much of the population seemed aware of the discrepancy. As we saw in the previous chapter, the end of rationing in December 1947 brought great hope and expectations that quickly faded into disappointment

---

[135] TsDNI f. 13, op. 4, d. 313, l. 18.

[136] TsDNI f. 13, op. 4, d. 313, l. 18.

[137] TsDNI f. 13, op. 4, d. 232, ll. 9, 23–24, 26, 33.

with the continuation of bread shortages. When rationing ended, eight single mothers from Mill No. 3 returned to pick up their children at an orphanage, extending thanks to Soviet power for "saving the lives of their children at a difficult time" and adding, "now we're in a position to raise them our-selves."[138] In a matter of months, however, such joyous spirits turned sour. Amid the spring 1948 bread crisis a report noted that most of the predomi-nantly female workers at three plants, many of them single mothers, felt that rationing should be restored.[139] Of course, these sentiments stand in stark contrast to complaints noted earlier that perceived rationing as the main problem before its cessation in December 1947, which highlights the varied and often contradictory nature of views held by the public. There were also reports of workers passing out from hunger and their children going days without bread. In one case, a young single woman machinist at DGTF told co-workers, "I haven't had any bread for eight days and I don't have any hopes of getting any."[140] In these texts, workers, like party leaders, commonly put their comments in terms of their own "family rhetoric." For them, however, the emphasis was on the difficulties of having a family (or of being alone), as well as the "lack of care" for the population shown by party leaders and the overall negative impact of party policies on them and their families. Those with the largest families complained the loudest. Commentaries overheard by informants and recorded in *svodki*, furthermore, did not differ greatly from workers' public statements to party officials about the famine measures, the lack of bread, and the negative impact of state policies on them and their families.

Reflecting official propaganda on the issue of national identity, several interviewees remembered "genuine friendship" among the city's various na-tional groups, including the only Armenian respondent.[141] In open meetings with party representatives people also occasionally touched on matters of na-tional identity, including acknowledging the disproportionate suffering of Jews during occupation. Several workers, for example, asked party agitators why the Nazis treated Jews so harshly, a fact that clearly did not escape the

---

[138] TsDNI f. 13,op. 4, d. 315, ll. 3, 11. See also ll. 24, 54, 59–60, 79.

[139] TsDNI f. 13, op. 4, d. 415, ll. 159–60. The three in question are a food processing plant, the Mikoyan Shoe Factory, and a factory that made construction materials. As noted in the previous chapter, rationing was illegally resumed in some stores.

[140] TsDNI f. 13, op. 4, d. 415, l. 159. See also ll. 146, 159, 160, 164, 187, 204–05, 242. See also TsDNI f. 13, op. 4, d. 392, l. 213.

[141] On the "genuine friendship" between nationalities see interview by author with Karina Abramian, 8 June 1995; Nina Nikitichna K., 17 March 1995; Ol'ga I. Pecher-skaia, 4 June 1995; Svetlana Semenova, 16 April 1995; Aleksandra Ermolenko, 16 April 1995.

population's attention.[142] Shortly after Stalin's toast to the Russian people someone asked why he "singled them out above all other nationalities" in the country, a question that must have been on many people's minds.[143] Commentaries on national identity were also less benign. Basing her observation on the stereotype that Jews did not fight in the war, one worker in May 1948 expressed surprise that Jews in Palestine had fought so successfully. She asked, "Are the Jews there different from the ones here?"[144] Elsewhere another worker was more explicit; in a discussion with the secretary of her factory's party organization, the worker reportedly said that "the majority of the leaders of our government are Jews, so we will never have a good life." When the party secretary tried to explain to her the error of her views she retorted, "I heard such opinions from people like you!" This comment, a glaring example of the Judeo-commune syndrome, suggests the existence of anti-Semitic sentiments among those in power as well as among society at large, contradicting the picture of society as "one friendly family" painted by the party's public record.[145] In their memoirs Karol and Leder note a sharp rise in anti-Semitic sentiments in the postwar period, both officially and among the population at large, and several interviewees also recalled the prominence of anti-Semitic sentiments among the population at this time.[146] Mariia Zhak said that anti-Semitism had been very strong prior to the 1917 Revolution, but then either subsided or "was under the surface" for many years afterward. However, "it reappeared and strengthened during the war and after."[147] Both she and her son Sergei remembered the strong sense of anti-Semitism they faced during evacuation, and Sergei said that a neighbor called him a "dirty Yid" not long after their return to Rostov in 1945. He did not notice anti-Semitism in the schools, but was confronted with it on the street. In either 1947 or 1948 someone came up to him in the street, made an anti-Semitic remark, and punched him before he even realized what was happening.[148]

A number of people remembered the disproportionate suffering of Jews at the hands of the Nazis, and several encountered clear examples of anti-Semitism in everyday Soviet life. Svetlana Semenova said that Russians hid Jews during occupation to save them from the Germans. Her family lived on the outskirts of town, and once during occupation her grandmother saw a

---

[142] See, for example, RGASPI f. 17, op. 88, d. 331, l. 8; TsDNI f. 13, op. 4, d. 92, l. 280; RGASPI f. 17, op. 88, d. 331, l. 94.

[143] RGASPI f. 17, op. 88, d. 426, l. 124.

[144] TsDNI f. 13, op. 4, d. 415, l. 84.

[145] TsDNI f. 13, op. 4, d. 233, l. 99. In this case, the party secretary did remove this worker from her position. See Weiner, "Making of a Dominant Myth," 641.

[146] Leder is particularly emphatic on this point. See *My Life in Stalinist Russia*, 279 and 295–306.

[147] Interview by author, 6 March 1995.

[148] Interview by author, 7 March 1995.

truckload of bodies, the Jewish victims of the German occupants, being taken to the ravine for burial.[149] Genadii Ermolenko said that everyone in Rostov knew that the Germans "rounded up" all Jews remaining in the city in August 1942 and shot them on the outskirts of town. Anti-Semitism was strong among Russians, he recalled, and there was a common stereotype that "cowardly" Jews had not fought in the war and thus that Russians had "saved" them from annihilation at the hands of the Nazis.[150] Oleg Pianiatsev also remembered this prominent stereotype during and after the war.[151] Karol, whose father was Jewish, recalls a number of anti-Semitic remarks and incidents in Rostov during the war and afterward. During his stint in the Red Army, 1941–42, he remembers the soldiers referring to a Jewish officer as a "dirty Yid." In another clear example of the "Judeo-commune" syndrome, a truck driver asked Karol and several friends amid the German onslaught and disorderly retreat in July 1942, "Why do you want to get yourselves killed for the Bolsheviks and the Jews who have been sucking our Christian blood since their damned revolution? Another, different Russia is soon going to be re-born, and it will need you. Come with me; I'll hide you. I shall obtain civilian clothes for you. You will want for nothing. Trust me."[152] He and his Cossack friends were repulsed by the offer and returned to the front lines to continue their service in the Red Army.

Karol's memoir tells us a great deal about perceptions of national identity during the war and reconstruction. He recalls that the first time he heard about the genocide of Jews he did not believe it, much as we saw in Valentina Bogdan's account previously. In August 1942 a Jewish man on a train explained to Karol, "The Germans are killing all of us without distinction, men and women, young and old alike. In every town and city large or small, they round up the Jews, take them to the fields and force them to dig communal graves, in which they are buried after being shot." Several years later, Karol and friends were unhappy with Stalin's 1945 toast to the "great Russian people" because, they felt, so many "non-Russians killed during the war [deserved] a little bit of gratitude from our supreme commander-in-chief [too]." His friend Chourik "claimed that Stalin had been drunk" when he gave the toast. Karol's father-in-law, a Don Cossack, did not know of Karol's Jewish ancestry and often made anti-Semitic remarks. After listening to a favorite

---

[149] Interview by author, 16 April 1995.

[150] Interview by author, 16 April 1995. An internal report noted that 59,000 Jews and almost 25,000 Armenians had received awards for their efforts during the war (compared to 2,183,000 Russians). Among recipients of the prestigious "Hero of the Soviet Union" award there were 3,390 Russians compared to 54 Jews. TsDNI f. 13, op. 4, d. 187, l. 80. Ermolenko claimed that Armenians opened cafes and stores for the Germans during occupation.

[151] Interview by author, 17 April 1995.

[152] Karol, *Solik*, 157.

song, his father-in-law said, "Stupid Hitler, why does he kill the gypsies, who sing so well? He would have done better to slit the throats of a few more Yids." He also expressed the opinion that "Jews engage in commerce and not in warfare." Karol asserts that Cossacks were particularly anti-Semitic and that there was a rumor "once widely current among [them]" that Stalin's real surname, Djugashvili, meant "son of a Jew" in Georgian. Karol's wife, Klava, also a Don Cossack, explained to him about the prominence of anti-Semitism among them: "they [Cossacks] drink of this poison along with their mother's milk." In 1946 at the corner of one of Rostov's busiest streets Karol saw a disabled veteran giving a "typical anti-Semitic speech: the Jews are in command, while the Christians, reduced to the role of simple executors, carry out their orders." A policeman directing traffic nearby did nothing to stop this public display of blatant anti-Semitism (a further illustration of the "Judeo-commune" syndrome) in the streets of Rostov.[153]

The recollections of interviewees and memoirists complement the image of Soviet society brought to light in archival sources, and the popular record illuminates perceptions of the regime's "family rhetoric" held by society at large. A number of workers publicly expressed doubts over women's "equal" status and the party's ability to "take care" of the population. Once again women have a strong voice in these texts, which posit popular views of "family relations" at odds with official definitions. Women with illegitimate children wondered what exactly constituted a "family," and others asked for the punishment of men who abandoned their wives, implying that alimony payments should be reinstated because otherwise men would not take responsibility for their actions. People shared the party's distinction between loyal and disloyal families while wondering how the niceties of marriage and divorce laws would apply to them and doubting the regime's ability to "provide adequate care" to the population. Often phrased in terms of family concerns, the popular record reveals a primary focus on economic issues and strong criticism of party policies, which are seen as contradictory and detrimental to workers' interests. Those posing harsh questions and making critical comments, moreover, often identified themselves as having large families, which further exposes the gap between the regime's "family rhetoric" and the reality endured by the population. In addition, clearly not all Soviet citizens accepted the official depiction of a "single family" of Soviet nationalities, with anti-Semitism existing alongside expressions of national "friendship." This reflected in part the regime's ambiguity regarding disproportionate Jewish suffering during the war and German occupation. There is also strong evidence of the "Judeo-commune" syndrome, the belief that Jews were a prominent force in the communist leadership and that this was a bad thing, as well as of

---

[153] Karol, *Solik*, 108, 157, 168, 282, 308-310, 312, 315. Klava defended Jews' record in the war, telling her father, "You know perfectly well that not only do the Jews fight very courageously in the present war, but that they also did it in biblical times" (312).

the stereotype that "cowardly" Jews "did not fight" in the war and were saved by the heroic Russian people.[154]

❧ ⚘

The similarities and differences between the party's records are instructive. Publicly as well as behind closed doors, party leaders described society in familial terms with women, the families of soldiers, demobilized troops, wounded war veterans, and children all playing prominent roles in the drama of "reconstruction." "Family rhetoric" in the press defined social sexual difference explicitly with descriptions of Soviet society in familial terms, and implicitly through an underlying paternalism while also equating all national groups as part of one "Soviet family." Public material portrayed the party in a fatherly role while associating women with the dual roles of domesticity and industrial production, constructing gendered meanings of "family" and "care." The party's internal record likewise shows that predominantly male party leaders looked upon women as both producers *and* reproducers, perhaps mainly due to the lack of labor power stemming from the war. Archival material reveals that party leaders defined "family" along political lines and anticipated worker opposition to party policies. As for national identity, the press initially acknowledged differences but mostly blurred distinctions in a single "Soviet family" construct. These sources indicate the existence of Jewish and Armenian religious groups in Rostov, and show that some Jewish party members preferred to be "Russian" in official documents, suggesting a perception that Russians received preferential treatment (and/or that Jews were discriminated against). Numerous sources (Leder, Karol, the Zhaks, etc.) point to a rise in anti-Semitism in the USSR after the war, as policies discriminating against Jews undermined rhetoric of "national unity" and "brotherhood." Official rhetoric aside, the Soviet regime was a lot like the police officer in Karol's account who stood by without acting while the disabled veteran delivered his "typical" anti-Semitic rant.

The word "family" rouses strong emotional feelings, and has entered political discourses across historical and cultural boundaries. "Family rhetoric" is an important part of the regime's discursive myth based on party ideology's configuration of social classes, gender, and national identity, which obscures other, conflicting systems of social construction at operation on the local level. One of the ways it does this is by shaping public opinion, yet the documents available here also give voice to popular complaints over the impact of party policies on families. As we established in chapter 2 and reiterated here, families faced a difficult time during "reconstruction," and, official "family rhetoric" notwithstanding, people often expressed their interests in terms at odds with the views and policies of party leaders, especially women and those with large families. In the popular record, workers and others

---

[154] Gross, "A Tangled Web," 105.

(many of whom identified themselves as single mothers) responded to state policies in terms of family rhetoric, displaying a preoccupation with material conditions. Official "family rhetoric" obscured the voices of discontent within the single "Soviet family" but did not douse them completely. Some workers, evidently unconvinced by the unifying language of the ruling ideology, defined themselves and their interests against the nomenklatura in positions of power, expressing a separate class consciousness vis-à-vis the ruling elite. The war experience, furthermore, sharpened the rifts and divisions in society beneath the "single Soviet family" construct by giving rise to collaboration, an issue dealt with by most combatant nations in World War II, but especially those that fell under occupation. The regime labeled collaborators "freaks" of the family, which we will examine in the next chapter.

Figure 1. Librarians sifting through the bombed out ruins of Rostov's main library for books that survived the bombing, February 1943

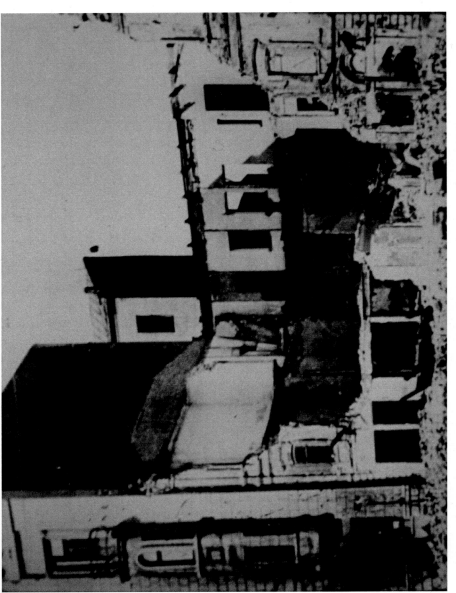

Figure 2. Ruins along Voroshilovskii Street in downtown Rostov, 1943

Figure 3. Bombed-out buildings near the center of Rostov-on-Don, 1944

Figure 4. Bombed-out buildings near the center of Rostov-on-Don, 1943

Figure 5. Bombed-out buildings near the center of Rostov-on-Don, 1943

Figure 6. A broad view of the destruction of Rostov's city center, 1943

Figure 7. Railway bridge across the Don River destroyed by the Nazis, 1945

Figure 8. A broad view of the wartime destruction of Rostov-on-Don, including the railway bridge across the Don River, 1945

Chapter Five

"Every family has its freak":
Perceptions of Collaboration in Occupied Soviet Russia

"Every family," in the words of a Russian proverb, "has its freak." During and after World War II the proverb was used to refer to Soviet citizens who sided with or assisted Nazi occupying forces. A cloud of suspicion hung over the country. German rule varied greatly from country to country in Europe— even from region to region within the same country—as did local reaction to it; but throughout the occupied areas, Nazi administration depended on local officials, police, and security units recruited from the native population to maintain order and quell resistance.[1] Thus, after liberation every formerly occupied country had to come to terms with acts of treason and collaboration among its populace. The ways in which societies dealt with this issue have been well studied for Western Europe (especially Vichy France), and increasingly so for Eastern Europe.[2] In the USSR, as noted, the Stalinist regime's

---

[1] For a discussion of Nazi occupation of the Soviet Union, see Barber and Harrison, *Soviet Home Front*, 113–16.

[2] See, for example, Klaus-Peter Friedrich, "Collaboration in a 'Land without a Quisling': Patterns of Cooperation with the Nazi German Occupation Regime in Poland during World War II," *Slavic Review* 64: 4 (Winter 2005): 711–46; Lloyd, *Collaboration and Resistance in Occupied France*; Gross, *Neighbors*; Deák et al., *Politics of Retribution*, including the essay by Deak, "A Fatal Compromise? The Debate over Collaboration and Resistance in Hungary"; Rab Bennett, *Under the Shadow of the Swastika: The Moral Dilemmas of Resistance and Collaboration in Hitler's Europe* (New York: New York University Press, 1999); Mazower, *Dark Continent*, 229–37; Claudia Kuretsidis-Haider and Winfried R. Garscha, eds., *Keine "Abrechnung": NS-Verbrechen, Justiz und Gesellschaft in Europa nach 1945* (Leipzig-Vienna: Akademische Verlagsanstalt, 1998); Tadeusz Piotrowski, *Poland's Holocaust: Ethnic Strife, Collaboration with Occupying Forces and Genocide in the Second Republic, 1918–1947* (Jefferson, NC: McFarland Press, 1998); Kenney, *Rebuilding Poland*; Bennett, *End of the War in Europe,*; Martin Conway, *Collaboration in Belgium: Leon Degrelle and the Rexist Movement, 1940–1944* (New Haven: Yale University Press, 1993); Gerhard Hirschfeld and Patrick Marsh, eds., *Collaboration in France: Politics and Culture during the Nazi Occupation, 1940–1944* (Oxford: Oxford University Press, 1989); Gerhard Hirschfeld, *Nazi Rule and Dutch Collaboration: The Netherlands under German Occupation, 1940–45*, trans. Louise Willmot (Oxford: Oxford University Press, 1988); Gross, *Polish Society under German Occupation*; Peter Novick, *The Resistance*

"family rhetoric" emphasized national unity and the party's paternal care, but evidence shows that collaboration was widespread and systemic within the vanguard party as well as society. Soviet leaders saw the war as a test of one's true feelings toward the regime, a way of judging the trustworthiness of every citizen or even entire nationalities. A person's whereabouts and activities during the war followed him or her throughout "reconstruction," as applications for work, party membership, government assistance, and the like requested information about what one and one's family did during the war.[3] The acknowledgement and discussion of collaboration further undermines the "single Soviet family myth" while exposing a major divide in society created by the war.

This chapter looks at the "freaks" in the Soviet "family," highlighting subtle differences in the perception of "collaboration" in society through an analysis of the language in a variety of sources. It is impossible to determine how many people helped the Germans during occupation, held pro-Nazi views, or actively betrayed the USSR. It is also impossible to establish the extent to which those who did were punished after Soviet control was reestablished, or the degree to which people were wrongfully accused.[4] My point is not to argue the "truth" of specific cases revealed in the archives but to focus on the attitudes expressed on collaboration by those in power as well as by the population at large. Recent scholarship on occupied Europe emphasizes the ambiguity between the two extremes of ardent resistance and enthusiastic collaboration. In northern France, many people under Nazi rule were apolitical, their decisions concerning how to cope with the Germans driven mainly by a desire to continue living.[5] For decades a limited "'binary vision"—resister/ collaborator, good/bad—dominated research of Vichy France, but the reality was far more nuanced and complex.[6] In looking at Vichy and Europe as a whole it is important to distinguish between "collaboration"—working with

---

versus Vichy: The Purge of Collaborators in Liberated France (New York: Columbia University Press, 1968).

[3] On the war as a litmus test for the loyalty of Soviet citizens, see Weiner, Making Sense of War, chap. 2.

[4] A recent publication of the Russian Federal Security Service states that, between 1943 and 1953, more than 320,000 Soviet citizens were arrested in the USSR for collaborating with the Germans during the war, including 12,196 people in the Rostov-on-Don region. Of course, arrest for collaboration does not necessarily mean guilt of collaboration. See O. B. Mozokhin, "Statistika repressivnoi deiatel'nosti organov bezopasnosti SSSR na period s 1921 po 1953 gg." Available on the Federal'naia sluzhba bezopasnosti (FSB) web site at http://www.fsb.ru/new/mozohin.html (accessed December 2005).

[5] Taylor, Between Resistance and Collaboration.

[6] Jean-Pierre Azéma and François Bédarida, eds., Le régime de Vichy et les Français (Paris: Fayard, 1992), 67, cited in Taylor, Between Resistance and Collaboration, 2. See also Sarah Fishman et al., eds., France at War: Vichy and the Historians (New York: Oxford University Press, 2000); and Diamond, Women and the Second World War in France.

or assisting the occupying power out of necessity and/or a will to survive—and "collaborationism"—enthusiastically aiding the Nazis due to an ideological affinity with their views.[7] The vast range of options between the extremes of resistance and collaboration constituted a "moral gray zone," with people forced to make difficult choices for the sake of survival.[8]

Among historians of the Soviet Union, Amir Weiner's groundbreaking study of Ukraine and Hiroaki Kuromiya's exhaustive study of the Donbas region examine collaboration during and after the war.[9] Both show that in the postwar years the line between heroes and villains in the Soviet Union remained unclear, with some unjustly repressed and several decorated heroes later revealed as betrayers of the Soviet cause. The Stalinist regime's focus on the internal threat posed by collaborators, moreover, dashed the population's hopes for a postwar political liberalization.[10] Those in power saw collaboration as a significant problem, labeling the worst offenders "betrayers of the motherland" (*izmenniki rodiny*), the Russian equivalent of the "collaborationists."[11] In addition, prisoners of war were considered disloyal based on Mili-

---

[7] Yves Durand, "Collaboration French-style: A European Perspective," in Fishman, *France at War*, 61–76. See also Stanley Hoffman, "Collaborationism in France during World War II," *Journal of Modern History* 40: 3 (September 1968): 375–95.

[8] See Rab Bennett, *Under the Shadow of the Swastika*, chap. 3.

[9] Weiner, *Making Sense of War*; and Kuromiya, *Freedom and Terror*. See also Kate Brown, *A Biography of No Place: From Ethnic Borderland to Soviet Heartland* (Cambridge, MA: Harvard University Press, 2004); Martin Dean, *Collaboration in the Holocaust: Crimes of the Local Police in Belorussia and Ukraine, 1941–44* (New York: St. Martin's Press, 2000); and Boterbloem, *Life and Death under Stalin*.

[10] On the population's hopes for a postwar liberalization, see Zubkova, *Russia After the War*; Dunham, *In Stalin's Time*; Fitzpatrick, "Postwar Soviet Society"; and Karol, *Solik*.

[11] Another term encountered more often is *predatel'*, the literal translation of which is "traitor," but in a very broad sense. It included those who worked for, assisted, and/or gave information to the Germans, its meaning falling somewhere between "traitor" and "collaborator." Numerous historians note the prevalence of collaboration and the strong anti-Soviet sentiments that rose to the fore during Nazi occupation. Martin Dean, for example, shows that there were plenty of volunteers for the German occupying police force in western Belarus and Ukraine (*Collaboration in the Holocaust*, 27). Kees Boterbloem points out that "collaboration with the Nazis was common in many parts of Eastern Europe, including Russia," and also notes an "anti-Soviet mood" in Kalinin oblast (*Life and Death under Stalin*, 48, 58). Vera Tolz argues that so many Ukrainians and Russians collaborated with the Germans it was impossible to deport large numbers of them due to what the regime called "technical difficulties." Tolz, "New Information about the Deportation of Ethnic Groups in the USSR during World War 2," in *World War 2 and the Soviet People: Selected Papers from the Fourth World Congress for Soviet and East European Studies, 1990*, ed. John Garrard and Carol Garrard (New York: St. Martin's Press, 1993), 164. See also Alexander Dallin, *German Rule in*

tary Order No. 270, which equated being taken prisoner with treason, stipulating that the families of prisoners would suffer dire consequences. Repatriated Soviet citizens—mostly youth—returning from work in Germany also fell under suspicion.[12] In the eyes of the regime, exposure to German propaganda and life abroad cast doubt on their faithfulness to Soviet power, even though a majority were forcibly conscripted and wanted to return home.[13] By the end of 1941 roughly 40 percent of the Soviet Union's population was in occupied territory, and their loyalties were suspect because of contact with the Germans and exposure to enemy propaganda.[14] Some worked during occupation, housed German troops, or otherwise "assisted" them, although not necessarily voluntarily.[15] Some fought against the Germans but, as Weiner points out, even they had to account for their actions after the return of Soviet power.[16]

Russia, 1941–1945 (New York: St. Martin's Press, 1957), and Barber and Harrison, *Soviet Home Front.*

[12] One source cites 3,738 in the city by September 1945. TsDNI f. 13, op. 4, d. 148 (Repatriation), l. 161. Another source, however, cites a total of 3,086 repatriated citizens in Rostov as of the same date. This source adds that for Rostov oblast as a whole, 37,185 people were forcibly taken to Germany, 6,680 of whom had returned by the end of July 1945. *Gosudarstvennyi arkhiv Rostovskoi oblasti* (GARO) f. 3737, op. 6 (Rostov City Soviet), d. 40, ll. 3, 4. Those with relatives living outside the country were also suspect.

[13] Kuromiya and Brown show that the Germans portrayed their campaign to raise workers for Germany as a great opportunity, and consequently the first wave of young Russians who went to work there often did so voluntarily. But word quickly spread that working and living conditions for the conscripts in Germany were horrible, and thereafter the Germans forcibly conscripted young people. See Kuromiya, *Freedom and Terror,* 272–73 and 299–300; and Brown, *Biography of No Place,* 217.

[14] As Boterbloem notes regarding Kalinin oblast, "It is impossible to establish how many people deliberately stayed behind to welcome the Germans instead of attempting to flee" (*Life and Death under Stalin,* 55). Many communists were caught behind the lines because of the poor organization of evacuation or were left behind by the NKVD to organize partisan activity. In an interview Mariia Zhak, who was born in 1901 and lived in Rostov most of her life, remembered that not long after the return of Soviet power, First Obkom Secretary Boris Dvinskii was removed "for the poor organization of evacuation." On the NKVD keeping party members in occupied territory to organize partisan activities, see Weiner, *Making Sense of War,* 52; and Boterbloem, *Life and Death under Stalin,* 47.

[15] As Kuromiya notes, occupation policies obliged residents to turn in Jews, partisans, and communists or risk death themselves, but by no means did everyone who stayed in occupied territory assist or work for the Germans. Also, he points out that many Soviet citizens in occupied territory worked out of necessity in order to survive, not out of any particular affinity for the occupying power (*Freedom and Terror,* 263 and 275). See also Weiner, *Making Sense of War,* 7–8; and, with regard to being forced to work to survive in Vichy France, see Taylor, *Between Resistance and Collaboration,* chap. 1.

[16] Weiner, *Making Sense of War,* 90.

The war, of course, heightened concern for security—as did the Cold War when it developed—and cast strong suspicions on "strangers" at a time when there were a lot of strangers due to the dislocation caused by the conflict. Hundreds of thousands of people moved into and out of Rostov during and after the war with the mobilization of the entire country. Not all of them were eager to defend Soviet power. When he gave his first address to the population following the German invasion almost two weeks afterward, Stalin said "there must be no room in our ranks for whiners and cowards, for panic-mongers and deserters."[17] The Soviet regime confiscated personally owned radios because it did not want people listening to German propaganda,[18] while Soviet citizens of German descent, including the entire population of the Volga German Autonomous Republic, were uprooted and deported at the beginning of the war. During the conflict, several other national groups were also exiled for their alleged collaboration with the Nazis.[19] After the Red Army's victory at Stalingrad in early 1943 the front gradually began moving west all the way to Berlin. At war's end an estimated five million Soviet citizens were outside the country's borders, three million POWs, forced laborers, and defectors in the West (mostly Germany), and two million in the Soviet-occupied regions of Eastern Europe.[20] Thousands of demobilized soldiers settled in Rostov and elsewhere between 1945 and 1948, many of whom had also been abroad.[21] The country was filled with internal refugees, people displaced from their homes and left with few if any possessions, many of them searching for lost relatives. As we have seen, the war destabilized the life of literally every Soviet citizen, and from the point of view of those in power, there were many people in the country whose behavior during the war and occupation was problematic to say the least.

---

[17] Cited in Treadgold, *Twentieth-Century Russia*, 347.

[18] On this point, see Karol, *Solik*, 75; see also Merridale, *Ivan's War*, 88, and Werth, *Russia at War*, 181.

[19] The groups exiled during the war were the Chechens, Ingush, Crimean Tartars, Karachay-Balkars, Meskhetians, and Kalymuks. On the deportations, see Tolz, "New Information"; Terry Martin, "The Origins of Soviet Ethnic Cleansing," *Journal of Modern History* 70: 4 (December 1998): 831–61; Roy Medvedev, *Let History Judge: The Origins and Consequences of Stalinism* (New York: Columbia University Press, 1989); N. F. Bugai, ed., *Iosif Stalin – Laverentiiu Berii: "Ikh nado deportirovat'."* Dokumenty, fakty, kommentarii (Moscow: Druzhba narodov, 1992); and N. F. Bugai, "K voprosu o deportatsii narodov SSSR v 30–40-kh godakh," *Istoriia SSSR*, no. 6 (1989): 135–44.

[20] Filtzer notes that by the end of 1947 just over 5.4 million of a total of 5.8 million Soviet citizens abroad had been repatriated (*Soviet Workers and Late Stalinism*, 24).

[21] As of January 1946, 2,704 demobilized troops were in Rostov, and that number would increase steadily in subsequent months. RGASPI f. 17, op. 122, d. 146, l. 27.

Collaboration and the Public Voice of Power

Less than a month after the city's liberation in February 1943, talk of treason already found its way into *Molot*, which wavered in its treatment of the issue at first but then penned a harsh stance and a broad portrayal of "collaborators." The first story with an underlying theme of collaboration, "Translator," appeared three weeks after liberation.[22] A party agitator described how he chatted with a group of people recounting their heroic acts of resistance during occupation. He noticed that one young woman sat silent and asked her what she had done. "Nothing special," she responded, someone else "nastily" (*so zloboi*) commenting, "she was a translator for the fascists." Then a young pilot in the group told how once, after being shot down, he and a co-pilot hid among Soviet civilians. They were eventually saved, he explained, by obtaining documents with the German commandant's signature smuggled out by a Russian accomplice in his office. "When the woman was asked to save two Soviet pilots," he said, "she gladly agreed and risked her own life to secure the necessary documents." He had not met her and asked anyone in the room who knew L. G. Kugusheva to "please pass a sincere, heartfelt thanks to her from me!" The silent young woman who had worked as a translator was, of course, L. G. Kugusheva. The pilot added that she had saved 14 other Soviet aviators in the same manner.

This article set a tone of tolerance, acknowledging the "gray zone" between the extremes of resistance and collaboration. The piece clearly insinuates that not everyone who stayed behind or even worked for the Germans was in the wrong, since the group was discussing acts of resistance and a woman who worked for the commandant turned out to be a heroine. It is acceptable to have worked for the Nazis, in other words, *if* you were an active agent for Soviet power. The commentary suggests that people should not be unfairly judged nor suspicion cast too widely. One could just as easily have secretly carried out an act of heroism as an act of treason. The translator was loyal to the Soviet cause, which implied that her service to the enemy was forced upon her. Nonetheless, evidence was required to confirm the translator's acts of bravery; those at the meeting who knew her assumed that she had betrayed the country. In this narrative, Kugusheva sat silent through most of the meeting; she did not look for recognition, and her good deeds were acknowledged solely by luck. The pilot, a man, spoke for Kugusheva, and it took his testimony to clear her name. She "risked her life," just like the pilots themselves. The story also shows tolerance toward the pilot, who, after all, had been in occupied territory and used documents signed by the German commandant to escape. Not only is he free from suspicion, but his words cleared someone else who had fallen under unjust suspicion.

---

[22] *Molot*, "Perevodchitsa," 7 March 1943.

Subsequent pieces in the local press assumed a much harsher tone toward treason. Two days after "Translator," a front-page editorial urged "greater Bolshevik vigilance" against traitors. "Hitler's bandits," it began, succeeded in attracting "anti-Soviet riff-raff" to their service. "Every family has its freak. There were some among us who betrayed the fatherland and helped the Germans." The editorial described the "unmasking of a certain Koren'kov," an "elder" (*starosta*) in the Cossack village (*khutor*) Alekseevo near Rostov. He had given the Germans a list of pro-Soviet peasants, all 19 of whom were shot. "There were also more than a few cases of treachery in Rostov," it continued, "and our mission now is to unmask agents of the enemy, fishing them out to the very last one."[23] In a dire warning, the piece concluded that it would be foolish to assume the Germans did not leave behind spies in Rostov, calling for "Bolshevik vigilance" from each and every citizen in the unmasking of Nazi agents. In mid-March 1943, *Molot* announced the arrest of people, "possibly fascist agents," accused of selling poisonous alcohol left behind by the retreating Germans.[24] An editorial in May, "The Strengthening of Vigilance—A Military Law," recounted how two young women were arrested in Stalingrad oblast after liberation.[25] The two had "befriended" (*sblizilis' s*) Nazi soldiers, and when the latter were forced to retreat, the women allegedly agreed to spy for them. "Their intense curiosity and inquiries after the arrival of the Red Army," the article assured, "did not go unnoticed." It called on workers to "diligently pay attention to others [and] piously guard the interests of the Fatherland by unmasking enemy agents. Spies," it warned on a strong cautionary note, "are sometimes sent out disguised as civilians running from the Germans or as Red Army soldiers escaping German capture."

In early August 1943, German troops were ousted from Novocherkassk, the former Cossack capital, and afterward a revealing story appeared in *Molot*. Entitled "Traitors" ("Predateli"), it began with the testimony of Sukhoruchenko, "a small man with beady eyes" who tried to explain why his arrest as a German agent was a mistake. "How am I traitor," he asked, "when I myself suffered in the jails of the Gestapo?" He tried to evacuate but did not get far and was forced to return, thereby "accidentally" winding up in occupied territory. "The whole time I actively fought against the Germans," the speaker assured his accusers. But his "cowardly eyes darting from person to person" gave him away as he tried to see what was written in the file on the table, and

---

[23] *Molot*, "Vyshe bol'shevistskuiu bditel'nost'!" 9 March 1943, p. 1.

[24] *Molot*, "Reshenie Ispolnitel'nogo komiteta rostovskogo oblastnogo soveta," *Molot*, 8 May 1943, p. 2. For the announcement of arrests of those selling the poisonous alcohol, see *Molot*, "V Oblastnom upravlenii militsii," 17 March 1943, p. 2. The announcement adds that some people are still selling the poisonous alcohol. For a similar warning about the sale of bad medicine on the market, see *Molot*, 14 March 1943, p. 2.

[25] *Molot*, "Usilenie bditel'nosti—Zakon voennogo vremeni," 16 May 1943, p. 2.

the "scoundrel" (*merzavets*) could not "hide from the truth." Sukhoruchenko "knew quite a few communists and Soviet patriots," and the file on the table reportedly held the names of 20 people he had turned in to the Gestapo. All of them were shot, and were now "on the conscience of this person." But is he really "a person," the author wondered, resoundingly answering in the negative and describing him instead as "vile filth." According to the article, in a desperate attempt to cover his tracks, Sukhoruchenko pasted bills calling on people to support the Red Army when it was about to retake the city. His effort to "paint himself out to be a patriot," however, proved unsuccessful.

Sukhoruchenko was not alone in his villainous deeds. He recruited his friend Buturlinov to work for the German police as well, and "that drunkard, linked to German spies already for many years," betrayed several loyal communists. Minina, a "loyal and patriotic communist," found out that Sukhoruchenko worked for the Germans and was determined to warn as many "comrades" as possible. Unfortunately, "thinking that he carried out communist activities," she cautioned Buturlinov, who immediately turned her in to the Gestapo. After excruciating torture, the article informed, Minina was shot. The most evil informant was "a certain Lishafaev," who "was a workaholic" and "spied without a break." The Germans even trusted him to work independently, and he did not disappoint, hunting down and arresting a number of leading communists. Among his victims was Belousov, who had been secretly sent into Novecherkassk to help out the partisans there. He and a number of other victims of Lishafaev's misplaced diligence were executed. These three "betrayers of the motherland" tried unsuccessfully to escape with the retreating Germans but were cut off by the approaching Red Army. The "scoundrels" tried to confuse the investigators and hide their evil deeds, but these men had the blood of innocent Soviet patriots on their hands. Faced with strong evidence of their guilt, the three confessed to "betraying their motherland by voluntarily and consciously serving the cause of the enemy." Thus, the author opined, they deserved to be executed; their guilt could not be softened by "circumstances." The article ended by assuring us that the Military Tribunal issued the only possible and just sentence to these three traitors—death by firing squad.

While focusing on a few specific examples, these accounts define collaboration broadly and promote a harsh stance on this issue.[26] The piece on Stalingrad warned of "intensely curious" characters in liberated areas and ended by casting suspicion on anyone escaping from the Germans. The article "Traitors" portrays "anti-heroes" and subhuman "scoundrels," indicating that traitors hid among the people, tried to disguise their acts, and even tried to present themselves as patriots. The demonization of such "vile filth," moreover, is completed by their juxtaposition with their victims—many of whose names

---

[26] On the regime's broad understanding of collaboration, see Penter, "Collaboration on Trial," 784.

we learn—honest, faithful patriots and communists. One's portrayal of one's actions during occupation was largely constructed and thus required corroborating evidence, which cast doubt on people whose activities were unaccounted for. Suspicion was reinforced by a call to spy on others. In addition, while not openly saying so, the article strongly implies that there were traitors in the party's ranks. Sukhoruchenko and Buturlinov knew "quite a few communists and Soviet patriots" and seemed to have inside information on underground communist activities in Novocherkassk. One of their victims thought that Buturlinov "carried out communist activities." The piece implies that "good" communists were martyred for the cause while "bad" communists—those who betrayed them—survived.

The article on Novocherkassk, furthermore, was significant because of that city's history as the Cossack capital and a center for White opposition during the Civil War. This piece did not specifically mention Cossacks, but most people in the lower Don region would have made such an association, just as the references to *starosta* and *khutor* in the previous article would have provoked a similar association. While such articles hinted at Cossack disloyalty, other public pronouncements loudly proclaimed Cossack loyalty. A *Molot* report on a bond drive in 1943, for example, relayed the success of Cossacks gathering funds for a tank column bearing their name. "Don Cossacks have a score to settle with the Hitlerites," the correspondent wrote. "The fascist scoundrels threatened the most sacred of all things for Cossacks—their motherland and their freedom. They tried to poison the consciousness of Cossacks with their pernicious propaganda while turning them into slaves. It did not work!"[27] Even such emphatic proclamations of loyalty, however, implied the opposite. This piece implicitly associated the "sacred freedom" of Cossacks with Soviet (as opposed to German) rule, which did not correspond to the history of opposition in the region. It also acknowledged German propaganda aimed specifically at the Cossacks in an effort to "poison their consciousness." But, alas, Cossacks remained "loyal" to "their" (read: Soviet) "motherland," presumably all of them since they were dealt with as a whole. This was highly significant given that at the time entire nationalities were being deported because of their alleged traitorous behavior during the war. *Molot* articles celebrating Cossack loyalty—which, as we will see, contrasts sharply with internal party documents—signaled that no such treatment would be forthcoming for them.

The press did openly question the loyalties of some women citizens, associating sexual promiscuity with traitorous behavior. The party press portrays collaborators, the regime's primary internal other during the war and immediately after, in gendered terms. The article about the women in Stalingrad oblast portrays them as disloyal for "befriending" (read: sleeping with) the enemy. They "betrayed" the motherland with their bodies ("horizontal col-

---

[27] *Molot*, "Vsenarodnaia podderzhka novogo zaima," 8 June 1943, p. 1.

laboration"), as women were held to a different standard of "faithfulness."[28] In August 1943, *Molot* published an article entitled "Wives" by a party agitator at the front, P. Nikitin, whose duty included "honest, open discussions" with the troops.[29] Often, he noted, the topic of discussion is "our wives." Soldiers at the front were proud of their wives for their "help to the Red Army, their stoicism in the face of sacrifice, and their faithfulness." But sometimes the author heard about "other women, weak souls" who were disloyal "to their motherland" for a "minute of happiness" and who "think only about themselves." The author compared two good wives to a bad one to illustrate his point. Sergeant Bel'kov, who died at the battle of Leningrad, had an exemplary wife. She responded to the news accordingly: "I lost the dearest person on earth to me, Nikolai Bel'kov, with whom I lived twelve years. We worked together at the same factory, at the same rolling press, were both Stakhanovites, shared the same difficulties and joys." After calling on the troops to avenge her husband's death, she added, "don't worry about me." The second positive example was the wife of Lieutenant Serdiuk, who was fatally wounded in the same battle. Her letter came from the "pure heart of a Russian woman who recognizes that a wife's honor to a soldier at the front is like the honor of a patriot to the motherland. 'Don't you worry about me,'" she wrote to her wounded husband, "I'll guard my love for you. I will not defile it." Such letters, Nikitin maintained, filled the hearts of their readers with pride and inspired them to carry out new heroic acts in battle.

"However," he continued, "we are all disgusted by those women who live only for themselves, who could not wait." These women, who were "like weeds growing among the collective, no longer have the right to be called the wives of soldiers at the front." As an example the author reproduced, with his permission, a letter by Sergeant Shcherbakov to his wife Taisia in Rostov. "The Germans destroyed our beloved city," the sergeant wrote, "but we will rebuild, and Rostov will be even better, even more beautiful. But," he continued, "what you've destroyed can never be restored. You stole the childhood of my son, throwing him to the mercy of fate, in order to live with another man." After quoting two more letters—one from co-workers and one from their son—as proof of her disloyalty, he assured his wife that their son "will love his father for defending the motherland." Even if he should die in battle, Shcherbakov maintained, he knew "that the Motherland-mother (*rodina-mat'*)[30] he defended would nurture and raise my son." Shcherbakov's ex-wife, Taisia, Nikitin states, "is not fit to be a wife or a mother." Soon, he concluded,

---

[28] As Merridale states, "Soviet morality judged them [women] by a double standard, condemning behavior that would be admired, or at least condoned, in men" (*Ivan's War*, 240).

[29] *Molot*, "Zheny," 11 August 1943, p. 4.

[30] The term *rodina-mat'* emphasizes the view of the "motherland" as a surrogate mother.

the battlefields will stand silent, people will place flowers before the graves of the fallen and say, "Sleep, heroes, we avenged your death, we served the motherland with honor," which wives who help the Red Army with their selfless labor will have the full right to say. "And," the author asked, "what will the former wife of Sergeant Shcherbakov say? She will not be with us."

This portrayal of "wives" links loyalty to one's husband with loyalty to the country. It is a question of "honor," which has strong gendered connotations since a woman's honor has historically been associated with her virginity before marriage and her faithfulness during wedlock. While it gave voice to the "good" wives by excerpting their letters, the article did not grant an avenue for Taisia to explain her actions, condemning her on the word of her son and former co-workers. There was no indication that she left her husband for a German, just "another" (presumably Soviet) man. Nikitin juxtaposed the weakness, selfishness, and individualism of this antiheroine with the strength, selflessness, and sacrifice of "pure" women who suffered along with the collective, leaving little room between those extremes. He does not question whether men were loyal to their wives, whether or not they "waited,"[31] nor does he identify the two positive examples by name—they were defined through their husbands, whose names (the diminutive in one case) were given. These women were synonymous with the nameless, faceless crowd, the overwhelming majority of Soviet women who worked hard and endured endless sacrifices without asking for recognition. We do, however, learn the name of the bad example, Taisia (a rare name), which personalizes and individualizes her while at the same time demonizing her. The fact that she should not "be considered a wife and mother," as we have seen, had economic implications since it meant she would not be eligible for government assistance. Finally, the haunting conclusion that "she will not be with us" after victory suggested, at the very least, that, because of her dubious actions, she would not have the right to celebrate the victory secured in part by "faithful" Soviet women.

That long-awaited victory came in May 1945, and less than three months later *Molot* published an article by L. Savel'ev entitled "Vigilance—The Holy Obligation of the Soviet People," which set a very harsh tone for the postwar period.[32] This piece indicated that there would *not* be a postwar relaxation in Soviet society and that an atmosphere of crisis would be maintained. The author reminded readers of Stalin's claim that "successes, like everything else in

---

[31] The men's sacrifice was that they risked their lives (and in two of the cases lost their lives) for the country. There definitely were troops at the front who "betrayed" their wives. Tumarkin quotes a passage from Svetlana Alekseevich, *War's Unwomanly Face* (Moscow: Palmira, 1988), 40–41, that after the war wives who stayed behind often despised women who served at the front, suspecting that they had slept with their husbands (Tumarkin, *Living and the Dead*, 184).

[32] *Molot*, "Bditel'nost'—sviashchennyi dolg sovetskikh liudei," 27 July 1945.

the world, have their dark side," leading to self-gratification, extreme self-confidence, and an undue degree of relaxation. Now, Savel'ev continued, when the country was returning to peace and nursing its wounds from the war, "the Soviet people should be especially vigilant." "Intense vigilance," he reiterated "is considered one of the most important obligations of a Soviet patriot." Toward the end of the war when they realized their defeat was inevitable, the German fascists created "spy networks to prepare for and instigate a third world war." Such a plan should come as no surprise, Savel'ev asserted, because the Germans had done the same thing at the end of World War I, which contributed to the outbreak of the Second World War.[33] As they fled a recently liberated town, the Germans left behind well-trained agents like Nina K., an energetic "activist" who turned out to be a spy. Tales of her arrests by the Gestapo and escapes from Nazi jails during occupation were merely a "mask meant to solidify her reputation as 'someone who suffered at the hands of the Germans.'"

Enemy agents, Savel'ev warned, are potentially everywhere. He noted that they were planted among the "crowd" of people returning from German capture, casting strong aspersions toward POWs and repatriated Soviet citizens. "Examples and facts of enemy activities obligate Soviet people to constantly be vigilant and strictly guard military and state secrets." He defined these as "information about Soviet military strength or that would facilitate a military attack against the country," such as "the number of troops, the country's resources, the system of transportation, etc." But, Savel'ev cautioned, "it is impossible to include everything that might be considered a military or state secret," implying a very broad understanding of the term. Enemy agents strove to penetrate the party, government, and military, to acquaint themselves with responsible and highly placed administrators with information on the country's military and economic strength. The obligation to protect state secrets and the responsibility to unmask enemy agents, moreover, belonged to everyone, from soldiers and party administrators to such "unnoticed" workers as couriers and custodians. Spies, the author cautioned, were very well trained and clever in their work. They knew how to glean helpful information from "careless comments" and they knew how to role-play, often posing as soldiers or administrators. They obtained information by "overhearing" conversations and through "chance acquaintances with talkative administrators on the train." They glanced at the desks of their superiors hoping to read the texts of official documents. The best way to guard against enemy agents and their activities, Savel'ev concluded, was to keep one's papers in order and one's tongue in check, not giving spies the slightest chance to obtain useful information.

---

[33] He claimed that they choose agents who will be useful to them not only now, but for the next 15–20 years when the fascists will likely try again to drag the world into a bloody conflict.

The first article about collaboration in the local press after liberation acknowledged some of the nuances and complexities involved with this issue, but subsequent pieces dealt with it from a straightforward resister/collaborator, good/bad point of view, casting a wide net of suspicion over society. Yet the warnings in these texts that enemy agents could be lurking anywhere contradicted the concentration on collaborators as an "isolated few" or "specific individuals." This reflected the dilemma of presenting collaborators as the main internal enemy at a time when many people—including party members—were potentially collaborators. Words alone could not free one from suspicion because people constructed stories about their actions—there was an assumption of guilt that had to be negated with evidence. Furthermore, the gender-coded language used to discuss collaboration cast traitorous women as "weaklings" who betrayed the country with their bodies, putting their "selfish [read: sexual] desire" for a "moment of happiness" above all else. The feminization of collaborators in the press may reflect the carefully constructed nature of this source, with the material therein holding women to a double standard of loyalty; "bad" wives did not "wait," did not remain loyal to their husbands at the front, while good wives were "faithful" and "honorable," quiet, selfless in the face of sacrifice ("don't worry about me"). They worked endlessly to support the Red Army or, like the men at the front, "risked their lives" to help the cause.

Furthermore, *Molot* trumpeted the loyalty of the Cossacks while casting doubt on POWs, repatriated citizens, and those who stayed in occupied territory. It dehumanized "traitors," and hinted (but did *not* explicitly state) that Communist Party members (like the "activist" Nina K.) were among their number. Significantly, the issue of collaboration is barely mentioned in the local press after 1945, and especially after August 1946 when Andrei Zhdanov, one of Stalin's top aides, launched the campaign to cleanse the Soviet arts and sciences of those who "kowtowed to Western culture." It seems plausible that the regime did not want to publicly air its "dirty laundry" on such sensitive matters in the context of the developing Cold War and amid the armed uprisings underway after the war in the Baltic states and Ukraine.[34] Also, as we will see from classified reports, the regime was having difficulty replacing even the people it deemed "untrustworthy," another reason it probably did not want to dwell on this problem publicly (such concerns may likewise explain why there was no explicit mention of treasonous party members in the local press). Thus, while collaboration remained a topic of conversation for

---

[34] Martin Dean notes that the "vast majority" of the more than 300,000 alleged collaborators arrested in the USSR in the postwar years were tried and sentenced "in closed session before military tribunals in a deliberate attempt to play down the massive scale of collaboration for both domestic and foreign consumption." Dean, "Where Did All the Collaborators Go?" *Slavic Review* 64: 4 (Winter 2005): 791.

party leaders at least until 1948, as I illustrate below, there was minimal discussion of this issue in the press after 1945.

Collaboration and the Hidden Voice of Power

Collaboration was also a prominent theme in the internal party record, which was molded by the same ideological assumptions as the public pronouncements. The center set a harsh tone early when the Supreme Soviet in April 1943 passed a decree requiring public hanging for all "traitors of the motherland." Signed by M. Kalinin among others, it specified that the bodies be left to dangle for several days so that "everyone can see what happens to such scoundrels."[35] Party leaders worried about assuring the "purity" of members—the sincerity and strength of their "call" to the communist cause.[36] The party had ordered all members to evacuate, so those who left accused those who stayed behind of disobeying orders. Complicating matters further, many members in occupied territory burned their party cards—breaking a key rule of membership—because the Nazis reportedly executed communists.[37] Others showed up to "register" with the Germans and/or turned over their party cards to the Gestapo, which cast even more doubt on their faithfulness to the Soviet cause. After the return of Soviet power in February 1943, the city's party organization began the daunting task of sorting the loyal from the disloyal in its ranks. Party leaders at the *raikom* level representing urban and rural districts were required to reconfirm members of the nomenklatura for their positions,[38] and all members who stayed had to reregister and explain why to their district branch, which heard each case and decided the person's fate. The file was then passed to the city party committee (*gorkom*), which upheld or overturned the decision, and then to the oblast party committee (*obkom*) for a final decision.[39]

---

[35] RGASPI f. 17, op. 3, d. 1047, ll. 232–33. It is not clear why the three traitors from Novocherkassk were sentenced to death by firing squad instead of public hanging in accordance with this decree.

[36] See Weiner, *Making Sense of War,* chap. 2.

[37] On members burning their cards, see Kuromiya, *Freedom and Terror,* 265.

[38] As noted in the introduction, the city party's nomenklatura consisted of all obkom, gorkom, and district (*raikom*) secretaries, heads of raikom departments such as *agitprop* (agitation and propaganda) departments, Komsomol (Communist Youth Organization) secretaries, newspaper editors and prosecutors. All members who stayed had to prove they had a good reason, and the poor organization of evacuation was *not* a suitable excuse for winding up in occupied territory.

[39] Weiner shows how existing networks of political alliances or cliques skewed this process from the outset—there was no such thing as an "objective" review procedure (Weiner, *Making Sense of War,* chap. 2).

Rostov's local party leaders often talked tough about collaborators, including those within the party. As we will see, however, they also recognized the complexity of the issue and acknowledged the "moral grey zone" for at least some alleged collaborators. Also, for various reasons the party did not always live up to the harsh image that it projected. At times local leaders emphasized the *lack* of a "moral gray zone" between the two extremes of collaboration and resistance—either one defended the motherland, ready to die doing so if necessary, or one collaborated with the enemy, even if just by staying in occupied territory, which automatically cast doubt on one's loyalty. At a closed meeting Comrade Soval'ev recommended firing former prisoners of war in positions of leadership because "during the struggle for the fate of our motherland they wound up on the wrong side of the lines."[40] He noted as well that the coach of Rostov's soccer team, Gofman, was a POW and had been excluded from the party, adding "one wonders whether this explains our shameful performances on the soccer field."[41] A 1945 report cited M. A. Zakharov, who reportedly maintained his post as director of the tobacco factory (DGTF) during occupation, as an example of a highly placed collaborator. The factory had been completely destroyed during the battle for Rostov in 1942, so, this account maintained, the Nazis set up production in a neighboring building with the help of Zakharov, other plant leaders, and several workers who stayed in occupied territory. Zakharov nonetheless continued as director after occupation, completely neglecting the material needs of the plant's workers. The district party bureau finally fired and replaced him in August 1943 and only then did the plant's cafeteria open.[42] In countless reports and meetings, local leaders demonized collaborators like Zakharov by contrasting them with "patriotic," "loyal" Soviet citizens.[43] One report suggested replacing those who worked for the Germans with those who "exhibited loyalty to the motherland during the war."[44]

At a conference two weeks after liberation, Comrade Pastushenko, second-in-command of the obkom, urged delegates to be vigilant in the investigation of party members who stayed behind. "Of course," he warned, "many will not admit that they showed up to register [with the Germans]," so district secretaries would have to confirm their stories from other sources.[45] Initial concerns in Rostov focused on those in control of the city's housing, many of

---

[40] TsDNI f. 13, op. 4, d. 214, ll. 24–25.

[41] TsDNI f. 13, op. 4, d. 214, ll. 24–25.

[42] TsDNI f. 13, op. 4, d. 56, ll. 10–11.

[43] Another highly placed collaborator, the former director of the zoo, was accused of trying "to protect his circle of friends who actively worked for the Germans." In late 1944 his replacement purged the staff of those "who do not inspire political trust." TsDNI f. 13, op. 4, d., l. 91.

[44] TsDNI f. 13, op. 4, d. 102, l. 90. In the district 76 people were promoted.

[45] TsDNI f. 13, op. 4, d. 29, ll. 22–23.

whom had assisted Nazi forces, including informing them where Jews and communists resided. Comrade Kaliagin of Andreevskii district described how, at a meeting after liberation, housing administrators "sat there like wet chickens, feeling very bad because they handed over [to the Nazis] lists of communists and Jews." He noted that they "removed" (*ubrali*) 10 staffers but that at least 20 more housing administrators had worked for the Germans. [46] Also at the conference, the procurator for Rostov oblast, Comrade Polozkov, lamented that "not one of the administrations of housing has helped to expose those individuals who worked for the Germans."[47] Several internal reports focused on housing organs and showed the prominence of collaboration in this realm. One in April 1943 stated that during their brief reign the Germans granted the best apartments for "services" (*uslugi*), and thus district secretaries needed to check passports and confirm the lawful residency of all citizens.[48] A report in September complained that 2,954 people still inhabited apartments with orders issued by the Nazis.[49] Housing, as we have seen, was in high demand in Rostov during and after the war and the bureaus in charge of it were tainted by the collaboration of many administrators.

Delegates at the February 1943 conference also called for thorough investigations of communist members who stayed in occupied territory, setting the agenda for much of the inter-party discussion of the next few years. Kaliagin's account of the check-up on communists in his district is revealing:

> The majority of the communists who remained here said they were outside of the city, leaving, but were picked out and told to return. Of those who simply stayed, they did so because they were ill or members of their family were ill. The majority kept their party cards intact. During discussion several of them obviously felt very embarrassed.

Like the spies described in *Molot*, the implication here was that people constructed stories to justify their presence in occupied territory, their "embarrassment" stemming perhaps from an inability to convince skeptical party leaders who evacuated. Higher-level local party leaders at the conference like Comrade Kocheriv of the Rostov obkom, meanwhile, called for vigilance in the check up on party members that remained behind. "Undeniably more stayed than have so far registered," he maintained, and "we must work doggedly to check those communists [because] we don't know if they went to the German commandant, Gestapo, or police." Kocheriv instructed raikom bureaus to obtain specific information about how members wound up in occu-

---

[46] TsDNI f. 13, op. 4, d. 29, l. 12.

[47] TsDNI f. 13, op. 4, d. 29, l. 39.

[48] GARO f. 3737, op. 8, d. 34, l. 29.

[49] TsDNI f. 13, op. 4, d. 23, l. 49. For another report on collaboration among housing bureau staff, see also TsDNI f. 13, op. 4, d. 184, ll. 18–19.

pied territory and what they did, a daunting task for understaffed bureaus.[50] He also relayed the obkom's decision not to create party organizations from among those members until the raikom bureaus "examine the personal behavior of every communist who stayed."[51] Comrade Pastushenko relayed the words of Obkom First Secretary Dvinskii, who was not in attendance, to the delegates: "We absolutely should not delay in carrying out this matter like we did last time," Dvinskii allegedly said, a reference to the check up of communists who did not evacuate when the Germans took Rostov-on-Don for a week in November 1941.[52]

Party meetings and reports frequently dealt with the investigation of members who stayed in occupied territory, with constant complaints that it was being carried out too slowly. Comrade Batina admitted at the conference that she had not heard explanations from the 60 communists, mostly old men, who remained behind in Leninskii district, adding that one-third of them had lost or destroyed their party cards.[53] A month after the conference, a gorkom protocol complained that the investigation was going very poorly, with only 23 percent of the cases settled. The slow process hampered the formation of primary party organizations.[54] An early report indicated that between March and October 1943 the gorkom examined the activity of 3,000 communists who stayed in occupied territory, excluding 1,000 of them from the party and allowing the remaining 2,000 to stay, some with and some without censure.[55] In late 1944 the gorkom protested to the Andreevskii district party apparatus that it was taking too long to confirm the loyalties of leading members of the nomenklatura, 12 of whom had been in occupied territory.[56] Iablokov, secretary of the Proletarskii raikom, noted that the check-up on members was being dragged out because some of the communists returning to Rostov-on-Don

---

[50] On the problem of the understaffing of party bureaus, see chap. 8.

[51] TsDNI f. 13, op. 4, d. 29, ll. 19–20.

[52] TsDNI f. 13, op. 4, d. 29, ll. 22–23. It is not clear why Dvinskii, the leading figure in the oblast party organization, was absent from the conference.

[53] TsDNI f. 13, op. 4, d. 29, l. 15. Comrade Demov explained that when he talked to the 59 communists in his district who remained behind, he would "need to ascertain why they did so and what they did during occupation."

[54] TsDNI f. 13, op. 4, d. 20, l. 75.

[55] TsDNI f. 13, op. 4, d. 44, l. 294. A decree from an October Conference declared that "in the near future it is necessary to conclude the check up on communists who stayed in occupied territory and purge the party of all unreliable, unstable, and 'hanging on' (opportunistic) elements." TsDNI f. 13, op. 4, d. 44, l. 11.

[56] TsDNI f. 13, op. 4, d. 101, l. 30. One of the 12 was the director of a school during German occupation and another had worked in a cafeteria. This source also noted that as of November 1944, 14 out of 16 leaders in the Oktiabr'skii district Housing Department stayed in occupied territory and 7 worked for the Germans, 2 in positions of leadership, l. 69.

had been in occupied territory elsewhere. Also, he complained that in many cases communists did not voluntarily register with party bureaus, forcing district secretaries to find them and get an explanation.[57] Those members were obviously not too eager to become involved in party affairs.

In addition to housing, party reports also focused on education as a field tainted by collaboration. A 1945 investigation concluded that 60 of 67 (89.5 percent) of Rostov's top education administrators stayed in occupied territory and 45 (75 percent) worked for the Nazis, which for the Soviet regime was an act of collaboration regardless of the circumstances.[58] The report cited several specific examples of collaborationists, including the regional inspector of schools, who hung portraits of Adolph Hitler in his office during occupation and distributed fascist literature. A historian at the Pedagogical Institute allegedly "destroyed Soviet literature, worked on religious questions for the Germans, and published disgusting articles in the vulgar German newspaper *Voice of Rostov*."[59] A number of people in education "who do not inspire political trust" were replaced, a separate report states.[60] However, treason among educators remained a prominent issue in 1948 when the gorkom released another report on the matter, finding that of the 2,087 teachers currently working in Rostov, 953 (46 percent) of them stayed in occupied territory, 237 of them (29 percent) worked for the Germans, and 68 of those (29 percent) occupied leadership positions. The report listed several examples of untrustworthy teachers still on the job, including one who allegedly told her students during occupation, "look at all the military machinery of the Germans — the Red Army will never return!" Another teacher admitted to covering posters of Stalin and Lenin with pictures of fascist leaders, and yet another wandered the streets of Rostov in rags during occupation "begging bread from the Germans like a hopeless tramp" and shouting in German, "Look at me — I am a Soviet teacher."[61] Despite all this, the report concluded, since 1943 only twelve teachers had been replaced, while many more suspect educators remained in their positions.[62] These accounts show the extent of the investigations against people under suspicion, reveal a fetish with categorizing and quantifying "collaboration," and acknowledge an implicit distinction between collaboration and collaboration*ism*.

---

[57] TsDNI, f. 13, op. 4, d. 39, l. 3. For other accounts of the slow process, see also TsDNI f. 13, op. 4, d. 29, l. 13; TsDNI f. 13, op. 4, d. 45, l. 78; TsDNI f. 13, op. 4, d. 53, l. 229.

[58] TsDNI f. 13, op. 4, d. 16, l. 27. It adds as well that 6 of the school administrators (1 percent) occupied leading roles in the department of fascist propaganda.

[59] TsDNI f. 13, op. 4, d. 44, l. 2.

[60] TsDNI f. 13, op. 4, d. 16, l. 27.

[61] TsDNI f. 13, op. 4, d. 430, ll. 8–9. It added that after liberation he went door to door begging for bread from his students. His "unclean outward appearance," moreover, "makes people sick and is a mockery of our education system."

[62] TsDNI f. 13, op. 4, d. 430, l. 15.

Reports on collaboration among the city's finance and trade organizations also exhibit a penchant for reducing this problem to decipherable categories and numbers. A gorkom protocol in July 1943 lamented that of 144 administrators in the city's departments of finance, 136 (94 percent) stayed under German rule, while 26 (19 percent) of them worked for the Germans. The former director of local trade, for example, was executive director of banking in Rostov during occupation, while the city's former chief accountant was in charge of setting prices for industrial goods under the Nazis. After occupation, furthermore, the leader of the City Financial Department failed to "clean out" his administrative apparatus of individuals "who do not inspire political trust."[63] Checkups on several food plants and trade organizations exposed people in positions of leadership who worked under German rule.[64] Other documents reported that the "overwhelming majority" of leading workers in the city's health clinics and pharmacies stayed during occupation and worked for the Germans, and that 12 of 26 people in positions of leadership in Andreevskii district's food and trade organizations did so as well.[65] In five large local organizations, an average of 42 percent of the employees stayed behind, although very few actually worked for the Germans (see table 5). One report lamented that the gorkom had previously "recommended the expulsion of such people but that the situation remains unchanged and they are still working there."[66] Several documents spelled out one reason it was so difficult to replace alleged collaborators: there was a lack of qualified personnel to take their positions.[67] Thus, a recurring theme in many party reports is frustration with not being able to replace people perceived as collaborators.

---

[63] TsDNI f. 13, op. 4, d. 44, l. 8. This report added that even the city's postmaster worked energetically for the Germans, and that the director of the dye-laundry factory worked in that capacity under the Germans, "demanding from the workers in the factory discipline and higher production."

[64] TsDNI f. 13, op. 4, d. 23, l. 45. At the Bread Factory 24 of 29 stayed and 2 worked in leading positions under German rule; at the Macaroni Factory 19 of 22 leaders stayed, 4 of whom did the same work during occupation; and at the food-processing plant *Smychka*, 22 of 26 stayed and four worked. For other examples of people in positions of leadership during occupation, see also TsDNI f. 13, op. 4, d. 45, l. 78; TsDNI f. 13, op. 4, d. 47, l. 4; TsDNI f. 13, op. 4, d. 101, l. 7.

[65] TsDNI f. 13, op. 4, d. 45, l. 60. The 12 in the Andreevskii district food organization who worked during occupation included Georgiev, who helped with bread distribution during German rule, Baitser who worked as a food inspector, and several others who managed cafeterias or otherwise assisted the enemy.

[66] TsDNI f. 13, op. 4, d. 46, l. 13.

[67] For reports on this problem, see ibid., d. 102, ll. 27–28; d. 45, l. 60; d. 46, l. 14; d. 47, l. 4; d. 55, ll. 69–70; d. 64, ll. 32, 58–59; d. 75, l. 38; d. 102, l. 14, 27–28; d. 171, ll. 3, 6; d. 176, ll. 2–3; and d. 330, l. 137.

Table 5. Numbers of Employees who Stayed in Occupied Territory
and Worked for the Germans During Occupation

Organization	Total # of Employees	# Who Stayed Behind	# Who Worked for the Germans
City Financial Dept.	144	136 (94%)	26 (19%)
Rostpishchtorg	474	134 (28%)	14 (3%)
Nakhpischtorg	567	152 (27%)	7 (1%)
City Trade Org.	311	201 (65%)	21 (7%)
City Ration Bureau	193	84 (44%)	11 (6%)
Total	1689	707 (42%)	79 (5%)

Sources: TsDNI, f. 13, op. 4, d. 22, l. 77; TsDNI, f. 13, op. 4, d. 23, l. 45; TsDNI, f. 13, op. 4, d. 44, l. 8. TsDNI, f. 13, op. 4, d. 221, l. 20.

Another reason for the slow replacement of "untrustworthy" figures was protectionism. Echoing the report from three years earlier, an investigation in early 1946 found that "the staffs of trade organizations are still far from cleaned of people who do not inspire political trust." The report complained that in Rostov's trade organizations, only 192 collaborators had been replaced. In just one trade organization, 201 of 311 (65 percent) employees were in occupied territory and 21 (7 percent) worked for the Germans.[68] Another report noted that, despite this situation, the city's stores and trade organizations removed 9 communists, 12 demobilized troops, and 2 wounded war veterans from their positions. Those in charge made decisions over who to keep and who to let go "not according to political qualities, but according to acquaintance and nepotism."[69] The director of the city's main trade organization was fired and excluded from the party because he held up the replacement of "untrustworthy" workers. A separate verification of Krupzavod in January 1946 showed that more than 20 employees worked during German rule, but that the plant leadership had not removed a single person, adding "the situation is the same in the remaining enterprises in the district."[70] At a party plenum in May 1946, Obkom First Secretary Aleksandriuk explained that many leaders

---

[68] TsDNI f. 13, op. 4, d. 309, ll. 17–18. The organization in question was *Rostproshtorg*. Others listed were *Rostpishchtorg*, where of 474 employees, 134 stayed in occupied territory, and 14 worked for the Germans; and *Nakhpischtorg*, where of 567 employees 152 stayed and 7 worked for the Germans.

[69] TsDNI f. 13, op. 4, d. 291, ll. 145–46. The report states that of 473 workers in the city's stores and trade organizations, 139 (29 percent) stayed in occupied territory.

[70] TsDNI f. 13, op. 4, d. 251, ll. 1–2.

did not want to replace "untrustworthy" staff because, he said, "it's easier to work with them, they are afraid and are thus very agreeable, quiet, and always trying to please their boss."[71] A year later the replacement of collaborators was still proceeding slowly, a gorkom protocol complained, "especially in several specific organizations."[72] Even the local police force was suspect; the gorkom concluded that, because of their actions during occupation, "many employees [of the city police] do not inspire political trust and are morally corrupt." It recommended that 100–200 police officers be replaced by "honest, capable employees."[73] There were several other such reports about various organizations, some of which specified that collaborators had finally been replaced and removed from the party.[74]

This material is filled with tough talk regarding collaboration; in the rhetoric of local leaders, one either defended the interests of the motherland or one did not—working for the Germans for the sake of survival or falling prisoner to them in the war were not justifiable excuses. Add to that the fact that *everyone* who stayed in occupied territory was suspect—including party members because they disobeyed orders to evacuate—and the result was discord in the local party apparatus between communists returning from evacuation or the front and those who remained behind. The former were in charge of Rostov's post-liberation party apparatus while the latter found themselves under investigation. In the official inquiries, most party members who were in occupied territory were cleared and only a few labeled "traitors," which shows again an acknowledgement of the distinction between collaboration and collaborationism. Yet some deemed by the regime to be collaborators who "did not inspire political trust"—a phrase peppered throughout these documents—remained in their positions as late as three years after victory— long after the regime ceased openly discussing this issue in the press—suggesting a degree of tolerance toward them in practice. This was due in part to the lack of qualified personnel, but also to protectionism or, as Aleksandriuk's comment suggests, the politics of *kompromat* ("compromising material")— wielding political power over someone through the control of negative

---

[71] TsDNI f. 13, op. 4, d. 214, l. 83. See also TsDNI f. 13, op. 4, d. d. 251, l. 2. That report noted that "in the party raikom there is an apprehension about replacing people," and gives the example of one factory, Krasnyi Don. There only 37 of over 1,000 workers were demobilized troops, only 16 of whom occupied leading positions. Twenty-four of them worked in the plant prior to the war, and only 11 of them were communists. For more reports on party leaders protecting those below them who stayed in occupied territory, see also TsDNI f. 13, op. 4, d. 221, ll. 222–23; TsDNI f. 13, op. 4, d. 291, ll. 187–88.

[72] TsDNI f. 13, op. 4, d. 230, l. 108.

[73] TsDNI f. 13, op. 4, d. 330, ll. 218–19.

[74] See, for example, TsDNI f. 13, op. 4, d. 221, l. 20; TsDNI f. 13, op. 4, d. 230, ll. 17 and 69; TsDNI f. 13, op. 4, d. 375, ll. 85 and 105.

information about them. Also, the party may have shown a degree of leniency because it did not want to look bad in the public's eye by exposing a high degree of collaboration among its ranks, and/or because local party leaders sympathized with the complexities of life under German occupation—they recognized the "moral gray zone" in some people's decisions and actions under very trying circumstances. Those who worked for the Germans and/or turned over their party cards were dealt with more harshly, but even they fared relatively well, especially compared to the repression of the late 1930s.[75]

Party leaders seemed obsessed with quantifying collaboration, keeping count of those in occupied territory who destroyed their party cards, registered with the Gestapo, or committed treason. At the February 1943 conference one speaker observed that in his district "there were instances when members of the party handed their party cards over to the Gestapo," while the party secretary of another district lamented that the majority of the 86 registered communists there had destroyed their party cards.[76] Comrade Sokolov reported "one case in which a communist turned out to be a traitor and went to work for the German police."[77] Several months later another district party bureau had registered 174 party members who stayed in occupied territory, keeping 118 of them (68 percent) in the party without penalty, censuring 42 (24 percent), and expelling 14 (8 percent). A report in late December gave the breakdown for the city for 1943: 2,200 members, nearly one-third of the local party apparatus, stayed in occupied territory, of whom 2,049 (93 percent) had already registered with district headquarters. Of these, the report informed, 356 (17 percent) were expelled by district bureaus.[78] At a gorkom plenum in April 1944, Comrade Iablokov updated the statistics, noting that a total of 2,213 communists stayed in occupied territory, of whom 428 (24 percent) had been expelled, adding, "it might be necessary to reconsider some cases as

---

[75] Kuromiya and Boterbloem show that while repression remained a prominent feature of Soviet political life in the postwar years, there was no return to the scale of repression witnessed in the late 1930s. See Kuromiya, *Freedom and Terror*, 299–300; and Boterbloem, *Life and Death under Stalin*, 153.

[76] TsDNI f. 13, op. 4, d. 29, l. 13. See also l. 12.

[77] TsDNI f. 13, op. 4, d. 29, l. 17. He further noted that the Germans shot 27 communists from their party organization, but did not connect these deaths to the traitor in their ranks. For a similar report on Stalinskii district, see TsDNI f. 13, op. 4, d. 29, l. 19. For a report on the City Department of Health, see TsDNI f. 13, op. 4, d. 29, l. 38. This report noted that an investigation of all workers was carried out and that "only separate individuals left with the Germans."

[78] Of the 2,200 who stayed in occupied territory, 233 (11 percent) registered with the Gestapo, 50 (2 percent) worked in various leading positions, 351 (16 percent) worked in non-leading roles, 23 (1 percent) were "unmasked" as fascists, and 16 voluntarily left with the Germans. Finally, 667 (30 percent) destroyed their party cards, 6 turned theirs into the Gestapo, and, the report noted, none of these communists took part in underground partisan activity. TsDNI f. 13, op. 4, d. 96, l. 68.

more information of their behavior during occupation becomes known."[79] A much higher percentage of cases heard later led to expulsion because they involved members who did not register with their party bureaus or who left with the Germans. For example, in October 1944, the gorkom heard the cases of 17 party members from one district who "voluntarily left with the Germans" and thus were not present at the hearings; all of them were excluded.[80]

The quantification of collaboration continued in October 1945, when the Central Committee assailed the Rostov obkom for poor work checking up on communists who stayed behind. For the oblast as a whole between May 1943 and September 1945, the report states, the obkom heard 11,429 cases, expelling 7,124 (62 percent), keeping 2,758 (24 percent) in the party without penalty, and censuring 1,500 (13 percent).[81] Thirty-seven percent (2,652) of the expulsions were for "betrayal of the motherland, active work on behalf of the Germans, improper behavior during occupation, etc.," 31 percent (2,224) for registering with the Gestapo, 20 percent (1,396) for failing to take measures to evacuate, and 12 percent (852) for "passiveness in the struggle against the enemy." At a micro level, a local report in January 1946 described a check-up on 26 enterprises and organizations in one district where "up to 200 people actively worked for the Germans."[82] The report noted that at the factory *Krasnyi Don* 21 people worked for the Nazis during occupation and continued to hold positions of leadership. A gorkom check-up on city and district ration-card bureaus cited the lack of the "necessary political qualities" among the staff as a major problem. Of the 193 employees of the city ration bureau, 84 (44 percent) stayed in occupied territory, and 11 (5 percent) of those worked for the Germans, including some people in top positions.[83] According to another report, even a district secretary from the Proletarskii raikom worked with enthusiasm for the Nazis, "producing up to three days' labor [in one day] for the Nazis." The secretary, moreover, was overheard saying that Soviet power had ended once and for all.[84]

Talk regarding collaboration was often tough, but party members exhibited a more tolerant attitude at times, acknowledging the "gray areas" between the extremes. At an April 1945 meeting of Rostov's teachers to exchange experiences in the study of Marxism-Leninism, one comrade defended

---

[79] TsDNI, f. 13, op. 4, d. 74, ll. 119–26.

[80] TsDNI f. 13, op. 4, d. 96, ll. 134–35.

[81] RGASPI f. 17, op. 122, d. 98, l. 90. The math does not add up, with 47 cases unaccounted for. Again the passage of time accounts for the higher expulsion rate because the worst cases were heard last.

[82] TsDNI f. 13, op. 4, d. 251, ll. 1–2. For reports at this time on Stalinskii and Kirovskii districts, see TsDNI f. 13, op. 4, d. 147, ll. 1, 16, 145.

[83] TsDNI f. 13, op. 4, d. 221, l. 20. For a similar report, see also TsDNI f. 13, op. 4, d. 47, l. 3.

[84] TsDNI f. 13, op. 4, d. 44, l. 83. For similar accounts and comments, see also l. 82.

those like herself who fell under German rule. "We all know," she began, "what war is, but people who were evacuated did not see the horrors that those comrades who stayed in occupied territory had to live through."[85] A report explaining the poor growth of the party cell in one factory stated, "there are good comrades that stayed in occupied territory," but, unfortunately, those people could not get the necessary recommendations and were hesitant to apply for party membership.[86] At a party plenum one speaker likewise noted that the poor growth of party cells was due to the large number of people who were under German rule. "I think," he said, "that not all those who remained in occupied territory worked for the Germans. Our task is to figure out which ones did and get rid of them."[87] Obkom Secretary Aleksandriuk, the highest figure in the Rostov oblast party hierarchy, expressed a tolerant view toward those that stayed but did not work for the Germans. Pointing out that millions of people were in occupied territory, Aleksandriuk stated, "we can't discount all of them, so we must determine how people behaved during German rule." Many of those who remained, he added, were women with small children, the wives of troops at the front. On the other hand, Aleksandriuk continued, the party should "kick out" those who worked for the Germans, drawing a very clear distinction.[88]

At the same time, however, local party leaders in Rostov often complained that *too much* tolerance was shown to those who stayed behind, sending a truly contradictory message. Occasionally, for example, party cells and district party organizations overlooked incriminating evidence when accepting new members. A central report on this problem cited the example of a worker at Krasnyi Aksai excluded by the Rostov gorkom for failing to evacuate, destroying her party card, and working for the Germans. The Rostov obkom, according to this account, reversed the decision "without any basis," keeping her in the party.[89] At the local level, a gorkom report blasted the Leninskii district branch for similar mistakes. A. Pecherskii, who had been a POW for two years during the war, and I. I. Zlatkov, an instructor "who actively worked for the Germans," were accidentally allowed into the party until the gorkom intervened.[90] In another case a district party organization belatedly discovered that a member "agitated against Soviet power" and had

---

[85] TsDNI f. 13, op. 4, d. 186, l. 10.

[86] TsDNI f. 13, op. 4, d. 181, l. 38.

[87] TsDNI f. 13, op. 4, d. 143, l. 77.

[88] TsDNI f. 13, op. 4, d. 214, ll. 82–83.

[89] RGASPI f. 17, op. 122, d. 98, l. 101. The report specified that she "had an opportunity to evacuate but did not take it," staying in occupied territory twice, and "did not fight the occupants."

[90] TsDNI f. 13, op. 4, d. 230, l. 42.

ties with the Germans during occupation.[91] A police officer in another district was arrested twice by the Germans and registered with them, and a member of the *Molot* party organization worked for the Germans as a typesetter. Both had been left in the party by their district organization, but the gorkom intervened and "corrected" these "mistakes" by expelling them.[92] The Stalinskii district likewise let three new members into the party who, it turned out, had worked for the Germans, a mistake noted in several other districts as well.[93] Lower-level party representatives walked a tight rope in trying to fulfill central decrees on party growth while being certain of the loyalties of new members.[94]

Finally, this material shows that behind closed doors some questions were raised among party leaders regarding Cossack loyalty, which is not surprising given the history of opposition to Soviet rule among Don Cossacks. The Germans formed a "Cossack Hundreds Brigade" in the lower Don region for Soviet citizens with pro-Nazi sentiments.[95] At the Conference in February 1943, a local party leader posed a revealing question to the representative of a rural district adjacent to Rostov: "were there any Cossacks in your district that served in the German Army?" "There were, and right now the appropriate organs are dealing with that."[96] In the concluding speech at the conference, Pastushenko said that after liberation he was in a Cossack village near Rostov where he found several party cards among captured German documents. He summoned the party members to whom they belonged and "every

---

[91] TsDNI f. 13, op. 4, d. 70, l. 185. The source claimed that while working as director of Training School No. 8 (FZO), Maletskii illegally gave his wife a position there as well. The gorkom excluded Maletskii for working in a factory under German rule and "behavior unworthy of a Soviet citizen." For a similar report about a separate case, see TsDNI f. 13, op. 4, d. 63, l. 137.

[92] TsDNI f. 13, op. 4, d. 45, l. 135. The report also listed Morozova from the party organization of the Bread Factory, who "hung out with German officers" during occupation. Oktiab'rskii district expelled three members for "actively working for the Germans," adding that three more had left voluntarily with Nazi troops. TsDNI f. 13, op. 4, d. 45, l. 5. For more reports on the investigation of party members in the fall and winter of 1943, see also TsDNI f. 13, op. 4, d . 39, l. 60; TsDNI f. 13, op. 4, d. 56, l. 64; TsDNI f. 13, op. 4, d. 63, l. 137.

[93] TsDNI f. 13, op. 4, d. 143, l. 187. See also TsDNI f. 13, op. 4, d. 29, l. 14; TsDNI f. 13, op. 4, d. 63, l. 192.

[94] I examine difficulties and problems in the party in chap. 8.

[95] Two Rostovians identified in one source, a father and son, reportedly served in the brigade and left with the Germans when Soviet troops advanced. TsDNI f. 13, op. 4, d. 145, l. 79. The Germans organized Soviet prisoners into battalion-sized combat units to fight against Stalin's forces, with as many as a million troops by 1943. Captured Soviet General Andrei Vlasov led the most famous battalion.

[96] TsDNI f. 13, op. 4, l. 36. The speaker added that he summoned the secretary of the German police to present the necessary lists.

single one of them lied, claiming they had destroyed their party cards."[97] Pastushenko's experience underlined party leaders' suspicion of Cossacks, who could not be trusted (or were even less trustworthy than the rest of the population). At a later party gathering an obkom secretary reported on traitorous activity in Novocherkassk, the former Cossack capital, noting that a group *within the party* "turned out to be simply traitors who gave other communists up to the Gestapo and eventually fled with the Nazis."[98] Also, more than 40 communist party cards were found in the Gestapo files when the Germans fled Novocherkassk, many more than were discovered in neighboring cities.[99]

Party reports and the minutes of closed party gatherings indicate a fetish to quantify collaboration, show that the party's investigations of collaboration centered on specific fields, and raise questions about Cossack loyalty. While the problem was certainly not limited to housing, trade and finance, and education, there is clearly disproportionate weight given to these areas in internal investigations. The reports do not explicitly state any reasons for this, but we can surmise a few. Housing, trade, and finance were beneficial positions to be in because of the control granted over money and items in scarce supply and high demand. People in these fields may have thought they would be in an advantageous situation to assure survival—even prosperity—under German rule.[100] The motivations for those in education who stayed and worked for the Germans are more difficult to ascertain. Perhaps some did so out of love for pedagogy, determined to teach no matter who was in power. Some probably taught or continued in their administrative capacity for the money and the increased chances for survival under trying circumstances, although the pay for teaching during occupation was probably not very high. No doubt some taught during occupation because they supported the Nazis' anti-Soviet and anti-Semitic views—"collaborationists" (as distinct from "collaborators")—though we cannot establish how widespread such sentiments were among So-

---

[97] TsDNI f. 13, op. 4, d. 29, l. 22.

[98] TsDNI f. 13, op. 4, d. 44, ll. 300–01. The report on Novocherkassk specifies that a party member there who turned out to be a German agent divulged strategic information about the party underground, leading to the execution of a number of partisans. It does not, however, name the figure, and thus there is no name to check against the *Molot* story "Traitors" described above. "There were many communists," the speaker elaborated, "who lost their heads and turned up at the German police or at the Gestapo and did everything they were ordered to do."

[99] TsDNI f. 13, op. 4, d. 44, l. 301.

[100] Later chapters show that those in trade and finance with access to goods and money were often involved in illegal trade before, during, and after the war and that housing was subject to corruption after the return of Soviet rule. On people vying for positions in trade and food organizations for the purpose of engaging in illegal trade, see Hessler, *Social History of Soviet Trade*, chap. 7; and Karol, *Solik*, 359.

viet educators.[101] These sources, furthermore, hint at a tendency among party leaders to question the loyalty of Cossacks, their suspicions based on a history of anti-Soviet sentiments in the lower Don region.

Popular Opinion on Collaboration

There is considerable overlap between the views expressed by the public and the material we have already examined. People who sacrificed a great deal during the war were sympathetic to the regime's negative portrayals of collaborators, but there are also subtle differences between the views found here and those in the previous sources. Taken together, this material reveals the ways workers and others in Soviet society perceived collaboration and the party's handling of it. For example, people in society at large realized that there were collaborators in positions of power and felt they were being dealt with too leniently, while at the same time many believed that the regime treated those who had been in occupied territory too harshly. They recognized, in other words, the "gray area" between the extremes, the nuances and complexities involved in explaining people's behavior (in some cases their own) under extremely difficult circumstances. In May 1945, a worker complained that several people who actively worked for the Germans currently held leadership positions in his factory. "Why haven't some measures been taken against them?" he asked.[102] "Several citizens who voluntarily left with the Germans are now returning," someone said at a separate meeting over a year later. "Will they stand trial as betrayers of the motherland?"[103] These queries show support for a harsh stance against collaborators, but question whether such policies are in fact being carried out, which mirrors the party's discussions behind closed doors.[104] Interviewees echoed the negative sen-

---

[101] Brown shows that in Ukraine members of the urban and rural intelligentsia were more likely than peasants to support the main Ukrainian nationalist organization (OUN) because, she suggests, "they had been trained to think in taxonomies, especially in the national taxonomies of both Soviet progressive reform and repression." As a result, she continues, members of the intelligentsia had been taught "to believe in the power of origins, to think that one's national affiliation mattered above all else." One might suggest a similar explanation for the apparently strong tendency toward collaboration among educators in Soviet Russia, although clearly the overtly anti-Semitic aspects of Nazi propaganda represent a complete rejection of the more progressive aspects of Soviet nationality rhetoric and policy from the prewar period (Brown, *Biography of No Place*, 215).

[102] RGASPI f. 17, op. 88, d. 426, l. 98.

[103] Ibid., l. 149. Elsewhere in the city a worker asked, "Why are betrayers of the motherland returning [from Germany] and why are they free, instead of in Siberia?" (ibid.).

[104] Mark Mazower notes that in Europe as a whole, "[i]n many countries tensions quickly emerged between the slow pace of official justice and popular expectations." He notes that this was especially true in Italy and France, and gives the following

timent toward perceived collaborators. Svetlana Semenova, aged 12 at the beginning of the war, stayed in Rostov with her mother, and she favorably compared her own family with neighbors that voluntarily left for Germany in 1942 and then returned after the war with lots of money. "How can one describe such people?" she asked, referring to them as "fascists."[105] Several respondents looked more favorably on the Germans than on Russians who helped them. Genadii Ermolenko, who participated in Rostov's partisan movement at the age of 13, said "the Germans did not touch us ... [but] *politsai* [Soviet citizens who worked for the German police] harassed us constantly and we hated them."[106] Karina Abramian, an Armenian, recalled going to the market one day during occupation to buy fruit for her young son. A Russian policeman began calling her a "Jew" in German (*jud*) and arrested her. However, when the German police commandant saw "Armenian" stamped on her passport he let her go and became angry with the Russian policeman.[107]

At the same time, archival sources and interviews point to concern over the party's perceived heavy-handed treatment of repatriated citizens. At a meeting in February 1946 someone queried, "Why does the government treat repatriated citizens so poorly?"[108] Later that year someone wanted to know, "why don't they accept repatriated citizens at institutes?"[109] These questions implicitly criticize the government's policies. People supported a harsh stance

---

breakdown for various countries: "In Norway, for example, the entire membership of the pro-Nazi Nasjonal Samling—some 55,000 people—was brought to trial. But few of these were sentenced to more than five years in jail. Only 25 death sentences were carried out and by 1957 the last life prisoner had been released. In the Netherlands, over 200,000 cases were investigated, resulting in some 40 death sentences actually carried out. Again, most prisoners were released by the early 1950s. Although French courts tried over 300,000 cases, and sentenced over 6,700 to death, the actual numbers executed or jailed were relatively low. A series of amnesties reduced the number in prison from 29,000 in 1946 to fewer than 1,000 in 1954" (*Dark Continent*, 231–32).

[105] Interview by author, 16 April 1995.

[106] Interview by author, 16 April 1995. "Fascism is fascism," Ermolenko added, "but I never witnessed any horrible acts by the Germans during occupation."

[107] Interview by author, 8 June 1995. She said the Commandant yelled at him "you don't capture those you need to capture, but you arrest those you do not need to." She also said that the man who arrested her was an acquaintance who for some unknown reason pretended not to know her.

[108] TsDNI f. 13, op.4, d. 259, l. 124.

[109] TsDNI f. 13, op. 4, d. 313, l. 18. Someone at a workers' club before a showing of *An Education of Feelings* (*Vospitanie chuvstv*), a war film among Stalin's favorites, said: "It would be more interesting to see how my comrades who stayed in occupied territory and were shipped off [to Siberia] are being treated there." The party representative writing this report noted that because the lights were out he was unable to identify the person making this statement. TsDNI f. 13, op.4, d. 393, l. 110.

against perceived collaborators but also recognized the prominence of the problem among party members and did not wholly agree with the regime's broad definition of "collaboration."[110] Interviewees often portrayed relatives, friends, and acquaintances as the victims of unjust treatment by the Soviet government. Svetlana Semenova's aunt, for example, was forcibly taken to Germany for slave labor during the war, and after being repatriated she had "problems" getting into Rostov State University, which Semenova considered unfair.[111] According to Oleg Pianiatsev, "Many paths were closed to those returning from German capture." His uncle was a POW, freed with the return of the Red Army to the lower Volga region but then arrested by the Soviet military and sent to serve in a penal battalion.[112] Genadii Ermolenko's family was forced to house two German officers during occupation, and he complained that the Soviet government treated them unfairly for this afterward, forcing them to move into a smaller apartment.[113] Svetlana Chernysheva returned to Rostov from evacuation in 1943 at the age of 16 and remembers that a lot of her classmates were in Rostov during occupation. She acknowledges that there was an "official" distinction between those who stayed and the evacuees, but she adds that "among the people" (*narod*) there was no difference.[114]

The unpublished memoir of S. I. Emel'ianenko, a Soviet pilot shot down in occupied territory and captured by Nazi forces, reveals official and popular views toward collaboration. His plane shot down in enemy territory, Emel'ianenko was captured in November 1942 by Rumanian troops. A party member since earlier that year (he "hid" his party document after being shot down but before being captured[115]), he was approached by a Moldavian prisoner,

---

[110] In one interesting account a teacher reported that "impressionable students" who saw the film *Ivan Groznyi*, Sergei Eisenstein's highly politicized film romanticizing the 16th-century tsar, were "too attracted to the character Kurbskii," portrayed as a traitor in the film. "They paid attention to his looks, his clothes, etc.," Iablokova stated, "and it was difficult to convince them that he was a betrayer of the motherland, a traitor." TsDNI f. 13, op. 4, d. 186, l. 14.

[111] Interview by author, 16 April 1995. Semenova also told about another aunt who purposely scraped her legs with salt and garlic to avoid being mobilized for work in Germany.

[112] Interview by author, 17 April 1995. Penal battalions had the toughest assignments at the front and, of course, a very high casualty rate. "It is a miracle he survived," Pianiatsev added.

[113] Interview by author, 16 April 1995. He remembered that their names were Kurt and Hans, and, showing that the war transcended borders in ideological terms, Ermolenko said that Kurt was a communist.

[114] Interview by author, 15 March 1995. "The majority," she said, "could not leave because of circumstances."

[115] Interview by author, 23 May 1995.

Shcherba, who found out he was in the party. The two conspired to escape; however, Shcherba was a provocateur and turned Emel'ianenko in, after which two Rumanian officers beat him badly with the butts of their rifles. Several weeks later, on Christmas day, he tried to sneak off from a marching column but was caught. Despite orders to execute those attempting escape, the soldier who caught Emel'ianenko shot above his head and let him go because he did not want to kill anyone on the holiday. "I remained alive," Emel'ianenko writes, "but in territory filled with occupying forces."[116] He once again set off for the front lines, asking for food and lodging from Soviet peasants along the way.[117] In January 1943 one woman in a Cossack village agreed to feed him. Her husband returned home and, to Emel'ianenko's dismay, he was wearing the armband of the *politsai*. The host demanded "with an authoritative tone" to see Emel'ianenko's documents, stating that he was obligated to turn him in. After a moment's silence Emel'ianenko responded, "It's too bad that we live in a time when we Russians have no mercy for one another." His host hesitated, then took out a bottle of moonshine (*samogon*) and two glasses, insisting that his guest drink with him.[118]

Like many people escaping captivity (about whom, as we have seen, there were public warnings), Emel'ianenko's fortunes did not greatly improve once he finally reached the Soviet side of the front lines in March 1943. He wanted to rejoin the Soviet forces immediately but was sent to Rostov-on-Don for medical treatment. In Rostov he reported as required of all escapees to the NKVD, where he was told that his "character" would be investigated. Not allowed back into the army, in April 1943 he was sent to work in a coal mine alongside German, Czech, and Hungarian prisoners of war in "camp-like" conditions. A loyal Soviet pilot, Emel'ianenko was distraught that his allegiance fell under question. "It was like a heavy weight crushed my soul," he recalls, "but there was nothing I could do about it." Expelled from the party, he met victory in the coal mine,[119] where he continued to work until 1948. After moving home to Rostov-on-Don he remained under suspicion, recalling in an interview that he was not allowed to work at Rostsel'mash or as a helicopter pilot because he had been a prisoner of war.[120] In his unpublished memoir, Emel'ianenko remembers Leonid Kononov, who shot himself rather

---

[116] S. I. Emel'ianenko, "Traditsionnyi vopros," unpublished memoir.

[117] He notes that people were afraid to help, however, because of "hired informers" and a strict German order that anyone abetting Soviet troops would be shot (unpublished memoir).

[118] They fed and lodged him, and the following morning the host even gave Emel'-ianenko a note so he could stay with a relative in the next village.

[119] Emel'ianenko informs that 11 German officers in captivity hanged themselves in the mine when they heard of the German surrender and Hitler's death.

[120] Interview by author, 23 May 1995. This despite, as we saw in chap. 3, a severe lack of labor at Rostsel'mash and constant efforts to mobilize workers for the plant.

than be taken prisoner, which is what the Soviet regime encouraged. But Emel'ianenko instead clung to life against difficult odds, traveling weeks in enemy territory with little food. In his recounting of events, his own actions stand in stark contrast to the real "traitors" he encountered, the implication being that the treatment he received from the Soviet government after the war was undeserved. He also paints a clear picture of the "moral gray zone" in the form of the *politsai* who helped him.[121]

Questions of Cossack loyalty arise in this and other such sources, just as in the internal party record. Ekaterina G. Karotskova grew up in a Cossack village (*stanitsa*) and was ten years old when German troops occupied it in 1942. She recalled in an interview how relieved she was to see that the Germans "did not have horns as I had expected, but rather were people just like us." Several Cossacks and others in the village who "had been so 'loyal' [*predannyi*] to the Soviets now became such 'loyal' *politsai* working for the Germans! These people," she opined, "were worse than the Germans themselves."[122] In her memoir, Elena Kozhina remembers strong support for the Germans among Cossacks in the village of Kuschevka, about eighty kilometers from Rostov.[123] At the age of eight she and her family escaped the siege of Leningrad in February 1942 on a train headed south. Her brother, sister, and grandmother all died of hunger along the way, leaving only Elena and her mother to take up residence in the hut of an old Cossack woman in Kuschevka. Kozhina's mother ardently supported the communist regime, as did her father, a Red Army soldier at the front, and she recalls that the Cossacks were very hostile to them. The village fell to the Germans in late July 1942 (three days after Rostov was occupied), and Kozhina and her mother were unable to escape. "The villagers," she recalls, "greeted the Germans with bread and salt," a traditional show of hospitality. They hated the collective farms Stalin imposed on them in the 1930s, and the Germans had dropped leaflets promising to get rid of them. The Cossacks hoped that the Germans

---

[121] Emel'ianenko was let back into the party and rehabilitated fully in 1957, and in recent decades his tale of bravery on the run from occupying forces has made him a local hero in Rostov.

[122] Interview by author, 5 March 1995. Karotskova said of the Germans, "Some of them were kind, some evil." Of the *politsai* she said they left with the Germans as Soviet forces advanced, but she heard that the Nazis shot them along the road, adding that in her opinion justice was thereby done. Dean reiterates that "for local inhabitants the collaborators whom they knew personally often generated more hatred than German officials they were unable to name," which, he adds, was "a familiar refrain encountered in trials of Belarusan collaborators, and especially among Jewish survivors" of the Holocaust ("Where Did All the Collaborators Go?" 793).

[123] As noted in chap. 4, Karol's account shows that Cossacks tended to be especially anti-Semitic, which explains in part why some were sympathetic to the Nazis (as well as the anti-Soviet views held by many, as illustrated by Valentina Bogdan and her father).

would return their land to them and grant them a degree of autonomy, as before 1917. Once Kozhina's mother was reading a newspaper in the presence of several Cossack women when she proclaimed, "They say we shot down eight aircraft." After an uneasy pause the Cossacks asked, "whom do you call 'we'—the Soviets or the Germans?" Her Cossack hostesses asked Kozhina's mother, "Why do you stand up for your damn Bolsheviks?... If you want to obey such people, go ahead, but we think differently. We remember our Cossack freedom!"[124] Such sentiments among the Don Cossacks directly contradict the press report that associated Cossack "freedom" with Soviet rule, while the prominence of anti-Soviet and pro-German sentiment among the villagers contrasts sharply with the proclamation of Cossack loyalty in the local press.

Kozhina's mother faced the same dilemma as many other party members in occupied territory—whether or not to register with the Nazi authorities. The Germans hung posters in Kuschevka stating that all residents had to report to the commandant's office with their passports in order to register. Noncompliance was punishable by death. After vacillating over what to do, Kozhina's mother went to register, returning with a German stamp on her passport. "How can we be worse off," her mother reasoned, "because of this ink stain?" The ink stain did, however, have a negative impact after the war: "because Mama's passport was stamped by the Germans, she [was] denied a Leningrad residence permit."[125] Kozhina depicts an interesting encounter between her mother and an official at "The Big House"—a building in Leningrad that housed the secret police—in the ensuing bureaucratic struggle to lay claim to their former apartment. "He held Mama's passport with two fingers and shook it with contempt.... 'A German commandant's stamp! A fascist stamp! And you, a Soviet citizen, permitted this to happen? In your Soviet passport? How?'" Her mother explained that not doing so was cause for execution, but the official accused her of "selling out" the Motherland. "Afraid to die, were you?" he asked. "One must fight to the death for the Motherland!"

---

[124] Kozhina, *Through the Burning Steppe*, 11. Karol's wife Klava recalls that the pre-Revolutionary Cossack Ataman Petr Krasnov, who had fled abroad at the end of the Civil War in 1921, came back to recruit a new Cossack White Army. "Yes, yes," she told Karol, "I also believed he had been dead for a long time, and yet, I swear to you, there he was parading in Novocherkassk, in Rostov and in the Kuban. At that time a lot of people, thinking that Stalin had lost the war, thought that they could achieve Cossack autonomy within the German Reich." He further notes that Klava spoke without hatred for the "foolish" Cossacks who hoped for autonomy, but for women who sided with the Germans, "whom she calls 'witless whores,' she has no pity" (*Solik*, 287).

[125] Kozhina, *Through the Burning Steppe*, 36–37.

They were eventually allowed to stay in Leningrad because Kozhina's father was in the Red Army, but her mother was never allowed to teach again.[126]

These sources reveal something about popular representations of collaboration during and after the war, including the nuanced and complex aspects of this issue emphasized by scholars. Popular attitudes toward collaboration differed in important ways from the party press and its closed discussions of the issue. People in society at large acknowledged the "gray zone" of behavior during occupation more readily than did the regime. Kozhina's mother, for instance, was a true believer in Soviet power, yet she fell under suspicion for allowing the Germans to stamp her passport rather than risk death. This account shows her action in a sympathetic light, of course, and she is portrayed as a victim of her interrogator's harsh inquiries. In addition, while we have seen that the party carried out a thorough check of members who stayed in occupied territory *without* airing this dirty laundry publicly, workers and others were nonetheless keenly aware that many party members collaborated with the Germans, and that—like everyone else (perhaps even more so)— party leaders constructed stories about their actions during the war. They perceived the problem of collaboration but associated it with the party itself, turning a critical eye back upon the leadership. Thus people internalized the party's public pronouncements on collaboration but found fault primarily with those in charge whom they saw as tainted by the problem. Interviewees reinforced this view by constructing a good vs. bad scenario, much like the party's public rhetoric, only in their versions the dichotomy is inverted, with the Soviet government in the wrong and unjustly suspected Soviet citizens in the role of victim. They also favorably compared German occupying forces with their Russian accomplices.

Finally, the interviews and memoir accounts are particularly telling with regard to attitudes among Cossacks of the lower Don region during the war. Not all Cossacks hated Jews or supported the Germans in the war; for instance, as noted in previous chapters, Valentina Bogdan's brother Alexander was a loyal Red Army soldier, while Karol's wife was not anti-Semitic and married someone who was part Jewish. Karol's father-in-law, although rabidly anti-Semitic, supported the Soviet side in the war. Yet the general picture of Cossack sentiments clearly contradicts the loyal image of them projected by

---

[126] Ibid., 39. She does not clarify her mother's fate within the party. "People who had lived in occupied territory," she notes, "forever lost their access to many careers— 'educating the rising new generations' chief among them" (41). This observation, as we have seen, does not correspond to the situation in Rostov where, as revealed in internal party reports, many teachers remained on the job after liberation. Leningrad, however, was a different story because it was closer to the center of power and it was never occupied. Also, many educators no doubt perished during the siege and had to be replaced anyway—someone who had been in occupied territory elsewhere like Kozhina's mother would have stood out there much more than in Rostov.

the local press. The Stalinist regime engaged in a propaganda struggle for the "hearts and minds" of the Don Cossacks—naming tank columns after them, for example—but this material suggests that many Cossacks remained hostile to Soviet power. On the other hand, the Nazis reneged on their promise to abolish the collective farms, and thus no doubt undermined their legitimacy among the Cossacks as well.[127] Nonetheless, the evidence presented here certainly supports the contention that there were strong anti-Soviet sentiments among the Don Cossacks. In light of this material, in fact, it seems likely that an unspoken assumption of Cossack *disloyalty*, which was "well known" according to Leder and widespread according to Kozhina, underscores the discussions of party leaders behind closed doors in which they raised questions about the Cossacks.[128] Party leaders shared a great deal of skepticism with society at large regarding the Cossacks' role during the war, while the local press inaccurately portrayed the Cossacks as a whole as "loyal, patriotic" Soviet citizens, presumably because they were not targeted for exile or repression and because the regime wanted to secure their support for the war and reconstruction efforts.

❧ ❧

The regime emphasized the threat posed by collaborators, publicly constructing an internal other, an archetypal "antihero," someone unwilling or too cowardly to risk their life for the country, thereby creating an atmosphere of suspicion that necessitated strong governmental measures and negated any hopes for an immediate postwar liberalization. The local press metaphorically depicted collaboration in gendered terms by associating it with feminine qualities and contrasting it with masculine heroism. Workers and others largely agreed with the negative portrayal of collaborators, but the evidence reveals a subtle divide in the perception and representation of this issue between party leaders and the population at large. Among themselves, local party leaders displayed an "us" and "them" mentality toward the population and, confirming their concerns, some people were critical. Also, while the party's tough public stance against collaborators appealed to many, popular perceptions of who should be handled harshly were based on the realization—supported by closed party documents but *not* openly admitted in the press—that some party members collaborated with the Germans. Thus the local party apparatus came under dual assault: people criticized it because "true" traitors, sometimes within the party leadership itself, were dealt with too softly while those perceived as innocent victims of Nazism were treated too severely. Based on the evidence presented here, there would have been

---

[127] On the Germans reneging on this promise, see Dallin, *German Rule in Russia*, chap. 15.

[128] I discuss Leder's recollections of anti-Semitism among the Cossacks above in chap. 4. For this specific point, see Leder, *My Life in Stalinist Russia*, 192.

popular support for the relaxation by Nikita Khrushchev in the mid-1950s of policies punishing repatriated citizens, POWs, and others unjustly repressed as collaborators. Also, the party's public assurances of the Cossacks' unquestioned loyalty contrasted with a widely-shared assumption of Cossack *disloyalty*, a discrepancy that reflected a history of anti-Bolshevism in the lower Don region. Finally, the creation of a treasonous "internal other" construct—the "freak" in the Soviet "family"—shifted hostility toward a common enemy that transcended the class divide in Soviet society between workers and the party elite, thereby obscuring that class divide. This is partially true also for another important "internal other" construct to be examined in the next chapter: "speculators."

Chapter Six

"People Without A Definite Occupation":
The Illegal Economy and "Speculation"

K. S. Karol remembers a thriving illegal market economy in Rostov during and after the war, recalling that the worst problem for him and his circle of friends was the "crash of the official economy." At the start of the war Karol condemned his landlady for trading on the black market, but by 1944, he says, "all of us had become her emulators with even more sophisticated rackets to help us get by."[1] *Speculation*, the buying and reselling of goods for profit, was a focal point of discussion at the top of the country's power structure as well as among the population at large. The language used to discuss the production and distribution of goods in any society carries considerable political weight; during the Cold War, economic activity was associated with "freedom," a relative term construed in different ways by the competing powers. In the West, the right to own property is a core principle of "democracy," with goods produced and distributed on the basis of a "free" market regulated by supply and demand, a system most Westerners see as superior. Theorists on the other side of the Cold War divide held to a different outlook, believing a centrally planned economy superior because it avoided the periodic crises of capitalism.[2] They described Soviet "socialism" in terms of the expanded economic rights and social equality stemming from "collective ownership" of "socialist property." In their view, such a system created the conditions necessary for the "free" development of each individual citizen.[3] As with the other issues examined here, however, theory did not mesh with

---

[1] Karol, *Solik*, 282.

[2] As American journalist Harry Schwartz observed, "Russian economists and political leaders are fond of claiming superiority for their own dictatorial organization on the ground that it avoids economic crises and depressions to which capitalist economies such as that of the United States are subject." Schwartz, *Russia's Postwar Economy* (New York: Syracuse University Press, 1947), 113.

[3] The Communist Party published a pamphlet in 1943 entitled "The Basic Rights and Obligations of Citizens in the USSR." It states that "Socialist Democracy creates the conditions for the maximum development of initiative and creative ability among the working masses in the struggle for a new socialist social structure." GARO f. R-3737, op. 8, d. 34a, l. 82.

practice. The official "planned" economy was in a state of crisis (at least) from July 1941, when rationing began, until it ended in December 1947, and a market economy flourished in the Soviet Union in the war and postwar period.

This chapter examines divergent perspectives on "speculation" between 1943 and 1948. Illegal economic activity was not unique to the Soviet Union; during World War II most countries, including the United States, rationed goods and/or placed restrictions on sales and prices, and all of them faced problems with forbidden trade. Black market deals were common whenever and wherever demand and the means of payment exceeded the supply of something. In the United States black-market transactions were carried on extensively in meat, sugar, tires, and gasoline.[4] In Britain, meat and dairy products, clothing, liquor, and many other items were rationed and became popular black-market commodities.[5] In occupied Belgium (1940–44), the illegal economy "expanded day by day," economist Raoul Miry recalled just two years after the war, due to the "effective consent of all citizens." Illegal trade thrived on the margins of an inadequate and tightly controlled rationing system, while those involved risked harsh penalties, including hard labor in Germany.[6] Also, as we have seen, because of the devastation wrought by the war in much of Europe, rationing—and along with it illegal market activity—continued in most countries for years after the war. Workers in Poland stole goods from their factories to sell on the illegal market, thereby supplementing their meager wages, while "other workers produced goods for black market sale during work or used machines after work for this purpose." Workers had to take part in the illegal economy to survive, while the Polish Workers' Party manipulated the issue to its advantage by scapegoating speculators, "who were both easily recognizable to workers and a convenient target for the state."[7] In Japan, too, by the end of the war goods were disappearing from stores except for rationed food items, and many people turned to the black market to survive despite the threat of severe penalties.[8]

---

[4] See Marshall B. Clinard, *The Black Market: A Study of White Collar Crime* (Montclair, NJ: Patterson Smith, 1969).

[5] See Angus Calder, *The People's War: Britain 1939–1945* (New York: Pantheon Books, 1969); Zweiniger-Bargielowska, *Austerity in Britain*.

[6] Raoul Miry, "The Black Market," in *Belgium Under Occupation*, ed. Jan-Albert Goris (New York: Moretus Press, 1947), 65–66. He lists items for sale on the black market in occupied Belgium as clothing, kitchen utensils, flashlights, letter paper, mustard seeds, cigarettes, coffins, turnips, iodine, and, of course, all sorts of foodstuffs (66).

[7] Kenney, *Rebuilding Poland*, 87, 91–92 and 191–92. Kenney adds that, for the postwar period, "What workers could afford (on ration cards) was not always available, but what was available (on the free market) they could not afford" (90). On the prominence of the black market in Poland during the war and German occupation, see Friedrich, "Collaboration," 723.

[8] Dower, *Embracing Defeat*, 97–102 and 139–48.

The Soviet Union, of course, experienced this phenomenon in its own ideological, historical, and cultural context. After NEP an informal economy of
small-scale manufacture and trade remained, becoming "nearly universal
during World War II."[9] Small private businesses sprang up after the war,
many of them shielded by "cooperatives," while legal collective farm markets
provided a cover for illegal transactions.[10] The police largely tolerated "speculation," Julie Hessler maintains, because it was a means of survival for people
during the war and because small-scale trade was so widespread that arrests
were impractical, leading to a "survivalist consensus."[11] Because prices were
high at the wartime bazaar, ordinary citizens either had to sell possessions or
barter items in exchange for food. Hessler cites interviews to show "informal
trade as a universal occupation" during the war. At the end of the war, increasingly profitable entrepreneurial ventures arose, leading some officials to
argue for legalization (a postwar NEP) and taxation. The regime, however,
followed a restrictive course; concern over illegal enterprise grew in the
months prior to the aforementioned 1948 crackdown.[12] The second economy
continued and thrived again during the L. I. Brezhnev years (1964–82); economists studying the period highlight the illegal economy's systemic roots,
citing the "planned shortages," low state prices, and inefficient distribution
system of the Soviet economy.[13] Shortages *necessitated* illegal trade, but "those

---

[9] I agree with Julie Hessler that, "legal or illegal, the history of private enterprise must
count among the biggest gaps in Soviet history today." She documents that Soviet citizens spent between one-third and one-half of their incomes on the legal free market in
all but a few years of Stalin's rule. Hessler, "A Postwar Perestroika: Toward a History
of Private Enterprise in the USSR," *Slavic Review* 57: 3 (1998): 516–17. For the prominence of the black market economy during the occupation of Minsk, see Uwe Gartenschläger, "Living and Surviving in Occupied Minsk," in *The People's War: Responses to
World War II in the Soviet Union*, ed. Robert W. Thurston and Bernd Bonwetsch
(Urbana: University of Illinois Press, 2000), 18.

[10] Fitzpatrick shows this for the 1930s also (*Everyday Stalinism*, 60–62).

[11] Hessler, *Social History of Soviet Trade*, chap. 6.

[12] Hessler states that the main topic of Stalin's "special files" (*osobaia papka*) in 1947–48
was violations in trade, speculation, and other economic crimes. "Ultimately," she indicates, "the response was to clamp down on the private economy — to reestablish, and
in one respect to constrict still further, the bounds of toleration formulated in the period following NEP" (*Social History of Soviet Trade*, chap. 7). She notes as well that after
1949 illegal market activity tailed off to near what it had been prior to the war.

[13] James R. Millar, *The Soviet Economic Experiment*, ed. Susan J. Linz (Urbana: University of Illinois Press, 1990), 199–215; Vladimir Treml and Michael Alexeev, "The
Growth of the Second Economy in the Soviet Union and Its Impact on the System," in
The Postcommunist Economic Transformation: Essays in Honor of Gregory Grossman, ed.
Robert W. Campbell (Boulder, CO: Westview Press, 1994), 221–48. Treml and Alexeev
suggest that the Soviet Union's official and unofficial economies "developed a certain
modus vivendi allowing them to coexist without overt conflict or even to support and

in power" then blamed "speculators" for *creating* shortages. People found large-scale speculation to be "immoral and reprehensible," but other types of illegal economic activity "acceptable," such as purchasing goods on the black market, moonlighting as part-time vendors, giving bribes, or "tipping" state service sector personnel for better service.[14]

The USSR had a long history of "speculation," which emerged during War Communism and existed in one form or another throughout the Soviet period.[15] Lenin's New Economic Policy in the 1920s widened the bounds of legal economic activity considerably, thereby diminishing the realm of illegal economic activity. Even after the Stalin Revolution of 1928–33, legal limits remained wide, though there was a progressive restriction of trade in the 1930s.[16] A "shadow" market economy thrived between 1943 and 1948 as an important part of an overall survival strategy for people at a very trying time.[17] Access to scarce goods and materials, which included almost everything, was crucial to the illegal economy, and people in positions of responsibility were linked to a private realm of production and distribution. Highly mobile and usually better supplied than state stores, the illegal economy benefited from payoffs and bureaucratic "oversight." Corrupt party officials and others diverted goods from the official state economy to the illegal market, which contributed to the acute shortages of many items in state stores, which in turn further fueled illegal economic activity.[18] The market especially

---

complement each other." They sum up the systemic roots of the second economy thusly: "The Soviet-type economy probably could not survive for any significant period of time without some second-economy activities greasing its wheels" (238). Joseph Berliner observed that the official Stalinist economy could not have functioned without the second economy because factory managers depended on the market to procure supplies for production, employing numerous "pushers" or procurement agents to obtain the necessary goods. Berliner, *Factory and Manager in the Soviet Union* (Cambridge, MA: Harvard University Press, 1957). On the government's planned shortages and the systemic roots of the illegal economy, see also Schwartz, *Russia's Postwar Economy*, 111.

[14] Treml and Alexeev, "Growth of the Second Economy," 223. These authors also point out strong regional variations in second-economy activity, with southern Russia the most active part of the Republic.

[15] On the history of the market economy in the Soviet Union until Stalin's death, see Hessler, *Social History of Soviet Trade*.

[16] See Hessler, "Postwar Perestroika," 516–42.

[17] On survival strategies during occupation and war, see Gartenschläger, "Living and Surviving in Occupied Minsk"; and Richard Bidlack, "Survival Strategies in Leningrad during the First Year of the Soviet-German War," in Thurston and Bonwetsch, *People's War*.

[18] As Sheila Fitzpatrick notes for the 1930s, "Goods leaked out of every state production and distribution unit at every stage from the factory assembly line to the rural cooperative store" (*Everyday Stalinism*, 59).

flourished and assumed widespread proportions during crises like the war and the postwar famine. Second-economy involvement varied among households, so while some enjoyed the higher incomes that came with illegal trade, others lacked that income and were further penalized by having to pay higher black market prices for at least some goods.[19]

The Soviet regime instituted a number of policies to strengthen the official economy vis-à-vis speculation, though, as we will see, they were often poorly implemented and did not always have the desired results. Ideally, goods were supposed to be distributed and services rendered through state-owned stores and shops, with uniform prices fixed for everything. Ration cards, a crucial part of anyone's survival strategy, became another form of currency for exchange.[20] Also, cooperatives had considerable autonomy in the production and distribution of goods. In the summer of 1944, "commercial stores" opened in a number of cities, including Rostov, in an attempt by the government to compete with the market economy and slow down inflation. Goods were sold without restrictions but at prices unaffordable to most workers at official wages.[21] Many people had a second income of some sort, participating out of necessity in the illegal economy as vendors, consumers, or both. Most "speculation" occurred in the open at the city's markets (bazari), where farmers (kolkhozniki) and others could sell goods without restrictions.[22] After years of relative leniency toward market activity, at the end of this five-year period the regime moved toward stifling commerce. In December 1947, it ended rationing and implemented a monetary reform intended in part to hurt speculators. Stalin himself, according to A. G. Zverev, finance minister at the time, drew up the reform amid great secrecy, sending out detailed instructions to regional party leaders stamped "Open only when instructed." But, as Zverev puts it, "the curiosity of certain local party functionaries overcame their official obligations, and the secret was revealed quite early."[23] In April 1948, the

---

[19] See Treml and Alexeev, "Growth of the Second Economy," 228.

[20] A number of people interviewed described ration cards as their link to survival at uncertain times. In his autobiography of life in Rostov K. S. Karol states, "[F]ood-ration cards represent a kind of supplementary currency that one uses at will" (Solik, 94).

[21] Prices in commercial stores were initially set at anywhere from 23 (for meat) to 136 times (for sugar) the prices on rationed goods (Kravis and Mintzes, "Trends in Prices," 34). On high prices in commercial stores in Rostov, see Karol, Solik, 325.

[22] For the 1930s Fitzpatrick states that "the most important of all sites of speculation was the kolhoz market" (Everyday Stalinism, 61).

[23] A. G. Zverev, Zapiski ministra (Moscow: Politizdat, 1973), 233, 235. The measure merged commercial stores with regular state stores. As we will see, the premature release of the information had major implications for the realization of the reforms.

government greatly restricted market activity and replaced top tax administrators who had lobbied for legalizing and taxing the "illegal economy."[24]

Also, as we noted in chapter 2, real wages were very low during and after the war, and hopes for postwar economic improvements were postponed by the famine, during which the government raised prices on rationed goods and decreased rations for dependents. Rationing, which began in July 1941, continued until December 1947, its cessation accompanied by a monetary reform. In early 1948, a number of Soviet cities, including Rostov, experienced bread shortages, revitalizing the black market just prior to a government crackdown against it. In examining illegal economic activity in the Soviet Union, I am not suggesting that a "superior" market economy would have somehow saved Soviet citizens from the travails of hunger and poverty during and after the war.[25] My purpose is not to judge Soviet policy, but to examine its implementation and show how people perceived economic forces during this difficult time. Of course, the difference between legal and illegal economic activity is always partly a linguistic matter, a juridical line that often blurs in practice, and such activity in the Soviet Union is complex and difficult to pin down by its very nature.[26] People at the time summed it up in one word, "speculation" (*spekuliatsiia*), the historical and cultural meanings of which interest me here.[27] This term demarcated the line between legal commerce and illegal economic activity resulting from the state's inability to satisfy consumers' needs, and I examine official and popular views of speculation in this crucial five-year period of "reconstruction."

---

[24] See Hessler, "Postwar Perestroika," 541.

[25] This, like most other modern famines, was what Amartya Sen describes as an "entitlement famine" in that it was avoidable and rooted in the inefficient and unequal distribution of food. Sen argues that all modern famines are profoundly "unnatural" and political in nature because enough food exists in even the most dire situations to feed everyone, but elites, who have high entitlements, make crucial decisions—not releasing emergency supplies, exporting grain, refusing charity, hoarding food for the market, etc.—that adversely (and often fatally) affect those with low entitlements. Sen, *Poverty and Famines: An Essay on Entitlement and Deprivation* (Oxford: Clarendon Press, 1981).

[26] This can be seen from the varied titles used to describe it: "second economy," "shadow economy," "underground economy," "black market," etc.

[27] Economist Gregory Grossman's definition of the Soviet Union's second economy captures the essence of "speculation": "all production and exchange activity that fulfills at least *one* of the two following tests: (a) being directly for private gain; (b) being in some significant respect in knowing contravention of existing law." This definition allows for change, which the laws regarding production and exchange often did. Grossman, "The Second Economy of the USSR," *Problems of Communism* 26: 5 (1987): 25–40.

"Speculation" in the Party Press

The party's public record portrays rampant speculation throughout this five-year period. Reports in *Molot* indicated that countless items could be obtained at "speculative prices," including ration cards, bread and food items, water, soap, candy, cigarettes, spirits, matches, lighters, kerosene, firewood, coal, building supplies, glass, fabric, linen, clothing, dye, movie and theater tickets, train tickets, spare tractor parts, textbooks, paper, and notebooks.[28] In a 1943 editorial, an official of the oblast judicial system notes that "speculation of bread and grain flourishes at the city's central market absolutely unpunished. The police," he adds, "carry out an insufficient struggle against speculation."[29] In 1945 the paper reported on private bread kiosks operating in the city "which only profit speculators."[30] The following year an article lamented that one could not even attend a movie because of speculators. The author went to the theater "Victory" to see a film, but the cashier announced there were no more tickets. He returned for an evening showing, but again all the tickets were sold. It was only when a "twiggish teenager" offered to sell him tickets that the author understood the root of the problem. "Around the theater," he writes, "you see the same faces every day—full-time speculators of tickets. It would be interesting to know," he continued, "how these tickets fall into the hands of speculators and why the police do not take notice of this outrage."[31]

The newspaper also reported examples of corruption that made rampant speculation possible.[32] As part of its coverage of crime, *Molot* announced the arrests of speculators and corrupt officials on its last page; after citing the name(s) of those involved and describing their operations, often in detail, the reports included the sentences meted out. For example, two announcements in 1943 described the activity of a group of "thieves and pilferers" at Krup-

---

[28] *Molot*, 8 March 1943, p. 4; *Molot*, 26 December 1943, p. 4; *Molot*, 1 August 1945, p. 4; *Molot*, 19 October 1945, p. 4; *Molot*, 3 January 1946; *Molot*, 4 October 1946, p. 4; *Molot*, 10 February 1948, p. 4; *Molot*, 18 April 1947, p. 4; *Molot*, 16 May 1947, p. 4; *Molot*, 3 January 1946, p. 4; *Molot*, 12 April 1947, p. 4. *Molot*, 19 December 1947, p. 4; *Molot*, 27 January 1948, p. 4; *Molot*, 10 February 1948, p. 4; *Molot*, 13 February 1948, p. 4; *Molot*, 29 February 1948, p. 4; *Molot*, 20 March 1948, p. 4; and *Molot*, 21 April 1948, p. 4.

[29] *Molot*, 26 December 1943, p. 4.

[30] *Molot*, 7 February 1945, p. 4. The report includes a poem: "An unpleasant rumor has reached us / And we will tell it loudly / A number of private kiosks have appeared / We don't know who's exploiting such dark talents / Which only profit speculators."

[31] *Molot*, "U kassy kinoteatra," 3 January 1946, p. 4.

[32] Regarding speculation in the 1930s, Fitzpatrick states, "Big-time operators often had 'connections' with store managers or warehouse personnel (or were themselves store managers) and systematically collected goods at the back door" (*Everyday Stalinism*, 60). Chapter 8 concentrates on party corruption separate from speculation.

zavod No. 1, which processed grains into cereal for the Soviet army. At the head of the "villainous group" was the director of the factory himself, the "scoundrel" Katsiiaev, allegedly a professional criminal who assumed a false identity after liberation and worked his way into the party—thus he was not a "real" party member. He oversaw the theft of grain with fictitious order forms and sold it through two speculators. The entire leadership of the factory was involved (in all, five persons), and the article adds that they "gave bribes left and right," though it does not report who received those payoffs. The court sentenced Katsiiaev to death, while his associates received ten-year terms.[33] The director of a Machine Tractor Station in Rostov oblast pilfered grain from nearby farmers, turned it into flour with the assistance of a guard at the Macaroni Factory, and then traded the flour for gas and oil in a small town near Rostov.[34] In a particularly tasteless affair, the manager of Store No. 22, two assistant managers, and three employees systematically soaked fresh bread in water so it would weigh more, then peddled it at the market.[35] A group of railroad employees at the Nakhichivan-Don Station "agreed among themselves" on the theft of six sacks of barley and sugar, which they then sold at the bazaar through two speculators.[36] There were many examples of people in positions of power involved in speculation.[37]

Reports in the media paint at least a partial picture of how the illegal market operated. Accounts in *Molot* assailed speculators for buying up goods in state stores and shipping them out of town, which, as we will see, was an important part of the process.[38] One woman "traveled all over town" to buy up fabric, which she and a cohort sold in a nearby village, and another speculator admitted that for years he went to various cities with a partner, bought up goods, then resold them for a profit in Rostov.[39] A railroad inspector "made a deal" with a kolkhoznik to transport potatoes to a speculator in Rostov.[40] An article in September 1947 exposed major "problems" at the main train station. The author noted that at one train car "a man approached the conductor and, instead of a ticket, slid a small packet into his hand." The man had given the conductor a bribe, for which both were arrested. The passenger was

---

[33] *Molot*, 28 August 1943, p. 4; and 6 October 1943, p. 4.

[34] *Molot*, 26 November 1943, p. 4.

[35] *Molot*, 16 March 1947, p. 4. See also *Molot*, 19 December 1947, p. 4.

[36] *Molot*, 16 April 1944, p. 4.

[37] See, for example, *Molot*, 26 December 1943, p. 4; *Molot*, 2 April 1944, p. 4; *Molot*, 19 July 1944, p. 4; *Molot*, 29 September 1946, p. 4; *Molot*, 11 October 1946, p. 4; *Molot*, 4 February 1947, p. 4; *Molot*, 6 June 1947, p. 4.

[38] See for example *Molot*, 26 December 1943, p. 4; *Molot*, 18 January 1947, p. 4; *Molot*, 19 December 1947, p. 4; *Molot*, 13 February 1948, p. 4; *Molot*, 29 February 1948, p. 4; *Molot*, 20 March 1948, p. 4; *Molot*, 21 April 1948, p. 4.

[39] *Molot*, 18 April 1947, p. 4; *Molot*, 16 May 1947, p. 4.

[40] *Molot*, 2 February 1947, p. 4.

sentenced to five years, the conductor to two years. It turns out the station was a nest of corruption, with a number of railway employees taking "large bribes from speculators to set aside train tickets for them." The director was removed from his position and given a five-year correctional labor term for "negligence."[41] Meanwhile, in an apparent follow up on speculation at the "Victory" movie theater, *Molot* announced the arrest of a woman in charge of ticket distribution because she was "in cahoots" with speculators. She received a seven-year sentence.[42] Despite repeated calls to "strengthen the struggle against speculation," it continued to be a major problem after the end of rationing and monetary reform in December 1947.[43] *Molot* presents these random cases as moral narratives, passing harsh judgment on those involved while conveying the sense that those participating in speculation on a *full-time basis* are, like collaborators, isolated individuals—in contrast to those engaging in petty or part-time illegal trade. The draconian sentences handed down to full-time speculators, moreover, seem intended to send a strong warning.

Local reports further enlighten us on the second economy's modes of operation, while the announcement of the monetary reform and the end of rationing revealed the regime's public stance on "speculation." These accounts often identify "speculators" as "housewives,"[44] or youth,[45] and *Molot* also describes workplace pilfering as one of the means by which goods were diverted to the illegal market. Several employees at a paper factory, for ex-

---

[41] *Molot,* 17 September 1947, p. 4. For another article on railroad employees taking bribes, see also *Molot,* 30 June 1946, p. 4.

[42] This was in two reports: "Spekuliantka biletami," *Molot,* 11 March 1947, p. 4; and "Proisshedshii," *Molot,* 12 April 1947, p. 4. For other stories of highly placed people conspiring with others in the illegal economy, see also *Molot,* 26 November 1943, p. 4; *Molot,* 26 December 1943, p. 4; *Molot,* 2 April 1944, p. 4; *Molot,* 16 April 1944, p. 4; *Molot,* 19 July 1944, p. 4; *Molot,* 13 November 1945, p. 4; *Molot,* 9 January 1946, p. 3; *Molot,* 29 September 1946, p. 4; *Molot,* 4 October 1946, p. 4; *Molot,* 11 October 1946, p. 4; *Molot,* 18 January 1947, p. 4; *Molot,* 4 February 1947, p. 4; *Molot,* 6 June 1947, p. 4.

[43] See *Molot,* 19 December 1947, p. 4; *Molot,* 27 January 1948, p. 4; *Molot,* 10 February 1948, p. 4; *Molot,* 13 February 1948, p. 4; *Molot,* 29 February 1948, p. 4; *Molot,* 20 March 1948, p. 4; and *Molot,* 21 April 1948, p. 4.

[44] See, for example, *Molot,* 26 December 1943, p. 4; *Molot,* 19 October 1945, p. 4; *Molot,* 9 January 1946, p. 4; *Molot,* 29 September 1946, p. 4; *Molot,* 18 January 1947, p. 4; *Molot,* 9 February 1947, p. 4; *Molot,* 11 March 1947, p. 4; *Molot,* 18 April 1947, p. 4; *Molot,* 19 December 1947, p. 4; *Molot,* 3 March 1948, p. 4; *Molot,* 21 April 1948, p. 4; *Molot,* 28 April 1948, p. 4.

[45] See, for example, *Molot,* 7 December 1943, p. 2; *Molot,* 3 January 1946, p. 4; *Molot,* 14 May 1948, p. 3. In May 1944, the executive committee of the Rostov city soviet passed a decree banning "underage trade" near movie houses, theaters, on the street, at the central marketplace, and in other public areas. *Molot,* 31 May 1944, p. 4.

ample, stole notebooks and sold them at the market.[46] Speculators even infiltrated barbershops, according to *Molot*, which announced that many barbers charged "arbitrary prices," including one who took 20 rubles for a shave. "How did he reach such a sum," the author wonders, "when the official price is five rubles and all barbershops are obligated to charge it?" The head of the trust overseeing such services, the article adds in conclusion, seemed "indifferent" to these many flaws.[47] Meanwhile, *Pravda* announced the monetary reform and the end of rationing on December 15, 1947, explaining these measures as a means to curb inflation and undermine speculators while proclaiming that they would lead to a dramatic rise in living standards.[48] For those with lots of cash on hand, one ruble of the new denominations was exchanged for ten rubles of old money (wage rates stayed the same), while savings accounts up to 3,000 rubles were exchanged on a one-to-one basis.[49] Money contributed by the population in government bond drives, meanwhile, was exchanged on a three-to-one basis.[50] Monetary reforms, the decree elucidates, were common in countries after a major war, but whereas workers bore the brunt of such reforms in capitalist countries, "in the USSR the liquidation of the consequences of war and the monetary reform will not be carried out on the backs of the people." The reform, however, required "sacrifice" by the population, the announcement admitted, because all segments of society will lose in the ten-to-one exchange of cash on hand, but the rate hits speculators hardest, is for the common good, and "will be the last sacrifice" the population must endure.[51]

---

[46] *Molot*, 27 January 1948, p. 4. For more on workplace pilfering, see *Molot*, 13 November 1945, p. 4.

[47] V. Zarin, "Ha gorodskie temy," *Molot*, 16 April 1943, p. 2.

[48] *Pravda*, 15 December 1947, p. 1. The measure maintained wages at their current level and lowered the price of bread, groats, macaroni, and flour relative to their rationed prices; it maintained rationed prices for meat, fish, fat, sugar, salt, baked goods, potatoes and other vegetables, while establishing the prices for dairy products, fruit, and most manufactured goods somewhere between their rationed and commercial prices. The decree set the prices for basic food items as follows: rye bread 3 rubles per kilogram; wheat bread 4.40 rubles per kilogram; butter 64 rubles per kilogram; meat 30 rubles per kilogram; sugar 15 rubles per kilogram; milk 3–4 rubles a liter; and eggs 12–16 rubles for ten (Schwarz, *Labor in the Soviet Union*, 225).

[49] Anything over 3,000 up to 10,000 was exchanged on a three-to-two basis, and the exchange rate for sums over 10,000 was two-to-one.

[50] This was a significant loss to a population that was, as we saw in chap. 3, sometimes pressured to contribute.

[51] Although the announcement did not mention the peasantry, many peasants also had huge hoards of cash and few if any had savings accounts, so they too were no doubt targeted by and were definitely hurt by the terms of exchange. On this point, see Filtzer, *Soviet Workers and Late Stalinism*, 77–78.

A press campaign in 1948 assailing those "few people without a definite occupation" coincided with the regime's clampdown on the market and "speculators." A mid-May editorial constructed a moral narrative, contrasting the "tremendous love of labor," "mass heroism," and "exceptional labor achievements" of millions of "Soviet patriots" with the "anti-social, parasitic life style" of a "very few." "Work," the author opined, is "socially useful, productive activity," the party having transformed labor into "a source of inspirational creativity, honor, and glory."[52] Speculators shun "work" and "live off the labor of others," their attitudes exhibiting "traces of capitalist consciousness carried over from the distant, accursed past into our bright, heroic epoch." The author cites several examples, including a man "with sly, cowardly eyes" that, unknown to neighbors and friends, sold goods illegally for many years. One woman involved in speculation was lured to it by "dark personalities" at "dances and parties," and another quit her job at the Mikoyan Shoe Factory and began associating "with the wrong crowd." Warning that such people "live side by side with us," the editorial called on Soviet citizens to monitor their neighbors, just as it had with regard to collaboration. "The Soviet family," it noted, cannot tolerate "the slightest stain on the moral purity of our socialist society."[53] A follow-up editorial two weeks later asserted that the first piece struck a chord with Soviet citizens, who were concerned about "the few individuals leading parasitic lives in our labor-loving family."[54] Citizens, according to this piece, wrote countless letters to *Molot* exposing speculators. An excerpt from one declared, "We should condemn loafers who live off the government and people," adding "the police should struggle with speculation more energetically" — the words of officialdom in the letters of the "masses." Another letter writer fingered his neighbor as an example of a "lowly speculator" because he "does nothing but travel around with his wife all day and carry out trade." The flood of letters, the author concluded, "indicates the high level of patriotism and consciousness of the Soviet people, who put the interests of their dear Motherland above all else."

Designed to generate public support for the party's course, the press shows that the illegal economy was very prominent, linking it explicitly to

---

[52] *Molot*, 14 May 1948, p. 3. "The party," the piece continued, "has forever banished unemployment, uncertainty in the future, and hunger." By contrast, several pieces described speculation as a selfish, immoral act contrary to the common good, the antithesis of "socialist labor." See, for example, *Molot*, 9 January 1946, p. 3; *Molot*, 4 October 1946, p. 4; *Molot*, 14 May 1948, p. 3. In this rhetorical construction people engaged full-time in the black market were officially "unemployed" even as their illicit businesses were often booming.

[53] *Molot*, "O liudiakh bez opredelennykh zaniatii," 14 May 1948, p. 3

[54] *Molot*, "O liudiakh bez opredelennykh zaniatii," 28 May 1948, p. 3. For a report on meetings with workers where the first editorial was discussed, see TsDNI f. 13, op. 4, d. 415, ll. 80–82.

corruption and implicitly to police acquiescence. However, it conceals the systemic roots of the problem by focusing on and demonizing the individuals involved. Portrayed as social pariahs or "antiproletarians," speculators made a convenient scapegoat for the many problems that plagued Soviet society during reconstruction. *Molot* assumed a harsh tone in random cases of "speculation" presented as moral narratives, passing judgment on "twiggish teenagers," "scoundrels" with "sly, cowardly eyes," and "parasites" who deserved harsh treatment. Speculators were the selfish non-working few amid a labor-loving majority, as these pieces contrast the "bright, heroic" present and future with "dark personalities" amid "the wrong crowd" from the "accursed past." The announcements of arrests focused on full-time speculators, implicitly contrasting them with those engaging in petty or part-time illegal trade. There was little variation in the depiction of speculators over this five-year period, but the rhetorical attacks on them intensified during the regime's crackdown on the market in 1948. The press campaign accompanying the crackdown attempted to mobilize popular opinion against speculators during the bread crisis and the regime's restriction of trade, but the official view was riddled with contradictions. The warning that speculators "live right next door to us," for example, contradicted the claim that they were an isolated few. This illustrates the regime's difficulty in denouncing traders when almost everyone was involved in trade to some degree. The glorification of "work" —as understood by those in power—contrasts sharply with the depiction of "those without a definite occupation," who "live off the labor of others" (which actually mirrored the position of party bureaucrats themselves). The public party record sends the message that conditions would be better (i.e., bread, sugar, butter, etc. would be in the stores) if only speculators would join the workforce and live honestly. This view (while not entirely invalid) obscures the roots of black-market activity in a corrupt party bureaucracy and a persistent shortage of goods—that is, the state's inability to satisfy the population's needs—which *necessitated* and perpetuated "speculation."

"Speculation" in Closed Party Discussions

More spontaneous and less restrained than the press, the party's closed record brings speculation into focus from another angle. In their conversations behind closed doors, party representatives appropriate public language on "speculation" but frame the discussion differently, revealing how the illegal economy functioned, the widespread corruption fostering it, an implicit acceptance of speculation, and that people from all walks of life were involved in illegal trade. A report of the city party committee noted that often speculators "don't let real kolkhozniki get to the bazaar," buying up all their produce "wholesale" at the train station.[55] The situation was so bad at times

---

[55] TsDNI f. 13, op. 4, d. 415, l. 26. See also TsDNI f. 13, op. 4, d. 297, l. 8.

that fewer kolkhozniki brought goods to Rostov.[56] Meanwhile, party investigations exposed payoffs to those in charge of the city's markets allowing speculators to sell goods.[57] Another report showed a direct link between the legal economy and speculation, emphasizing the importance of access to goods in the functioning of the illegal economy. It notes that "in several cases" people in charge of warehouses, stores, cafeterias, and restaurants worked with speculators to sell goods.[58] Party documents reveal how speculators managed to avoid work. While editorials in *Molot* extolled the virtues of labor, some people bribed officials to elude their "patriotic duty" of employment. A speaker at one party meeting, for example, complained that many speculators got "help" shunning work, like a woman who received a certificate from a "respectable person" saying she was employed at Factory No. 86, when in fact she sold fried fish all day. The same woman had previously offered a party administrator a 3,000-ruble bribe to free her from a factory assignment.[59]

In closed meetings local party officials echoed the press on the meaning of "work" in Soviet society while begrudgingly accepting the market as a necessity at times. Linking work with patriotism, one gorkom secretary referred to speculators as "unused reserves" of labor and called on factory directors to mobilize them. With the "necessary political effort," he argued, "those comrades" would go to work "not because the police practically dragged them there, but because they wanted to carry out their patriotic duty."[60] An internal party report lamented that many people "do not work," and that "some of them are engaged in unproductive, useless labor"—full-time "speculation."[61] At the same time, oblast Procurator Polozkov candidly admitted at the City Party Conference in February 1943, "we can't break up the market right now" because "they are still counting sacks of flour and people are going to trade."[62] He described an "interesting evolution" of the city's store managers during the two evacuations and occupations of the city. "These people" (*eta publika*), he claimed, hid items both times when people were fleeing, selling them later at great personal profit, then opened up cafes and snack shops for German troops during occupation. Many of them, he asserted, were again becoming store managers under Soviet sovereignty, recommending that the City Financial Department should keep them from assuming their previous positions.[63] Polozkov's stance with regard to the role of market forces in post-

---

[56] See, for example, GARO f. 3955, op. 1, d. 11, l. 53.

[57] TsDNI f. 13, op. 4, d. 24, l. 60.

[58] TsDNI f. 13, op. 4, d. 297, l. 8.

[59] GARO f. 3737, op. 4, d. 1397, ll. 2–3. See also GARO f. 3955, op. 1, d. 1, l. 6.

[60] TsDNI f. 13, op. 4, d. 85, l. 54.

[61] TsDNI f. 13, op. 4, d. 104, l. 17. See also TsDNI f. 13, op. 4, d. 252, l. 34.

[62] The Russian phrase is *torgat' poka budut*.

[63] TsDNI f. 13, op. 4, d. 29, l. 39.

liberation Rostov is interesting. On the one hand, he clearly did not like private enterprise, linking it to treason and threatening to at least partially suppress it; but on the other hand he explicitly admitted the necessity of a market economy due to the breakdown of the official economy and the severe shortage of goods. Thus he exhibited the leniency (in terms of prosecution at least) toward illegal economic activity that was common among oblast procurators.[64]

Subsequent party reports corroborated Polozkov's claims about the city's store managers and further exposed the split in official attitudes toward market activity. Several months after the procurator's comments a checkup of the trade and food industries revealed that 94 percent of their workers stayed in occupied territory and that almost half of them worked for the Nazis, the implications of which we saw previously. This report stated that the trade and food industries "are run through with 'shady speculating elements,' who during occupation opened private cafes, stores, cafeterias, shops, etc."[65] The manager of Store No. 47, for example, worked for the Nazis in an exclusive buffet but hid this fact after liberation and received a promotion.[66] Meanwhile, at a party plenum in 1945 the director of Factory No. 359 displayed a curious attitude toward the market, prompting a strong reaction. He reportedly said "it would be good if trade organizations suggested numbers for the demand (of goods) on the market. Factory directors and the managers of trade organizations could meet and discuss the goods it would be possible to manufacture from material leftover in factories and for which there is a demand on the market." The proposal, according to the minutes for the meeting, was met with "laughter" and the comment, "where do you live?" From the perspective of his audience, members of the local power structure, this factory director crossed the line between the Soviet Union's "planned" economy and a purely market (capitalist) economy based on the principle of "supply and demand." The joke was lost on the speaker, however, who responded, "comrades, it's one thing to know where we live, but another thing to know the demand for necessary goods on the market. There is nothing wrong with trade organizations helping us [factory directors]," he assured them, "and there is nothing funny in what I am saying."[67]

Indeed the market was no laughing matter; the "illegal" economy operated so openly and was so closely linked to "legal" economic operations that it is best described as an appendage of the official state economy. Several sources indicated that the illegal economy was better stocked than the official

---

[64] On this point, see Hessler, "Postwar Perestroika."

[65] TsDNI f. 13, op. 4, d. 16, l. 28. For another gorkom report on this issue, see also TsDNI f. 13, op. 4, d. 21, l. 110.

[66] TsDNI f. 13, op. 4, d. 44, l. 8.

[67] TsDNI f. 13, op. 4, d. 290, l. 26.

sector of the economy.[68] In 1947 the gorkom found that "the speculation of both food items and manufactured goods has strengthened and assumed widespread proportions," adding that due to the inadequate struggle against them "speculators operate openly in the city's streets and markets."[69] The illegal economy was highly mobile, as several times people in state-owned cars were caught transporting goods after work.[70] Trains were vital to the black market's operations; a speaker at one gathering insisted that many of the "tens of thousands" of people at the central market every day "are not ours" but are "outsiders" who have come from elsewhere via train to engage in illegal trade.[71] According to a gorkom investigation, the director and several employees on Train No. 61 accepted bribes and allowed passengers on board without tickets. They even stopped the train with the emergency brake to allow the speculators to unload their cargo.[72] The transport of goods was an important part of illegal economic activity usually accomplished with a bribe.[73] The police also received payoffs. Whereas *Molot* hinted at police complicity, internal party documents leave no doubt. In June 1946, a police officer was caught taking 2,000 rubles from a speculator selling paper.[74] A 1947 investigation concluded that in one district there were "perversions" in the police's work against speculation, and another report noted that "instead of struggling against speculators, police in one store connived with them [*igrali im na ruku*]" by letting them jump ahead in line.[75] At a closed party meeting in November 1948, Comrade Pototov stated the problem in explicit terms, albeit not in his own words: "People say, 'not only do the police *not* struggle against

---

[68] Deliberating on the shortage of instruments and materials desperately needed for production at one meeting, someone pointed out that "on the private market it's possible to buy anything." TsDNI f. 13, op. 4, d. 30, l. 151 ob. See also TsDNI f. 13, op. 4, d. 24, l. 59.

[69] TsDNI f. 13, op. 4, d. 297, l. 8.

[70] See, for example, TsDNI f. 13, op. 4, d. 291, ll. 66, 123–24; TsDNI f. 13, op. 4, d. 292, ll. 38, 82; TsDNI f. 13, op. 4, d. 294, ll. 151, 208; GARO f. 3737, op. 4, d. 1397, l. 3; GARO f. 3737, op. 4, d. 1397, l. 3.

[71] GARO f. 13, op. 4, d. 1397, l. 10.

[72] TsDNI f. 13, op. 4, d. 294, l. 159. Train No. 61 is on the Rostov-Sochi line. This case involved three passengers with several tons of flour and five more with cargo weighing 550 kilograms. In a separate incident a baggage handler accepted bribes to transport goods illegally. TsDNI f. 13, op. 4, d. 296, l. 28.

[73] See also TsDNI f. 13, op. 4, d. 130, l. 52; TsDNI f. 13, op. 4, d. 293, l. 78; TsDNI f. 13, op. 4, d. 296, l. 38; TsDNI f. 13, op. 4, d. 147, ll. 100–01.

[74] TsDNI f. 13, op. 4, d. 233, ll. 44–44 ob.

[75] TsDNI f. 13, op. 4, d. 297, l. 8; and TsDNI f. 13, op. 4, d. 415, ll. 126–29. For other reports on police misconduct or negligence, see also TsDNI f. 13, op. 4, d. 63, l. 56; TsDNI f. 13, op. 4, d. 297, l. 9; TsDNI f. 13, op. 4, d. 392, l. 213; TsDNI f. 13, op. 4, d. 415, ll. 80–82; GARO f. 3955, op. 1, d. 1, l. 38; GARO f. 3955, op. 1, d. 11, l. 53.

speculation and bribery, they actually shield it and are in cahoots with it."[76] These sources give meaning to the oft-heard refrain "lack of struggle against speculation."

Party documents also reveal a realm of private production, in which party members were clearly involved. Along with an accomplice, one party member—an old Bolshevik—embezzled funds from a pensioner's fund to start a "private business." They bought goods at the market and secretly produced unspecified "forbidden items" to fulfill orders from a third party.[77] One party member "opened a leather shop" in his father's apartment and another bought fabric at the market and sewed sheets to sell for a profit.[78] In 1948, coinciding with the central government's hardening stance on private trade, a gorkom investigation concluded that speculators had infiltrated a number of cooperatives "to carry out private production." Owing to few checkups by those in control, this report notes, a number of the city's kiosks and snack shops were privately owned and operated, as noted in *Molot*. The report cites ten examples and states that "there are more," suggesting that the problem was widespread.[79] One party member in an electrical repair shop was caught working on items for personal profit and recommending "an acquaintance" (read: speculator) with items for sale.[80] Confirming another *Molot* report, in 1945 a Central Control Commission inspection found that a number of barbers and beauticians "actually operate private businesses," and a raikom investigation added that barbers bought the materials for their work themselves at "speculative prices," which no doubt explains why their prices were so much higher than the "fixed" price.[81] Market forces, in other words, determined even the price of a shave. A report from one district noted that artisans illegally produced handicrafts and worked with speculators to sell them.[82] Illustrating how complex and far-reaching illegal economic operations were, one local party administrator bought coal in Rostov, transported it to a kolkhoz in Krasnodarskii *krai* and exchanged it for flour and animals, then sold the meat and flour back in Rostov.[83]

Internal party material shows strong involvement in the illegal economy by those in power, while closed discussions that talk around the problem of

---

[76] TsDNI f. 13, op. 4, d. 337, l. 55.

[77] TsDNI f. 13, op. 4, d. 395, ll. 219–20.

[78] TsDNI f. 13, op. 4, d. 320, l. 19; TsDNI f. 13, o. 4, d. 394, l. 172.

[79] TsDNI f. 13, op. 4, d. 392, ll. 40–41.

[80] TsDNI f. 13, op. 4, d. 291, l. 214.

[81] For the central report, see RGASPI f. 17, op. 122, d. 34, l. 47. For the local report, see GARO f. 3955, op. 1, d. 1, l. 79. For similar material on other services, see TsDNI f. 13, op. 4, d. 30, l. 152 ob.; TsDNI f. 13, op. 4, d. 74, ll. 83–84.

[82] GARO f. 3955, op. 1, d. 1, l. 38.

[83] TsDNI f. 13, op. 4, d. 291, ll. 6–7.

corruption are informative for what they strongly imply. The party expelled the director and the main accountant of a canning factory for diverting supplies to a full-time speculator.[84] The director of Rostov's Cafeteria Trust, the focus as we saw of countless complaints over its "poor service," illegally sold apples at the market with an assistant. A school director exaggerated the number of students at her school, ordered extra bread ration cards, then sold them "for speculative prices" through two students.[85] There were countless reports of theft or pilfering by managers and employees of state stores,[86] and throughout this five-year period there were many, many accounts of people in positions of responsibility conspiring in illegal economic activity.[87] Aspersions were cast in the direction of the city's ration-card bureau and its director, Comrade Trusov. Speaking at the City Party Conference in February 1943, Oblast Procurator Polozkov contended that, due to poor control, ration cards for bread were frequently stolen and sold. He relayed two examples of corruption in district ration bureaus and added, "These are only the ones we know about."[88] According to a union leader, a checkup by workers on the allocation of ration cards in the city's factories exposed a 30 percent rate of misappropriations by those in charge of distribution.[89] Demobilization further complicated matters, a gorkom report noting that "due to insufficient control over the distribution of coupons for manufactured goods intended for soldiers and their families," many ration cards "wound up for sale at the market."[90] An inspection revealed that over the course of 1946, 795,829 extra cards (in a city of about 450,000) with a value of 566,000 rubles were printed.[91] Whereas, by law, city ration-card bureau administrator Trusov and his asso-

---

[84] TsDNI f. 13, o. 4, d. 292, l. 82.

[85] TsDNI f. 13, op. 4, d. 292, ll. 21–22. See also TsDNI f. 13, op. 4, d. 392, l. 87. According to another report, the head of a food trust "suggested to two store managers that they sell sugar at the market for speculative prices." TsDNI f. 13, op. 4, d. 296, l. 74.

[86] See, for example, TsDNI f. 13, op. 4, d. 1, ll. 362–63; TsDNI f. 13, op. 4, d. 294, l. 164; TsDNI f. 13, op. 4, d. 299, ll. 97–98; TsDNI f. 13, op. 4, d. 392, ll. 159–60.

[87] See, for example, TsDNI f. 13, op. 4, d. 14, l. 46; TsDNI f. 13, op. 4, d. 24, l. 60; TsDNI f. 13, op. 4, d. 70, l. 35; TsDNI f. 13, op. 4, d. 75, ll. 22 and 24; TsDNI f. 13, op. 4, d. 219, ll. 199–200; TsDNI f. 13, op. 4, d. 220, ll. 244, 257; TsDNI f. 13, op. 4, d. 291, ll. 173, 187–88; TsDNI f. 13, op. 4, d. 292, ll. 38, 127, 131; TsDNI f. 13, op. 4, d. 293, ll. 71, 76, 130, 135, 137, 147; TsDNI f. 13, op. 4, d. 294, ll. 207–08; TsDNI f. 13, op. 4, d. 296, ll. 72 and 74; TsDNI f. 13, op. 4, d. 299, l. 39; TsDNI f. 13, op. 4, d. 394, l. 172; TsDNI f. 13, op. 4, d. 395, ll. 38–39.

[88] TsDNI f. 13, op. 4, d. 1, ll. 362–63. For a report on corruption in district ration card bureaus, see TsDNI f. 13, op. 4, d. 297, l. 8.

[89] TsDNI f. 13, op. 4, d. 77, ll. 26–28. The 30 percent rate was based on 998 out of 2,700 cases. For more on ration card corruption, see also TsDNI f. 13, op. 4, d. 70, l. 122.

[90] TsDNI f. 13, op. 4, d. 149, l. 89. See also GARO f. 3950, op. 1, d. 2, ll. 64–65.

[91] For the estimate of Rostov's population in 1946, see TsDNI f. 13, op. 4, d. 260, l. 59.

ciates should have burned these cards, they failed to do so, and the cards (which, as we know, were an alternative form of currency) were systematically stolen and sold.[92] This report does not directly accuse Trusov of wrongdoing, saying only that he was guilty of negligence or "loss of party vigilance."

At the Eighth City Party Conference in January 1945, Procurator Polozkov gave a revealing account of economic corruption. He told how a deserter from the Red Army arrived in November 1943, made contacts with "criminal elements," and then appeared at the city ration-card bureau claiming to represent "some sort of military organization with 152 people" and asking for rations of bread, groats, sugar, sweets, and alcohol. In over a year, he received 76,000 rubles worth of goods at government prices, which, according to the procurator, translated into 1,726,000 rubles at market prices at a time when the average worker's wage was between 300–500 rubles a month.[93] "One wonders," Polozkov rhetorically commented, "how this criminal was able to trick so many leaders. When he showed up at Trusov's office, the latter met him calmly and quickly registered his 'organization.'" In June 1944, the ration-card bureau did ask to see a certificate confirming the existence of this military organization, which the criminal in question was able to obtain with relative ease from an assistant to the city commandant. Polozkov concludes his tale on an accusatory note: "These communists, leaders of government organizations, lost their party vigilance and were captive to [v plenu] a criminal."[94] Short of a direct accusation of criminal wrongdoing on Trusov's part, these harsh words implicitly acknowledged what everyone in the audience would have understood: corruption was widespread and people in positions of authority frequently profited from a "lack of vigilance."

These documents also reveal tolerance of illegal economic activity because of the economic hardship at its root. The gorkom reversed several decisions of lower party bodies to expel members for illegal economic activity, among them the school director who used students to peddle ration cards and the old Bolshevik who embezzled funds to start a business. Taking into account the latter's longevity in the party, the gorkom allowed him to stay in its ranks.[95] More often, however, economic reasons were given for reversing expulsions. An illustrative case is that of a party member and head of the per-

---

[92] TsDNI f. 13, op. 4, d. 221, ll. 45, 50.

[93] TsDNI f. 13, op. 4, d. 130, ll. 47–49. The information on wages comes from Karol, *Solik*, 295.

[94] TsDNI f. 13, op. 4, d. 130, ll. 47–49.

[95] TsDNI f. 13, op. 4, d. 395, ll. 219–20. For other examples of reversed decisions and lighter sentences, see also TsDNI f. 13, op. 4, d. 75, l. 22; TsDNI f. 13, op. 4, d. 146, l. 1; TsDNI f. 13, op. 4, d. 220, ll. 22–23; TsDNI f. 13, op. 4, d. 291, ll. 66–67, 214; TsDNI f. 13, op. 4, d. 293, ll. 130–31; TsDNI f. 13, op. 4, d. 295, l. 65; TsDNI f. 13, op. 4, d. 392, l. 87.

sonnel department at a leather-processing plant.[96] In 1945 the district bureau excluded her for stealing four pieces of leather to sell on the black market, but the gorkom reinstated her because she had a sick child and elderly mother to support. Fired for illegally obtaining ten kilograms of honey to sale at the market, an instructor at a training school "had no means of existence," so he illegally sold items his brother had brought from Germany.[97] The district bureau excluded him for losing his "party honesty," but, taking into account his "financial difficulties," the gorkom reversed the decision.[98] An eight-year veteran and "master baker" at Bread Factory No. 1 explicitly linked workplace theft and illegal trade to economic hardship. She told her comrades at a closed party meeting she was glad workers commonly stole bread to sell at the market because, she claimed, they only earn between 80–100 rubles a month and "no one worries about salaries."[99] This is an admission of economic causation not readily made in the party press. Also, this internal party material reveals tolerance of and leniency toward illegal economic activity—a "survivalist consensus" as Hessler calls it—that contrasts sharply with the celebrated arrests of big-time speculators in *Molot*.

Internal party documents also indicate that workplace pilfering was another survival strategy for workers at least somewhat overlooked by those in power.[100] During the first ten months of 1944, the Mikoyan Shoe Factory reported 73 cases of theft of leather and other items and, in December, the director was fired for not dealing with "mass pilfering" from the factory.[101] The Champagne and Wine Factory reported that workers stole 101 bottles of spirits in January 1945.[102] A report by Moscow concluded that in Rostov "a significant number of tractor parts were pilfered [from the factories] and sold at the market at speculative prices." The report added that the theft of deficit tractor parts at some places "took on a mass character," including one trust where "hundreds of thousands" of pieces were stolen.[103] A gorkom investigation uncovered "systematic" workplace theft over the course of 1946 from Bread Factory No. 1, noting that one worker sold more than 37,000 rubles worth of stolen bread at the market. The report also noted widespread worker

---

[96] TsDNI f. 13, op. 4, d. 218, ll. 10–11.

[97] On the importance of stolen German goods on the Soviet black market, see Merridale, *Ivan's War*, 238.

[98] TsDNI f. 13, op. 4, d. 220, ll. 22–23.

[99] TsDNI f. 13, op. 4, d. 193, l. 4.

[100] Even though workers were usually searched when leaving factory grounds, many found ways to get goods out, no doubt by either sharing with or otherwise compensating guards. See Karol, *Solik*, 275.

[101] A total of 17,138 rubles worth of goods were pilfered. TsDNI f. 13, op. 4, d. 89, l. 30; and TsDNI f. 13, op. 4, d. 102, l. 3.

[102] TsDNI f. 13, op. 4, d. 199, l. 105.

[103] RGASPI f. 17, op. 122, d. 116, l. 14.

theft from a food-processing plant and a machine-tools factory.[104] Military factories No. 168 and No. 359 also suffered "mass theft of material and finished products" (this in an allegedly "totalitarian" society).[105] Several employees at a paper factory were arrested for peddling pilfered goods, an incident noted in *Molot*.[106] In 1947, the gorkom found that "mass-scale pilfering" from the workplace continued in the city's factories, remaining at a "very high level" as of October.[107] Many workers, in short, looked upon "collective property" as their own, just as party officials looked upon their positions as a way to earn money.

Closed party material further shows that "speculators" came from all walks of life, lured to market activity because of harsh material conditions and low wages in the official economy. At a party meeting, someone cited "resistance" to efforts to bring the "nonworking population" into the factories, noting that people earned more speculating. Another speaker agreed that the problem was the "seduction of the market," where people could earn up to 300 rubles a day compared to 200 rubles a week in the factories.[108] As we have seen, women greatly outnumbered men, and the second economy became an important survival strategy for many of them, especially single mothers. Moreover, rank-and-file party members and demobilized troops, groups that overlapped to a significant degree, were prominent among those seduced by the market. One party member and war veteran "systematically sold tobacco," and another "did not work" for four years because he "sold goods at the market" all day. When pressed, the latter finally took a job *as a security guard*.[109] Several months after the beginning of demobilization in the fall of 1945, local party organs complained that former workers returning from the war did not return to their old jobs.[110] According to a highly critical

---

[104] TsDNI f. 13, op. 4, d. 292, l. 6.

[105] TsDNI f. 13, op. 4, d. 219, l. 119. A worker at the latter plant handed in his resignation in the fall of 1946, threatening that if factory leaders did not accept it he would resort to workplace theft to make ends meet. TsDNI f. 13, op. 4, d. 232, l. 23.

[106] TsDNI f. 13, op. 4, d. 291, l. 174.

[107] TsDNI f. 13, op. 4, d. 300, ll. 53–54. For reports on workplace theft at other factories, see TsDNI f. 13, op. 4, d. 56, l. 99; TsDNI f. 13, op. 4, d. 83, l. 7; TsDNI f. 13, op. 4, d. 193, ll. 4, 36–37; TsDNI f. 13, op. 4, d. 218, ll. 10–11; TsDNI f. 13, op. 4, d. 220, l. 205; TsDNI f. 13, op. 4, d. 221, ll. 28–29; TsDNI f. 13, op. 4, d. 270, l. 14; TsDNI f. 13, op. 4, d. 294, ll. 207–08; TsDNI f. 13, op. 4, d. 322, ll. 3–4.

[108] GARO f. 3737, op. 4, d. 1397, ll. 2–3.

[109] Security guards, as we have seen, were often involved in the theft of goods for sale at the market. TsDNI f. 13, op. 4, d. 296, l. 30. For examples of other rank-and-file party members involved in speculation, see also TsDNI f. 13, op. 4, d. 218, l. 99; TsDNI f. 13, op. 4, d. 220, ll. 22–23; TsDNI f. 13, op. 4, d. 291, ll. 21–23; TsDNI f. 13, op. 4, d. 295, l. 65; TsDNI f. 13, op. 4, d. 320, l. 32; and TsDNI f. 13, op. 4, d. 394, l. 172.

[110] TsDNI f. 13, op. 4, d. 205, l. 4.

report by Moscow officials in December 1946, only 48 percent (3,098 of 6,381) of demobilized troops in three Rostov districts had been assigned jobs, and "part of the demobilized forces arriving in the city participate in speculation at the market." This account further elucidated that, for Rostov oblast as a whole, only 63 percent (57,363 of 91,052) of demobilized troops had been assigned jobs as of December 15, 1946. It concluded by obligating the Rostov obkom to "take decisive measures with demobilized troops who refuse their assigned jobs and continue to carry out speculation at the markets."[111] A follow-up investigation several months later found that demobilized troops in two districts were still not "mobilized" for factory work.[112]

Disabled veterans, divided into three categories, with group I the most seriously impaired and group III the least, were active in the illegal economy, in part because their sacrifices for the war effort made it more difficult for the authorities to prosecute them.[113] In one party report during the war, a district secretary wrote that it was difficult to find jobs for disabled veterans because many of them wanted to be speculators.[114] An investigation by the Central Control Commission in Moscow found that, in Rostov oblast as a whole at the end of 1944, as many as 57 percent of group II and 25 percent of group III war invalids remained "unemployed." The report noted that many disabled veterans find the low pay for unskilled labor unsatisfactory and "prefer to live by speculation."[115] Local party reports likewise indicated that many wounded war veterans carried out "trade and speculation" full-time.[116] Pointing again to the mobility of the market economy, one wounded war veteran allegedly proposed to another that he join their "trust," which traveled to Ukraine to buy up goods for resale in Rostov.[117] On the first day of the unrestricted sale of goods in December 1947, a report claimed that a "war invalid" infiltrated a store on the outskirts of town, gathered a group of people and instructed them to buy up all the sugar.[118] Thus, party discussions behind closed doors convey that many rank-and-file party members, demobilized troops, and

---

[111] RGASPI f. 17, op. 122, d. 146, ll. 27–29.

[112] TsDNI f. 13, op. 4, d. 221, l. 222.

[113] Nina Tumarkin shows that they were treated leniently, arguing that wounded war veterans in particular had considerable social "capital" after the war (*The Living and the Dead*, chap. 5).

[114] TsDNI f. 13, op. 4, d. 104, l. 17.

[115] RGASPI f. 17, op. 122, d. 71, ll. 195–96. To put the numbers into context, the report added that for the Russian Republic as a whole, more than 10,000 disabled veterans were denied pension payments because they refused to take up assigned jobs.

[116] TsDNI f. 13, op. 4, d. 104, l. 17.

[117] "Trust" is set off in quotes in the original. TsDNI f. 13, op. 4, d. 130, l. 52. See also TsDNI f. 13, op. 4, d. 30, l. 151 ob.; TsDNI f. 13, op. 4, d. 130, l. 52; TsDNI f. 13, op. 4, d. 145, l. 92 ob.; TsDNI f. 13, op. 4, d. 252, l. 34; TsDNI f. 13, op. 4, d. 291, l. 21.

[118] TsDNI f. 13, op. 4, d. 309, l. 17.

wounded war veterans preferred a life of speculation to low-paying assigned jobs in the state economy.

On opposite ends of the age scale, young people and pensioners were also active in the illegal economy. Hidden party documents lamented that the city's youth were falling under the "dark influences of the street" and engaging in speculation.[119] According to one report, over 2,000 children were detained at the city's marketplaces in the first half of 1946.[120] Meanwhile, a district soviet again displayed tolerance based on the harsh material conditions of an elderly woman involved in illegal trade. The soviet waved her fine for selling sunflower seeds on the street because she lost two sons during the war and she was raising an orphaned grandson on a pension of a mere 160 rubles a month.[121] Young and old alike participated in petty trade for the sake of survival while the authorities (many of them involved themselves) mostly looked the other way during the period of "reconstruction," 1943–48.

The party's hidden record frames its discussion of this issue differently from its public texts. The public record exhibits a harsh tone against speculators while deemphasizing economic woes and systemic corruption, but, behind closed doors, party leaders admitted that widespread corruption was at the root of the problem, displayed a high level of tolerance for illegal economic activity, and conceded that economic need drove many to "speculation." Police corruption partly explains the leniency shown speculators during this period, adding to Hessler's notion of a "survivalist consensus." Payoffs to police, who earned pitiful wages like everyone else, were an important part of the illegal economy, a type of business expense, with the cost undoubtedly passed on to consumers. The tolerance shown speculators in closed party proceedings contrasts sharply with the harsh sentences trumpeted in *Molot*, reflecting that almost everyone participated in the illegal economy to some degree. Whereas the party press focuses attention on full-time or professional "speculators," internal party documents show that people from all walks of life engaged in illegal trade, including rank-and-file party members, demobilized troops, disabled veterans, women, young people, and pensioners, mostly on a part-time basis to supplement their meager incomes. Meanwhile, full-time speculators vilified in the press benefited greatly from payoffs and bureaucratic "oversight." Denounced by party propaganda, professional profiteers were linked to people in positions of responsibility—the higher the position, the more likely they were to be in the party—whose *access* to scarce goods put them in a position to profit. Not all of them did, but the record shows that a significant number of party officials were involved in illegal eco-

---

[119] See, for example, TsDNI f. 13, op. 4, d. 63, l. 56; TsDNI f. 13, op. 4, d. 69, l. 144; and TsDNI f. 13, op. 4, d. 415, l. 81.

[120] TsDNI f. 13, op. 4, d. 220, l. 89.

[121] GARO f. 3955, op. 1, d. 11, ll. 16–17.

nomic activity, overseeing at times small private businesses with goods and materials diverted from the official state economy.

Popular Opinion on "Speculation"

Along with interviews and a memoir account of black market activity in Rostov, lists of questions posed at public meetings and informant reports help fill out our picture of the varying perceptions of "speculation." In accordance with our other sources, interviewees recalled a flourishing black-market economy during the war and after. Genadii Ermolenko remembered that "people sold anything and everything they could." Eighteen years old in 1946, he worked with his father making shoes in their apartment, for which "they had many orders." A neighbor informed on the business in 1949, and Ermolenko said that to avoid the two-year prison sentence for illegally producing goods, his father paid the Chief Inspector of the city's Financial Department a bribe. While a few "major speculators" were looking to "get rich," Ermolenko says, "most people were just trying to get by," making the same distinction as the party's public record.[122] Svetlana Semenova stated that "speculation was very strong," especially, she added, "among party administrators." As an example Semenova cited a neighbor who worked in the district courts as a secretary and received extra ration cards from her boss, a highly placed official, which she then sold at the market.[123] V. I. Akimenko was an 18-year-old student at the Rostov Art Institute who in 1946 received a monthly stipend of 150 rubles, enough to buy one loaf of bread at market prices. He stood in line at kiosks from 3:00 a.m. to buy bread to resell for a profit at the central market.[124] Thus while many people engaged in illegal trade to some degree out of necessity — to "get by" — they, like party leaders, distinguished themselves from and vilified "major speculators" who were out to "get rich."

K. S. Karol's account offers fascinating insights into the operation of the illegal market. He notes that when he returned to Rostov in 1944 prices at the kolkhoz market were extremely high. "A kilo of bread," he informs, "costs as much as a skilled worker earns in a week, and the prices are spiraling upwards."[125] The USSR, he explains, settled into a dual economy: a "fairly inexpensive" official one "marked by a penury of goods" and another one, "parallel to the first" but "better supplied, free of restrictions as to how much [one] can buy, but characterized by galloping inflation." Elaborating further on eco-

---

[122] Interview by author, 16 April 1995.

[123] Interview by author, 16 April 1995.

[124] Interview by author, 20 May 1995.

[125] Karol, *Solik*, 91. Prices were so high on the market, he adds, that his wife Klava "prefers to put up with a slight hunger rather than buy food on the black market." He notes about "the authorities": "Preoccupied with their impotence when faced with the problems of supplies, they appear to encourage [the second economy]" (91, 314).

nomic life during "reconstruction," he writes, "it is almost as if, in switching from one market to another, we were changing country and entering a world where everything has increased in prices a hundredfold." He also recalls the opening of "commercial stores" in 1944 that "for exorbitant prices that bear no relation to the workers' official incomes, offer practically everything without coupons [ration cards]." Karol's attitude toward the illegal economy was ambiguous. As noted above, initially he criticized the woman he rented a room from for selling ration cards provided to her every week by a suitor. She responded that "her customers come from all walks of life—even men in uniform," which put her conscience at ease.[126] Eventually Karol was also drawn into illegal trade, although unwillingly because, as someone who genuinely believed in socialism, he did not approve of such machinations. He draws a picture in which almost everyone is involved in some questionable—if not outright illegal—economic activity to survive. "In spite of their modest official wages of between 300 and 500 rubles a month," he informs, some people "were clearly not short of money." His wife, Klava, for example, filled in occasionally as a cashier in a café, and the director, a close friend, "helps her to fix her till so that she makes from it much more than her wages." A dancer for the Rostov Theater lived by speculating the two tickets granted her for each performance.[127] Karol sums up the economic situation in postwar Russia thusly:

> In theory we were living in a society in which the interests of the individual merged with those of the collectivity—this was one of the cardinal points of Soviet doctrine. In practice, however, the collectivity evidently didn't care a fig about our individual interests and we repaid it fully in kind, especially where "socialist property" was concerned. By behaving in this way we were … simply manifesting our elementary needs: the will to survive, to satisfy our hunger, to dress ourselves decently, and to be able to go out to the entertainments of our choice.[128]

These sources also further illuminate the connection between workplace pilfering and speculation, as well as the high degree of mobility of those involved in underground trade. Ermolenko began working at Krupzavod in 1945 and pilfered grain to sell at the market during the famine. "People dragged everything they could out of all the factories to sell," he said, adding,

---

[126] Ibid., 91, 94–95, 321, 325.

[127] Ibid., 291, 294–95. The dancer, his friend Kolia's fiancée, thereby earned an extra 60 rubles a night, or roughly 1,500 rubles a month, a sizable income at the time. Karol further notes that he and his friends were among the consumers who paid high prices to speculators for theater tickets.

[128] Ibid., 282.

"What else was there to do?" Karol likewise notes widespread workplace pilfering, despite the fact that workers leaving factories were searched.[129] In late 1945, Karol and several friends agreed to load fish onto a freight car, for which the port manger allowed each of them to load up with fish and walk out of the premises twice. "The guards," he writes, "pretend not to notice that our greatcoats, not needed at this time of year, literally flutter about on our backs, as the fish which are still alive try to leap out of our pockets." By prior arrangement, two women "wholesalers" met them at a nearby gate and purchased the fish for one-third of the market retail price.[130] Karol and his friends each earned roughly 1,000 rubles, about twice the average worker's monthly salary in the official economy, for this act of "pilfering." He adds that "the authorities close their eyes" to all these "suspicious deals."[131] Separate from this fishy deal, Karol's close friend Kolia hatched a plan to take advantage of their travel privileges as veterans by buying and selling goods between Tiflis, the capital of the Georgian Republic, and Rostov. "Given the huge disparity of black market prices in these two metropolitan centers," his friend explained, "we could make vast sums of money out of each return journey." He remembers that they gave bribes to train conductors to ride on top of the train.[132] Karol once profited nicely from a trip to Moscow, which he describes as a universal practice. Taking along a sack of sunflower seeds, Karol sold them for a hefty profit and bought up cloth and underwear in Moscow to sell in Rostov.[133] Ermolenko likewise recalled that "people constantly went to Moscow to buy things" and "were always looking to buy something somewhere that they could then sell for a profit somewhere else." These sources, in short, reinforce a large part of the picture of "speculation" drawn by public and closed party materials.

Archival material further shows that workers and others were largely receptive to the portrayal of professional speculators as a social nemesis, sharing the distinction between full-time speculators and those involved in petty trade for the sake of survival (which, of course, included many of the workers themselves).[134] They often assailed speculators for buying up goods in state stores (which obviously required the cooperation of store managers). The two official stances toward the market, leniency vs. a harsh stance, are discernible here as well, with workers' comments definitely weighted in favor of clamping down on full-time speculators. Echoing party leaders, at the beginning of

---

[129] Ibid., 275.

[130] Unhappy with the price paid for their fish, Karol observes, "a good Soviet citizen who gives herself to commerce behaves no differently than a bourgeois profiteer of the worst kind" (ibid., 327).

[131] Ibid., 328.

[132] Ibid., 263, 271–72.

[133] Ibid., 337.

[134] Kenney shows that this was the case in Poland as well (*Rebuilding Poland*, 90, 191).

the famine in 1946 several workers stated at a public meeting that "rationing norms for those who work should be increased, while bread should be denied to those who are able to work but do not."[135] Someone else bemoaned that speculators "accumulate money at workers' expense."[136] Similar comments aping the official line in the party press are encountered often in these sources, and widespread dissatisfaction with professional profiteers was undoubtedly genuine.[137] Here as elsewhere, however, I am more concerned in diagnosing the "unhealthy" comments made by workers on this subject. As a rule, people expressed their sentiments on speculation in markedly different terms from those of party leaders, proposing alternative ways to overcome pricing and distribution problems. Some threatened to (and in numerous cases did) "leave work," which often meant becoming a speculator. Several cafeteria employees, for example, told their boss after the decision to lower rations in September 1946, "We will not work without bread; we'll go sell goods at the market."[138] A worker at a shoe shop reportedly said he would have "to think of something 'on the side' because it's not possible to live on one's salary alone," and two workers at Factory No. 359 declared, "we'll have to leave the plant and find other work."[139] Whereas the regime portrayed "work" as a hallowed "patriotic duty," many of those engaged in it saw it in much more practical terms, judging their jobs solely by whether or not they paid them enough to survive.

People also measured living standards by market forces, exhibiting little faith in rationing or commercial stores. An employee at Bread Factory No. 1, for example, lamented publicly that "our workers [do not receive] enough to live on considering prices at the market."[140] A summary of a meeting with workers in one district stated that many of them expressed the following opinion: "The stores aren't open for us, but for do-nothings (*bezdel'nikov*) and speculators."[141] As for ways to solve the problem, several people suggested selling more food items at the plant because, as one worker declared at a factory meeting, "from the stores they wind up with speculators at the ba-

---

[135] TsDNI f. 13, op. 4, d. 233, l. 27.

[136] TsDNI f. 13, op. 4, d. 315, l. 3.

[137] Karol describes an uncle who merely repeated everything he read in *Molot* (*Solik*, 137).

[138] TsDNI f. 13, op. 4, d. 232, l. 33. See also TsDNI f. 13, op. 4, d. 232, ll. 3–4, 7, 9, 23 and 63; TsDNI f. 13, op. 4, d. 415, ll. 146 and 160; and RGASPI f. 17, op. 122, d. 188, l. 21 and 26.

[139] TsDNI f. 13, op. 4, d. 232, ll. 47, 63.

[140] TsDNI f. 13, op. 4, d. 193, l. 4. See also TsDNI f. 13, op. 4, d. 29, l. 1; TsDNI f. 13, op. 4, d. 232, ll. 2, 18, 28, 33–34, and 51; TsDNI f. 13, op. 4, d. 315, ll. 22, 76, 79; TsDNI f. 13, op. 4, d. 343, l. 88; TsDNI f. 13, op. 4, d. 415, l. 164.

[141] TsDNI f. 13, op. 4, d. 315, l. 14.

zaar."[142] A frequently heard suggestion was that store hours be extended so people could buy goods when they left work.[143] During the 1948 bread crisis, some advised that the government set prices for state goods according to those at the market to combat speculation, or even that it allow the "free sale" of goods "so that they would become cheaper."[144] One worker reportedly asked in 1948, "Why do city authorities break up the sale of goods by speculators at the market, which only leads to higher prices?"[145] These comments reflect the same difference of views apparent at the top levels of leadership—a harsh stance calling for a clamp down against illegal trade as opposed to an approach that allows and uses the market to the population's benefit.

Significantly, people publicly acknowledged the ties between corrupt police, party officials, and the illegal economy. At a factory meeting, one worker claimed that, rather than dispersing people illegally selling bread, police "took money" from them.[146] A worker and demobilized soldier complained that he notified the police twice about a "young speculator" in his housing complex, but that they "did nothing about it." A rank-and-file party member said he personally saw speculators elsewhere bribe the police to leave them alone.[147] Another report noted that, among workers at the fish-processing plant, "there is talk that instead of a struggle with speculators the police discredit themselves."[148] Workers and others also explicitly linked corrupt party leaders to speculation, especially during the monetary reform in December 1947. The exchange rate, one ruble of the new denominations for ten rubles of old money, was designed to adversely affect those with lots of cash on hand, i.e., speculators. As already noted, though, regional party leaders revealed the plan prematurely and, in response, people went on a spending spree in the first two weeks of December. They made an informed business decision, realizing it was better to have their money tied up in goods. This was, moreover, a nationwide phenomenon that involved thousands descending on Moscow to buy up goods in the country's best stocked city.[149] Three days before the official announcement of the reform, workers at a meeting in the Mikoyan Shoe Factory complained that, "thanks to the talkativeness of several leaders, the whole town knows about the upcoming reforms, as a result of which

---

[142] TsDNI f. 13, op. 4, d. 233, l. 3. See also TsDNI f. 13, op. 4, d. 343, l. 88; TsDNI f. 13, op. 4, d. 415, ll. 204–05.

[143] TsDNI f. 13, op. 4, d. 232, ll. 7, 9, 23–24, 26–28, 33, 39, 44, 47–48, 51, 55, 63-64; TsDNI f. 13, op. 4, d. 233, ll. 47, 77.

[144] TsDNI f. 13, op. 4, d. 232, ll. 3–4.

[145] TsDNI f. 13, op. 4, d. 415, l. 120.

[146] TsDNI f. 13, op. 4, d. 233, ll. 44 and ob.

[147] TsDNI f. 13, op. 4, d. 415, l. 82.

[148] TsDNI f. 13, op. 4, d. 219, l. 71.

[149] On this point, see Filtzer, *Soviet Workers and Late Stalinism*, 79–80.

those with lots of dishonestly-earned money are buying up everything." Strengthened by a call to arrest "those divulging state secrets," this statement strongly implies a connection between "talkative leaders" and those "with lots of dishonestly-earned money," displaying the perception that the city's party organization was corrupt.[150]

Soviet citizens, moreover, were keenly aware of the inability of the official economy to supply their needs, and publicly expressed concern over disparities between themselves and speculators. Comments were hostile to full-time speculators—as in the party's public record—but often with the added caveat that the regime was not doing anything to solve the problem. In late 1945, for example, a housing administration employee posed a straightforward question to a party agitator: "Why is it that in Rostov speculators live better than workers and when will this problem be dealt with?"[151] There were numerous questions at public meetings about the "lack of struggle" against speculation by police.[152] People asked why youth were allowed to sell goods at the bazaar rather than being brought into the workforce.[153] On the first day of the unrestricted sale of goods in December 1947, a policeman assured people in line at one store that "the government knows what it's doing, there is enough bread for everyone." Customers, however, remained uncertain, asking questions like, "Won't speculators strangle us by buying up everything in the stores?" Others worried about shortages "creating conditions for speculators to prosper." During an open meeting, a metal worker at Rostsel'mash proclaimed, "At the appearance of the slightest difficulties in government stores they [speculators] will be able to inflate prices at the bazaar."[154] After the end of rationing workers complained because, they claimed, speculators were indeed undermining sales by buying up everything.[155] One worker expressed the thoughts of many when, during the spring 1948 bread crisis, she asked, "Why haven't city authorities done something about bread lines and speculators?"[156] Such complaints remained prominent well into the summer. According to a report from Andreevskii district in July, workers were "extremely dissatisfied that speculation still has not been eradicated."[157] Full-time speculators clearly profited at people's expense, so it is not surprising that many

---

[150] TsDNI f. 13, op. 4, d. 298, l. 26. I elaborate on party corruption in chap. 8.

[151] TsDNI f. 13, op. 4, d. 233, l. 60.

[152] See, for example, TsDNI f. 13, op. 4, d. 30, l. 150; TsDNI f. 13, op. 4, d. 30, l. 151 ob.; TsDNI f. 13, op. 4, d. 233, l. 68.

[153] See, for example, TsDNI f. 13, op. 4, d. 92, l. 282.

[154] TsDNI f. 13, op. 4, d. 315, ll. 14, 22, 76, 79; TsDNI f. 13, op. 4, d. 343, l. 88. See also TsDNI f. 13, op. 4, d. 232, ll. 47, 91.

[155] TsDNI f. 13, op. 4, d. 309, ll. 17, 50–52.

[156] TsDNI f. 13, op. 4, d. 415, ll. 118, 142, 146–47, 159–60, 164, 187, 204–05, 242.

[157] TsDNI f. 13, op. 4, d. 290, l. 26.

were receptive to the regime's negative portrayal of "those without a definite occupation." However, their comments exhibited little hope in the regime's ability to solve this problem.

People also pointed out that, at times, party policy benefited speculators. During the monetary reform in December 1947, for example, workers and others asserted that the lengthy (one-week) exchange period helped speculators. The government ended the circulation of old rubles three days after the reform began, and people flocked to the exchange points with sacks of old rubles to exchange. On December 18 anywhere from 300 to 1,000 people waited at several banks to exchange money, with more than 100 people in line at the city's central bank. An average of 600,000 rubles in old money was taken by the banks, compared to only 275,000–300,000 rubles for the two previous days.[158] Proving once again the pervasiveness of illegal economic activity, a form of speculation even developed in the lines; those near the front exchanged money for those at the back at a rate of 15 or 20 to 1. "This upsets workers," one summary of questions notes: "Many express their wish that the government would cease the exchange of money now because at this point only speculators are exchanging money."[159] According to another report, a group of workers was pleased with the decision to end the circulation of old money, saying, "Now speculators can use their bundles as wallpaper." When they found out speculators could still exchange their old money, however, "their excitement turned to disappointment." One of them argued, "The government should have set up exchange points not at banks, but at factories, where speculators would not have been able to exchange anything." Several others pointedly asked in public meetings, "Why doesn't the government hurt speculators by ceasing the exchange of money?"[160] Thus, people publicly proposed alternatives as to how the government might achieve its stated goal of undermining speculators (which, as presumed by the questions, the government was not doing adequately).

Comments noted in svodki paralleled statements in public meetings. One informant reported the "common complaint" among people in his district that speculators bought everything in the stores while they were at work. In 1945, an employee at Bread Factory No. 1 was overheard saying, "Speculators live well and will continue to live well because they buy up goods in the stores and resell them for three times as much, whereas we workers don't have time to buy the things we need."[161] These sources point to the greater availability of goods at the market; an informant reported a worker saying, "I

---

[158] TsDNI f. 13, op. 4, d. 315, l. 22.

[159] TsDNI f. 13, op. 4, d. 315, ll. 17–18

[160] TsDNI f. 13, op. 4, d. 315, ll. 20, 22, 30, 39.

[161] TsDNI f. 13, op. 4, d. 232, l. 51. For similar comments, see also ll. 2, 18, 28, 33–34.

can't find sugar in the stores, but at the market they're still selling it."[162] After bread rations were cut in the fall of 1946, an informant observed "unhealthy attitudes" among recently "mobilized" workers at the Mikoyan Shoe Factory, "especially demobilized troops," who said things like, "They forced us to work, [but] don't even give us bread."[163] Workers and others had numerous qualms about the monetary reform and couched their concerns in revealing terms, according to these sources. Recorded opinions include a common refrain that "the money workers had on their person should have been exchanged ruble for ruble with the new money, at least the sum of a month's salary."[164] In line at exchange points, "isolated individuals" were overheard complaining, "We lost a great deal with the monetary exchange," or asking "perplexing questions" like, "Why are speculators able to exchange tens of thousands of rubles that they have in the bank?" People also complained about the three-to-one exchange for government bonds; a worker at DGTF said he considered this to be "incorrect because it hurts workers not speculators." A worker at Rostsel'mash likewise noted, "speculators receive their 3,000 rubles in full, but workers who gave up their savings to the government as bonds lose out."[165] Workers' comments reveal a perspective at odds with the official explanation of these reform measures, while the interpretation of their views by district party secretaries marginalize worker opposition as the "perplexing" views of "isolated individuals."

There is some overlap between party records and popular opinion; people were receptive to the regime's negative portrayal of professional speculators and occasionally "spoke Bolshevik." Thus, the regime's efforts to shape popular opinion on this issue were at least somewhat successful, if only because they fell upon a sympathetic audience. The popular record, however, also differs in important ways from party texts. Workers and others declared their lack of faith in the official economy to supply their needs, saw the black market as an alternative to low-paying factory jobs, and proposed alternative policies to undermine speculators. Workers recognized that some party leaders profited from access to scarce items, so many of them pilfered goods and channeled them to the illegal market as part of their own strategy of survival. People were *dependent upon* a second income to supplement their meager official wages and cooked up all sorts of schemes. Largely accepting the party's

---

[162] TsDNI f. 13, op. 4, d. 415, l. 55.

[163] TsDNI f. 13, op. 4, d. 232, l. 4.

[164] TsDNI f. 13, op. 4, d. 315, ll. 3–4, 14. This opinion was reported among workers at DGTF and Factory No. 309, among other places. One woman in line was distraught because she had kept 10,000 rubles she saved at home, thus losing most of it in the exchange. Also, one account noted the opinion of a worker at DGTF that when stores opened for free sale "there will be nothing left for workers except a few dirty items because speculators will buy up everything."

[165] TsDNI f. 13, op. 4, d. 315, ll. 14, 40, 52, 67.

public demonization of "speculators" and the dichotomy between petty and full-time speculators, workers and others perceived the systemic roots of the illegal economy in the persistent shortages of goods and in the link between corrupt officials and professional speculators, factors obfuscated by the party press. People were keenly aware, for example, that the monetary reform did not have the intended effect on speculators precisely because they were "in cahoots" with corrupt party officials, who divulged this important state secret prematurely. Like Karol's friend Kolia, many understood that one's position in the official economy was key to one's position in the illegal economy, determining how one could participate in and profit from hidden deals. Karol's account also shows that "pilfering" was at times an informal form of payment. In addition, while the two lines toward market activity spelled out above are apparent in these texts, these commentaries clearly favor a harsh stance toward professional profiteers. That position, however, is underlined with a realization that corrupt officials and police were *working with* speculators rather than enforcing laws against illegal trade. Thus, while there is some overlap between party and popular records, the latter frame discussion of this issue at odds with official views, exhibiting distinctly different perspectives of Soviet economic life.

The various sources examined here illuminate the illegal economy from several angles, reflecting an ongoing dialogue on this issue between those in power and their subordinates. During the war and postwar years, "speculation" was far-reaching and deeply rooted in the Stalinist system, and it was particularly pervasive during crises like the postwar famine. Many people were involved in illegal trade, but corrupt officials often benefited disproportionately because of their access to scarce goods. The "shadow economy" operated openly, was highly mobile, involved people from all walks of life, and was closely linked to workplace pilfering. The campaign against speculators, publicly dubbed "people without a definite occupation," intensified in the spring of 1948, coinciding with the crackdown on market activities. "Speculators" became the regime's primary "internal other" construction at this juncture, the media attacks against them intended in part to divert working–class hostilities away from party bureaucrats. Shaped by the same ideological assumptions, the press and the party's record behind closed doors both defined "speculation" within narrow confines, obscuring the systemic roots of the black market by associating work with patriotism and speculation with "unemployment." *Molot* scapegoated speculators as antiproletarians, an internal other largely to blame for economic difficulties. Moral narratives for public consumption turned attention away from economic hardship contributing to widespread speculation and tried to show that local authorities (who were part of the problem) were dealing with the issue. That material emphasizes speculation's negative impact on people's daily life, showing how it affects everything from a trip to the barber to bread sales. Contrary to public pronouncements, however, closed party sources show that many people were involved in illegal trade to some degree, expose economic hardship as a primary cause for speculation, and exhibit a large degree of tolerance toward it.

Among society at large, workers and others realized that, despite the vilification of "speculators" in the press, party officials conspired with this internal other to profit at the expense of the very population whose interests they ostensibly represented. Many people declared their lack of faith in the official economy, viewed the black market as an alternative to low-paying factory jobs, pilfered goods for sale on the black market, and saw the link between a corrupt party bureaucracy and the illegal economy as part of the problem. While accepting the demonization of full-time "speculators," they saw small-scale trade as a crucial part of an overall strategy of survival. Many Soviet citizens, moreover, questioned the ideological assumptions shaping the way those in power saw and projected the country's economy, implicitly defining their own identity and interests vis-à-vis local party leaders. The comments of workers and others lead one to wonder whether the regime's crackdown on market activities in spring 1948 was a response to swelling popular opinion against professional speculators (and their corrupt party cohorts). Soviet popular culture was negatively predisposed toward those engaged in speculation "to get rich," as opposed to those trying to survive. The regime tolerated illegal trade to a significant degree until the end of rationing and monetary reform, but then took decisive steps against the market. This move coincided with the public mood at the time as recorded in lists of questions posed by workers and others at meetings with party representatives and in *svodki*. For scholars this raises a familiar question: what exactly is the relationship between media and popular opinion?[166] Did those in power *shape* popular opinion through their monopoly control over the press, or were they merely *reacting to* popular opinion through the press and in creating policy? The contention here is that it was a two-way street, that, contrary to the totalitarian model, the regime did take popular opinion into account in shaping (and timing) its policies. As noted earlier, both sides in the Civil War responded to information gathered by informants in their newspaper editorials.[167] The evidence suggests that this practice continued in the Soviet period as part of an ongoing class dialogue, a point I develop further in the next chapter on a series of postwar elections.

---

[166] Robert Darnton examines this relationship in 18th-century France in "The Forbidden Best-Sellers of Pre-Revolutionary France," in *The French Revolution: The Essential Readings*, ed. Ronald Schechter (Oxford: Oxford University Press, 2001). In the Soviet field regarding this question, see Brooks, *"Thank You, Comrade Stalin!"*; and Kenez, *Birth of the Propaganda State.*

[167] See Holquist, "Anti-Soviet *Svodki* From the Civil War," 447.

Chapter Seven

"What sort of democracy is this?": The "Myth of the War" and Soviet Elections

The right to cast a vote is, of course, a primary feature of citizenship and democracy. The dominant political discourses on both sides of the Cold War exalted the public's right to vote as an essential part of their own form of "democracy."[1] For most Westerners, democracy rests on a balance of powers and includes various "inalienable" political rights, the right to own property, elect representatives, etc., standards by which they judge all other socio-political systems.[2] Soviet theorists, however, measured political reality from a different vantage point. The 1936 Stalin Constitution allegedly granted "citizens" (*grazhdane*)[3] social and economic rights along with the right to elect representatives to organs of the "workers' and peasants' state," defining the Soviet Union in theory as a "socialist democracy." As with their Cold War adversaries, Soviet ideologues measured all other governments from this perspec-

---

[1] Political authority is linguistic authority (and vice versa), and a crucial aspect of any government is the way it defines itself to its citizenry. Craig Brandist explains, "In a socially stratified setting the prevailing national language is subject to the power relations and hierarchy of society in which a dominant discourse imposes itself on others, presenting itself as universal and ideal." Brandist, "Gramsci, Bakhtin and the Semiotics of Hegemony," *New Left Review* 216: 2 (1997): 94–109.

[2] Frederick C. Barghoorn, for example, states that "Western-style constitutional democracy is the least harmful to human liberties of all forms of government." Barghoorn, *Détente and the Democratic Movement in the USSR* (New York: Free Press, 1976), 41.

[3] David Hoffmann notes that, in the mid-1930s, "[c]itizenship replaced class as the most operative category [in Soviet society], and all loyal Soviet citizens were portrayed as equal contributors to socialism." Hoffmann, *Stalinist Values: The Cultural Norms of Soviet Modernity, 1917–1941* (Ithaca, NY: Cornell University Press, 2003), 149. Karen Petrone states that the Stalin Constitution "expanded Soviet rhetoric by bringing western conceptions of civil rights to the forefront, guaranteeing freedom of speech, association, the press, and religion and offering protection against arbitrary arrest. It also identified universal, secret, direct, and equal suffrage as a central tenet of Soviet democracy." Petrone, *Life Has Become More Joyous, Comrades: Celebrations in the Time of Stalin* (Bloomington: Indiana University Press, 2000), 180.

tive, considering their system superior as the rule of the majority of the population (workers and peasants) versus Western "capitalist democracies" or dictatorships of the bourgeoisie. Of course, there was absolutely nothing truly democratic about the fundamentally flawed and repressive Stalinist system, but, legitimate or not, this outlook shaped Soviet political discourse, limiting the framework for how problems in society were discussed. The master narrative of "socialist democracy" wrote social and political problems out of the picture, implicitly denying the possibility of mass discontent while eliminating discordant voices. Yet, as we have seen in previous chapters, such voices were not completely silenced. A series of postwar election campaigns designed to show popular support for the regime and its policies also reveal dissatisfaction with Communist Party rule, a gap between the "ideal" Soviet "socialist democracy" and the ways in which many in society perceived Soviet political "reality."

This chapter looks at the postwar election campaigns—and the "myth of the war" that underlay them—to see how people both at the top of the sociopolitical hierarchy and at the bottom felt about Soviet "socialist democracy." Elections in the aftermath of the Second World War were common among the combatant nations. Postwar elections in Western Europe were "borne by rhetorics of national reconciliation and new beginnings" and brought powerful evidence of broadly based reforming desires. New constitutions in France (1946), Italy (1947), and West Germany (1949) restored parliamentary democracy, civil rights, and the rule of law.[4] In Eastern Europe, on the other hand, the Red Army's presence "overshadowed" postwar reconstruction and distorted the elections, which "ranged from thoroughly corrupt in Poland to genuinely free in Czechoslovakia."[5] The parliamentary elections in January 1947 in Poland—where World War II began—took on great significance for the developing Cold War. The allied powers agreed at Yalta that with Poland's "complete liberation by the Red Army," a multi-party coalition government, the Polish Provisional Government of National Unity, should be formed until "the holding of free and unfettered elections as soon as possible on the basis of universal suffrage and secret ballot."[6] Of course, the elections

---

[4] Geoff Eley, *Forging Democracy: The History of the Left in Europe, 1850–2000* (Oxford: Oxford University Press, 2000), 289–90. The constitutions of France and Italy enfranchised women for the first time. Ely shows that Communist parties of the various European countries fared well in the first postwar elections, including in France, where they tallied 26 percent of the vote, and Italy where they received 19 percent.

[5] Ibid., 305–06.

[6] The coalition government included the Moscow-supported Polish Worker's Party, the Polish Socialist Party, and the Polish Peasant Party. The February 1945 Yalta Agreement further specifies, "in these elections all democratic and anti-Nazi parties shall have the right to take part and to put forward candidates." The Avalon Project of Yale Law School, http://www.yale.edu/lawweb/avalon/wwii/yalta.htm (accessed May 2007).

were anything but "free and unfettered"; results were fixed through intimidation and fraud, allowing the communists to consolidate power. Voter apathy, exhaustion, and the struggle for daily survival contributed to the communist victory.[7] The reinforcement of the occupying Red Army by three million troops, some of whom actually participated in the voting, sealed the deal. "Opposition activists were harassed, jailed, or even killed, and [the Polish Peasant Party] PSL lists were declared invalid in many of its strongholds." The election marked the end of a hopeful period of state-society relations in Poland and facilitated the communist imposition of control.[8]

Communism, of course, was already established in the Soviet Union, which had a history of elections. The official name "Union of Soviet Socialist Republics" illustrates the significance of the elected soviets or councils that originated in the 1905 Revolution.[9] Early Soviet constitutions disenfranchised "alien elements"[10] and weighted voting rights toward urban workers, but the 1936 Stalin Constitution, celebrated as "the most democratic constitution in the world," granted universal suffrage and civil rights to all.[11] J. Arch Getty analyzes the drafting of the Constitution and the 1937 elections in order to examine the "workings of Stalinist politics, Soviet society, and the interactions between them."[12] Soviet leaders, he assures, took the constitution and the elections very seriously, and Stalin played a major role in the process. Central leaders presented a draft of the constitution to the press in June 1936, initiating a "national discussion" of it. They wanted "to use it to praise the Soviet regime and its accomplishments," but "citizens" and "voters" raised ques-

---

[7] Kenney, *Rebuilding Poland,* 117. Kenney shows that the communist-dominated Polish Provisional Government engineered temporary improvements in living standards just prior to the elections, and also notes that workers and others in society used the election campaigns to complain about their harsh material conditions.

[8] Ibid., 54 and 56. "Poland's leaders," he adds, "hoped their election victory and the new three-year plan would give them greater authority; the workers, however, now realized that the state was directly responsible for working and living conditions" (117).

[9] They reappeared following the fall of the tsar in February 1917, and one of the rallying cries for the Bolshevik Revolution in October was "all power to the soviets."

[10] The 1918 Constitution of the Russian Republic denied the right to run as candidates or to vote in soviet elections to persons using hired labor for profit and/or those living off unearned income (dividends, profits, rent, etc.); private traders and middlemen; priests and monks; former employees of the tsarist police state apparatus; and members of the Romanov family.

[11] Because industrialization and collectivization had "eliminated landlords, capitalists, and rich peasants [*kulaks*]," the Constitution proclaimed, "there are no longer antagonistic classes in [Soviet] society ... [that] consists of two friendly classes, workers and peasants."

[12] Getty, "State and Society Under Stalin," 18.

tions over "bread and butter" issues, crime, and religion.[13] The final version included only minor changes—"the vast majority of suggestions and proposed additions were completely ignored."[14] The regime did respond to voters' complaints, however, recommending that local party organs increase bread deliveries to collective farms and speed up the construction of housing. Initially, Getty adds, party leaders considered conducting contested, multi-candidate elections.[15] However, in October 1937 about two months prior to the elections, the party's Central Committee secretly reversed this aspect of the electoral rules, probably because of the threat (perceived or real) that "enemies" would try to nominate candidates.[16] The regime presented this abrupt change to single candidates "as the result of social and political unanimity." Getty sees its decision to cancel the multi-candidate aspect of the elections as a sign of the regime's weakness. "The 1936 Constitution and 1937 elections," he states, "illustrate the limits of state power in its interaction with a vast, multifaceted society."[17]

---

[13] Ibid., 23, 26, and 28. According to Getty, "a central memorandum admitted that 300,000 religious institutions still existed and 600,000 persons worked in them" ("State and Society Under Stalin," 31). Fitzpatrick states that "Orthodox and sectarian activity was also widely reported, with an emphasis on Tolstoyan and Baptist activity" (*Everyday Stalinism*, 181). Petrone also sees the significance of religion among voters' concerns in discussions of the 1936 Stalin Constitution and elections the following year (Petrone, *Life Has Become More Joyous*, 185–87).

[14] Hoffmann likewise notes that, "while the final version" of the Stalin Constitution promulgated in December "did include a number of changes, there is no indication that they were based on popular opinion." He calls the discussion of the draft constitution "an exercise in controlled participatory politics" (*Stalinist Values*, 153). However, as Petrone states, "the celebration of the constitution and the elections opened up a space for political and economic discussions in the Soviet Union both within and outside of the boundaries of Soviet orthodoxy" (*Life Has Become More Joyous*, 201). Perhaps the most accurate depiction of the Soviet political system is Diane Koenker's concept of the "participatory dictatorship" that took shape in the 1920s based on an unequal dialogue between workers and the regime. Looking at the Printer's Union, Koenker states that "the participatory element is important here. ... Workers did talk back to their union leaders, whether vocally, through satire, or in their behavior. The balance of power of course was unequal: the regime controlled jobs and therefore welfare and security" (Koenker, *Republic of Labor*, 171).

[15] "Archival evidence on these events," Getty states, "suggests that the center devoted great attention and energy to the preparations for contested elections" ("State and Society Under Stalin," 29 and 31).

[16] Ibid., 31. The regime adopted the term *bloc* to describe candidates for the elections, Getty asserts, to cover its reversal on the issue of multi-candidate elections (32).

[17] Ibid., 35. Getty elsewhere links the elections, which coincided with the height of the purges in 1937, with the intensification of political repression. Getty, "'Excesses Are not Permitted': Mass Terror and Stalinist Governance in the Late 1930s," *The Russian Review*, no. 1 (2002): 124–26. On the Stalin Constitution and the elections, see also Fitz-

The Stalin Constitution established a bicameral Supreme Soviet as the highest organ of state power, with a Council of the Union elected directly from equal districts (one deputy per 300,000 people), and a Council of Nationalities with deputies from each republic and autonomous region. Delegates, elected to four-year terms, kept their regular jobs (usually within a local party apparatus) but attended brief yearly sessions, while a Presidium elected by both houses issued decrees when it was not it session.[18] Below the Supreme Soviet stretched an expansive network of soviets on republic, regional, city, and district levels, with over 60,000 soviets in all and some 1,500,000 local deputies throughout the country elected to two-year terms. Elections to the various levels of soviets were postponed because of the war, but in August 1945 the Central Committee of the CPSU called for elections to the Supreme Soviet to be held in February 1946, republic-level soviets in February 1947, and city and district soviets in December 1947. The decision set into motion an almost continuous series of campaigns that lasted for over two years. The Central Committee's proclamation clarified that the elections were needed "to sanction the policies of the CPSU"; this is a telling phrase because, in fact, the soviets at all levels had become merely rubber-stamp bodies endorsing decisions reached by the central party leadership behind closed doors.[19] Though the elections were for meaningless political organs, party leaders expended a great deal of time, resources, and energy carrying them out. Voters had no choice in the elections and little was decided by them, yet government officials went to great lengths to ensure unanimous voter participation.[20] People were expected to attend meetings and cast a ballot, so willingly or not the campaigns took on some meaning for everyone. Rather than dismiss the elections on the obvious grounds that they were mere political formalities, we should examine their ideological context and reconstruct the meanings people at the time ascribed to them.

The election campaigns offer another window onto life in the Soviet Union during this crucial period of "reconstruction." Important propaganda tools for those in power, the elections offered an opportunity to propagate and validate the ideology of power, including the regime's mythologized

---

patrick, *Everyday Stalinism*, 180–82; *Stalin's Peasants*, 280–85; and Ellen Wimberg, "Socialism, Democratism and Criticism: The Soviet Press and the National Discussion of the 1936 Draft Constitution," *Soviet Studies*, no. 2 (1992): 313–32.

[18] The Stalin Constitution entrusted executive and administrative authority to a Council of People's Commissars (renamed the Council of Ministers in 1946).

[19] See *Pravda*, 16 August 1945, p. 1. For a description of the Soviets and their role, see Roy Medvedev, *Let History Judge*, chap. 3. As Fitzpatrick notes, "[T]he national parliament to which deputies were elected had no real political power" (*Everyday Stalinism*, 180).

[20] On this point, see Hoffmann, *Stalinist Values*, 155; and Petrone, *Life Has Become More Joyous*, 176–79.

version of the war. The campaigns began months before the elections with posters, banners, red flags, and party slogans decorating Rostov's streets. Party agitators, mostly young rank-and-file party members with full-time jobs, fanned the city to hold mandatory meetings with the electorate, explaining voting procedures and theories behind the elections while fielding questions and listening to complaints. They reported extensively on the mood and concerns of the electorate, filtering the voice of the voting public up through the power structure, while also organizing and carrying out the elections. On election day voters stood in line at the polling sites, in schools, factories, and public buildings, showing their passports with residency stamps to members of the voting commission, who checked their names against registration lists and gave out ballots. Although non-communists were on the ballot as part of the "Communist and non-party" bloc, as in 1937 the CPSU selected and approved candidates through party and trade union organizations, and once the selection was made there was no further contest. The name of the single candidate was listed, and voters either returned their ballots with no mark, indicating that they supported the party's candidate, or invalidated the candidacy by crossing out the listed name. "Secrecy" was guaranteed because people could go into booths to mark their ballots.[21] Though the elections merely confirmed decisions that had already been made, the regime wanted to prove claims of unanimous support, so refusing to vote was a strong form of protest.

The Elections in the Party Press

The party's public record depicts the elections as an expression of "socialist democracy" wherein citizens control their government, with the war experience heavily influencing campaign rhetoric. The USSR's "highest form of government," according to the Stalin constitution, was based on the "state of the proletariat and peasantry." Basic economic rights were guaranteed, including the right to work, education, rest, and maintenance in sickness and old age, while Article 125 assured basic political freedoms. Of course, as we will see, the party acted as intermediary between citizens and "their state," and, as we have already seen, the state did *not* adequately supply the population's material needs nor grant basic rights to its citizens. A Central Committee Proclamation on the eve of the elections to the Supreme Soviet reminded readers that the party "comprises the most advanced and conscious members of Soviet society [who] pursue the interests of all working people."[22] The party,

---

[21] On this point, see Getty, "State and Society Under Stalin," 35.

[22] *Pravda*, 2 February 1946, p. 1. Article 126 of the 1936 Constitution states: "The most active and politically conscious citizens in the ranks of the working class, peasants, and intelligentsia voluntarily unite in the Communist Party of the Soviet Union, the vanguard of the working people in their struggle to build communist society and the

moreover, led the most "democratic" country in the world; a *Molot* article contrasted "Soviet and Bourgeois Democracy" to illustrate this point. The basis of the Stalin Constitution, it explained, was "already existing socialism," meaning "the liquidation of exploitation and exploiting classes, the end of inequalities between an impoverished majority and wealthy few."[23] There were those in the party, as we shall see, who openly disavowed claims of Soviet "socialist democracy," and undoubtedly others who harbored doubts. But there were also many people, party and non-party alike, who accepted the basic tenets of the prevailing political master narrative, which shaped the contours of political discussions in postwar Soviet society.

The election campaigns gave form to an early myth of the war with a strong Stalinist flavor.[24] The notion that the Soviet Union "saved humanity" from "Hitlerist banditry" underlies this early war myth, formulated in part by Stalin himself when he addressed the Soviet people for the first time after the German invasion, on July 3, 1941. The Red Army would fight not only to defend its own soil, he said, but "for the freedom of all peoples under the yoke of German fascism."[25] Four years later on victory day, May 9, 1945, *Molot* proclaimed that the Soviet Army, under the guidance of the "wise and beloved Comrade Stalin," deserved "endless glory as the saviors of humanity!"[26] Triumph, it added, proved the "superiority" of the Soviet Union's socialist system. In one of his most significant postwar speeches, given on the eve of the elections in February 1946, Stalin emphasized the war as a test of the socialist system that legitimated Soviet power. "The war showed," he said, "that the Soviet social structure is a genuine structure of the people" and "the best form of social organization compared to any non-Soviet social structure."[27] A Central Committee Proclamation prior to elections to the Supreme Soviet clarified that the war was about "the life or death of the Soviet state and people, about whether or not the Soviet Union would be enslaved or free.

---

leading core of public and state organizations." *Constitution (Fundamental Laws) of the Union of Soviet Socialist Republics* (Moscow, 1957), 103.

[23] *Molot,* "O Sovetskom i burzhuaznom demokratizme," 5 February 1947, p. 3.

[24] On the myth of the war that takes shape as the war is still raging, see Merridale, *Ivan's War,* 188 (and, more generally, chap. 6, "A Land Laid Waste").

[25] The USSR's alliance with Nazi Germany prior to June 1941 is obviously conveniently forgotten in this view. Stalin's speech is cited in Karol, *Solik,* 77.

[26] *Molot,* "Sovetskii narod torzhestvuet pobedu," 10 May 1945, p. 1.

[27] *Pravda,* 10 February 1946, p. 1. A *Molot* article on the eve of the elections a year later explained: "Victory proves that the Soviet state, created by the people and under the leadership of the Bolshevik Party, is the best possible form of social organization." *Molot,* "O Sovetskom i burzhuaznom demokratizma, 5 February 1947, p. 3.

Under Stalin's call the masses rose to the defense of the Motherland."[28] The early myth of the war, therefore, included a conceptualization of the Soviet Army as "saviors" of the world, a belief that the USSR triumphed because of the inherent superiority of its socialist system, and the notion that the country won the war due to Stalin's guidance.

This myth took shape in tales of the city's "liberation" from Nazi occupation, reports of the ritualistic meetings arranged for Red Army troops returning home from the war, and, of course, accounts of annual victory day celebrations. The February anniversary of Rostov's liberation coincided closely with the first two elections—those to the Supreme Soviet and republic-level soviets—so it received a lot of attention around election time. Talks, lectures, and celebrations were held every year to remember the event, the equivalent of a local victory day. In 1946 *Molot* ran a piece on the anniversary by Marshall R. Malinovskii describing how his forces liberated Rostov-on-Don. "Within three hours after the operation began," he elucidated, "we were in the streets of Rostov looking in the tear-filled, joyous eyes of the population."[29] The city's liberation was celebrated even before the end of the war, in 1944, when Nikolai Fedunov, commander of partisan forces, gave a lengthy talk recounting his experiences. In August 1942, he said, "filthy lies circulated in our beloved city that Comrades Stalin and Kaganovich had killed Voroshilov and left the Soviet Union, flying to America and handing Moscow over to German command." Even the partisans were shaken by this, he added, some of them asking, "what are we fighting for when even Comrade Stalin has abandoned us?" Fedunov said he told the partisans, "even if Comrade Stalin did abandon the Soviet Union the Russian people would fight to its last breath. But I am completely convinced that under no circumstances would Comrade Stalin, an iron-willed man, leave Russia behind. He would die at his post in his homeland!"[30] Fedunov's speech, which emphasizes Stalin's "iron-willed" leadership, implicitly suggests the *possibility* that Stalin might have left (or died), even as it negates that possibility with assurances of his manhood (i.e., that he would remain at his post and fight to the death as any good soldier is expected to do).

Ritualistic meetings of troops returning from the front, which became closely intertwined with the election campaigns, also helped define and prop-

---

[28] *Pravda*, 2 February 1946, p. 1. For similar accounts, see also *Pravda*'s tribute to victory, 9 May 1945, p. 1. The party press, as we will see, also emphasized the wartime experiences of candidates to the elections.

[29] R. Malinovskii, "Osvobozhdenie Rostova," *Molot*, 13 February 1946, p. 2. Also in *Piat' let spustia*, 4.

[30] For the text of the speech, which was delivered in public, see TsDNI f. 13, op. 4, d. 116, ll. 113–20. For the rumors about Stalin, see l. 114; see also Johnston, "Subversive Tales?" 62–78

agate the early myth of the war.[31] Demobilization began in August 1945 with the release from the Red Army of soldiers over 40 years of age, and trainload after trainload shortly poured into cities throughout the country. The returning troops were met with banners, posters, and pamphlets about the elections, as well as candidates, representatives of district party organizations, delegations of workers, and usually an orchestra. This was, of course, in addition to family members awaiting loved ones, hoping they would be on the next train. District party bureaus took turns organizing the celebrations, which were planned in intricate detail. A *Molot* report of August 1945 noted that 1,000 people came to the city's main train station to meet demobilized troops, many from a Rostsel'mash delegation. "At exactly 1:00 an echelon of demobilized troops marched out onto the train station platform to band music and a jubilant crowd," the author stated. "Many of the soldiers had countless medals pinned to their chests," he added, "and vowed to do their best to help Rostov rebuild," linking victory to postwar reconstruction.[32] Troops returning from the war faced a devastated city in desperate need of rebuilding, and the press reports of these ritualistic events tie the great achievement past to the great challenge ahead. An early myth of the war was taking shape, a Stalinist interpretation of how the war *should* be remembered. The regime tried to mold and shape collective memories of the war and use them to political advantage, particularly by glorifying Stalin's personal role, a crucial chapter in the late Stalinist personality cult.[33] Also, postwar "reconstruction" was linked to and thus *part of* this developing myth of the war, as we saw in chapter 3.

Victory day celebrations constituted an important part of the myth trumpeted during the election campaigns. The day after victory *Molot* told how people gathered around radios and public speakers to hear Stalin's long-awaited address to the Soviet people. Comrade Stalin, the author noted, "had correctly said even at the most difficult time of the war that one day we would be celebrating victory in our country's streets. That day arrived." This statement of assurance implicitly carried with it a suggestion of doubt—Stalin never wavered in his belief, but what about everyone else? "And then," the report continued, over the radio came the "familiar, beloved voice of our chief, a voice that strikes a chord deep in the heart of each of us." "The war in Europe is over," Stalin proclaimed, "and the period of peaceful development

---

[31] On the celebrations for returning demobilized troops, see Merridale, *Ivan's War*, 355–62.

[32] *Molot*, "Pobediteli vozvrashchaiut k Rodnomu Rostovu," 16 August 1945, p. 2.

[33] Tanja Penter notes that "the Soviet government in the immediate postwar years tried to establish an official memory discourse on World War II that had very little in common with the real experiences and memories of the population who lived under German occupation," although, she adds, the postwar trials of alleged collaborators "provided a podium for alternative memory discourses that differed from the official Soviet discourse" (Penter, "Collaboration on Trial," 789).

has begun." He declared May 9 a day of celebration, but second-shift workers "came to their beloved factories anyway to express their joy and their love for Comrade Stalin."[34] Below the piece are two photos, one of a brigade of Red Army troops marching through the city's streets and another of a huge public meeting in the central square. A year later *Molot* reported on Victory Day festivities, though the accounts are not as long as the ones for May Day and the anniversary of the Revolution. Beneath a photo of two people receiving war medals, the paper noted large public meetings to celebrate victory. Veterans of the war spoke, a jazz orchestra played in the central park,[35] two "agitation cars" (*agitmashini*) with public speakers circled the city and regaled residents with speeches and music, and presents were given to the families of soldiers and wounded war veterans.[36] Another report noted that Stakhanovites speaking at factories "thanked Comrade Stalin, organizer of our victory, and vowed to over-fulfill the fourth five-year plan."[37] The paper reported annually on V-E Day, though the coverage remained less extensive than that for May Day and the anniversary of the Bolshevik Revolution, both of which were state holidays, whereas V-E Day was not.

The war records of candidates for the elections were touted in official biographies that created a "good communist" image of leaders with unquestioned ability, honesty, and loyalty. Printed as leaflets and widely distributed at factories and elsewhere, the biographies of party candidates for elections to the Supreme Soviet depicted a certain breed of communist. The portrayal of Boris Aleksandrovich Dvinskii set the pattern. Dvinskii, former first secretary of the Rostov obkom, was running as Taganrog's representative for the Supreme Soviet. Born in 1894, he was orphaned at age 13 with the death of his father, a clerical worker. A bright young boy, Dvinskii worked his way through school by tutoring "bourgeois" students. When he finished studying at Moscow University in 1917 he went to work as a teacher, receiving his first position in the government bureaucracy in 1918. After supporting the Bolshevik cause in the Civil War he joined the party in 1920. In the 1930s he worked in a central bureau in Moscow, from where he was sent to serve as second and soon first secretary of Rostov oblast in early 1937.[38] He received the highest medal, the Order of Lenin, in 1941. During the war years, the biography informed, "the oblast organization of Bolsheviks under Dvinskii's leadership solved the problems of mobilizing people and resources." Dvinskii returned to Rostov-on-Don the day of its liberation and, thanks to his guidance, "reconstruction took on a genuine mass character." In September 1944

---

[34] *Molot*, "Sovetskii narod torzhestvuet pobedu," 10 May 1945, p. 3.

[35] Shortly thereafter "jazz" would be denounced as a Western perversion of music.

[36] *Molot*, "Segodnia na ploshchadiakh i ulitsakh Rostova," 9 May 1946, p. 4.

[37] *Molot*, "Prazdnovanie dnia pobedy v Rostove," 11 May 1946, p. 1.

[38] As noted in chap. 1, the top of the local party leadership in Rostov oblast was purged, which explains Dvinskii's rapid advancement at the time.

he was moved to a position in the State Procurement Bureau. His biographer assured readers that Dvinskii "fulfills the obligations of a people's candidate and deputy of the Supreme Soviet" because he is "tightly bound to the workers of Rostov oblast."[39]

The biographies of other candidates for the Supreme Soviet raised similar themes. Petr Il'ich Aleksandriuk was born into a family of landless peasants in 1904, losing both parents by the time he was 13. His relatives finally received "long-awaited and hoped-for land" in 1918, and Petr became involved in political activities. He received an education, finishing the Pedagogical Institute of Krasnodar in 1928, and began moving up the party hierarchy. As first secretary of a rural district in Rostov oblast he received a medal in 1938, exhibiting the attributes of a "true party leader" and "pupil of Stalin." During the war he "organized partisan columns along the Don," receiving two medals for his efforts. After liberation Aleksandriuk remained "inseparably tied to the working masses," receiving three more medals for successfully carrying out grain procurement in 1944. He replaced Dvinskii as first secretary of the Rostov obkom in September 1944. The handbill assured voters that he was "a fervent and faithful son of the party, a humble, decisive leader who gets things done."[40] Nikolai Petrovich Kucherenko was born in 1903 to a family of middle-peasants and was also orphaned at 13. He studied mechanics in the Red Army in the late 1920s, and in 1930 he moved to Rostov to help in the construction of Rostsel'mash, where he settled in as an exemplary worker and shop foreman. Kucherenko, according to this account, wanted to go to the front when the war began, but plant leaders said he was needed in production. He evacuated equipment with the German advance, maintained a leadership role in the plant while it was in Tashkent, and helped rebuild Rostsel'mash after the liberation of Rostov. Kucherenko had "the excellent traits of a Russian man [chelovek][41]—a firm character and patience," apparent in his rise from a peasant background to become a "faithful son of the Bolshevik Party." Most of the official biographies told a similar tale.[42]

Public biographies for celebrity figures and women, moreover, did not deviate from the norm. Well-known author Mikhail Aleksandrovich Sholokhov was a candidate for the Supreme Soviet from Rostov Oblast.[43] Born in 1905 in a Cossack village, his father an official in the government bureaucracy, Sholokhov started writing at age 18, publishing his first book in 1925.

---

[39] GARO f. 3737, op. 8, d. 32, l. 3.

[40] GARO f. 3737, op. 8, d. 32, l. 7.

[41] The term chelovek can mean either "man," "woman," or (more generally) "person"; the word is of masculine gender.

[42] GARO f. 3737, op. 8, d. 32, l. 2. Kucherenko was the candidate to the Supreme Soviet for Rostov's Proletarskii district. For other biographies of candidates to the Supreme Soviet, see also GARO f. 3737, op. 8, d. 32, ll. 1, 6–7, 10.

[43] Millerovskii district.

The biographer assured that he "learned about life not from books, but from experience" as a worker, writing the classic *Quiet Flows the Don* (*Tikhii Don*) in his spare time for 14 years. This book, "satiated with Bolshevik ideals, social-ist realism and popular sentiments (*narodnost'iu*)," marked the highest level of Soviet literature. A party member since 1932, during the war Sholokhov was a correspondent for *Pravda*, receiving several medals. He remained a popular man of the people, the biography concluded, and a worthy candidate for the Supreme Soviet.[44] While there were no women candidates from Rostov oblast, an obituary in *Molot* for party leader Anastasia Kondrat'evna Krasikova fol-lowed the same pattern. Head of propaganda for the gorkom at the time of her death in 1946, Krasikova was described as a "faithful daughter of the Bol-shevik party." Born in a rural area to an impoverished Cossack family, she received an education "with great difficulty" under the tsar and became a teacher in 1912. After the revolution she carried out party propaganda work among young Cossacks, joining the party in 1920. In the 1930s she completed the Institute of Journalism, writing for *Molot* several years thereafter. During the war she "carried out major work in mobilizing the masses to help the front," receiving numerous medals for her efforts. Krasikova, who played a major role in organizing the election campaigns, was, according to her official biography, a great orator and tireless agitator "very well respected by the workers of Rostov."[45] She is also obviously an example of a Cossack who strongly supported Soviet rule.

These biographies drew the "public face" of party leaders, beginning with the socioeconomic background of their subjects and charting the difficulties in their lives, always pointing out if they were orphaned at an early age. The party assumed the role of surrogate parent for these poor orphaned "sons" and "daughters" of Lenin-Stalin, another example of "family rhetoric" dis-cussed previously. There was an emphasis on social mobility under Soviet rule and no discernable gender variation in the biographies of public leaders (although, of course, women were much less represented at the highest eche-lons of power, as we saw in chapter 2). These figures worked their way up through talent to overcome all obstacles, receiving an education (often be-cause of the revolution), and in many cases specializing at institutes during the 1930s. They were representatives of the "Brezhnev generation" advancing through the party's ranks during the Stalin Revolution, often replacing the Old Bolsheviks and others in local party leadership decimated during the purges of the late 1930s (though, of course, this was not explicitly mentioned

---

[44] GARO f. 3737, op. 8, d. 32, l. 4. The biography quotes Sholokhov's own words on the importance of popular support for Soviet writers: "each of us constantly feels the guid-ing, gentle current of mass creativity."

[45] *Molot*, 22 October 1946, p. 4.

in the official biographies).[46] Dutifully listing awards and medals, these accounts noted the heroic deeds of party leaders during the war, be it at the front or in evacuation. In one case it was pointed out that a candidate "wanted to go to the front" but was held back because he was so valuable to production. A couple of the candidates allegedly "organized partisan groups" in the lower Don region during occupation, the biographers going out of their way to paint a heroic picture. According to these portrayals, the candidates demonstrated great skill, honesty, and unquestioned loyalty without exception, and were "closely tied to the masses," creating the ultimate "good" communist image with no room for flaws on the part of these public officials.

While celebrating the war experience and lauding candidates, campaign rhetoric also contrasted a dark, gloomy, prerevolutionary past to a bright Soviet future. Articles appeared in *Molot* in the days after each of the three major elections celebrating the joyous mood of the electorate. Reports on elections to local soviets were typical, including one authored by the mother of Aleksandr Efimov, a twice decorated war hero elected to the Supreme Soviet the year before. "On this happy day," the proud mother wrote, "one unwillingly remembers the distant past [when] there was hardly any bread and we went around hungry and dressed in rags" (a *very* ironic statement given the famine-like conditions of the time!) Soviet power opened the road to education and opportunity for her children, she added, and "the party helped me raise my son to be honest, courageous, and patriotic."[47] Another article reported on 70-year-old Vasilii, who had worked for over five decades at the Lenin Shipbuilding Plant (*Lenzavod*). At a meeting prior to the elections he told younger workers that life was much better now than under the tsar. He and his family, consisting of nine voting-age adults, were in line to vote by 5:00 a.m., among the first to arrive "to fulfill their obligation to the motherland." He said workers had absolutely no rights before the revolution, but now they elect their own leaders. Also, both his children had higher degrees, which would have been impossible under the tsar. Vasilii then paused and asked: "And in what other country is it possible to elect workers as ministers? Nowhere! We voted for these candidates," he concluded, "because we know that they are from the same family of workers as ourselves."[48] In Taganrog an elderly worker standing in line to vote reportedly said, "before the revolution they called this street 'the devil's pit.' Now it looks totally different with a streetcar line, walkways, and schools."[49] Soviet power, in short, meant progress, upward mobility, and better conditions for the masses.

---

[46] Sheila Fitzpatrick, "Stalin and the Making of the New Elite, 1928–1939," *Slavic Review* 38: 3 (1979): 377–402.

[47] *Molot*, "Slovo materi," 22 December 1947, p. 2.

[48] A. Kutsko, "Vsei sem'ei," *Molot*, 22 December 1947, p. 2.

[49] *Molot*, "V noch' pod 21 dekabria," 22 December 1947, p. 2.

These themes are further apparent in narratives about the bright happy future. In the days prior to each of the elections *Molot* published "letters to the editor" endorsing candidates. These letters established the worthiness of the party's nominations in the words of co-workers and colleagues, including one signed by a party agitator and employee of the city's transportation trust strongly advocating K. G. Garkushenko for election to the Rostov City Soviet. The author wrote that he had known the candidate for 15 years, watching with other long-time employees as "in front of our very eyes this young man grew into a skilled specialist," completing an engineering institute in 1930. Garkushenko, his friend stated, works by example, staying at the job day and night when necessary to overcome problems and provide the city with much needed transportation. Owing in part to his example "in the near future Rostov will become the most beautiful city in the Soviet south."[50] The city's future was on display in the form of an architectural model at one voting precinct during the December 1947 elections, giving people a chance to see what they were voting for. "Broad streets, high buildings, new workers' suburbs, theaters, and squares," *Molot* detailed, "how beautiful it will be in the new, prosperous Rostov! Every Rostovian thinks about the future of our native city," the piece continued, "and all are sure it will become even more beautiful in the near future." As more and more people arrived in a steady stream to vote, the report concluded, they did so "with a strong feeling of civic pride, convinced that the people's candidates can and will make our native Rostov even better."[51] From a dark past of tsarist despotism the Soviet people were allegedly on their way to a communist future of boundless prosperity.

Topping off the master narrative or "grand fiction" of the election campaigns was the public announcement of voting results in the press. Stalin and other central leaders were often nominated as symbolic candidates to the local soviets, their names appearing on ballots throughout the country. And, of course, they usually did very well; *Pravda* described the December 1947 elections to local soviets as being "like a holiday" for workers at Rostsel'mash, who unanimously cast their ballot for Stalin, Molotov, and Mikoyan.[52] A subsequent article proclaimed, "[E]lections to local soviets are a clear demonstration of the complete moral and political unanimity of the Soviet people."[53] The day after voting for the Supreme Soviet, *Molot* declared that 99.9 percent chose the official bloc of party and non-party candidates.[54] While, as we will

---

[50] *Molot,* "Golosuite za kandidatom kommunistov," 20 December 1947, p. 1. The piece concludes that workers in their Stalinskii district voting precinct "unanimously support Garkushenko as our candidate."

[51] A. Zelentsova, "Za budushchee rodnogo Rostova," *Molot,* 22 December 1947, p. 2.

[52] *Pravda,* "Slovo stroitelei kombainov," 22 December 1947, p. 2.

[53] *Pravda,* "Vybory v mestnye sovety—iarkaia demonstratsiia polnogo moral'no-politicheskogo edinstva sovetskogo naroda," 24 December 1947, p. 2.

[54] *Molot,* 23 December 1947, p. 1.

see, the official numbers were not to be trusted, a large "majority" of voters did undoubtedly drop their ballots in without marking out the candidate's names. Yet local party leaders felt compelled to stretch the numbers to the edge of total unanimity, with opposition to party rule reduced to a small fraction of one percent. Thus, on paper the elections had indeed "sanctioned the policies of the CPSU," as the Central Committee proclamation requested; it was, however, a constructed "majority," the pre-packaged, guaranteed result of the campaign and the ways in which the elections were carried out.[55]

The 1936 Stalin Constitution theoretically established the country as a "socialist democracy" with basic political freedoms *plus* economic rights, and elections to the soviets, with their long history rooted in spontaneous worker revolt, were important expressions of the country's ostensibly "representative" and "democratic" political system. The campaigns provided a chance to propagate victory as a result of Stalin's leadership, a sign of the system's legitimation and superiority, and an indication of the Soviet Union's role as "savior." An early Stalinist myth of the war trumpeted his wise guidance while linking victory to the challenge of reconstruction. This myth included rituals like local celebrations of "liberation" from Nazi occupation, mass meetings of soldiers returning from the war, and annual celebrations of victory day. Biographies of candidates to the elections, meanwhile, constructed mini-myths of heroic deeds during the war as part of a "good communist" archetype. In another example of "family rhetoric" the party assumed a paternal role for these orphaned "children of the revolution," and through them for the population at large. These "representatives" of "socialist democracy" were supposedly intertwined with the masses, whose interests were assumed to be the same as those of the figures in power, as indicated by the generic terms used to describe people in society like "voting public" or "citizens." Public party material on the elections, furthermore, stressed social mobility and progress while contrasting the harsh prerevolutionary past with the bright Soviet future ahead. The underlying message of such texts is that no matter how bad things might be now, they used to be even worse, and, of course, the situation will improve because the people themselves are in power. Campaign rhetoric constructed and propagated a paradigm of power in various ways, imposing the regime's understanding of political, social, and economic "reality" on the country's political discourse at this crucial juncture in its history.

---

[55] In reference to the 1937 elections to the Supreme Soviet, Getty cites a secret telegram from Georgii Malenkov, a key aide to Ezhov and a Central Committee operative, to all local electoral commissions. The tallied votes were to be communicated to Moscow before being passed on to the press. ("Even though they faced the electorate uncontested," Getty notes, "the Moscow leadership apparently feared they might lose.") "Given Malenkov's insistence that his office control all reporting of vote counts," he further states, "we can wonder whether the reported totals bore any relation to reality" (Getty, "State and Society Under Stalin," 35).

Discussion of the Elections Behind Closed Doors

Party representatives filtered their views of Soviet society through the ideological assumptions of the public record, but also perceived and often acknowledged the population's economic hardships. Addressing a meeting of
party agitators before the elections, gorkom secretary Comrade Stepanov berated the primary party organization and union at one factory for not dealing
with problems in daily life faced by workers. Activists there did not know
how well the factory cafeteria functioned, who in their plant was in need of
immediate monetary assistance, nor how many workers' children could not
go to school because of a lack of clothing. He reminded his listeners that "the
interests of our party and those of our people are one and the same." Stepanov cited countless other examples as well. The walls of one worker dormitory were either covered with ice or had water constantly flowing down them
and, he noted, the mass transit in the city operated inadequately, causing
major complications for workers. "Comrades," he declared, "you all clearly
understand that in isolation from these burning issues of the day (*zlobodnev-
nye voprosy*), our mass-political work [during the campaigns] loses all meaning and becomes abstract (*bespredmetnyi*)."[56] Thus party discussions behind
closed doors acknowledged problems left out of campaign rhetoric for the
public, while the ruling ideology imposed itself and its limitations on the conversation: Stepanov concluded that ultimate blame lay not on harsh material
conditions—economic "rights" constituting a crucial part of Soviet "socialist
democracy"—but on the failure of specific inattentive members of the "vanguard" party to overcome workers' material problems.[57]

The party's internal record also reduced the Soviet political arena to an
"us" and "them" scenario—focusing on repatriated citizens among others—
that contrasts sharply with the image of complete "political unanimity" presented in public texts. Discussing the campaign for elections to the Supreme
Soviet, Rostov obkom member Comrade Cheburakov underscored the threat
posed by "enemy elements." Up till now, he mused, agitational work has not
done enough "to reveal demagogues, put an end to unhealthy attitudes, and
carry out a decisive struggle against pernicious rumors." He described a
scene after a recent campaign meeting when several workers in a corner expressed "unhealthy attitudes." "What sort of democracy is this," they reportedly asked, "when we have to vote for a person we don't know, who they

---

[56] TsDNI f. 13, op. 4, d. 213, ll. 78–80. Stepanov adds that the cafeterias at Krasnyi
Aksai, Lenzavod, Rostsel'mash, and Military Factory No. 168 were cold and dirty and
lacked dishes and spoons for patrons, and that workers' dormitories in these and other
factories were also in terrible shape, issues that we saw in chap. 2 as well. For further
discussion among party leaders linking campaign work with material conditions, see
also TsDNI f. 13, op. 4, d. 144, l. 194.

[57] I develop this point further in the next chapter on Rostov's local party apparatus.

force upon us, and we're not allowed to write in our own candidate?" Cheburakov added his concern about the negative influence repatriated citizens had on "backward workers" with their tales of comparative wealth in Germany.[58] He called on propagandists to unmask enemies "who are likely to become more active during the campaign and attempt to undermine the elections by discrediting the candidates and instilling distrust in the electorate."[59] At another closed gathering Comrade Krasikova, head of the gorkom's agitprop department, warned agitators, "many repatriated citizens returned to our country with enemy attitudes and we will have to work closely with them."[60] Elsewhere a party representative said, "many repatriated citizens lag behind (*otstaiut*), expressing enemy attitudes, praising life abroad, and spreading pernicious rumors. Enemy elements work among them," the speaker added, clearly delineating between "us" and "them" in his description while encouraging propagandists to "work with them" and "convince them of the superiority of the socialist system compared to capitalism."[61]

Internal documents further show that leaders of the "superior socialist system" did not want to look bad at election time, as was also the case in 1937 and in the 1947 Polish elections. During one of Rostov's frequent bread supply crises in December 1945, someone at a gorkom meeting said the long bread lines were unbearable during preparations for elections to the Supreme Soviet. Later that month, noting that local police organs had not done enough to combat Rostov's rising crime rates, the gorkom added 150 new officers to the police force just before the election. The decree called for an improved effort, "especially since during the election campaign crime helps activate enemy elements opposed to the party's political agenda."[62] A gorkom report noted that police work improved in February 1947, but that the struggle with crime weakened immediately afterward.[63] There were fleeting improvements in living standards during the campaigns. According to an agitator's report, residents of one housing complex pointed out that during the previous two campaigns electrical service to their area was good but was cut off again shortly afterward. The agitator promised to see to it that the improvements

---

[58] Catherine Merridale also points out that Soviet veterans were prone to make such comparisons. See *Ivan's War*, 286 and 354.

[59] TsDNI f. 13, op. 4, d. 187, ll. 45, 49. For similar expressions of worry by party leaders about the negative influence of repatriated citizens on voters, see TsDNI f. 13, op. 4, d. 144, l. 197.

[60] TsDNI f. 13,op. 4, d. 252, l. 8.

[61] RGASPI f. 17, op. 122, d. 198, l. 184. Rumors they spread include that Ukraine would be given to America as repayment for lend-lease material. For an excellent discussion of the role and importance of rumor in the postwar USSR, see Johnston, "Subversive Tales?"

[62] TsDNI f. 13, op. 4, d. 149, ll. 145, 168–69.

[63] TsDNI f. 13, op. 4, d. 293, l. 95.

were permanent.[64] At the central level consideration of public opinion was apparent in the timely decision to end rationing one week before elections to local soviets, hardly coincidental given Stalin's promise to do so a year-and-half earlier (and, as we saw, his failure to do so on the 30th anniversary of the Bolshevik Revolution).[65] The party's obvious solicitousness prior to the elections indicates a responsiveness by party leaders to some of the difficulties facing voters (albeit on a superficial basis and in a piece-meal fashion); it is, as Getty notes for 1937, a sign of the regime's weakness.

The public's concerns were funneled up the party's ranks by agitators who compiled countless reports about their interactions with voters. According to a gorkom document, in the months prior to elections to the Supreme Soviet, 1,562 party agitators carried out 80,460 discussions, 87 evenings of questions and answers, 118 consultations, and 183 seminars in Rostov.[66] A secretary in the Staliniskii district party branch summed up their position at an agitprop meeting, stating that agitators not only answered questions about electoral laws and the Stalin Constitution, but also had a chance to study voters' lives.[67] Examples of their "great" work among the electorate are numerous in these narratives. In Kirovskii district a resident complained about the lack of heat in her apartment to an agitator, who saw to it that the problem was fixed, "earning the trust of voters in the area and thereafter being welcomed by the electorate as a guest."[68] This statement implicitly suggests that party agitators did not always share that trust and were not necessarily always welcomed. In another case an agitator helped find an apartment for a worker and his family who for five months had been living in a cold corridor.[69] One agitator even saved the life of a young woman who attempted suicide due to her "difficult living conditions."[70] In still another instance an agitator convinced an estranged husband to return to his wife, turning the woman from someone "almost anti-Soviet in outlook" into an enthusiastic voter and supporter of the Communist Party.[71] In these accounts agitators provide a link between the party and the electorate by fulfilling the promises

---

[64] TsDNI f. 13, op. 4, d. 233, l. 18. Most of the residents worked at Krasnai Aksai.

[65] In his February 1946 speech on the eve of elections to the Supreme Soviet, Stalin announced that rationing would end "in the near future," but, as we have seen, the famine foiled plans to end it that year.

[66] TsDNI f. 13, op. 4, d. 213, l. 140. Getty shows that central leaders constantly berated local party organizations for poor work in organizing the election campaigns.

[67] TsDNI f. 13, op. 4, d. 144, l. 196.

[68] TsDNI f. 13, op. 4, d. 187, l. 103.

[69] TsDNI f. 13, op. 4, d. 259, l. 24. For other examples of agitators helping meet the demands of voters, see also TsDNI f. 13, op. 4, d. 221a, l. 169; TsDNI f. 13, op. 4, d. 253, l. 5; TsDNI f. 13, op. 4, d. 213, l. 46.

[70] TsDNI f. 13, op. 4, d. 253, l. 5.

[71] TsDNI f. 13, op. 4, d. 252, l. 26.

of official political rhetoric, going above and beyond their role as propagandists spreading the party's line on the upcoming elections.

Internal party discussions also reveal, however, that not all party activists were enthusiastic about the campaigns. Someone at a party meeting in February 1946 complained that several agitators were not carrying out their work, appearing only rarely at the headquarters of their voting precincts.[72] Most agitators, over two-thirds of whom were either party members or candidate party members, campaigned for the elections in addition to their usual work load, and there were limits to what they could do. Party activists faced the same problems as everyone else, and they were susceptible to attacks while making their rounds in a town which, as we saw in chapter 2, was inundated with criminals. The assistant director of the Leninskii agitation and propaganda (agitprop) department told a party meeting that muggers stole the clothes off of an agitator, an incident that caused a great deal of consternation among other agitators in that district. The representative of one district party branch relayed how an entire delegation of agitators came to him and demanded weapons, saying, "if you don't give us weapons, we will not go out agitating at night."[73] No wonder that, as we will see, one of the citizenry's main concerns during the elections, voiced again and again in meetings with party representatives, was crime—even the party's own agitators feared the streets in carrying out their duties.

Also, contrary to public reports in the local press, meetings with demobilized troops were often poorly arranged. An investigator from Moscow found that the Rostov oblast party organization did an inadequate job organizing the meeting of demobilized soldiers.[74] A follow-up report by the gorkom noted that due to poor organization of the meetings "a small number of workers participate"; as few as 100 people met one trainload of demobilized troops. Another echelon of returning troops on August 1 was not met at all, while the meetings were often so poorly organized that workers had to wait for hours before anyone arrived.[75] The difficulties uncovered in these internal reports contrast sharply with the enthusiastic press reports of the meetings.

Party leaders also discussed religion, a potential ideological threat or challenge to Marxism-Leninism, as they had in the first elections a decade earlier. This issue came up well before the election campaigns, as in 1944 a gorkom secretary cautioned that religious influences were growing, and at a meeting the following year a speaker lamented that young people were turn-

---

[72] TsDNI f. 13, op. 4, d. 213, l. 140.

[73] TsDNI f. 13, op. 4, d. 221a, ll. 170, 195.

[74] RGASPI f. 17, op. 122, d. 146, l. 27.

[75] TsDNI f. 13, op. 4, d. 148, l. 35.

ing to religion.[76] Several internal reports noted church weddings and other religious acts by party members, for which they were either censored or excluded.[77] One account cited as proof of the "low cultural level" of the voting masses the tale going around town that a woman's icon was miraculously renovated.[78] At a closed party meeting with agitators, Comrade Krasikova told those present they should "teach people to hate religion." The number of believers was growing, she noted, and "workers think God helped us win [the war]—that earlier we conflicted with God but now are at peace with Him." Krasikova complained that in their campaign work agitators no longer even pronounced the term "anti-religious propaganda," although "religion is still an opiate of the masses."[79] Reports from polling sites indicated the influence of religion on the elections, especially among older voters. An 81-year-old woman "crossed herself in a religious manner" and said, "May God help the elections go smoothly."[80] The report couched this statement amid positive comments about the elections and did not criticize the woman's religious beliefs. In the December 1947 elections an elderly man is said to have "crossed himself and the ballot box according to an old Russian tradition," referring to a practice rooted in rural *zemstvo* elections during tsarist times.[81] These detailed accounts of voters' actions indicate the strength of religious feelings among some while also showing that party representatives at the polling sites were watching people closely.[82]

---

[76] TsDNI f. 13, op. 4, d. 65, l. 40; and TsDNI f. 13, op. 4, d. 186, l. 16. The latter speaker further complained that teachers were not doing anything to stop religious conversions.

[77] See TsDNI f. 13, op. 4, d. 218, l. 10; TsDNI f. 13, op. 4, d. 227, l. 71; TsDNI f. 13, op. 4, d. 254, l. 92; TsDNI f. 13, op. 4, d. 295, l. 105; TsDNI f. 13, op. 4, d. 297, l. 45; TsDNI f. 13, op. 4, d. 298, ll. 10, 20, 40; TsDNI f. 13, op. 4, d. 299, l. 73; TsDNI f. 13, op. 4, d. 413, l. 33; TsDNI f. 13, op. 4, d. 415, l. 38. Zubkova also shows the significance of religious sentiments at this time (*Russia After the War*, chap. 7).

[78] TsDNI f. 13, op. 4, d. 415, ll. 63–64.

[79] TsDNI f. 13, op. 4, d. 184, l. 53.

[80] TsDNI f. 13, op. 4, d. 259, l. 25.

[81] TsDNI f. 13, op. 4, d. 343, l. 3. The author would like to thank E. Willis Brooks for bringing this traditional practice to my attention. For other accounts of elderly voters crossing themselves in this tradition, see also TsDNI f. 13, op. 4, d. 253, l. 7; TsDNI f. 13, op. 4, d. 335, l. 75.

[82] The perceived problem of religion remained after the elections; a report from August 1948 complained that religious groups held meetings in the street and that 20–30 percent of the city's population attended church. TsDNI f. 13, op. 4, d. 427, ll. 21–22. For more on religion in the party, see also TsDNI f. 13, op. 4, d. 1, ll. 301–03. Comrade Ivanov at the Seventh Rostov City Party Conference in October 1943 complained: "A large group of communists were corrupted by religion [during the early days of the war]. Very many went to church, organized choirs, baptized children. They were all young members of the party and men were the majority."

Closed party material exposes the rule of force behind the rhetoric of "socialist democracy" and indicates difficulties with campaign work. Voters undermined secrecy, according to one report, by dropping their ballots into the boxes without going into the booths. When agitators reminded them of voting procedures, many responded, "I wish to openly give my vote for a worthy person."[83] This "widespread practice" had obvious implications for those who *did* go into the booths: perhaps they did so to mark out the candidate's name or write negative comments on the ballot. One account noted that at a polling site in December 1947, a police officer "made an unpleasant impression" on voters by standing next to the ballot box.[84] That "unpleasantness" stemmed from a perception of the rule of force underlying electoral rhetoric. For their part, local party leaders found the election results in February 1947 unpleasant as well. While 100 percent of Rostov's approximately 298,000 registered voters reportedly participated, "only" 98.41 percent voted for the approved candidates, a percentage in the lower-middle range of the average for the Russian Republic as a whole. In all 4,757 people voted against official candidates in this election. A gorkom report expressed "disappointment" that so many crossed out the names of the pre-approved candidates, the author blaming it on the fact that "district and primary party organizations failed to inspire all levels of the population with Bolshevik agitation."[85] In other words, not everyone was "convinced" by the sheer superiority of the ruling ideology. The system itself and the trying material circumstances in the country were not seen as causes of discontent; instead the fault lay with the insufficiencies in the agitprop departments of the "vanguard" party.

The party's internal record differs from official campaign propaganda in a number of ways. While conceding the importance of economic difficulties, internal party texts stop short of casting doubt on the material underpinning of Soviet socialism by recognizing poverty as the primary cause of mass discontent. Instead, problems stem from poor "mass political work" and inadequacies in dealing with "enemy elements" (including repatriated citizens) who spread "pernicious rumors" to "backward" workers. Party leaders constructed an "us" and "them" scenario to describe their relationship with at least part of the voting public. Their reading of society rested on the assumption that the enlightened voice of the Communist Party of the Soviet Union determines what is in the best interests of the working class, embodying and expressing working-class consciousness. Consequently, anyone speaking against party policies is by definition opposing the best interests of the working class and lagging behind in "consciousness," even members of that working class. Also, party representatives showed concern over their public image

---

[83] TsDNI f. 13, op. 4, d. 335, l. 72. For more information on irregularities in voting, see TsDNI f. 13, op. 4, d. 213, l. 140.

[84] TsDNI f. 13, op. 4, d. 343, l. 4.

[85] TsDNI f. 13, op. 4, d. 291, l. 180.

at election time, indicating some responsiveness on their part to the population's needs (the state *wants* society to like it). Reports on the good deeds of party agitators illustrated how they won voters' trust by dealing with these needs and solving problems largely written out of the party's public record on the elections. These accounts expose the very weakness of the system whose strengths they are intended to show; citizens, some of them hostile to Soviet power, are asked (told) to vote for the party's candidates though they have no electricity, no housing, and little hope for the "bright and happy future" ahead. Agitators themselves displayed apathy and/or apprehension toward the campaigns, party leaders perceived strong religious sentiments among the population as a threat—God, *not* Stalin, won the war!—and, public proclamations of unanimity notwithstanding, a number of voters crossed out the party's candidates.

Popular Perceptions of Soviet Elections

Judging from their recorded comments, many in the population at large saw Soviet "socialist democracy" and the war experience from a different point of view. As with most issues examined here, the elections elicited both avid support for the regime and a great deal of apathy and skepticism. Many people accepted that victory was a confirmation of their "way of life"—that the tremendous sacrifices for the cause were not in vain. Similar to the celebratory local media accounts described above, agitator reports stressed voters' enthusiasm in the polling lines as young and old competed to vote first. According to one depiction, a 63-year-old woman who had worked at DGTF for 32 years stood in line all night to guarantee her position up front in December 1947. She reportedly stated, "I received freedom from Lenin and Stalin and I will not give it up to anyone." At another polling site an 18-year-old voting for the first time arrived at three in the morning to cast her ballot first, stating: "Every person has a joyous day in life they remember forever, and for me today is just such a day!"[86] Svetlana Chernysheva turned 16 in 1946 and thus was too young to vote, but in an interview she recalled the commotion and remembered wishing she too could cast a ballot. She said she had no doubts about Soviet power or the legitimacy of Soviet rule, considering victory a "validation of the system" (*samo soboi razumeiushcheesia*).[87] It is impossible to determine how many people felt this way, but clearly there were Soviet citizens who enthusiastically supported the regime in the wake of victory.

Others, however, were less enthused, their indifference to the elections exposing cracks in the regime's master narrative of "socialist democracy." An

---

[86] TsDNI f. 13, op. 4, d. 343, l. 60. For other examples of people trying to vote first, see ll. 2, 11.

[87] Interview by author, 15 March 1995. For a similar opinion, see also interview by author with Nina K., 17 March 1995.

agitator from Andreevskii district reported difficulty getting some citizens to attend meetings, and an elderly woman asked, "Why should I attend? I know that when I'm invited on election day I will deposit my ballot and be done with it." People at the meeting "convinced" the elderly voter, the author of this report relayed, and she promised to attend the next meeting, though she complained the whole time that her head hurt. Another woman refused to attend, stating "my husband will tell me everything, so I don't need to study and I have nothing to talk with you about."[88] These reports explained voter apathy as a result of "poor political work" among the masses. In an interview Mariia Zhak, in her forties after the war, said people were glad to go vote because of the food and concerts at precinct headquarters. "Everyone understood that [the elections] were ridiculous," she maintained, "but people simply got together and voted." Genadii Ermolenko said the elections were "a game." "One had to go vote and that was it. God forbid one didn't go vote," he added, "then you had to explain why and there were problems as a result."[89] Karol remembers the February 1946 elections in his memoir. He too states that electoral precincts held buffets, concerts, and even handed out meat rations to entice voters. His friend Kolia, who had recently joined the CPSU, was a campaign agitator whose "duty is to make sure that all the voters go to the polling station," part of a socialist competition between agitators. On election day Karol recalls being bitter that he had to rise early on a Sunday, but that he did so anyway because of his friend Kolia's position. "We could have refused to take part in the rite, but it would have been dangerous, and what have we lost by it? One or two hours of Sunday rest." Most people, he notes, did not even bother to read the voting slip, but "at least six of us" went into the booth to cross out the name of the district candidate, who they did not like. Karol's wife Klava created a diversion in line so no one would notice when Karol slipped into the booth to cross out the candidate's name. The next day, however, *Molot* announced that no one cancelled the candidate's name.[90]

Just as the regime used the elections to propagate its ruling ideology, workers and others used them to voice complaints about crime and material conditions, issues of secondary importance in the party records on the elections. People questioned some of the basic aspects of Soviet "socialist democracy." Chief among voters' concerns was crime, a topic that, as we saw in

---

[88] TsDNI f. 13, op. 4, d. 253, l. 69. For other examples of people refusing to attend campaign meetings, see TsDNI f. 13, op. 4, d. 233, l. 112.

[89] Interview by author, 16 April 1995. He also remembers the buffets at election sites.

[90] Karol, *Solik*, 365–66. The candidate in question, Boris Ponomarev, eventually climbed all the way to the Soviet Politbureau. Karol notes that his friend Kolia declined all responsibility in the voting fraud, since he had not taken part in the count. Kolia claimed that he too voted against Ponomarev because he did not like the candidate and because he wanted to act in solidarity with his friends.

chapter 2, came up often in question-and-answer sessions with the public, including during the election campaigns.[91] A party activist reported that crime hampered campaign work because voters were afraid to walk the streets at night and thus did not attend meetings after dark.[92] Other problems also aggravated voters, who berated agitators with "sharp questions," as the head of the agitprop department in one district put it, concerning daily life.[93] One party member refused to vote due to the difficult material conditions his family endured. "I have become a stepson of Soviet power," he said. "All that's left for me to do is buy a rope and hang myself."[94] It is impossible to determine how many party members shared such sentiments because most would never state such opinions openly, but evidently not everyone in the "vanguard party" shared the representation of Soviet reality put forward by the party press. Workers at Rostsel'mash said they intended to vote for Kucherenko, the candidate for Supreme Soviet in their district, but demanded to know why they could not find salt, matches, sugar, and kerosene.[95] The secretary of the party organization at one factory told colleagues that workers asked countless seemingly minor but very difficult questions: "'Why does Tram No. 1 run so poorly? Why do we have to wait anywhere from forty minutes to an hour for a bus?'"[96] A voter complained in one campaign meeting that the constitutional guarantee of the right to work was not upheld because he could not freely change his place of employment. In another someone wanted to know why people were not granted the freedom to publish ideas that "do not correspond to our ideology."[97] An accountant at the fish-processing plant stated his opinion at a public gathering that the country still needed to be democratized, i.e., that it was not already a "democracy."[98] These comments and actions cast doubt on the ruling ideology's claims of "socialist democracy," holding the regime accountable while shedding light on the gap between rhetoric and "reality" as some people saw it.

---

[91] For lists of questions posed about crime, see TsDNI f. 13, op. 4, d. 221a, ll. 177–78. See also TsDNI f. 13, op. 4, d. 233, l. 93; TsDNI f. 13, op. 4, d. 259, l. 124; TsDNI f. 13, op. 4, d. 313, l. 18.

[92] TsDNI f. 13, op. 4, d. 253, l. 8.

[93] TsDNI f. 13, op. 4, d. 221a, l. 169.

[94] TsDNI f. 13, op. 4, d. 313, l. 17. For more on party members refusing to vote, see also TsDNI f. 13, op. 4, d. 259, l. 43.

[95] TsDNI f. 13, op. 4, d. 259, l. 124. See also TsDNI f. 13, op. 4, d. 221a, l. 169; TsDNI f. 13, op. 4, d. 233, ll. 1–3; TsDNI f. 13, op. 4, d. 253, l. 22; TsDNI f. 13, op. 4, l. 196.

[96] TsDNI f. 13, op. 4, d. 221a, l. 183. For other complaints by workers on daily matters, see also TsDNI f. 13, op. 4, d. 230, l. 15; TsDNI f. 13, op. 4, d. 335, ll. 27 and 103; TsDNI f. 13, op. 4, d. 233, l. 48; TsDNI f. 13, op. 4, d. 302, l. 8; and TsDNI f. 13, op. 4, d. 313, l. 18.

[97] TsDNI f. 13, op. 4, d. 259, l. 75, and TsDNI f. 13, op. 4, d. 428, l. 135.

[98] See TsDNI f. 13, op. 4, d. 343, ll. 78, 109.

There was also a gap between official and popular understandings of the political and class nature of Soviet society. Looking back on it from the perspective of the 1990s, S. I. Emel'ianenko said in an interview that he saw the Soviet system as undemocratic because "once someone worked their way up to a position of leadership they were there for life." Also, while agreeing with the tenets of "socialist democracy," he maintained there was more like a "half democracy" in the USSR because in many instances district party secretaries "could do whatever they wanted without recourse or accountability."[99] After a 1946 lecture on the political meaning of the elections a worker at the Rostov train station asked, "is there a difference between Soviet and bourgeois democracy?"[100] At another such gathering in a garment factory a worker wanted to know, "Do we have class struggle in the Soviet Union?" One confused voter inquired, "Is our government right now a dictatorship of the proletariat or of the working class?"[101] Such questions came up often, as did those having to do with working-class–peasant relations, the last remaining friendly classes in the Soviet Union according to the Stalin Constitution. A trainee at a school for railroad workers pointedly stated, "Why do they allow kolkhozniki (peasants) to sell their goods so expensively and buy bread and manufactured goods so cheaply? Won't they soon be rich while we go hungry?"[102] In Kirovskii district someone asked, "Is there a contradiction between the working class and the peasantry at the current time?"[103] Agitators occasionally interviewed party members to make sure they understood the tenets of Soviet "socialist democracy," but many seemed uncertain about the country's class structure. One even tried to explain that while there were no classes in the Soviet Union, there was nonetheless an ongoing "class struggle" against the legacy of capitalism in people's minds.[104] Another party member put on the spot said at first "hesitantly" that there were no classes, changed his mind, then "sighed heavily" and said once again that classes did not exist.[105] These questions and answers indicate that while people were unclear about the officially defined class nature of Soviet society, they were at least vaguely aware of the existence of competing interests. However, no explicit connection was made (at least not publicly) between the nomenklatura's privileged position and the "class" structure under question.

---

[99] Interview by author, 23 May 1995.

[100] RGASPI f. 17, op. 88, d. 331, l. 82.

[101] TsDNI f. 13, op. 4, d. 180, l. 42. The latter question was part of a report compiled for the center as well. See RGASPI f. 17, op. 88, d. 426, l. 100.

[102] TsDNI f. 13, op. 4, d. 415, l. 141.

[103] TsDNI f. 13, op. 4, d. 415, l. 83.

[104] TsDNI f. 13, op. 4, d. 430, l. 23.

[105] TsDNI f. 13, op. 4, d. 431, l. 68.

People did, however, explicitly criticize the lack of candidates on the ballot. Zhak remembered a joke comparing the elections to God appearing before Eve and telling her, "choose yourself a husband," when, of course, Adam was the only choice.[106] One worker wondered aloud at a public meeting why there was always only one candidate on the ballot, an issue that came up several times.[107] When asked for whom she would vote, one young woman worker responded, "whomever they force on us."[108] Another voter knew of a former Supreme Soviet deputy who surrendered to the Nazis during the war, stating "and they also told us that he was a good man." Workers accused two candidates of being rude, and a worker at Military Factory No. 168 worried, "How will we vote for those candidates who we do not know at all?"[109] A woman said she heard that during evacuation candidate Kucherenko stole state money and ran off, as had former deputy Pozhkova. "Who," she meaningfully asked, "nominates such parasites as candidates?"[110] The answer, of course, was the Communist Party, the rhetorical question implicitly casting doubt on its rule and the legitimacy of the elections. While party leaders and agitators rejected all doubts as "backward," voters questioned important precepts of Soviet political theory, illustrating the skepticism of many toward Soviet "socialist democracy." Karol describes the elections as "an astonishing spectacle of self-mystification" by the Soviet regime. "Had I not witnessed it, I wouldn't have believed that they spend fortunes in this country on an electoral campaign, as though the (only) list of 'Party and non-Party Candidates' cannot fail to be elected." He also recalls a popular joke about "Japanese-style elections." A lecturer in the university's history department, Karol explains, criticized elections in Japan, where, he told students, party bosses paid cash for each vote. "The students privately aired their views in favor of 'Japanese-style elections,' declaring their readiness to sell their vote." He adds that everyone would have preferred an envelope with a few rubles to the posters and leaflets hung all over town.

The prevalence of religious sentiments is further apparent in the popular record. Questions about church-state relations began prior to the election campaigns, while the war still raged. Religion was a popular topic in the summer of 1944, when a list of inquiries noted several questions by different (unidentified) people: "Have the Bolsheviks come to peace with religion?" "Why

---

[106] Interview by author, 3 June 1995.

[107] TsDNI f. 13, op. 4, d. 313, l. 55. For other such comments, see also TsDNI f. 13, op. 4, d. 180, l. 101; and TsDNI f. 13, op. 4, d. 233, l. 26.

[108] TsDNI f. 13, op. 4, d. 335, l. 87.

[109] TsDNI f. 13, op. 4, d. 180, l. 104. For more questions and comments casting doubts on the Communist Party's candidates, see also TsDNI f. 13, op. 4, d. 259, l. 24; TsDNI f. 13, op. 4, d. 335, l. 103; TsDNI f. 13, op. 4, d. 233, l. 1; TsDNI f. 13, op. 4, d. 233, l. 2; TsDNI f. 13, op.4, d. 343, l. 113.

[110] TsDNI f. 13, op. 4, d. 259, l. 25.

is it that we've been given the freedom of religion precisely now, and why was there such a strong battle against religion in 1918–19?" "How will religion be looked upon after the war?"[111] Such questions implicitly suggest that the Soviet state might have been using religion to win the war, only to turn against it again afterward. A separate report noted that someone asked, "Is it possible for young people who believe in God and go to church to join the Komsomol?" Several people inquired if churches opened during occupation would remain so.[112] Someone in March 1945 straightforwardly asked, "Why is our government paying more attention to religion?"[113] During campaign meetings several people wanted to know if believers could run for office, including a man who asked if he could nominate the patriarch of the Orthodox Church.[114] Voters posed numerous questions about religion at campaign meetings: "How can you explain the fact that many great people (Pavlov, Roosevelt) are believers?" "Why is religious faith so widespread?" "Why did they open the churches?" "Can party members attend church?" "Does the slogan 'Religion is the opiate of the masses' still apply given that the state is now working with the church?" "Are schoolchildren forbidden from wearing crosses to school?"[115] Clearly religion was very much on the population's mind at this time, and voters used the election campaigns to try and clarify state policies toward this very important realm of daily life.

Religious issues aside, there were several public tirades against Soviet rule and the claims of the early myth of the war, with people "speaking truth to power" at considerable risk. At a campaign meeting in early February 1946, L. G. Aralova ironically and with "a considerable negative effect" on those present remarked, "Haven't the candidates for the Supreme Soviet already been chosen a long time ago, so why carry out this comedy?"[116] The agitator leading the meeting, the author assured, "very thoroughly and correctly responded." He explained that Aralova spied for the Germans during occupation and that she led a "wild" lifestyle, noting that "soldiers often spend the night at her place."[117] The agitator's response did not even address the

---

[111] TsDNI f. 13, op. 4, d. 92, l. 413.

[112] TsDNI f. 13, op. 4, d. 92, l. 280; and RGASPI f. 17, op. 88, d. 426, l. 135.

[113] RGASPI f. 17, op. 88, d. 426, l. 98. For more questions about religion, see also l. 41.

[114] TsDNI f. 13, op. 4, d. 180, l. 104. For other questions about the potential candidacy of religious figures, see also TsDNI f. 13, op. 4, d. 259, l. 24; TsDNI f. 13, op. 4, d. 335, l. 103; TsDNI f. 13, op. 4, d. 233, l. 1; TsDNI f. 13, op. 4, d. 233, l. 2.

[115] TsDNI f. 13, op. 4, d. 188, l. 72; and RGASPI f. 17, op. 88, d. 426, ll. 135, 186.

[116] TsDNI f. 13, op. 4, d. 259, l. 124. Zubkova documents evidence of this attitude on a national level as well. See Zubkova, "Obshchestvennaia atmosfera posle voiny (1945–1946)," *Svobodnaia mysl'*, no. 6 (April 1992): 12.

[117] TsDNI f. 13, op.4, d. 259, l. 124. The description sounds like a brothel. The report does not explain why, if she worked for the German police, she was not already in jail or in exile.

elections. Instead, he cast doubt on Aralova's character, associating her alleged traitorous behavior with sexual promiscuity, a theme we examined in chapter 5. At another campaign meeting demobilized soldier Volgin gave an "anti-Soviet speech," stating that NKVD personnel receive butter, sugar, and other items, while workers get only 200 grams of sugar and seldom see other goods. "A good master feeds his horse first," Volgin stated, "then forces it to work, and it's the same with people—feed them first, then set them to work."[118] His comments, the author of this report stated, were followed up by a "thorough discussion" with "backward voters" about the country's "temporary problems with the supply of goods."[119] Another report noted that a white-collar administrator held a loaf of rye bread up to a co-worker in the party and said, "You say you've built socialism, but look at the bread I eat. Tomorrow or the next day you will probably announce that you've already built communism!" When told to join the union at work, this same man responded that he did not want anything to do with such a band of scoundrels.[120]

Workers also publicly challenged important precepts of the early Stalinist myth of the war so central to campaign rhetoric. A report by a district secretary, Comrade Romanovskii, described an interesting scene after a lecture by a party agitator, Comrade Lebedeva, entitled, "Stalin on the Twenty-Seventh Anniversary of the October Revolution." Sixty-three-year-old metal worker Romaniuk "attracted the attention of the listeners" by posing a question to Lebedeva she "could not answer." "Why," Romaniuk asked, "did Comrade Stalin not destroy the enemy in the first days of the war, ... but instead allowed them to get deep in our country and destroy many cities and villages? In tsarist times," he added, "outside armies never got so deep into our territory." Romanovskii rescued Lebedeva by answering this obvious challenge to the myth of the war and the view of Stalin as military genius, explaining to Romaniuk that Germany, the strongest capitalist country in the world that had been preparing for war a long time, invaded the Soviet Union without warning.[121] There was, however, a glaring contradiction in his rebuttal: if Germany had long since been preparing for war, their invasion should not have come as such a surprise. A worker at Military Factory No. 106 in April 1948 claimed at a meeting that not Hitler but the Soviet Union started the war in 1941, a very direct challenge to the official version of events. The report added that this worker's character was "being looked into."[122] Another account stated that a "certain Pletnikov, who stayed in occupied territory and worked

---

[118] TsDNI f. 13, op. 4, d. 343, l. 109.

[119] TsDNI f. 13, op. 4, d. 343, l. 109.

[120] TsDNI f. 13, op. 4, d. 415, l. 60. His colleagues decided to remove him from his post.

[121] TsDNI f. 13, op. 4, d. 184, ll. 74–75.

[122] TsDNI f. 13, op. 4, d. 415, l. 73.

actively for the Germans," tore down an election banner on the street and stated his discontent with Soviet rule, for which he was arrested.[123] People publicly criticized Soviet power and Stalin's handling of the war. The descriptions of and responses to these occurrences by local party leaders, moreover, exposed the repressive apparatus backing up their rule as well as their perception of what constituted an "anti-Soviet" statement.

Citizens asked provocative "questions," refused to vote—a strong form of public protest—and wrote critical comments on election ballots, sometimes also in a very public fashion. After a 1947 talk entitled "Soviet democracy and its advantages over bourgeois [democracy]," a worker asked several "anti-Soviet" questions: "Why does our 'genuine people's government' let citizens die of hunger? What freedom is there when people at Rostsel'mash work like serfs—they want to leave, but are not allowed? What freedom is there when policemen attack women on the street and steal their food?" When the lecturer tried to find out her name, this citizen quickly headed for the door, saying, "I better get out of here before they arrest me." Her name was discovered and passed on to the security organs, who "immediately began an investigation of her character."[124] In the elections of February 1947, the mother of a disabled veteran told her neighbor she would not vote even if they threatened to kick her out of her apartment.[125] In one district a citizen categorically refused to vote, finally doing so only after an agitator visited his apartment for the sixth time. One woman set her dog on an agitator, and a man responded sarcastically to an agitator's invitation to vote, "[W]hat will I vote for, hunger?"[126] One man initially refused to vote on religious grounds but eventually agreed to cast the very last ballot. A woman in another district appeared in several reports for refusing to vote because of her religious beliefs. She would not even take a bread ration card from "cursed" agitators, saying she preferred "to beg for scraps."[127] Some people who did cast ballots wrote comments on them. For example, in February 1947 a note dropped into the voting

---

[123] TsDNI f. 13. op. 4, d. 259, l. 25. For instances of people elsewhere in the country tearing down election banners and otherwise displaying their discontent during the elections, see Zubkova, *Russia After the War*, 274–75.

[124] TsDNI f. 13, op. 4, d. 343, ll. 109–10. Another internal report cites an incident when a police officer was reprimanded for taking someone's bread. TsDNI f. 13, o. 4, d. 233, ll. 44 and ob. For other examples of anti-Soviet behavior and people speaking out at campaign meetings, see also TsDNI f. 13, op. 4, d. 214, l. 168; TsDNI f. 13, op. 4, d. 253, l. 69; TsDNI f. 13, op. 4, d. 259, ll. 25, 43, 75, and 128; TsDNI f. 13, op. 4, d. 343, l. 10.

[125] TsDNI f. 13, op. 4, d. 335, l. 87.

[126] TsDNI f. 13, op. 4, d. 253, l. 19. See also TsDNI f. 13, op. 4, d. 253, l. 7.

[127] TsDNI f. 13, op. 4, d. 343, l. 1. About the 52-year-old woman, see TsDNI f. 13, op. 4, d. 343, ll. 7, 9, 78. Examples of people not wanting to vote for religious and other reasons: TsDNI f. 13, op. 4, d. 253, l. 75; TsDNI f. 13, op. 4, d. 213, l. 30; TsDNI f. 13, op. 4, d. 343, ll. 8–9, 11.

box signed by demobilized captain Zolotov asked Garkushenko, the candidate endorsed by the *Molot* letter cited above, to pay more attention to the living conditions of workers.[128]

Anonymous notes on ballots assumed a more contentious tone, while informants recorded the opinion of one party member that democracy did not exist in the country. Despite the lack of "secrecy" at the polling sites one bold voter wrote on a ballot: "When will Russia eat white bread? When will serfdom finally end among the conquerors of Europe?" Another citizen marked out the candidate on the ballot and wrote, "Today I vote for bread and something to wear. Down with empty rhetoric. Down with hypocritical, pompous lies. The Communist Party is leading the country. We suffered, went hungry. Where are you leading us? You should understand that it's impossible to live like this any longer."[129] In a military voting precinct during the December 1947 elections two voters drew swastikas on their ballots. In those same elections at the Academy of Communications someone marked out the candidate's name, the head of the Academy General Murav'ev, and wrote, "Down with this thief and fascist," and another voter there crossed out Murav'ev's name and wrote "Zinoviev" in its place.[130] The gorkom looked into the case of N. I. Repko, a decorated veteran, party member, and former instructor of cultural-educational work at an FZO. Repko lost his job and was expelled from the party in January 1948 for "criticizing the party's leading role in the election campaign for the local soviets and slanderously maintaining that there is no democracy in our country." An informant overheard and reported his blasphemous statement, and the district party organization ousted Repko from the party, the gorkom subsequently upholding the decision.[131] Obviously not all voters, including not all those in the party, believed official rhetoric on "socialist democracy." A separate *svodka* noted that one worker at Military Factory No. 359 "praises life in the American–occupied zone of Germany and shows a photo he has of life in Germany."[132] As party leaders had feared, the elections led to expressions of doubt about the Soviet system by some citizens.

The recorded sentiments of the voting public reveal support for the regime and its political rituals—the ruling ideology trying once again to "manufacture consent"—but also indifference and opposition. Some strove to vote first, but most went because they had no choice. Critical of the party's leadership and doubtful of the theoretical underpinnings of "socialist democracy,"

---

[128] TsDNI f. 13, op. 4, d. 302, l. 9.

[129] TsDNI f. 13, op. 4, d. 302, l. 9.

[130] TsDNI f. 13, op. 4, d. 335, ll. 172–73. These accounts added that the incidents "are being looked into" or "have been passed to the proper organs."

[131] TsDNI f. 13, op. 4, d. 392, ll. 86–87.

[132] TsDNI f. 13, op. 4, d. 415, l. 73. The report noted that the worker is "under investigation."

the population at large was mostly concerned with material conditions. In these sources, moreover, there is a clear indication that religious sentiments were strong. In some cases voters publicly and harshly criticized the regime, while in others they "secretly" wrote negative comments on their ballots. Those openly berating the regime were promptly placed under investigation, fired from work, or arrested, their alternative interpretations of Soviet society marginalized by official "explanations" carrying the weight of power. These incidents provided a discursive challenge to party representatives, whose efforts to comprehend mass discontent exposed a significant premise of the ruling ideology: party leaders exhibited a superior level of consciousness confirmed by the war and by their position of power; they allegedly ruled in the interests of the working class, but at the same time "ahead of" or "above" many "backward" workers. Thus those resisting needed to be "convinced" and, conversely, a lack of support proved that not enough "mass political work" was being done to "persuade" voters. While undoubtedly people in the Soviet Union were attracted by rhetoric emphasizing the war experience and linking victory to postwar "reconstruction," many also considered the elections a "comedy," or were forced to participate, or went along out of fear. Beneath official rhetoric about "socialist democracy" the popular record exposes support mixed with apathy, dissatisfaction, and even hostility toward Soviet rule.

৵ ৶

Taken together the variety of sources examined here weave an intriguing tale of Soviet political life and the postwar election campaigns from several different angles. The party press trumpeted the elections as vital to the Soviet Union's "representative" government, adding an underpinning of "democracy" to the rhetoric of power. The campaigns, moreover, granted leaders an opportunity to play up the country's triumph over Nazi Germany as they utilized an early myth of the war focusing on Stalin's brave and unfaltering leadership to persuade voters of the legitimacy of Soviet rule. At the local level, official biographies of the candidates constructed a "good communist" image of party representatives who climbed the social ladder under Soviet power, exhibiting great honesty, ability, and determination. Party discussions behind closed doors, on the other hand, showed that amid the population's discontent and apathy, local leaders were concerned about the regime's public image and saw society in terms of an "us" and "them" scenario. Official language, moreover, utilized equalizing, unifying terms such as "citizens" and "voters" (*izbirateli*) that dissolved class, gender, and ethnic distinctions in Soviet society. Along with Karol's memoir and interviews, voters' recorded comments, questions, and opinions during the campaigns, people showed support, apathy, and opposition for the regime and its elections and critically called into question some of the basic elements of Soviet "socialist democracy." Workers and others used the elections to state their dissatisfaction with many basic aspects of everyday life and material conditions, which presumably would be taken care of in a "true" socialist democracy.

Political authority is linguistic authority, but voices often rise from the cracks in the master narrative to challenge official views, as was the case in these election campaigns. Defining democracy in economic as well as political terms, the regime constructed the war experience as proof of the superiority of the Soviet system, utilizing inspiring rhetoric of triumph to divert attention away from difficult material circumstances. The notion of "the state of the proletariat and peasantry" validated the government as a form of majority rule, even though the party held the reigns of power. The Stalin Constitution allegedly widened suffrage because only "two friendly classes" remained, but this actually denoted the de facto imposition of monopoly control in the political realm. The party's role as "vanguard" implicitly justified any policy it undertook, including its domination over the nomination of candidates. Party leaders discounted conflicting interpretations of Soviet society by defining as "true" workers those who (at least publicly) accepted party leadership, while dismissing those who did not as "backward," "unconscious" "enemies." The party solicited public support prior to elections, while confidential reports equated politics to a battle with "enemy elements," depicted heroic and unenthusiastic agitators, described measures taken against recalcitrant voters, and expressed "disappointment" with voting results. Party discussions behind closed doors acknowledged material hardship but focused on problems in propaganda work. Keenly aware of that material hardship, however, Soviet citizens used the elections to voice their complaints, another chapter in the prevailing class dialogue. Some voters greeted the campaigns with enthusiasm, others with apathy, and still others with hostility toward the "vanguard" party and its candidates, exposing once again the discursive gap and class divide that prevailed in Soviet society. It remains to be seen in the final chapter what sort of internal problems and difficulties faced the Rostov party branch and how the population perceived local party leaders.

Chapter Eight

"Right now you can't get anything done without a bribe": Problems in and Perceptions of the Soviet Communist Party

The creation of the "vanguard party" was Lenin's primary contribution to Marxism and 20th-century politics more generally. Early in the century, different conceptualizations of a revolutionary party split Russian Social Democrats, the Mensheviks preferring an open, flexible party structure to Lenin's idea of a tightly-knit, highly-disciplined group of "professional revolutionaries." The vanguard's role was to lead the working masses, who, Lenin maintained, would not rise above "trade union consciousness" if left to their own devices.[1] In his view the Bolshevik Party was not separate from the working class—it was the workers' conscious revolutionary voice in the struggle against tsarist rule. After October 1917, Lenin's "vanguard party" underwent a dramatic transformation from rallying popular opinion against the government to solidifying control, managing state affairs, and suppressing opposition. The change in name to the Communist Party of the Soviet Union (CPSU) in 1919 symbolized this metamorphosis. The party remained an exclusive organization with only about four percent (or less) of the country's population as members during most of Stalin's rule. Like many such organizations it had its own official ideology, Marxism-Leninism, complete with canonical texts. Party membership was key to those hoping to build careers, making its ranks susceptible to "opportunists"—those who exploited their position for personal gain. From the outset of the USSR's formation in 1921, central leaders assailed the poor work of party functionaries at the local level. The first "purges" or "cleanings" (*chistki*) of incompetent and corrupt officials occurred under Lenin's leadership. The Stalinist regime more thoroughly purged the ranks in the late 1930s with the arrest of many local party officials, including those in Rostov as we saw, and the war led to yet another transformation of the party.[2]

---

[1] See V. I. Lenin, "What Is to Be Done?" in *Collected Works* (Moscow: Progress Publishers, 1964).

[2] On the purges, see, for example, Getty and Naumov, *Road to Terror*; and Roy Medvedev, *Let History Judge*.

This chapter looks at how the local party organization functioned and how it was perceived during "reconstruction," with a particular focus on the problem of corruption within the party's ranks. Of course, like the other issues examined here, corruption is a widespread problem by no means limited to the Soviet Union, and the term itself is imprecise by its very nature. Two prominent scholars note that "corruption should be understood as part of a broader web of social relations, which form part of the exercise of political power." Political systems themselves "enable and often necessitate corrupt practices," which are usually "embedded in clientelistic structures" and serve "as a form of protectionism." Corruption is primarily political, moreover, "in the sense that it is the political structures themselves that enable and often necessitate corrupt practices." It is a betrayal of public trust by officials that "constitutes patterns of behavior dictated by the basic operation of government and political structures."[3] In Hungary in the postwar period, for example, corruption was a latent second system of redistribution that fed on the deficiencies of the first, official distributive system. For the population at large, paying bribes became part of a "survival strategy" in which people tried "to find loopholes in the rigid framework of an authoritarian system."[4] Also, like the different gradations of "speculation" and "collaboration," there were many different shades of "corruption." "The term corruption," Joseph Lapalombara writes, "can be and is applied to a very wide spectrum of human behavior and institutions." He defines it as "behavior by a public servant, whether elected or appointed, which involves a deviation from his or her formal duties because of reasons of personal gain to himself or herself or to other private persons with whom the public servant is associated." Corruption, he continues, "requires two or more parties to a transaction, at least one of whom holds a position of public trust and/or exercises a public role, and another (or others) of whom acts in a private capacity."[5] In the USSR there

---

[3] Stephen Kotkin and András Sajó, eds., *Political Corruption in Transition: A Skeptic's Handbook* (Budapest: Central European University Press, 2002), xvii. They argue that corruption has emerged as "a language of politics" in the post-Soviet era, "especially where not only a specific ideology (communism) but also the very notion of ideology has been discredited," xvii–xviii.

[4] Elemér Hankiss, "Games of Corruption: East Central Europe, 1945–1999," in Kotkin and Sajó, *Political Corruption in Transition*, 244.

[5] For corruption to exist "there must occur a deviation from a public role," and it "is not necessarily tied to a particular type of political regime"—it may occur in democracies as well as in repressive or dictatorial regimes. "Corruption is an elusive phenomenon [that] exists in a gray zone of social interactions." Joseph Lapalombara, "Structural and Institutional Aspects of Corruption," *Social Research* 64: 2 (1994): 325–50. Robert Klitgaard points out that there are always *three* actors involved in a corrupt transaction: a client, an agent, and a principal (usually the state) that authorizes the agent to act on its behalf. Klitgaard, *Controlling Corruption* (Berkeley: University of California Press, 1988), 69–74. See also Hankiss, "Games of Corruption." Admitting

were, for example, the *tolkachi*, whose function was to supply the plant direc-tor with *whatever* was needed but not included or delivered by the plan, which usually meant utilizing unauthorized sources of supply, almost always outside the scope of the official plan. Without them production would have stalled.[6]

The editors of an anthology on bribery and *blat* stress that practices of "unofficial exchange" are deeply rooted and "have been remarkably tena-cious throughout Russian history."[7] Certainly there was systemic corruption in the 1930s; some contend that the Stalin cult stemmed from party officials' need to see some direction and coherence in the disorder for which they were responsible.[8] Leaders were concerned over the "insufficient ideological train-ing" of cadres in the 1930s, which became a euphemism for disciplinary prob-lems, the assumption being that drunkenness, absenteeism, tardiness for work, etc. by party members could only be due to a poor understanding of Marxism-Leninism.[9] Worry over the "insufficient ideological training" of party cadres, many of whom joined during the war, remained a problem in the postwar period.[10] Adopting an open-door approach and paying little at-tention to ideological criteria, the CPSU took on many soldiers and veterans. As previously, the loosening of membership requirements raised the question of ideological purity in the party afterward.[11] Party corruption was deeply

---

that it is not all-encompassing, Hankiss posits a "working definition" of corruption as "an act in which a public official (or another person in a position to distribute public goods or services) breaks the rules of distributing a public good or providing a public service, rules for the enforcement of which he or she is responsible, in favor of a client, by whom he or she is rewarded for this breaking of the rules" (245). On the vague nature of corruption in practice, see also Alena Ledeneva, Stephen Lovell, and Andrei Rogachevskii, eds., *Bribery and* Blat *in Russia: Negotiating Reciprocity from the Middle Ages to the 1990s* (London: University of London Press, 2000).

[6] Berliner, *Factory and Manager*, 18–35.

[7] Ledeneva et al., *Bribery and* Blat, 2.

[8] Rittersporn, *Simplifications staliniennes*, chap. 6.

[9] Getty, *Origins of the Great Purges*, intro. and chap. 1.

[10] Cynthia S. Kaplan, *The Party and Agricultural Crisis Management in the USSR* (Ithaca, NY: Cornell University Press, 1987), chap. 4; Rigby, *Communist Party Membership*, 237. On changes in party composition, see also Cynthia S. Kaplan, "The Impact of World War II on the Party," in Linz, *Impact of World War II*, 160–64. Kaplan and Rigby indicate the decimation of local party leadership during the war and the changes of policy in response.

[11] The party was "militarized," as Rigby puts it, while the number of white-collar em-ployees relative to industrial workers and peasants also increased, leading to concern among party leaders. A central report noted that for the country as a whole between 1941 and 1946 the percentage of white-collar workers (*sluzhashchie*) in the party in-creased by 39.6 percent, while the percentage of workers decreased by 22.7 percent and the percentage of peasants by 16.2 percent. The report added that to regain its

rooted in the postwar period, part of a change in "the nature of the Soviet dictatorship" due to "the grueling demands of post-war reconstruction and the escalating animosities between East and West." The Soviet nomenklatura feathered its nest and lined its pockets in a sinister version of the "big deal" that includes its corrupt underside.[12] In addition, there was a secret and mostly muted campaign against bribery in 1946–47 amid a "tidal wave of everyday graft endured by the majority of the population desperate to make ends meet, but forced to placate state functionaries demanding payments for regular services." At the same time, however, there was a low incidence of prosecution and a great deal of tolerance for corruption within the party because leaders did not want to create undue embarrassment.[13]

There was a distinction between party and state in the Soviet political system, but the two overlapped to a significant degree, and ultimately power rested within the party apparatus, which is why I focus on it here. The CPSU was a complex and multi-layered entity comprised of different and competing interest groups.[14] In order to join, people had to be nominated by current members and needed three recommendations from members who had known them for at least one year. Nominees then went through a one-year probationary period as "candidate" members, after which they entered as full

---

prewar social composition the party would have to take on no more white-collar employees and take in a total of 1,495,384 workers and 683,867 peasants. RGASPI f. 13, op. 4, d. 189, ll. 119–21.

[12] Cynthia Hooper, "A Darker 'Big Deal': Concealing Party Crimes in the Post-Second World War Era," in Fürst, *Late Stalinist Society*, 143. "The 'rapprochement' between Moscow and the middle bureaucratic classes that took place after 1945," Hooper states, "was more sinister than the one Dunham describes, grounded as it was in a qualified indulgence of corrupt activities on the part of Soviet elites and a redefinition of the rules of party and state control sufficient to protect these elites from overly vigilant public scrutiny or unauthorized prosecution." On the "big deal," see Dunham, *In Stalin's Time*, intro.

[13] James Heinzen, "A 'Campaign Spasm': Graft and the Limits of the 'Campaign' against Bribery after the Great Fatherland War," in Fürst, *Late Stalinist Society*, 123. Heinzen summarizes a letter by P. I. Minin to Stalin, in which Minin writes that bribes "are given and accepted by people of the most varied professions and in the most varied forms," including mail carriers, railroad employees who take money to allow passengers to ride or claim packages, and even teachers and professors who take bribes to admit students into institutes or to pass exams. Elsewhere he compares perspectives on bribery from above and below in the Soviet social structure. See Heinzen, "Graft and 'the Art of the Bribe' in the Late Stalin period, 1943–1953: The View from the State and the View from Below," unpublished paper delivered at the 37th National Convention of the American Association for the Advancement of Slavic Studies, in Salt Lake City, 3–6 November 2005.

[14] Jerry Hough, *Soviet Leadership in Transition* (Washington, DC: Brookings Institution, 1980); and Jerry Hough and Merle Fainsod, *How the Soviet Union is Governed* (Cambridge, MA: Harvard University Press, 1979).

members, the process no doubt contributing to clientelism—you had to know someone in the club in order to join. Theoretically the party's proper functioning was based on Lenin's notion of "democratic centralism," that decisions within the party would be freely discussed by all members in a democratic and open process, but that once a decision was reached everyone was obligated to carry it out. In practice, however, central leaders concentrated decision-making power in their hands, relying on local representatives to implement central policies. Power flowed from the top down in a hierarchically-structured system in which people were accountable to those above rather than those below. Many of these officials, moreover, controlled access to scarce goods in demand, which led to corruption, cliquish politics (the formation of interest groups), and protectionism. The party publicly stated the need to overcome these problems repeatedly even as the system itself gave rise to them. In response to problems within the party, central leaders assailed members of the Rostov oblast party committee for various reasons; they in turn passed the criticism down to the city committee or gorkom and regional leaders, who found fault with the work of district party secretaries. They, in turn, focused their criticisms on primary organizations or party cells.[15] At the same time, as we have seen, there was a dialogue from the bottom up, party leaders compiling svodki on the "mood" of the population, including popular views of the party and local leaders.

Developments in Rostov's party organization mirrored those of the country as a whole in the postwar years (see table 6): growth mainly on the basis of demobilization. On the eve of the war there were 10,203 members in the city, a number that fell to just 500 in February 1943 at the time of liberation. By the end of March, 2,484 party members were in Rostov, and by October 1943 the figure had risen to 4,301.[16] The city's party organization grew steadily after

---

[15] Getty shows a similar pattern for the Smolensk party organization in the 1930s. See Getty, Origins of the Great Purges, intro. and chap. 1.

[16] TsDNI f. 13, op. 4, d. 39, l. 67; TsDNI f. 13, op. 4, d. 39, ll. 12–14; RGASPI f. 17, op. 88, d. 214, ll. 2, 8. For all the cities of Rostov oblast 4,188 of 14,649 (29 percent) of party members stayed in occupied territory. The October report listed the fate of Rostov's party members: 176 joined the Red Army; 1,473 were evacuated; 207 were shot by the Germans; 18 were forcibly relocated to Germany, while 22 voluntarily left with the Germans; 85 died during the war; and the largest share, 3,369, were missing and unaccounted for. See also ll. 14, 16, 18–20. Every party organization in the city felt the impact of the war. The Stalinskii district party organization had 516 members in July 1942, but only 261 a year later. Leninskii district's membership for the same period fell from 1,951 to 777. According to one report the party cell at a ship repair shop had 104 party members and 16 candidate party members as of July 20, 1942. A year later only 58 and 13 remained. TsDNI f. 13, op. 4, d. 56, l. 64. The report specified that the Germans arrested 10 communists during occupation whose fate was unknown; 5 left for Germany with the fascists; 8 were killed in the Red Army; 9 have not yet returned

the war, mostly because soldiers and veterans who were members settled there. Overall membership grew from 13,202 in January 1946 to 21,262 a year later, and to 23,407 by the middle of 1947. One report on the Leninskii district noted "the growth of our party organization from 950 to 1,922 in 1946 took place primarily due to the demobilization of Red Army troops" (649 of 972 new members or 67 percent were soldiers).[17] Despite the growth local party bureaus were understaffed and, as we have seen, had to deal with persistent shortages of basic goods and materials, a shattered infrastructure, labor shortages, and many other problems. Control over the production and distribution of goods amid difficult material conditions bred corruption, a problem so prominent it often found its way into the press, albeit in somewhat muted terms. As Cynthia Hooper states, "City and regional (oblast') leaders were

Table 6. Membership in the Rostov-on-Don City Party Organization

Date	Number of Party Members
June 1, 1941	10,203
July 15, 1942	9,651
February 1, 1943	500
March 31, 1943	2,484
July 1, 1943	3,826
October 31, 1943	4,301
January 1, 1946	13,202
August 1, 1946	19,478
January 1, 1947	21,262
July 1, 1947	23,407

Sources: TsDNI f. 13, op. 4, d. 39, ll.12–14, 67; TsDNI f. 13, op. 4, d. 56, l. 64; RGASPI f. 17, op. 88, d. 214, ll. 2, 8; TsDNI f. 13, op. 4, d. 227, l. 52; TsDNI f. 13, op. 4, d. 295, l. 119.

occasionally forced to initiate investigations into wrongdoing for the sake of appearances, but at such moments they typically punished lower-level officials for less serious offences in order to mask larger and more incriminating crimes."[18]

Party functionaries had the most direct contact with workers at the neighborhood (or district) and factory level. In large factories an entire party structure existed outside the realm of production, staffed by members of the nom-

---

from evacuation; 15 left for other party organizations; 6 had not appeared for registration; and 2 were missing.

[17] TsDNI f. 13, op. 4, d. 215, l. 17. Rigby shows that the party countrywide took on a high percentage of soldiers (Rigby, *Communist Party Membership*, 224–25).

[18] See Hooper, "A Darker 'Big Deal,'" 147.

enklatura. They carried out propaganda on a full-time basis, coordinating labor-union activity, organizing closed party meetings and open meetings with non-party workers, dealing with requests for material assistance and/or complaints by workers, as well as other functions. At the factory level members came into contact with non-party workers at meetings organized by party cells, and, as we saw, propagandists encountered voters during election campaigns. Also, bureaucratic control over housing, passports, ration cards, marriage, etc. necessitated direct contact between the representatives of power and their subjects. One can picture the (usually) overcrowded rooms of people in an informally-ordered line waiting, for example, to have their passports stamped to verify their right to receive aid as members of a soldier's family or to prove their claim to a disputed apartment. Government/party representatives dealing with these and other cases had to weigh each in terms of individual merit against standardized rules designed to protect "the collective good." Many (not all) of them were not above taking advantage of their positions of power for personal gain, a fact that did not escape the population's attention. An examination of official and popular perspectives on Rostov's party branch during "reconstruction" adds to our picture of the period.

Party Rule According to the Press

The party constructed a "good communist" archetype of flawless leaders during the election campaigns, but it also aired at least some of its dirty laundry publicly, constructing a "bad communist" image at fault for the many problems facing society.[19] A section in the local press called "Party life" reported on flaws in the "vanguard," exhorting communists to be better party members and explaining how to improve their ways. In April 1943, for example, an article entitled "Universally strengthen our contribution to the front" identified communists "in the advance guard of the heroic struggle" to "enthusiastically and steadfastly rebuild factories" in the city. But there was always room for improvement in "agitation-propaganda work," and "now, more than ever, it is necessary to carry the fiery words of Bolshevik truth to the masses."[20] An editorial entitled "What the party demands out of communists" explained what it takes to be a good member: "party discipline, which means to conscientiously, consciously fulfill all demands and carry out all decisions taken by the party leadership." It called on communists to learn "revolutionary theory" and "raise their ideological-theoretical level," highlighting

---

[19] On the dichotomy between the good and bad portrayal of communists in party propaganda, see ibid., 154–58.

[20] *Molot*, "Vsemerno usilivat' pomoshch' frontu," 1 April 1943, p. 2. Another piece demanded that communists "piously watch over discipline" and "maintain organization and order" in their work. *Molot*, "Sviato bliusti distsiplinu, sobliudat' organizovannost' i poriadok," 23 May 1943, p. 1.

their role as "the conscious vanguard of society" and reminding them that "Marxism-Leninism is the highest achievement of world culture." Every communist had the right to discuss party policies and propose their own ideas and suggestions, it illuminated, "but once the discussion is over and a decision is taken, all members are obligated to implement it without question, even those that personally voted against it."[21] Countless articles and editorials raised similar themes which, as we will see, were also prominent in party discussions behind closed doors in this five-year period.[22]

Molot implicitly responded to constant complaints over living conditions with articles, editorials, and letters on the inadequate work of factories, stores and cafeterias, housing administrations, etc. These pieces focused mainly on the shortcomings of individual party leaders to explain material difficulties. According to one editorial, a factory's failure to fulfill its plan was "usually explained by all sorts of objective reasons—the lack of fuel, electricity, labor power, etc. But," it continued, "our role as party leaders is to overcome deficiencies."[23] In the complicated reality of the Soviet system of production, that meant have the *tolkachi* wheel and deal to fulfill the plan. Other articles portrayed party administrators themselves as deficient, such as one that claimed leaders in the oblast' trade organizations "criminally squander goods."[24] A union leader published a letter calling for workers to take a more active role in overseeing the sale of goods in stores and demanding a "decisive battle against the cheating of customers that is common."[25] An article on the poor work of the city's cafeteria trust noted that several of its leaders "explain" problems as the result of the war and other such "objective reasons."[26] During a meeting at Rostsel'mash workers reportedly complained that a leader at the plant, "talked a lot about 'objective reasons'" for various shortcomings, "but

---

[21] *Molot*, "Chego trebuet partiia ot kommunistov," 18 March 1945, p. 2.

[22] See, for example, *Molot*, "Krepnet sviaz' s massami," 14 November 1943, p. 2; *Molot*, "Za strozhaishii rezhim ekonomiki!" 19 November 1943, p. 3; *Molot*, "Uchet partiinogo aktiva," 25 December 1943, p. 2; *Molot*, "Marksistsko-leninskaia ucheba rukovodia-shchikh kadrov," 16 February 1944; *Molot*, "O partiinoi distsipline," 15 November 1944, p. 2; *Molot*, "K novomu pod"emu partiinoi raboty," 6 January 1945, p. 1; *Molot*, "Partiinaia ditsiplina," 18 March 1945, p. 2; *Molot*, "Vazhneishii uchastok partiinoi raboty," 2 June 1945, p. 3; *Molot*, "Uluchshit' politicheskoe vospitanie torgovykh rabotnikov," 20 June 1948.

[23] *Molot*, "O kontrole partiinykh organizatsii nad deiatel'nostu administratsii," 20 January 1945, p. 3.

[24] *Molot*, "Vsemerno razvivat' torgovliu," 13 October 1943, p. 1. For more articles on the poor work of stores and broken trade rules, see also *Molot*, "Po sledam vystuplenii 'Molota,'" 14 October 1943, p. 4; *Molot*, "Prenebregaiut zaprosami pokupatelei," 21 July 1948, p. 2.

[25] *Molot*, 15 April 1943, p. 2.

[26] *Molot*, "Za strozhaishii rezhim ekonomiki," 28 April 1944, p. 3.

said nothing about measures being taken to assure the fulfillment of central directives." Workers at the meeting also pointed out major flaws in the work of Rostov's main train station, "especially in the sale of tickets," and, the article noted in passing, metalworker, Stakhanovite, and rank-and-file party member Comrade Riabchenko exposed "several bribe takers" within the plant's leadership.[27] It did not elaborate on this information, but the article clearly linked workers' interests with central directives while blaming factory leaders for a failure to implement them (and for taking bribes).

There were several reports about corruption in the city's housing administrations, which were, as we saw, tainted by collaboration as well. A report in early 1945 noted the upcoming trial of several former employees of the Andreevskii district department, who stood accused of taking bribes.[28] A month later the paper divulged the details. Comrade Boichenko, head of the district apartment bureau, had taken a payoff to illegally grant someone an apartment, but soon the oblast procurator found out about the "bribery." It proved to be only the tip of the iceberg, the report informed, with six employees of the district housing administration arrested for similar offenses.[29] A year later during the party's campaign against corruption, a report stated that the city procurator uncovered "numerous cases" of corruption on the part of employees in the city's housing bureaus. An apartment manager in Proletarskii district, for example, accepted money to illegally grant an apartment to someone, as did the manager of a housing complex in Stalinskii district and several other administrators as well.[30] An account in 1947 strongly insinuated wrongdoing in another housing-related scandal in Andreevskii district. "How does one steal an apartment in broad daylight?" the article asked. After noticing a pleasant apartment building in the district, it explained, Bel'chikov appeared before a housing official claiming that he had renovated a second-floor apartment in the building in 1937 and that thus it should belong to him. He had lost all documentation proving any claim to the apartment during the war, and neighbors who could have confirmed the story had been killed. Yet despite the lack of proof, the housing official, "trusting like a child," granted Bel'chikov the apartment, evicting its current residents. "It is not even necessary to say more," the author knowingly noted, "because we all already understand what happened." Awareness of corruption was so deeply rooted in

---

[27] *Molot*, "Rabochee sobranie po tekushchim voprosam," 10 October 1944, p. 2.

[28] *Molot*, "Sud nad vziatochnikami iz Andreevskogo Raizhilupravleniia," 27 February 1945, p. 4. On the prominence of corruption among housing administrations, see Heinzen, "A 'Campaign Spasm,'" 125–26.

[29] *Molot*, "Vziatochniki iz Andreevskogo raizhilupravleniia," 16 March 1945, p. 4.

[30] *Molot*, "V gorodskoi prokurature," 28 July 1946, p. 4. For a report on major embezzlement, see *Molot*, "Kaznokrady," 15 January 1947, p. 4.

people's perception of everyday life, in other words, that it became an un-spoken "truth" or shared assumption.[31]

The press often hinted at corruption and revealed protectionism within the ranks of the local party organization. A story on a July 1943 meeting of the Kirovskii party organization explained why district secretaries Alekseev and Kravchenko were removed from office. At the meeting Gorkom Secretary Grigor'ian "sharply criticized" these leaders for "poor organizational and mass political work." They became isolated from party members in the district, were unaware of membership numbers, and failed to check up on the implementation of party policies. Economic enterprises there operated poorly, but Alekseev and Kravchenko failed to take notice, preferring "to live peacefully" alongside those "that trampled on the state's interests." These district secretaries "protected party functionaries that did not fulfill orders from the Oblast Defense Committee."[32] Alekseev and Kravchenko, furthermore, "created a culture[33] of false pleasantries and groveling," and disappeared when problems arose. District party members at the meeting resolved to take strong measures to improve "organizational and mass party political work" in the district party organization.[34] A follow-up report a month later noted that under the new leadership of district secretary Comrade Kurkov, the local party branch was addressing these problems.[35] But flaws remained elsewhere; a piece about the Leninskii district complained that while its party organization made a number of good decisions, there was no effort to make sure that the decisions were carried out. "Only that," the article proclaimed,

---

[31] *Molot*, "Sluchai neobyiknovennyi," 19 October 1947, p. 4. The report added that district-level leaders had yet to do anything about this "outrage," and that Bel'chikov also managed to get a false document from a metal-working shop saying he worked there "with incredible ease." For other reports on problems in housing administrations, see also *Molot*, "Vsledstvie deistvii," 9 April 1943, p. 2; and *Molot*, "Plokhie khoziaeva," 30 June 1945, p. 4.

[32] Although not stated, there is almost certainly a link between the removal of the Kirovskii district party leadership and the scandal at Krupzavod No. 1, which was located in the district, at almost the same time (the public announcement came in August, less than a month after this story). As noted in chap. 6, the director of Krupzavod, Katsiiaev, was reportedly a "professional criminal" who wormed his way into party leadership by using false documents, then used his position as factory director to steal tons of grain and sell it through two speculators at the market. Krupzavod was supposed to be filling orders to make cereal for the Red Army. See *Molot*, 28 August 1943, p. 4, and 6 October 1943, p. 4.

[33] The Russian verb *kul'tivirovat'* has the root *kul't*, or cult, which has obvious connotations of a cult of personality.

[34] *Molot*, "Negodnyi stil' rukovodstva," 4 July 1943, p. 2.

[35] *Molot*, "Vnikat' v ekonomiku predpriiatii," 17 August 1943, p. 2. Kurkov gave "concrete leadership to party work among the masses" and had already greatly improved agitation work in the district.

"can explain why several leading factories have not taken on a single new member" this year.[36] Articles also assailed party organizations for sloppy record keeping. In April 1944, *Molot* ran a story about disarray in the party records of Stalinskii district, where about one-third of the membership was still waiting to be issued cards.[37]

Other *Molot* reports blasted party leaders for poor work and corruption, implicitly blaming material difficulties on "bad communists" who abused their power. The management of one small machine-tools plant, for example, was singled out because of its "office-bound style of leadership." In 1945 the plant fulfilled its plan by only 78 percent, and in an interview the factory's director admitted that problems remained. The author of this article, G. Iakushchenko, wrote that workers in the plant were "hurt" because of insufficient "guidance" from above, as a result of which "labor discipline in the plant is very low." In some cases workers in the plant had not been paid their wages in over a month. The list of problems was quite long, including a failure to create suitable living conditions for the workers, inferior propaganda work in the plant, and horrendous conditions in the factory cafeteria. Although factory leaders "repeatedly promised improvements," Iakushchenko concluded, "all of that has proven to be just empty words."[38] *Molot* noted the 1944 complaints of workers at Rostsel'mash about the train station cafeteria, and an account almost three years later reported that, indeed, the managing director, accountant, and others had "systematically stolen thousands of rubles."[39] Reports of petty corruption usually included sentences meted out to guilty parties in an effort to show the party was dealing with the problem. A typical account during the party's campaign against corruption involved Zagoitov, a party representative from Khar'kov, and I. A. Iankovskii, director of Leather

---

[36] *Molot*, "Pod znakom samokritiki," 10 October 1943, p. 2. Tishchenko also said that several organizations in the district were led by people "who do not inspire trust," a very prominent issue, as we have seen, in internal party sources.

[37] *Molot*, "Za obraztsovyi poriadok v partiinom khoziaistve," 7 April 1944, p. 3. It stated the secretary of one party cell failed to write up the minutes of party meetings, and when called upon to do so he hastily sent a list of eight months worth of meetings, all by memory and without the signatures of attending communists. For similar articles, see also *Molot*, "Podgotovka partiinykh sobranii," 11 September 1943, p. 2; *Molot*, "Bol'she vnimaniia rabote s det'mi," 7 December 1943, p. 2; *Molot*, "Poverkhnostnoe rukovodstvo," 27 July 1945, p. 3; *Molot*, "Partiinaia zhizn': Negodnyi stil' rukovodstva," 17 June 1946, p. 2; *Molot*, "Bol'she zaboty o demobilizovannykh kommunistov, 14 December 1946, p. 2.

[38] *Molot*, "Kabinetnyi stil' rukovodstva," 13 March 1946, p. 3.

[39] *Molot*, 10 June 1947, p. 4. They received sentences of 25, 10, and 8 years respectively; the story does *not* refer to the aforementioned 1944 account of a meeting at Rostsel'mash where complaints about the train station were leveled. For similar cases, see also *Molot*, 20 August 1943, p. 4; *Molot*, 26 December 1943, p. 4; *Molot*, 2 April 1944, p. 4; *Molot*, 20 March 1945, p. 4.

Factory No. 3 in Rostov. Zagoitov was supposed to receive several thousand meters of pigskin, but he offered Iankovskii a bribe for a better type of leather instead. The plan was soon discovered and Iankovskii received a seven-year prison sentence, while Zagoitov was still waiting "to be brought to justice."[40]

Nepotism was another common theme in public reports on shortcomings within the party. The 1943 piece on problems in the Kirovskii party organization noted that Alekseev and Kravchenko decided questions of production "in a family way" (po-semeinomu).[41] One account accused the city's cafeteria and restaurant trust of taking on new workers "according to acquaintance" instead of experience. It described how yet another visitor came into the office of Comrade Dubrovin, head of the trust's personnel department, with a letter in hand. The letter from Comrade Savin, head of the military department of Stalinskii district, reportedly read "according to our earlier agreement I'm requesting that you employ Comrade Filonenko, my relative." The next visitor to Dubrovin's office also had a note: "Ivan Fedorovich! In light of our friendship I ask that you find a good position within your apparatus for my person [svoika]."[42] Such letters were "a daily occurrence" in the trust; there were already over 100 such "letters of recommendation" in Dubrovin's office. There was no "concern for the political qualities of hired workers," as everything depended on connections. Comrade Stalin, the author reminded readers, railed against such practices in 1937, but unfortunately things at Rostov's Cafeteria and Restaurant Trust were still done "according to acquaintance."[43] The article did not accuse Dubrovin of taking bribes, but there was a subtle suggestion (or at least possibility) that he took money to find work for these people, i.e., "according to our earlier agreement." The implicit message is that corruption in the foodservice industry stems primarily from employees with "poor political qualities" hired through such connections (i.e., as conduits to the illegal market). Also, the word svoika, "my person," highlights the clientelistic nature of Soviet politics; utilizing one's connections to find work for someone, especially in the food industry, would create a loyal patron to call upon later for support. Nepotism is part of the ill-defined gray area of this issue, but as a rule it was dealt with separately from corruption in these texts.

---

[40] Molot, "Vziatochnik," 11 October 1946, p. 4.

[41] Molot, "Negodnyi stil' rukovodstva," 4 July 1943, p. 2.

[42] The word svoika has the connotation not so much of a blood relative of as a close friend and ally, i.e., "my person." Molot, "Za strozhaishii rezhim ekonomiki," 28 April 1944, p. 3.

[43] The term is po znakomstvu, not po blatu, a phrase with a similar meaning more common among the population at large.

The party's public depiction of a "bad communist" archetype obscured the root causes for the many difficulties facing the population at large.[44] While, as we have seen, biographies of party leaders constructed a positive communist archetype inextricably linked to the working masses (as Lenin had envisioned), the party's public narrative also depicted "bad" party leaders whose actions hindered workers' interests. Two completely different and seemingly unrelated images of party leadership emerge. Good communists won awards, were from poor backgrounds, and were upwardly mobile; bad communists took bribes, broke party rules on nepotism, and were generally incompetent. Their class background was not mentioned, but their dishonesty made them bourgeois by implication. Party editorials, meanwhile, vehemently railed against poor membership habits and explained how to become a better communist, placing a great deal of emphasis on ideological enlightenment—the "call" to the communist cause.[45] Meanwhile, *Molot* responded directly to issues of public concern raised by workers, dismissing material conditions as an "objective reason" for the failure to fulfill production plans. Never mind the lack of resources, equipment, electricity, workers, etc., factory directors and lower-level party leaders should show "persistence" and overcome all challenges like true Bolsheviks. Rejecting "objective reasons" such as the war and scarcity, these texts implicitly promoted a "subjective" reason for all shortcomings—poor (often corrupt) work by "bad communists"—while perhaps encouraging quasi-corrupt activity on the part of *tolkachi* and others. Poor party leadership compounded material hardship for the population in this portrayal; reports exposed corruption in housing and food administrations, two of the main areas of concern in the population's daily life. While acknowledging (even assuming) corruption, therefore, the party press muted its treatment of this issue and channeled discontent toward the shortcomings of specific lower-level party leaders, rather than toward dictatorial party rule and the fundamentally-flawed Stalinist system as a whole.

Internal Material on the Party

Internal party material overlaps with public rhetoric in a number of ways, but there are also significant differences. Criticism of a whole host of issues, including inadequate party growth, was passed down through the party hierarchy. Although party leaders at all levels encouraged growth to replace the decimated ranks, strict entrance requirements and a hesitance to take on people who stayed in occupied territory impeded recruitment. We have already seen an inability to bring women into the party in large numbers, and as

---

[44] I agree with Hooper that the regime was hesitant to reveal the depth of the problem of corruption to the public, touching mainly on superficial examples of a very deep-rooted problem, i.e., the scandal at Krupzavod in Kirovskii district.

[45] See Weiner, *Making Sense of War,* chap. 2.

noted the statistics also show a decline in the percentage of factory workers relative to office workers (*sluzhashchie*), a major cause of concern for party leaders.[46] A report on Leninskii district in late 1943, for example, complained that between March and October the district organization took on 25 new members and 47 new candidate members, but only six women and only five factory workers.[47] In the city as a whole in the first quarter of 1944, the party accepted 199 new members and 60 new candidate members, a total of 259, of whom only 60 (23 percent) were workers.[48] According to a 1947 gorkom report, several secretaries of party cells explained poor growth as the result of "an insufficient base for expansion" because so many workers stayed in occupied territory and thus could not get recommendations.[49] The report dismissed this, however, as "an inaccurate claim." Illustrating the dilemma for lower-level party leaders regarding recruitment and party growth, this same account criticized party organizations in the district for taking on new members who stayed in occupied territory.[50] The director of the Mikoyan Shoe Factory elaborated on this problem at one meeting, stating "there is still some fear in taking on members who stayed in occupied territory. At our factory," he continued, "most workers stayed and many of them worked for the Germans," adding that they would have to pick carefully among those that remained faithful to Soviet power.[51] The inadequate growth of the party (among segments *other than* demobilized soldiers in white-collar positions) was a prominent topic in these texts.

A shortage of personnel impeded the implementation of central directives and facilitated corruption, especially during the war. In early 1943 Oblast Procurator Polozkov said that a major reason for corruption was the lack of party inspectors to check-up on primary party organizations. "Despite the fact that energetic people work in positions of control and inspection the job is not done satisfactorily because these organizations are severely understaffed."

---

[46] For a central report on this trend nationally, see RGASPI f. 17, op. 122, d. 189, ll. 119–21.

[47] TsDNI f. 13, op. 4, d. 45, l. 136. Sixty-two were "professionals" (*sluzhashchie*).

[48] TsDNI f. 13, op. 4, d. 69, ll. 103–04. For similar accounts on the failure to bring in workers, see also TsDNI f. 13, op. 4, d. 71, ll. 177–78; TsDNI f. 13, op. 4, d. 217, l. 15; TsDNI f. 13, op. 4, d. 227, l. 54; TsDNI f. 13, op. 4, d. 287, l. 46; TsDNI f. 13, op. 4, d. 295, l. 120.

[49] TsDNI f. 13, op. 4, d. 230, l. 42. On the inability to receive recommendations, see TsDNI f. 13, op. 4, d. 20, l. 75; TsDNI f. 13, op. 4, d. 29, l. 14; TsDNI f. 13, op. 4, d. 75, l. 41; TsDNI f. 13, op. 4, d. 84, ll. 2, 8, 32; TsDNI f. 13, op. 4, d. 143, ll. 65, 77, 187, 189; TsDNI f. 13, op. 4, d. 181, l. 38.

[50] For similar contradictory accounts, see also TsDNI f. 13, op. 4, d. 63, ll. 135–37; TsDNI f. 13, op. 4, d. 131, ll. 75–76; TsDNI f. 13, op. 4, d. 143, ll. 59–60; TsDNI f. 13, op. 4, d. 287, l. 46.

[51] TsDNI f. 13, op. 4, d. 63, l. 192.

Inspectors were responsible for 2,024 various trade organizations in the city, he noted, which at the current level of staffing would take 11 years and 9 months.[52] As Hooper suggests, uncovering widespread, deep-rooted corruption via the Central Party Control Commission was *not* in the interests of party leaders *at any level*, so investigations were not a high priority. District party organizations were severely understaffed during the war and took several years to replenish afterward. As of May 1943, the Proletarskii district had 61 percent of the staff necessary to carry out its tasks, the Zheleznodorozhnyi district only 60 percent.[53] At a party conference in 1945 secretary Kurov responded to complaints of "bureaucratism" in getting help to soldiers' families by pointing out that the Kirovskii district had only two staffers to deal with over 2,000 families.[54] Higher-level party leaders, however, encouraged their subordinates to overcome such limitations. Obkom secretary Kobilev blasted district and city leaders at the conference for not providing school-age children with shoes and warm clothes. Singling out Comrade Andreev of the city soviet, Kobilev stated, "I understand that [he] faces tremendous difficulties," but still Andreev and others should deal with such questions "more energetically, less sleepily," especially with regard to the families of soldiers.[55] It was a common theme; at a party plenum several months later, Comrade Krasikova cited the situation at Factory No. 359, a plant that produced military goods, as an example of "criminally impersonal relations" toward soldiers' families. Despite central directives to provide aid, over the first three months of 1945 the factory's party organization examined only 22 of 147 requests for assistance.[56]

Internal party sources also reveal concern over the lack of ideological training of new members who did join, which leaders saw as a contributing factor to corruption and other problems within the party. Revealing again a penchant for quantification, one report noted that the city party organization in 1946 grew from 10,713 members and 2,489 candidate members to 17,868 and 3,393 respectively, an increase of 8,060 people. Fifty-four percent of its membership joined during or after the war, which "gives the gorkom a huge responsibility for their edification."[57] Obkom First Secretary Aleksandriuk

---

[52] TsDNI f. 13, op. 4, d. 1, ll. 363–65. Polozkov added that "Of 1,048 ration card distribution points in the city only 9 have been checked, and meanwhile ration cards continue to disappear."

[53] TsDNI f. 13, op. 4, d. 21, l. 81. For more on the lack of party personnel, see also GARO f. 3737, op. 8, d. 30, l. 13.

[54] TsDNI f. 13, op. 4, d. 130, l. 91.

[55] TsDNI f. 13, op. 4, d. 130, l. 74.

[56] TsDNI f. 13, op. 4, d. 150, l. 81.

[57] TsDNI f. 13, op. 4, d. 228, ll. 1–2. On the pressing need to educate new members, see also TsDNI f. 13, op. 4, d. 77, l. 110; TsDNI f. 13, op. 4, d. 214, l. 36; TsDNI f. 13, op. 4, d.

reminded listeners at a closed gathering: "The party demands that every communist raise his ideological-political level and put theory into practice in an exemplary way, exhibiting a high level of consciousness and discipline"—i.e., not being corrupt (or at least not *too* corrupt).[58] However, not all members in Rostov heeded these words, as central investigations illustrated. An inspector dispatched by Moscow chided the Rostov obkom for poor work educating demobilized soldiers in party ideology, citing the lack of "political-educational work" among them as the reason why some former troops now in the party "disrupt public order."[59] Another report from Moscow reiterated the call for better "agitation and propaganda work," noting that the oblast newspaper *Molot* was "not on a very high level."[60] Protestations of "poor ideological work" were passed down through the party's ranks. At a party plenum Obkom Secretary Kovalev cited it as the cause of a high turnover rate (32 percent in 1946) for positions of leadership in Rostov-on-Don's district party organizations.[61] "Why such a high rate?" he asked. Because party organizations spent too much time on questions of production and not enough on the one thing that will improve their productivity: "ideological work." The root of the problem, Kovalev insisted, was that cadres did not try to expand their horizons, forgetting Stalin's words that "the higher the ideological level, the higher the consciousness of cadres, the more fruitful their work." The workload of party functionaries, which would have obviously limited their time for study, was not considered in this commentary.

As in the 1930s, ideology was depicted as a panacea for the many problems facing the local party organization. An August 1944 Central Committee decree called on members of the intelligentsia, teachers, instructors, cultural workers, etc. to improve their ideological work.[62] Propagandists from the gorkom and/or district organizations fanned out to randomly test teachers and others on their knowledge of history, politics, and theory, and many fared poorly. Comrade Kashlinskaia, a party member and teacher at School No. 39,

---

217, l. 15. For a breakdown of membership growth in 1946 by city district, see TsDNI f. 13, op. 4, d. 230, ll. 2, 5, 34–36, 38, 43, 57–59, 85–86, 99–100.

[58] TsDNI f. 13, op. 4, d. 339, l. 14.

[59] RGASPI f. 17, op. 122, d. 146, l. 28.

[60] RGASPI f. 17, op. 88, d. 427, l. 6. Several months after this report, in November, 1945, Aleksandriuk filed a report to the center stating that the Rostov obkom had done a great deal to improve ideological work and adding that the quality of newspapers in the oblast had also improved. RGASPI f. 17, op. 122, d. 90, ll. 185, 187. For other reports from the center criticizing propaganda and agitation work in Rostov oblast, see also RGASPI f. 17, op. 122, d. 87, ll. 104–05.

[61] TsDNI f. 13, op. 4, d. 232, l. 17.

[62] The decree was a reaction to historical studies claiming the preeminence of Tatarstan in Russia's historical and cultural development and was part of a central crackdown on ideological questions throughout the country.

responded to a query about why World War I was called an "imperialist war" by saying "because it was fought by emperors."[63] At a closed party gathering, Comrade Krasikova of the gorkom blasted district propaganda departments for their poor work with teachers, many of whom "do not know the elementary truths of Marxism-Leninism."[64] "Poor ideological knowledge" acted as an effective explanation for a whole host of problems, including corruption, improper behavior by party leaders, and insufficient production by factory managers. Comrade Liashkov at a closed meeting contrasted two factories in Proletarskii district, one where the directors raised their ideological levels and overfulfilled their production quotas to another where the directors did not study and "the situation with production deteriorated."[65] A 1945 gorkom report noted that many party members claimed to be "working independently" on their ideological knowledge, but in fact "individual discussions revealed that they did no such work."[66] Higher-ups in the party, moreover, did not accept the lack of time as a viable excuse. According to a 1945 Andreevskii district report, factory directors often claimed "they are overwhelmed with work and don't have enough time for political studies. But," it continued, "clearly they underestimate the significance of Marxist-Leninist theory in practical life."[67] These reports show strong concerns for the theoretical level of party members well before Zhdanov's campaign for ideological purity, which began in earnest in August 1946.

Party leaders saw poor ideological knowledge as the cause of disciplinary problems within the ranks and, in accordance with a long-standing Soviet tradition, blamed accidents on irresponsible people in positions of power. A gorkom report in June 1944 noted serious deficiencies in the work of the party organization at the Mikoyan Shoe Factory, where study groups had not been organized and there were "few banners, placards, and wall newspapers." As a result of such "weak mass political and educational work," the report maintained, there were a number of disciplinary problems among the plant's party collective.[68] Owing to inadequate propaganda work by the party cell at the factory 15-let Oktiabra, director A. S. Kalabukhin surrounded himself with "his people," and began illegally raising goats on factory grounds.[69] The situation was even worse at the City Streetcar Depot, where in early 1945 a major

---

[63] TsDNI f. 13, op. 4, d. 181, l. 74.

[64] TsDNI f. 13, op. 4, d. 186, l. 16.

[65] TsDNI f. 13, op. 4, d. 214, l. 15.

[66] TsDNI f. 13, op. 4, d. 186, l. 159. For more on party members who studied poorly, see also TsDNI f. 13, op. 4, d. 180, l. 28; TsDNI f. 13, op. 4, d. 186, l. 28; TsDNI f. 13, op. 4, d. 430, ll. 22–23; TsDNI f. 13, op. 4, d. 431, ll. 66, 68.

[67] TsDNI f. 13, op. 4, d. 181, l. 74.

[68] TsDNI f. 13, op. 4, d. 72, ll. 53–54.

[69] TsDNI f. 13, op. 4, d. 395, ll. 38–39.

fire destroyed the administrative building and 43 cars, exacerbating an already acute transportation problem in the city. Accidents like these were "public" by their very nature—the population at large would have been well aware of such a serious fire, the consequences of which could not be easily swept under the rug.[70] An inquiry, the findings of which were not made public, claimed the reason for the fire was a "defective system of leadership," noting that the depot's director "systematically drank at work and even got others to drink too."[71] The fire was so damaging because the security guard on duty was asleep in one of the cars when it began. The guard was fired along with the managing director of the depot and the head of the streetcar trust. Several city and district-level reports in this five-year period attributed "poor ideological training" as the cause of many problems, including inadequate party growth, the failure to implement central policies and carry out party tasks, or even "hooliganism" and suicide.[72]

Soviet bureaucrats clearly defined their world with numbers, focusing considerable attention and concern on accounting issues. Many Communist Party members were missing after the war, while among those who survived a significant percentage were "inactive." Also, internal party material reported hesitation on the part of workers to join the CPSU and (in accordance with public revelations) exposed nepotism among those in power. A central report from June 1946 stated that in the Soviet Union 1,284,056 Communist Party members remained unaccounted for due to the war, part of the massive dislocation of population already discussed.[73] In addition many communists were reported as present but "inactive," meaning they refused to show up for party meetings or participate in party activities.[74] As we saw, many in the party who stayed in occupied territory were hesitant to even register with their district organizations afterward. Party documents further noted that people did not want to join the party, a sentiment, as we will see, corroborated in interviews. Speaking at a 1947 party plenum amid famine about the

---

[70] Mariia Zhak remembered that when she returned to Rostov from evacuation in October 1945, there were still no streetcars running because of the fire and her family had to walk home. Interview by author, 6 March 1995.

[71] TsDNI f. 13, op. 4, d. 149, l. 45.

[72] See, for example, TsDNI f. 13, op. 4, d. 45, ll. 77–78; TsDNI f. 13, op. 4, d. 55, l. 69; TsDNI f. 13, op. 4, d. 143, l. 65; TsDNI f. 13, op. 4, d. 146, l. 54; TsDNI f. 13, op. 4, d. 151, l. 9; TsDNI f. 13, op. 4, d. 180, ll. 8, 11, 13; TsDNI f. 13, op. 4, d. 188, ll. 20, 23; TsDNI f. 13, op. 4, d. 227, ll. 71, 167; TsDNI f. 13, op. 4, d. 252, l. 33; TsDNI f. 13, op. 4, d. 293, ll. 47–48; TsDNI f. 13, op. 4, d. 337, l. 52; TsDNI f. 13, op. 4, d. 393, l. 189; TsDNI f. 13, op. 4, d. 413, l. 28.

[73] For reports on missing party members, see also TsDNI f. 13, op. 4, d. 77, l. 110; TsDNI f. 13, op. 4, d. 219, l. 164; TsDNI f. 13, op. 4, d. 230, ll. 36, 57; TsDNI f. 13, op. 4, d. 295, l. 121; RGASPI f. 17, op. 122, d. 189, l. 97.

[74] See, for example, TsDNI f. 13, op. 4, d. 295, l. 117.

difficulty recruiting among workers, one district party secretary stated they avoided joining the party because of all the time required for meetings. "Right now," he said, "as soon as work ends they all run as quickly as possible to tend their gardens."[75] Among those who were in the party, nepotism or "familiness," as discussed in public, plagued the ranks as well. The chief doctor at the city's main medical clinic, for example, was accused of hiring two nieces as assistants and illegally putting another relative on the payroll as a "sanitary worker."[76] Nepotism was also reported at Rostov's Pedagogical Institute, where the director allegedly allowed his wife entrance as a graduate student without the proper test scores and illegally received a 5,000-ruble insurance payment.[77] As in the party press, closed party reports deal with nepotism separately from corruption, revealing a wide variety of issues and problems faced by the local "vanguard" party organization during "reconstruction."

The most glaring problem was party corruption, which was widespread during this alleged time of Stalinist "totalitarianism," even affecting the city's judicial system and police force. In 1945 a party member of 25 years was removed from his job in the oblast judicial system, expelled from the party, and sentenced to 5 years for accepting a bribe from a woman trying to lighten her father's sentence.[78] There were numerous reports and commentaries on the police, including one on the removal of the head of the city's first precinct for "taking bribes from the population."[79] I. F. Makarov, party member since 1929 and official for the city's sixth precinct, accepted money to provide a deserter from the Red Army with false documents, for which he was excluded from the party and sentenced to six years.[80] Another report stated that an officer took money from someone at the central market, a gorkom protocol cited "cases of immoral acts by several policemen," and a separate account indicated "a high rate of immoral acts" by policemen.[81] At a closed meeting in late

---

[75] TsDNI f. 13, op. 4, d. 181, l. 38.

[76] TsDNI f. 13, op. 4, d. 68, ll. 15–16. The quotation marks around "sanitary worker" are in the original source, indicating that in this case it was a purely fictitious position.

[77] TsDNI f. 13, op. 4, d. 392, l. 118. For more examples of "family relations" (nepotism) among party leaders, see also TsDNI f. 13, op. 4, d. 130, l. 42; TsDNI f. 13, op. 4, d. 221, ll. 2–3; TsDNI f. 13, op. 4, d. 429, ll. 89–90, 151.

[78] TsDNI f. 13, op. 4, d. 294, l. 141. Heinzen notes the dual position of the courts and judicial system during the campaign against bribery, since they were charged with implementing laws against corruption but were also a key target in the campaign (Heinzen, "A 'Campaign Spasm,'" 135–37).

[79] TsDNI f. 13, op. 4, d. 53, l. 229. In addition the head of the sixth precinct, Sudorenno, also a candidate member of the party, was demoted for "inappropriate ties with certain people."

[80] TsDNI f. 13, op. 4, d. 218, l. 20.

[81] TsDNI f. 13, op. 4, d. 24, l. 18; TsDNI f. 13, op. 4, d. 293, l. 95; TsDNI f. 13, op. 4, d. 330, l. 219. The officer caught taking money was sentenced to eight years and kicked

1945 Comrade A. M. Pototov repeated the "popular rumor" that police are on the take, noting that while this "may be an exaggeration, there is no smoke without fire."[82] At a party gathering in 1946, during the early stages of the famine, the director of Bread Factory No. 1 shared the exploits of two policemen who allegedly waited for workers outside the plant and searched them for pilfered bread. In one case the two officers asked a worker, "why don't you carry bread out? You want to live and so do we." The speaker named three more police officers who, he said, robbed the bread factory at night, and concluded his invective by calling for the "strictest possible measures against such people who ruin the name of the police."[83] These commentaries show how deeply rooted corruption was within the local power structure.

Internal party documents reveal rampant corruption in food services and housing administrations, two of the main foci of worker criticism addressed in the local party press. As we have seen, store managers and others with access to food supplies participated actively in the illegal economy through (or *as*) "speculators," a common transgression in this five-year period. In early 1943 Comrade Polozkov admitted that embezzlement was a huge problem in the city's bakeries, primarily the theft of grain by the leadership of Bakeries 7–10. He said that at the city's mills and grain-processing plants "criminal hands are reaching out from all sides" to get at supplies.[84] Scandal rocked the main food production and distribution organization in the city, Rostpishchtorg, in 1945. Noting that it was infiltrated by "countless scoundrels and thieves," the gorkom upheld a decision to fire the director for not fulfilling production plans, for "liberal" treatment of pilferers, and for holding up the replacement of "untrustworthy" workers. The gorkom likewise agreed to the expulsion of the assistant director of the food trust for inactivity, concealing transgressions of trade rules, misuse of his position for personal profit, and "systematic drunkenness."[85] In May 1947 the director of Nakhpishchtorg, a major food

---

out of the party but he chose to serve in the penal battalion at the front instead. For more on police corruption, see also TsDNI f. 13, op. 4, d. 53, l. 229; TsDNI f. 13, op. 4, d. 320, l. 19.

[82] TsDNI f. 13, op. 4, d. 337, l. 55.

[83] TsDNI f. 13, op. 4, d. 300, l. 29. Padraic Kenney notes that in Łódź, Poland in December 1946, "there were reports of attackers in police uniform robbing passersby of money and clothing," although he concedes that it is not clear if the culprits were truly policemen or imposters (*Rebuilding Poland*, 144).

[84] TsDNI f. 13, op. 4, d. 1, l. 362. These comments were made during the aforementioned scandal at Krupzavod. Polozkov also cited the widespread pilfering of leather from the Mikoyan Shoe Factory by factory leaders and workers alike as an example.

[85] TsDNI f. 13, op. 4, d. 291, l. 146. A year later M. K. Turok, party member and cafeteria manager at the factory Rabochii (Worker), was expelled from the party for pilfering butter. TsDNI f. 13, op. 4, d. 295, l. 106.

distribution organization, was released for misuse of his position.[86] A check-up on the city's trade organizations after the monetary reform in December 1947 revealed "serious transgressions of the principles of Soviet trade," including rigging scales, short-changing customers, and even illegally raising the official price for goods.[87] Corruption received a great deal of attention in the public press, but closed party material is more forthcoming, referring to people in important positions as "criminals," "scoundrels," and "thieves" while suggesting this as a reason for the inadequate work of such organizations.

The party bureaucracy also regularly discussed corruption among housing administrators behind closed doors. A gorkom protocol about the turmoil in housing organs in the Andreevskii district was revealing; as we have seen, *Molot* reported on several bribe-takers in February and March 1945. This internal document, however, clarified that a total of 11 housing administration employees in the district were involved and that they had distributed as many as 60 apartments for bribes or through acquaintances. The situation, it added, was also problematic elsewhere in the city, which the *Molot* piece did not note. Employees in the Leninskii district housing administration took bribes to distribute 28 apartments illegally, 6 apartments were illegally distributed in another district, and so on.[88] This material indicated a much more far-reaching problem than discussed in the public press, which lends credence to Hooper's assertion that the party did not want to expose the full extent of its problems publicly. Subsequent internal reports further indicate that corruption was a pervasive problem. T. D. Uspenskaia, a party member since 1928 who worked as a housing administrator in Proletarskii district, received a 700-ruble bribe in March 1946, for which she was expelled from the party and sentenced to two years.[89] A gorkom report later in the year complained that nothing was being done about widespread abuse of power, bribe taking, and the buying and selling of apartments by "loafers and dim wits undermining the work of housing organs."[90] The underlying assumption of this material is that if it were not for the actions of a few corrupt figures the party would be able to deal with difficulties and greatly improve material conditions. These are but a few examples of the countless corruption cases heard by the Rostov gorkom in this five-year period, suggesting that it was a systemic problem.[91]

---

[86] TsDNI f. 13, op. 4, d. 293, l. 53.

[87] TsDNI f. 13, op. 4, d. 299, l. 97.

[88] TsDNI f. 13, op. 4, d. 146, l. 62.

[89] TsDNI f. 13, op. 4, d. 291, l. 73.

[90] TsDNI f. 13, op. 4, d. 220, l. 304.

[91] For other examples of internal documents on corruption or the "misuse of one's position," see also TsDNI f. 13, op. 4, d. 56, l. 94; TsDNI f. 13, op. 4, d. 70, l. 10; TsDNI f. 13, op. 4, d. 75, l. 26; TsDNI f. 13, op. 4, d. 23, l. 82; TsDNI f. 13, op. 4, d. 102, l. 91;

Gorkom reports stop short of explicitly accusing district-level party leaders of accepting bribes and show leniency to many of those caught in cases of petty corruption. People at all levels were closely scrutinized and many were replaced in a revolving-door process. The removal of Zheleznodorozhnyi District First Secretary Mogol'skii was a case in point. An official quoted above in a *Molot* piece cited a "lack of ideological knowledge" as the reason for the high turnover rates among district-level leaders, but internal party documents show that several were replaced because of corruption (which, of course, the official may have equated with insufficient ideological enlightenment).[92] A gorkom check-up on insufficiencies in the district organization placed the blame squarely on Mogol'skii for "ruling bureaucratically, drinking systematically, and not allowing anyone to criticize him." His rule encouraged "lawlessness," the report claimed, but it did not implicate Mogol'skii in corruption. The gorkom demoted him for "losing his authority as district party secretary" but did not expel him from the party.[93] In September 1946 the gorkom exposed major problems in the Ordzhonikidzevskii district party branch; the first and second party secretaries, Comrades Tokareva and Kalmykov, "stood aloof from the criticisms of rank-and-file communists" and "failed to adequately respond to a number of signals of anti-government practices and the illegal abuse of power by factory leaders [in the district]."[94] It listed several examples, including the same Military Factory No. 359 cited above by Krasikova for "criminally impersonal relations" to soldiers' families. Although there was no indication that they directly profited, the report blamed Tokareva and Kalmykov for pervasive corruption because of their "distant and removed style of leadership." The gorkom censured Tokareva but kept her on as raikom first secretary, while it decided to remove Kalmykov from his position as second secretary but not expel him from the party.[95]

TsDNI f. 13, op.4, d. 176, ll. 1–2; TsDNI f. 13, op. 4, d. 214, ll. 35–36; TsDNI f. 13, op. 4, d. 220, ll. 9, 204; TsDNI f. 13, op. 4, d. 221, l. 39; TsDNI f. 13, op. 4, d. 227, l. 168; TsDNI f. 13, op. 4, d. 291, ll. 123–24; TsDNI f. 13, op. 4, d. 292, l. 127; TsDNI f. 13, op. 4, d. 293, l. 136; TsDNI f. 13, op. 4, d. 294, l. 136; TsDNI f. 13, op. 4, d. 315, l. 20; TsDNI f. 13, op. 4, d. 320, l. 19; TsDNI f. 13, op. 4, d. 392, ll. 19, 74–78, 87–88, 148, 158–59, 198, 202–07; TsDNI f. 13, op. 4, d. 393, ll. 11, 13, 37, 40–42, 57, 61, 67, 78, 99, 158, 162–63, 165, 187; TsDNI f. 13, op. 4, d. 394, ll. 61, 65, 67–68, 99, 101, 138, 152, 159, 171, 173–74; TsDNI f. 13, op. 4, d. 395, ll. 38–39, 141, 148–49, 152, 154–55, 158, 208, 212, 235, 265.

[92] More specifically, a separate gorkom report noted that of the 105 members of the nomenklatura replaced in 1946, 30 left "of their own wish," 30 were replaced for "doing a poor job," 14 were promoted to higher positions, 11 left to go study, and 4 were replaced for "compromising themselves." TsDNI f. 13, op. 4, d. 128, l. 15.

[93] TsDNI f. 13, op. 4, d. 53, l. 229.

[94] The report said they decided questions "according to the principle 'don't hang each other's dirty laundry out to air.'"

[95] TsDNI f. 13, op. 4, d. 221, ll. 3–4.

In other cases as well a high degree of tolerance for corruption was shown at the gorkom level, the suggestion being that the problem should be solved with more "theoretical work" (an implicit solution to all problems), rather than with a disciplinary approach.[96] A gorkom report exposing problems at the factory *Proletarskii Molot* cited "insufficient party-political work" by Comrade Shkitov, secretary of the factory's party organization, as the cause. Factory Director Minin, who often threw drunken parties, collected money from workers to purchase potatoes for them and then "used it for other purposes." He also approved the use of factory parts to repair a generator in another plant, for which he and others illegally received money. Shkitov, this account asserted, "had to have known" but took no measures to correct the situation. The raikom censured him "for loss of vigilance" and excluded Minin, but the gorkom reversed the decision, keeping Minin in the party with a reprimand.[97] In another example, the gorkom lessened the punishment of a party member since 1920 excluded by the Kirovskii raikom for illegally selling vodka.[98] In the summer of 1947 the gorkom released the city's main architect from his position for allegedly embezzling money, but there is no indication that it punished him further.[99] One report claimed that for the final quarter of 1946, the gorkom reviewed 57 cases of the "illegal use of power" by party members, upholding the exclusion of 36 while reducing the sentences of 21, or more than one-third.[100]

Meanwhile, those near the bottom of the party hierarchy often accused their superiors of corruption and protectionism, and there were hints of these problems at the highest echelons of the local power structure. In 1944 the gorkom heard the case of V. A. Sudakov, head of the personnel department of the Stalinskii district party bureau, who had been fired for refusing to work with the district party secretary, Comrade Zamuraev. Sudakov filed a complaint with the gorkom claiming that "half of the Stalinskii district party apparatus is corrupt [*razlozhena*]" and that "Zamuraev is part of an intimate clique of criminals." While upholding the decision to fire Sudakov, the gor-

---

[96] Getty shows the divergence of two distinct views toward disciplinary problems in the 1930s, one a more lenient approach emphasizing study (Zhdanov), and another harsher, more disciplinary approach (Ezhov) that wins out during the purges. See Getty, *Origins of the Purges.*

[97] TsDNI f. 13, op. 4, d. 146, l. 1. In another incident, A. I. Mozheiko, an instructor for party cadres, conspired to receive ten kilograms of honey "on the sly"; his district organization expelled him from the party for having "lost his party honor," but in this case too the gorkom reversed the decision and kept Mozheiko in the party. TsDNI, f. 13, op. 4, d. 220, ll. 22–23. For similar reversals, see also TsDNI f. 13, op. 4, d. 29, 1. 28; TsDNI f. 13, op.4, d. 176, ll. 1–2; TsDNI f. 13, op. 4, d. 220, ll. 9, 204.

[98] TsDNI f. 13, op. 4, d. 75, l. 22.

[99] TsDNI f. 13, op. 4, d. 294, l. 151.

[100] TsDNI f. 13,op. 4, d. 228, l. 12.

kom requested that he provide information to back up his accusations for further investigation. There is no indication, however, that Zamuraev or others in the Stalinskii district party organization were removed due to Sudakov's claims.[101] Lower and mid-level figures commonly made allegations of "clientelism" and "protectionism" from above. Comrade Sokolov, first secretary of Proletarskii district, complained in one meeting that an oblast-level union leader "removes production managers without the raikom's consent and replaces them with his own people." The district party branch informed gorkom leaders about these incidents, Sokolov added, but nothing was done about it, which implies that the protectionism may go even deeper.[102] District secretaries at a party conference in 1947 assailed gorkom leaders for merely passing down "paper directives" from the obkom but then not checking up on their fulfillment, another common theme in these sources.[103] Two party officials from Rostov wrote the Central Committee in 1947 to complain about the "abuse of his position" by A. A. Kozhin, a member of the Rostov oblast judicial system. A check-up by the center confirmed that someone illegally made goods for Kozhin and his friends, who also secured apartments in the center of town, and generally acted with rudeness and disregard toward the city's workers. Moscow's inspectors recommended that he be removed from his position in the oblast courts but not expelled from the party or severely punished, which again shows a great deal of tolerance toward corrupt party figures.[104]

One rank-and-file party member spelled out his view of internal party politics in no uncertain terms, and a document describing the selection of leaders for the Rostov gorkom largely validated his opinion. In a letter to G. M. Malenkov, a member of the Council of Ministers, in October 1945, Captain K. Anisimov boldly complained that centralized control over the appointment of party secretaries at all levels of the CPSU stifled party democracy. The Central Committee, Anisimov lamented, recommended candidates for obkom

---

[101] TsDNI f. 13, op. 4, d. 71, l. 82. Two months after the meeting a special session of the gorkom was held to consider the evidence but unfortunately no notes were recorded.

[102] TsDNI f. 13, op. 4, d. 130, l. 42. He also cited the example of a union leader in the oblast lumber industry who similarly put his associates in positions of power. For other accounts by district party secretaries claiming protectionism by gorkom leaders, see also TsDNI f. 13, op. 4, d. 151, ll. 130–31.

[103] TsDNI f. 13, op. 4, d. 408, l. 11. Another oft-heard criticism by secretaries of primary cells at meetings was that higher-level leaders never visited the factories to meet with workers. See, for example, TsDNI f. 13, op. 4, d. 408, l. 10.

[104] This information is from the *Komitet partiinogo kontrolia* (KPK—the Committee for Party Control) files available at the Hoover Institution. RGANI (*Rossiskii gosudarstvennyi arkhiv noveishei istorii*—Russian State Archives of New History) f. 6, op. 6, d. 1587, ll. 165–68. I would like to thank James Heinzen for bringing this material to my attention.

first secretary, who in turn recommended the leaders of lower-level party organizations. This accepted practice had negative consequences, he explained, because it meant that "party leaders look on the party masses 'from above,' as inferiors, scorning their opinions and wishes since, after all, their position did not depend on the party masses, but only on higher-standing party organs." As a result, party leaders often retreated into "careerism" and "bureaucratism," isolating themselves from the masses. Anisimov suggested that the practice of appointing party leaders from above be liquidated and rank-and-file members permitted to nominate their own leaders because only in such a case could true democracy flourish in the party's ranks and the country.[105] For Anisimov "democratic centralism" involved too much centralism and not enough democracy, and that was certainly the case in the selection of the Rostov gorkom in April 1948. Comrade Patolichev began the closed party plenum by announcing elections for first, second, and third secretaries of the Rostov gorkom and several other positions as well. From the floor someone said, "I propose Comrade Patolichev for first secretary." Patolichev followed this up by asking if there were any other proposed candidates, which there were not, and asking those that supported the proposal to raise their hands, which everyone did. The proposal was accepted unanimously, and the same process was repeated with Comrade Kozlov as second secretary and so on.[106]

Their appointment from above notwithstanding, oblast and city leaders came under fire with volleys of criticism from Moscow that mirrored discussions at the gorkom and district levels. As noted, Aleksandriuk replaced Dvinskii as first secretary of the Rostov obkom in September 1944, and unfortunately little information is available on that change in office. One can, however, follow Aleksandriuk's fall from grace, which may have been a consequence of the regime's secret anti-corruption campaign in 1946–47. Criticism of the new leader appeared as early as July 1945, when a report from Central Committee investigator N. Volkov to Malenkov noted that "Aleksandriuk does not show enough initiative and persistence in solving the very serious challenges of Rostov's reconstruction." These were, of course, the same criticisms leveled at lower-level party leaders within the oblast party organization. The report cited the slow rebuilding of Rostsel'mash and Krasnyi Aksai ("famous plants in this country") as examples of the obkom's inadequate work.[107] A subsequent report in late 1945 from Rostov (signed by Aleksandriuk) to Moscow admitted the slow reconstruction of many of the city's factories (including Rostsel'mash), explaining the problem as the result of conversion from military to civilian production and the poor supply of equip-

---

[105] RGASPI f. 17, op. 122, d. 87, ll. 123–24.

[106] TsDNI f. 13, op. 4, d. 388, l. 3.

[107] RGASPI f. 17, op. 88, d. 427, ll. 1–2.

ment and raw materials necessary for production (i.e., "objective reasons").[108] While central inspectors were already citing problems with his leadership at this early date, Aleksandriuk's relatively new position as first secretary of the Rostov obkom seemed safe for the time being. Serious problems, however, reemerged in subsequent months, foreshadowing leadership changes in the Rostov obkom in the fall of 1947.

In September 1946 Moscow again began to raise questions about the local leadership in Rostov. Noting that oblast leaders had not fulfilled a central directive in April on home construction for coal miners, a report claimed the reason was the diversion of materials to build homes for leaders of the oblast coal trust, *Rostovugol'*, most of whom "already have nice apartments." It named Comrades Shibaev and Datchenko, gorkom secretaries of two cities near Rostov-on-Don, as the main culprits. According to the report, rank-and-file party member Ivanov, a coal miner and father of seven, was refused material to build a home because of the alleged lack of bricks. At the same time, however, Datchenko and others were building their own homes, including Ivanov's boss, Surkov, who built *two* personal homes. To get the bricks Ivanov reportedly had to give Surkov a gold watch and two rings. Datchenko "did not pay attention to this and protected Surkov" because he himself was illegally building a home with Surkov's help. Meanwhile, Shibaev began building his home in a designated green area belonging to the city water trust, sparking protests from the leader of that department, Comrade Minenko. The report claimed that Shibaev phoned Minenko and said, "Today you are a boss [*nachal'nik*], but tomorrow you could be a worker. Today I am secretary, but tomorrow I might not be secretary. Do not interfere. I will build the home." In a subtle suggestion that obkom leaders might be complicit in these intrigues, the report stated that the Rostov obkom "has dealt with these problems far too slowly and has not taken any decisive measures" to correct them.[109] A subsequent report indicated that, despite these accusations, Shibaev maintained his position as of June 1947.[110]

Moscow's criticism of local leaders intensified in 1947—coinciding with the regime's secret anti-corruption campaign—because the oblast as a whole and Rostov-on-Don lagged behind the rest of occupied Russia in "reconstruction." In February Aleksandriuk, quoted above telling a group of party members that they needed to exhibit "a high level of consciousness and discipline," found himself once again responding to harsh criticisms. He ad-

---

[108] RGASPI f. 17, op. 122, d. 132, ll. 19–20. A month later another letter to Malenkov, this one written by central leader P. Parshin, confirmed Aleksandriuk's claims, admitting that equipment confiscated in Germany as reparations had not yet been shipped to Rostsel'mash because of difficulties in transportation. See RGASPI f. 17, op. 122, d. 105, l. 224.

[109] RGASPI f. 17, op. 122, d. 155, ll. 145–48, 152–54.

[110] RGASPI f. 17, op. 122, d. 194, ll. 98–101.

mitted that a whole host of problems still plagued the oblast party organization, including poor party-organizational work, weak links between the obkom and primary party organizations, and a "bureaucratic style of leadership."[111] A June report by Volkov painted a bleak picture of industrial production and stated that Aleksandriuk and other oblast leaders "look at party organs from the top down" and "completely ignore criticism from below."[112] Of course, as Anisimov's aforementioned letter revealed, this problem was endemic to the top-down nature of the Soviet political system. A report in August spelled the end of Aleksandriuk's tenure. Pointing out previous Central Committee warnings about "paper leadership and poor ideological-political work," the document complained that Aleksandriuk had not yet corrected these problems. Instead, he merely blamed his subordinates for persistent difficulties in production, the report continued, while ignoring major signs of corruption by party leaders in the oblast like the illegal use of material for housing construction by the party leaders cited above.[113] This account ended by listing "serious insufficiencies in Aleksandriuk's personality and leadership style," including his "calmness and serenity in the face of vitally important tasks going unfulfilled." His speeches at party plenums, moreover, "are superficial" and tend to end rather than spark further discussion. Less than a month after this report, Moscow dispatched Patolichev to replace Aleksandriuk, who was moved to another, presumably less demanding position.[114] Subsequent reports show that shortcomings in the oblast party organization remained, but criticism did not reach the level of that endured by Aleksandriuk in the months before his replacement.[115]

Behind closed doors local leaders discussed corruption and other problems within the "vanguard" party in more revealing terms than in the press. The sheer number of cases of the "illegal abuse of power" by party members suggests that corruption was a widespread, systemic problem, which party material for public consumption obscures by emphasizing "isolated incidents" stemming from "poor ideological knowledge." Some corrupt officials were caught and punished, which means they operated with limitations and at some risk; but, as with speculation and collaboration, petty corruption was largely tolerated and there was a significant degree of "protectionism" within the party's ranks. Hints of corruption at the highest levels of Rostov oblast's party organization foreshadowed the removal of Aleksandriuk as first secre-

---

[111] RGASPI f. 17, op. 88, d. 769, ll. 40–41.

[112] RGASPI f. 17, op. 122, d. 194, l. 100.

[113] RGASPI f. 17, op. 122, d. 205, ll. 78, 80–82. The report noted that the obkom took up this question "only after interference," suggesting again the possibility of protectionism at the obkom level.

[114] TsDNI f. 13, op. 4, d. 288, l. 85.

[115] For reports on problems after September 1947, see RGASPI f. 17, op. 122, d. 205, ll. 59, 63, 65.

tary during an anti-corruption campaign. With the notable exception of Captain Anisimov's letter to Malenkov, these texts mirror press reports by emphasizing defective *individuals* with their dishonesty, negligence, nepotism, and incompetence—rather than the fundamentally flawed and undemocratic nature of the top-down Stalinist system (as described by Anisimov). Democratic centralism in practice meant the center made decisions that were passed down the party structure but not always carried out, causing a lot of turmoil in intra-party relations. Policies emanating from Moscow were often contradictory and failed to take into account the difficulties faced by those implementing them. For example, while encouraging party growth, leaders at the same time called for caution in letting people join, which greatly impeded recruitment. Also, criticism of a variety of issues was passed down through the local party hierarchy, and closed documents deal with disciplinary problems in the party's ranks (especially drunkenness) more than the press. Like the party's public texts, internal material blames these shortcomings on "poor ideological training" or insufficient "mass-political work," broad euphemisms that made convenient excuses for a number of insufficiencies and operated as effective smokescreens for more substantive issues. Finally, as in the press, these sources dismiss the war and material conditions as "objective reasons" for the failure to implement central directives.

Popular Perceptions of the Party

Interviews, public statements of workers and others, and commentary recorded by informants give us some insight on how people perceived the party and its leaders. Mariia Zhak recalled that First Obkom Secretary Shiboldaev was arrested during the "repression" of 1937, clearing the way for Boris Dvinskii's advancement to the top of the local party apparatus. In contrast to biographical accolades during the 1946 election campaign claiming that Dvinskii "solved the problems of mobilizing people and resources" during the war, Zhak remembered that "people blamed him for the poor organization of evacuation." She said he told party members not to panic, assuring them that the Germans would not take Rostov, and as a result many wound up in occupied territory, while many others were caught trying to escape at the last minute. Meanwhile, she noted with a sense of irony, Dvinskii himself had no trouble getting away. Zhak's husband, Vinamin, a writer, joined the party in 1939 though he was not eager to do so; he joined after being invited to, she said, so as not to be "uncomfortable." Zhak relied on the good communist/bad communist dichotomous construction to describe her husband's ties to the party. Corruption, she said, was a problem and "we understood that not all party members held to the 'high goals' of party ideology," but Veniamin in contrast "was an honest communist who never abused his position to his advantage." S. I. Emel'ianenko similarly recalled that "not all party secretaries were bad, of course, but many were." If someone criticized their leadership, he stated, they could exclude them from the party "for drinking," and others would go along out of "fear."[116]

All but a few respondents remembered having positive feelings for Stalin. According to Zhak, her husband Veniamin "understood" about Stalin early on, in the 1930s. She remembered being very frightened when her husband criticized Stalin, even though he only did so when they were alone.[117] Genadii Ermolenko recalled that "people cursed Stalin quietly, among close friends and relatives," adding that he personally hated Stalin but would never say so in front of strangers.[118] Aleksandra Ermolenko recalled that her father, a prominent local artist, was offered party membership but "delicately turned down the offer [because] he didn't support the party" and did not think highly of Stalin. Her mother, she further recalled, was very religious and resented the party's history of repressing religion.[119] Detractors, however, were in the minority, as most accepted the officially promoted apotheosis of Stalin. V. I. Akimenko, a teenage art student after the war, recalled "all we heard about everywhere we went was 'Stalin, Stalin, Stalin,' so of course we believed in him."[120] Nina K. said people "considered Stalin a god" at the time and there were no criticisms about a "cult of personality" because "no one even knew such a thing existed."[121] According to Svetlana P. Chernysheva, who was born in 1930, "they raised us from childhood to believe in Stalin like a god, and I sincerely believed in his greatness."[122] Several people, including Aleksandra Ermolenko and Svetlana S. Semenova, both of whom were born in the mid-1930s, remembered that their families strictly forbade talk about Stalin at home because some of their relatives had suffered in the purges. As a result, they only heard praise for Stalin, which they had no reason to doubt. "There has never been a historical figure so completely loved as Stalin," Ermolenko stated, "whether or not it was justified."[123] People respected Stalin, says S. I. Emal'ianenko, because he did not abandon Moscow during the war. Stalin, however, trusted those around him too much, he added, like Beria who was "of the same nationality" and was more responsible than

---

[116] Interview by author, 23 May 1995.

[117] Interview by author, 6 March 1995. As we saw, Veniamin's May Day 1947 poem praising "the chief" was insincere.

[118] Interview by author, 16 April 1995.

[119] Interview by author, 16 April 1995.

[120] Interview by author, 20 May 1995.

[121] Interview by author, 17 March 1995.

[122] Interview by author, 7 March 1995.

[123] Interviews by author, 16 April 1995. Ermolenko said a teacher in one school went crazy after Stalin's death in March 1953, and Semenova, who was born in 1936, said the younger generation believed in Stalin especially strongly because they did not know about the purges.

Stalin himself for the repression of the late 1930s.[124] Several interviewees said they remembered crying when Stalin died in March 1953, and the majority maintained favorable opinions of him.[125]

Local residents also thought highly of N. S. Patolichev, who replaced Aleksandriuk as first secretary of the Rostov obkom in September 1947. Emal'ianenko remembered Patolichev as someone who "stood out not just because of his sense of justice, love of labor, and honesty, but because he was an exception among those who reached such a level of power."[126] Mariia Zhak likewise said Patolichev was "the only first secretary of the obkom that the people [narod] loved." The city's party leaders went around with guards, she elaborated, but he did not, which meant he could visit stores anonymously. Zhak told a legend about Patolichev, admitting she did not know whether it was true. He supposedly went into a store and asked for macaroni and, upon discovering that there were no bags, put out his hat and told the clerk to pour the macaroni into it. Then he called in the store's director and blasted him for selling macaroni in this manner.[127] Akimenko contrasted Patolichev with other party leaders who, he said, "just commanded others 'do this, do that,' but not him—he personally took up a shovel and did the work himself." He and others credited Patolichev with making the left bank of the Don a beach to rest at on weekends. Akimenko also remembered the same anecdote told by Zhak, only in his version grain rather than macaroni gets poured into Patolichev's hat.[128] True or not, the irony of this (evidently widely told) story was that someone in his position would even go into a regular store. Ol'ga Pacherskaia's daughters studied with Patolichev's children. She stated that "previously all party leaders brought their children to school in cars, but his daughters walked to school, even in knee-deep snow." Patolichev and his

---

[124] Interview by author, 23 May 1995. For a similar opinion about Stalin's associates being at fault for the purges, see also interview by author with Sergei Veniaminovich Zhak (Mariia Zhak's son), 15 March 1995.

[125] See, for example, interview by author with Iurii Alekseevich Petrovskii, 27 April 1995; interview by author with Ekaterina Grigorovna K., 3 May 1995; interview by author with Ol'ga Ivanovna Pacherskaia, 8 June 1995; interview by author with Nina I. Asetorova, 18 June 1995. Twenty-two years old when Stalin died, Svetlana Chernysheva remembered it as a devastating loss of someone dear and close. Interview by author, 7 March 1995. For other opinions on the popularity of Stalin, see also Dmitry Loza, *Fighting for the Soviet Motherland*, ed. and trans. James F. Gebhardt (Lincoln: University of Nebraska Press, 1998), intro.; Barber and Harrison, *Soviet Home Front*, 70–73.

[126] Interview by author, 23 May 1995. Emal'ianenko added, "People of course loved him, and he was very well respected in Rostov-on-Don." He further claimed that Patolichev's downfall was that he "did not accept the injustice of a system that did not allow for the periodic replacement of leaders," which led to the end of his career.

[127] Interview by author, 6 March 1995.

[128] Interview by author, 20 May 1995.

wife, she said, also worked alongside the rest of the population on *subbotniki*, "voluntary" work Saturdays when people cleaned the streets or did some other task. Pacherskaia specifically contrasted Patolichev with his predecessor Aleksandriuk saying, "he wasn't like him at all."[129]

In the archival record, many of the questions and comments by the populace dealt with the same themes party leaders raised behind closed doors, albeit often in a different tone. These sources highlighted the statements of rank-and-file members at the factory level, usually described as model workers and Stakhanovites, who tended to pose the toughest "questions" (critical comments) at meetings. A worker at Rostsel'mash reportedly said at a meeting that "factory leaders should demand more from shop foremen and other bosses (*nachal'niki*) and listen less to their talk about objective reasons" for difficulties in production, a phrase straight out of public party rhetoric.[130] In question-and-answer sessions with party representatives, workers commented on problems such as the failure to implement policies, the lack of assistance to those in need, and the immoral behavior of communists. Someone at an open meeting asked, "Why do district Soviet organs break government policies?"[131] At a campaign meeting a voter wanted to know, "Why do they pay so little attention to workers?" Another worker reiterated the same sentiment in clearer terms: "Why don't *party members* pay attention to us?"[132] In another meeting a Stakhanovite asked, "Why doesn't the [factory's] party organization deal more with the daily behavior of communists?"[133] The question suggested a tendency toward dubious acts by party functionaries, which, as we have seen, was indeed a problem. An issue for rank-and-file members was the lack of a party congress, which had not been held since 1939.[134] People were also curious about changes in local leadership, several at one factory in late 1947 wondering, "Why did they remove Aleksandriuk?"[135]

---

[129] Interview by author, 8 June 1995. For more interviews praising Patolichev, see also interview by author with Sevetlana Petrovovna Chernysheva, 7 March 1995; interview by author with Nina Nikitichnaia K., 17 March 1995; interview by author with Iurii Alekseevich Petrovskii, 27 April 1995. Acclamation for this leader can also be found in the documents of the time, including one *svodka* on May Day in Proletarskii district that reported widespread praise for Comrade Patolichev for improving workers' leisure time. TsDNI f. 13, op. 4, d. 415, l. 118.

[130] TsDNI f. 13, op. 4, d. 233, l. 85.

[131] TsDNI f. 13, op. 4, d. 331, l. 24.

[132] TsDNI f. 13, op. 4, d. 180, l. 44. Emphasis added. See also TsDNI f. 13, op. 4, d. 259, l. 24.

[133] TsDNI f. 13, op. 4, d. 92, l. 282.

[134] TsDNI f. 13, op. 4, d. 414, l. 72. This 1947 account notes that "several communists ask when will there be another congress." See also TsDNI f. 13, op. 4, d. 233, l. 60.

[135] TsDNI f. 13, op. 4, d. 233, l. 75.

Workers and rank-and-file party members, of course, were not privy to central reports condemning oblast leaders.

In questions and statements made openly at meetings with party functionaries, workers exhibited a keen awareness of corruption and often brought up issues of pay and working conditions. One worker asked, "Why isn't anything being done about bribery? Right now you can't get anything done without a bribe," the speaker continued, "everyone sees it but they can't do anything about it."[136] This question (comment), like the one above, constructed a "they" separate and apart from the person asking it, an amorphous entity that presumably had the power to do something about corruption but did not. Several workers at the Mikoyan Shoe Factory allegedly asked at one gathering, "Why don't they put an end to the misuse of one's position among food supply workers because these acts complicate difficulties for workers?"[137] As with the party material examined above, this question linked individual corruption with the population's economic difficulties. Also, we saw that housing administrators and the police were the focus of intense scrutiny in closed reports and occasionally in the press. Perhaps in response to public reports on the subject, a worker inquired at one meeting, "Why isn't the district housing bureau distributing apartments instead of illegally selling them?"[138] Expressing concerns over other matters, a policeman and party member at one meeting wanted to know, "Why aren't we supplied food and other goods along with workers of the secret police?"[139] This query expressed concern over pay and working conditions (major contributing factors to corruption), issues that were *not* emphasized in public and internal party material, both of which focused more on the shortcomings of individual leaders lacking sufficient ideological knowledge.

Statements overheard by informants revealed an "us" and "them" mentality among some workers who juxtaposed themselves to local party leaders, the flip side of the scenario we discussed in the previous chapter. Riabikov, a worker at Rostsel'mash, reportedly commended the Soviet ambassador to the United Nations for a speech to the organization. "If we spoke and criticized local leaders that bravely," he added, "life in Rostov and our factory would be much better."[140] While standing in line during the spring 1948 bread crisis, one woman deplored the fact that "they only bake bread for the bosses while workers stand in line for up to three days and can't get any."[141] At a textile

---

[136] TsDNI f. 13, op. 4, d. 92, l. 284.

[137] TsDNI f. 13, op. 4, d. 233, l. 35.

[138] TsDNI f. 13, op. 4, d. 313, l. 18.

[139] TsDNI f. 13, op. 4, d. 233, l. 60. Someone else at the meeting asked why policemen are required to work three hours more per day than factory workers.

[140] TsDNI f. 13, op. 4, d. 233, l. 85.

[141] TsDNI f. 13, op. 4, d. 415, l. 242. The word *nachal'stvo* might be translated as either "bosses" or "authorities."

plant a worker said, "When we stand in line for bread we don't see a single boss," adding that if they would join her for just a little while they would understand the extent of the problem and do something about it.[142] This *svodka* also reported that a cleaning woman cursed "the authorities" for "stuffing themselves while we workers are without bread."[143] A woman construction worker similarly declared, "communists live well and don't care about us; we stand in line for bread for a long time and have nothing to eat."[144] A woman worker at a garment factory blamed local leaders for the population's woes because "they don't take care of us like they should, but take good care of themselves and their friends."[145] At Rostov's fish factory two mother-heroines "cursed local authorities" for their difficult material circumstances.[146] Workers, in short, contrasted their position in everyday Soviet life to "them"—Communist Party members, "bosses," "local authorities"—who "take good care of themselves and their friends," an acknowledgment of protectionism within the party's ranks. Their commentaries also imply an expectation of "care" from above coupled with disappointment over not receiving it—they seemed keenly aware of the fact that the regime was not living up to its paternalistic rhetoric, and that corruption was part of the reason. The party press no doubt influenced popular opinion—the ruling ideology acting as a mediating factor in people's consciousness—but these sources show that at least some people in Soviet society consciously denounced local party leaders (albeit unwittingly to an informant) as a separate, elite entity.

Popular attitudes reflected the discussion of party-related issues at the top of the power structure. People at open factory meetings asked about problems with party leadership, displayed concern over corruption, and indicated that a reason for poor party growth was reluctance on the part of some to join. In many of their commentaries workers and others clearly delineated between themselves and Communist Party members or local authorities, displaying an "us and them" mentality. Also, those "below" focused on material difficulties and working conditions, while in some cases conceiving of the party in terms of the familiar "good" communist vs. "bad" communist dichotomy. The ultimate good communist was, of course, Stalin, who enjoyed almost god-like reverence. "Believers" greatly outnumbered a few critics, suggesting that much of the population at large—not just local officials—subscribed to the cult, especially the younger generation that did not remember the purges of the late 1930s. The cult no doubt gave people some direction, some cause for hope amid daily difficulties and despair. They *wanted* to believe in someone

---

[142] TsDNI f. 13, op. 4, d. 415, l. 142. I translate *nachal'nik* as "boss."

[143] TsDNI f. 13, op. 4, d. 415, l. 146.

[144] TsDNI f. 13, op. 4, d. 415, l. 147. For similar comments, see also TsDNI f. 13, op. 4, d. 415, ll. 118, 159.

[145] TsDNI f. 13, op. 4, d. 232, l. 61.

[146] TsDNI f. 13, op. 4, d. 232, l. 48.

"up there" watching out for them, a psychologically comforting idea and part of an overall strategy of survival. This notion was implicitly expressed in comments about leaders not "taking care" of people's needs. Meanwhile, Patolichev, described as an exception to the rule by interviewees, was popular precisely because he broke down the barriers separating local party leaders and the population, "impersonating" real workers in "regular" stores. The implicit message of the Stalin cult is that the dishonesty and incompetence of "bad communists" — the "bosses" workers actually had to deal with on an everyday basis — kept the god-like Stalin and his disciple Patolichev from solving people's daily needs.

№ ∂

It is impossible to say where exactly the line between classes in the Soviet system was located. It did not clearly divide party members from non-party workers because many workers were in the party; nor did it clearly divide workers from members of the nomenklatura, most of whom were from worker or peasant backgrounds. Nonetheless, it is clear that a line did exist in many people's perception of Soviet society between "them," Communist Party members (especially local party leaders), and "us," those at the bottom of the social order, the workers (and peasants) in whose name the "vanguard" party allegedly ruled. This is an inversion of local leaders' "us" and "them" perspective revealed during the election campaigns. Seeing Soviet society through the prism of the ruling ideology, local party leaders perceived of themselves as the "vanguard" of the working class and thus were less likely than workers to perceive a gap between themselves and their constituents. To the extent that those in charge did see this social divide, furthermore, they were inclined (following Lenin's lead) to explain it as the result of their own higher "consciousness," implicitly suggesting their superiority over those they intended to "lead" to the promised land of communism. In the party's public and internal narratives, "ideological knowledge" became the proposed solution for all problems and the lack of it a convenient explanation for those same problems. Dissatisfaction with subordinates in the party's hierarchy, furthermore, reflected the party's ideological framework — problems in a vanguard party state, after all, must be due to problems in the vanguard party. The Stalin cult (and support for local "good communist" leaders like Patolichev) acted as a salve for the many challenges facing local authorities and the population alike; it dissolved the class differences expressed in the "us and them" constructions of various texts, implicitly focusing blame on a "bad communist" archetype while absorbing all of society under the protective wing of the "wise chief" and his disciples.

There is a sinister side to the postwar "big deal" — systemic corruption and protectionism within the party' ranks. The political system fostered clientelistic structures and central leaders "came to terms" with most of the machinations of the local elite and its allied bureaucratic middle class, tolerating corruption and allowing some autonomy, albeit within bounds and against a current of centralization that had existed since the Stalin Revolution.[147] As with speculation and collaboration, the regime appears Janus-like, complaining publicly about corruption—albeit in muted terms—but then tolerating corrupt practices to a significant degree. The authorities acknowledged the obvious—if only because "everyone sees it," as one worker put it— to give the impression that it was dealing with the problem, when in fact only *significant* reforms of the political system could have addressed the root causes of corruption.[148] Many of the postwar Soviet middle class with whom the "big deal" was struck, moreover, were veterans who had joined the party during and after the war and who, as we have seen, had a strong sense of entitlement and wanted (demanded) higher-paying positions. Karol's friend Kolia joined the party in 1945 to get "in position in the race for posts of responsibility," he explained, because "it is the only means available, in our country, to carry out the struggle against suffering."[149] Transformed by two recent traumas—the purges of the late 1930s and the war—the party changed in the postwar period, adopting a greater degree of tolerance of corruption. Lenin's "professional revolutionaries" had, by the time of late Stalinism, evolved into "professional functionaries." However, popular pressures and sentiments apparent in the class dialogue of "reconstruction" created an undercurrent of reformist sentiment that finally came to the fore during the Khrushchev years. The same postwar reformist attitudes prevailing in Europe and noted in the previous chapter were apparent in the USSR as well, but it took Stalin's death before the impulse to reform could be realized. One of the key early reforms of the mid-1950s, as noted, was a relaxation of the harsh policies toward POWs and others with "suspect" behavior during the war, which effectively opened the way for more people to get in on the "big deal" until then mostly limited to war veterans like Kolia.

---

[147] On this point, see Hoffman, *Stalinist Values*, intro.

[148] Indeed, it should be noted that, when reforms were finally carried out under Nikita Khrushchev in the 1950s, they clearly did not go far enough to address these root problems—most of the changes were superficial rather than structural in nature. See Roy Medvedev and Zhores Medvedev, *Khrushchev: The Years in Power* (New York: Columbia University Press, 1978).

[149] Karol, *Solik*, 359.

Conclusion

"In my opinion this is all a fraud!"

I maintain that the party nomenklatura in the Soviet Union existed as a separate ruling class, its privileged position stemming from its control over the production and allocation of resources. In many cases corrupt officials profited from the distribution of goods in the illegal market or from bribes in this alleged period of "high" Stalinism. It is undeniable that an element of repression and fear backed up the Stalinist system, but the image presented here does not mesh with the idea of a society living in fear of a "totalitarian" state. These sources reveal a dialogue—both in words and in deeds—between the ruling elite and the working class. The party dutifully noted popular demands for better material conditions in report after report, and at times leaders responded to those demands, but ideological blinders kept them from acknowledging the systemic flaws at the root of the problem. Party texts conceptualized society in paternalistic "us" and "them" terms, a conscious expression of the elite's economic and cultural hegemony over the population. Languages of power also defined social sexual difference—implicitly in public texts, explicitly in internal documents and party policies—in ways that assured continued male domination of society, rhetoric to the contrary notwithstanding. Gauging by several sources, including *svodki* compiled at the local level, popular views varied widely, from genuine support for the regime and its supreme leader—the ruling ideology acting as a mediating factor to "manufacture consent"—to apathy and outright hostility. Common sentiments were recorded several times, such as complaints about exporting grain during the famine and tirades about "bosses" who do not have to stand in line for bread. Workers also resisted party policies by abandoning factory jobs and exercised considerable power within the "politics of productivity," occasionally protesting unpopular policies with work slowdowns or walkouts. The clear expression of worker dissatisfaction exposed in these documents shows the different ways people perceived Soviet reality on a daily basis. Some workers conformed with the regime's ruling ideology, but many expressed discontent with party policies and defined their own interests vis-à-vis the Communist Party and local authorities—an amorphous, omnipresent "they" in these documents—the representatives of the elite with whom workers interacted in the realm of production and through the bureaucracy.

In any stratified society an elite sits atop the social order in a position of privilege due to its control over economic *and* cultural production, the two being closely intertwined, and this includes the Soviet Union. People's perception of themselves in terms of their position in society, moreover, is imbedded deeply in a complex cultural context and a network of hierarchical power relations. Of course, one's station in life is closely linked to one's function within the realm of productive relations—defined broadly to include mental as well as physical labor—to what one does on a daily basis, be it as a factory director, an artisan, a peasant, a church scribe, professor, or factory worker. Often people do not explicitly see themselves in "class" terms; one of the most important aims of a dominant ideology is to diffuse or "explain away" the economic disparities rooted in the realm of production. It does this by focusing on flawed individuals rather than on the deficiencies of the system itself (i.e., the top-down, repressive nature of a fundamentally undemocratic political system); by constructing internal "others"—collaborators, speculators, "bad communists," etc.—to blame for all economic, social, and political ills; and by constructing myths of selfless heroism and sacrifice to gloss over material difficulties. The basic function of any ruling ideology is to manufacture consent while marginalizing dissent, goals achieved through a combination of propaganda and force (or the perceived threat of force, which makes its use unnecessary).

One's position was not set in the Soviet social order, as there was movement up and down with concomitant changes in perception. Workers became party bureaucrats, who could be demoted or even jailed for inadequate work or corruption (although, as we saw, those in power tolerated corruption to a significant degree). Peasants became workers, as demobilized troops from the countryside remained in the cities and rural youth were recruited through training schools, during this period of tremendous demographic change. The line dividing workers and the party nomenklatura was not always entirely clear, but people crossed it in both directions all the time, both in terms of what they did on a daily basis and in their perceptions of themselves and their position within the world around them. The Communist Party overlapped with the ruling elite to a significant degree, but the two were not synonymous. A rank-and-file party member who worked on the shop floor at a plant, for example, was in an entirely different position than the secretary of the plant's party cell. Reports on public opinion identify "rank-and-file" members as among the party's harshest critics. Their opinions were given special credence, as they in effect spoke for the "worker's conscience" of the party elite, which, again, was comprised of many former workers and peasants. Thus, the line between the ruling elite and the exploited classes did not cut between the party and the rest of society, but rather through the party itself.

The line between the elite and society also cuts through generations. On one side of that line stood the party elite of the Brezhnev generation, whose careers began in Soviet technical schools during the First Five-Year Plan and advanced during the purges.[1] Members of that age-group who survived the war now added that shared formative, myth-building experience to their collective identity as the state reimposed its control following a complete breakdown of the system under German occupation. A younger "war" generation born between 1923 and 1928, especially veterans, also joined the party in large numbers during and after the conflict and began to climb the career ladder. Elena Zubkova sees them as the embryo of the generation of the Twentieth Party Congress (1956) that returned from the war with high hopes for a political thaw and improved living standards and became a driving force behind de-Stalinization and the reforms of the Khrushchev period.[2] Catherine Merridale stresses that many veterans eventually became a conservative force and social support for the regime during the rule of Leonid Brezhnev (1964–82).[3] Both of these views are correct. Generational experiences like the war undeniably tied everyone of an age group together, but soldiers held a wide variety of views of the experience even while the war still raged. People, in other words, experienced the war differently, including soldiers, and not all of them necessarily emerged from it with a deep love for Soviet rule. On the other hand, *most* veterans of this generation no doubt bought into the Stalinist system, wanting to see their cause as just. Veterans clearly used their social capital to secure the best possible positions for themselves within the Stalinist system and did not necessarily question that system's overall contours. The spirit of this era among veterans of the younger generation is perhaps best embodied by Kolia, Karol's friend who said "everything here will have to change" but who also joined the party in 1945 mainly, he implied, for the sake of survival. Although we unfortunately do not know Kolia's fate, one gets the sense that he would have been supportive of Khrushchev's reforms but also perfectly comfortable as a member of the elite within Brezhnev's party apparatus, especially with the passage of time and gradual overall improvement in living standards.

For its part, the Soviet working class was being "remade" during the war and after. One of the focal points of this study is the intersection between class and gender in Soviet society; as Joan Scott evinces, languages of class are

---

[1] Fitzpatrick, "Stalin and the Making of the New Elite."

[2] Zubkova, *Russia After the War*, intro. The war became a common reference point for defining oneself and one's experiences within a cultural and historical context, and victory, as shown above, was perceived by many as a vindication of the ruling ideology and legitimation of the "vanguard's" rule. A short story from the period, for example, describes members of the party bureaucracy sharing stories about the "front," the term itself taking on strong cultural and political overtones. See "Nastoiashchii tovarishch" (True Comrade), *Don*, no. 11 (1948): 182–93.

[3] Merridale, *Ivan's War*, 374–77.

languages of gender.[4] The percentage of women in industry increased dramatically during the war and then decreased slightly after demobilization as men returned to the factories from the front, especially in the skilled-jobs sector. But in 1948 a larger number of women worked in industry than before the war, most of them at the bottom of the pay scale and many of them single mothers living in *extremely* difficult conditions. The percentage of women in the party and in positions of leadership, on the other hand, remained low because of a number of factors, including the "double burden" for women, which was worse than ever during the war and after. The party's public and internal record tied women to motherhood *and* economic production, hinting at their importance as both producers and reproducers. This was not the case in the countries of Western Europe, which separated these two roles for women, emphasizing the maternal role. The heroic, career-oriented, and highly masculinized depiction of "liberated womanhood" promoted in the party press did not resemble the everyday life of most women revealed more clearly in the party's discussions behind closed doors (nor, for that matter, did it resemble the "mother heroine" image also propagated by the regime). The discrepancy between rhetoric and reality in this case helps us understand why the new population policies failed to produce the dramatic increase in births that policy makers hoped for—there was to be no large scale Soviet baby boom.[5] Definitions of "loyalty" also took on gendered meanings during and after the war; wives were held to a double standard and betrayed their countries with their bodies. "Housewives," moreover, were pressured into the workforce and—labeled "non-working adult dependents"—implicitly vilified by reports of women "working like men." The model woman constructed in the party press was a *loyal*, patriotic, humble, quiet, caring, selfless worker, wife, and mother ("with a pure *Russian* heart") willing to accept any and all sacrifices. Women, meanwhile, had a major voice in the popular record, often expressing views at odds with party policies.

Demobilized troops, wounded war veterans, and youth from the countryside made up the rest of a variegated workforce, which was not totally powerless. The state never completely controlled labor because of worker resistance to party policies, especially abandoning jobs, a common act throughout this five-year period that peaked during the famine year of 1947 and declined thereafter. There was little difference between the population's public comments and statements reported by informants, as at times workers and others *publicly* challenged the party's claims, "speaking truth to power." Their bold-

---

[4] Joan Scott, *Gender and the Politics of History*.

[5] There was an increase in births, except in 1948 because the famine of the previous year greatly reduced the number of pregnancies. The reduction in births in 1948, however, was compensated by a significant rise in births in 1949. Nonetheless, population growth fell well below the hopes and expectations of those making policies. See Nakachi, "Population, Politics and Reproduction," in Fürst, *Late Stalinist Russia*.

ness, the social capital of victory, stemmed in part from the relative strength of workers within the "politics of productivity." This did not, however, translate into collective struggle against their bosses; resistance took on the form of individualized protest. As before the war, workers and others perfected survival skills outside the realm of state control, including workplace pilfering and illegal economic activity. At the same time, the struggle for survival depoliticized workers. Clearly the relationship between state and society was *very* complex; amid grim material circumstances workers had a great deal of room for maneuver in a tight labor market that allowed them to negotiate the best possible conditions of labor (which implicitly meant jockeying for position in the illegal economy). Demobilized troops were in a particularly strong position, especially vis-à-vis factory directors and others who remained in occupied territory. There was a perception in society of the "cocky war veteran" willing to speak his mind in public, and as several authors indicate there were also expectations for a better life after the war.

Significantly, the popular record inverts the "us" and "them" construction of party texts, construing an image of local party leaders as an aloof elite. Despite constant propaganda of a "workers' state" — which convinced some — many workers saw their "boss" (*nachal'nik*) as a privileged "other." This is an implicit acknowledgment of the exploitative nature of productive relations between workers and the party elite whereby the latter extracts surplus value from workers' labor, which is also implicitly demonstrated by workplace pilfering and workers' constant dissatisfaction with material conditions. They saw the party elite as an "other" in a number of ways, adopting but often inverting official language on several issues. They questioned, for example, the loyalty of some party leaders during the election campaigns, recognized the link between corrupt party officials and speculators, and in some cases even mixed their antipathy for the party elite with anti-Semitic stereotypes, such as the widely held view that Jews were "cowardly" and were "saved" by Russians or the "Judeo-commune" syndrome. Workers often pinpointed the contradiction(s) between public party rhetoric and their own perceptions of daily experience — thus they were in dialogue with an agenda set in the Stalinist press, which at the same time was in dialogue with popular concerns in an (unequal) dialectical relationship. The realization by workers of a gap between rhetoric and reality is sometimes framed as an "awakening experience," as in the case of one worker who refused to donate to bond drives after the monetary reform because he felt cheated by the exchange. This example, furthermore, illustrates that people's views evolve over time as they grow older, gain more experience, and/or learn more information. Worker comments often exposed a sense of deception or of being lied to, including the comment noted in the title: "in my opinion this is all a fraud." Specifically, that comment, made by a worker with a large family, referred to price increases on rationed goods during the early stages of the 1946 famine, which were offset by a small wage increase.

More broadly, however, I argue that such statements reflect the realization by workers and others that official explanations of everyday "reality" did not correspond to their own experiences, comprising a key part of the dialogue between antagonistic class discourses. My primary goal has been to give a voice to popular sentiments, which, with greater access to Soviet archives, are only now being added to the historical record. To understand their full significance, I maintain that we must recognize such voices for what they are—the expression of a separate working class consciousness vis-à-vis the party elite in this alleged "workers' state." Conversely, the party elite's response to these comments also shows the gap in consciousness or fundamental misunderstanding between those in power and society at large. An example is a report written by District Party Secretary V. Koliadin, who tried to comprehend the comment "in my opinion this is all a fraud" and other statements of dissatisfaction by workers within his own ideologically-determined worldview. Koliadin's interpretation offered a very simple explanation as to why a "significant number" of workers at the beer factory and elsewhere reacted so negatively to the price hikes on rationed goods at the beginning of the famine: the plant's party cell failed to fully spell out the "meaning" of the government's decision to workers. The disproportionately female workers at the low end of the pay scale and those with a lot of children, of course, understood perfectly well that the measure meant less bread for them and their families. As we have seen, in other summaries of the popular "mood," party secretaries characterized negative commentaries as reflective of "unhealthy, decadent attitudes" by "backward" workers and employees. Espousing an ideology that saw themselves as part of a vanguard party ruling in the interests of the working class, local leaders could only comprehend resistance and discontent by workers in these terms. Workers, on the other hand, acted first and foremost out of an instinct to survive—a postwar *homo sovieticus*[6]—bending or breaking whatever ideologically-driven dictates were imposed on them to achieve that end for themselves and their families.

The various texts examined here, read as distinct bodies of opinion or layers of discourse, elucidate the operations of power and ideology. To reiterate, ideology is a way of consciously categorizing perceptions of the material world and functions in a number of ways to *contain* and present "reality" within an explanatory framework. Shaped by a shared set of basic assumptions and beliefs, a ruling ideology is the dominant portrayal of society plus the rationalization (or containment) of problems propagated by those in power as the "official story" via its control over the press and other media. The specific features of a ruling ideology change in response to new social challenges and/or the changing goals/needs of the elite. Languages of power, furthermore, are in constant dialogue with voices of dissent that often invert or caricature official depictions of society. A ruling ideology responds to the

---

[6] See Fitzpatrick, *Everyday Stalinism*, 1–3.

concerns of workers and others by attempting to shape the contours of popular opinion on a whole host of issues. Party propaganda, for example, employed "family rhetoric" to present the elite's construction of how class, gender, and national relations in society should be and marginalize popular perceptions at odds with official views. It propagated the "myth of reconstruction" — an extension of the Stalinist "myth of the war" — that glorified the daily suffering and sacrifice of the population. The myth of "socialist democracy" underscored the Soviet political system, granting a "democratic" facade to a fundamentally undemocratic system based on one-party rule. Leninist tenets of the "vanguard" party became a *de facto* justification for policies disadvantageous to the workers allegedly in charge of a society based on "collective ownership."[7] Ideology is evoked as a panacea for all problems and," conversely, the lack thereof as the cause of those problems. The elite also worried about the perceived threats posed to their ideological supremacy by the growth of religion and the exposure of part of the population to the West.

Two final issues must be considered to fill out our picture of reconstruction in the Soviet Union: the *Zhdanovshchina*, a major domestic political campaign between 1946 and 1948, and the development of the Cold War over the same period. The *Zhdanovshchina* was an anti-Western ideological campaign that began in the autumn of 1946 when Andrei Zhdanov, head of the Leningrad branch of the party, harshly criticized the works of authors Mikhail Zoshchenko and Anna Akhmatova published in two Leningrad journals. The *Zhdanovshchina* was a negation of Western influences that had crept into Soviet culture during the wartime alliance, and the movement was built on the myth that the Soviet Union was a classless society.[8] The perceived enemies from within were labeled "cosmopolitans," those with a "worldly outlook" who kneeled before Western culture, ignoring the achievements of Russian history, the Bolshevik Revolution, and socialism. This domestic campaign for "ideological purity" in Soviet culture coincided with increasingly rigid relations with the former wartime allies. The Zhdanovshchina was limited to the literary and cultural fields and was, as recent research indicates, instigated solely at Stalin's behest. Zhdanov was merely a spokesperson for Stalin's attack on the cultural realm, and, in fact, since the initial attack was focused on two journals based in Leningrad, where Zhdanov had been party boss, the campaign was in some ways an attack on Zhdanov himself.[9] The campaign

---

[7] Djilas, for one, argued that the false claims of Soviet socialism rested on the myth of "collective ownership," which was just a smokescreen for the new class's control over the production and distribution of goods.

[8] See, for example, RGASPI f. 17, op. 122, d. 278, ll. 61–62.

[9] See Yoram Gorlizki and Oleg Khlevniuk, *Cold Peace: Stalin and the Soviet Ruling Circle, 1945–1953* (Oxford: Oxford University Press, 2004), 31–38. For a classic work on the *Zhdanovshchina*, see Werner G. Hahn, *Postwar Soviet Politics: The Fall of Zhdanov and the Defeat of Moderation, 1946–1953* (Ithaca, NY: Cornell University Press, 1982). For years

constituted a dogmatic reaction to an increasingly hostile international situation as the Cold War developed, especially after the Marshall Plan in 1947, when it became clear that American aid to the war-torn Soviet Union would not be forthcoming. As with "socialism in one country" in the 1920s and 1930s, the Soviet Union in the 1940s would have to undergo "reconstruction in one country" — although without explicitly calling it that.

The regime proclaimed the end of "reconstruction," measured by its own yardstick of achieving prewar levels of production for heavy industry, in 1947 for most of the country, and a year later in Rostov. As noted, however, actual physical reconstruction took much longer than that, more in line with the rest of Europe and Japan, i.e., the early-to-mid 1950s. Yet 1948 marked the end of the official period of "reconstruction" *as the regime defined it*, and since it was a myth created by those in power, that is really all that mattered. The timing, of course, coincided with the early stages of the Cold War, which was not an accident: the regime did not want to look weak in the world's eyes (and especially the eyes of the West) amid the developing Cold War. The same rationale explains why the regime kept the postwar famine secret from the West and exported grain according to prior agreement, leading to major complaints by workers. The myth of "reconstruction" morphed into the myth of the USSR as a Cold War "superpower," especially after the Soviet regime successfully tested a nuclear device in 1949. With the onset of the Cold War, moreover, the regime could not allow for a postwar "relaxation," as hoped for by many. Thus, unlike Western Europe after the war, there were no significant immediate postwar reforms in the USSR (as Fitzpatrick notes, there could be no de-Stalinization as long as Stalin himself was still in power).[10] The pressures for reform were present in the Soviet Union as elsewhere after the war, but they remained bubbling beneath the surface until after Stalin's death in 1953. The Stalinist regime's creation and manipulation of a myth of the war operated in part to keep pressures for reform at bay by linking society through a common, shared experience of suffering that culminated in a victorious vindication of the Soviet "socialist" system and its "great leader." Yet reform was just a matter of time, the pressure for change from below was too strong to overcome in the long run, especially since it no doubt grew stronger following Stalin's death.

The five-year period of "reconstruction" beginning with liberation from German occupation and ending in 1948 linked the war and immediate postwar periods as the Cold War developed. The 1948 Berlin air lift was clearly a crucial event in the early Cold War, and, as noted, a number of scholars see

---

rumors surrounded Andrei Zhdanov's death in August 1948 insinuating that Stalin had somehow played a part in his demise, but Zhdanov's son, Iurii Andreevich (who was also Stalin's son-in-law at the time), said in an interview that he witnessed his father's death and insisted that he died of natural causes.

[10] Fitzpatrick, "Postwar Soviet Society: The 'Return to Normalcy.'"

1948 as an important turning point in the USSR's domestic history as well.[11] A parallel can be drawn between this period and the 1920s. During the NEP the regime relaxed restrictions on the market as the economy recovered from years of war, revolution, and civil war. Once pre-1914 levels of production for heavy industry were reached in 1927, however, Stalin clamped down on the market and extracted resources from the countryside to fuel a massive, state-controlled industrialization campaign. That same year a war scare with Great Britain convinced Soviet leaders of the need to rapidly industrialize amid "capitalist encirclement." Similarly, in the 1940s the regime allowed informal markets (especially in foodstuffs) to operate relatively freely until the end of "reconstruction" in 1948, when heavy industry achieved prewar levels of production (or at least something close to it). From that point on, the regime tried to bring economic activity more firmly under its control, a task made all the more crucial by the rise of the United States as a new external "other" and a growing enmity that was clear by 1948. We could speculate as to the possibility of a different path by the Stalinist regime during this five-year period, and especially following victory in May 1945. Could the regime, for example, have maintained good relations with the West, relaxed internal political restrictions, and concentrated on improving living standards, as Karol, his small group of friends, and no doubt many others in the USSR hoped? Stalin's successor Nikita Khrushchev would eventually attempt to do all of these things, which indicates that there were social pressures from below for reform. The Stalinist system, however, proved incapable of reforming itself, either under Khrushchev or thirty years later during Mikhail Gorbachev's *perestroika* (restructuring) and *glasnost'* (openness) in the late 1980s, when the system collapsed under the weight of its own flaws and inefficiencies as well as the bankruptcy of its ruling ideology.

---

[11] Filtzer, *Soviet Workers and Late Stalinism*, intro. See also unpublished paper, Donald Filtzer, "The Regime and the Working Class During Late Stalinism, 1945–1953," delivered at the American Association for the Advancement of Slavic Studies National Convention in St. Louis, Missouri, in November 1999; Hessler, *A Social History of Soviet Trade*; Karl Qualls, "Local-Outsider Negotiations in Sevastopol's Postwar Reconstruction," in Raleigh, ed., *Provincial Landscapes*, 276–98; and unpublished paper, "Localism During National Reconstruction: A Case Study of Post-War Sevastopol, 1944–1953," delivered at the American Association for the Advancement of Slavic Studies National Convention in St. Louis, Missouri, in November 1999. On the significance of the period 1943–1948, see also William O. McCagg, *Stalin Embattled, 1943–1948* (Detroit: Wayne State University Press, 1978).

Selected Bibliography

Accampo, Elinor et al. *Gender and the Politics of Social Reform in France, 1870–1914.* Baltimore: Johns Hopkins University Press, 1995.

Acker, Joan. "Class, Gender, and the Relations of Distribution." *Signs* 13: 3 (Spring 1988): 473–97.

Andreev, E. M. *Naselenie Sovetskogo Soiuza, 1922–1991 gg.* Moscow: Nauka, 1993.

Aleksievich, Svetlana. *War's Unwomanly Face.* Moscow: Palmira, 1988.

Arad, Yitzhak et al., eds. *The Einsatzgruppen Reports: Selections from the Dispatches of the Nazi Death Squads' Campaign Against the Jews, July 1941–January 1943.* New York: Holocaust Library, 1989.

Aten, Marion, and Arthur Orrmont. *Last Train Over Rostov Bridge.* New York: Messner, 1961.

Azéma, Jean-Pierre, and François Bédarida, eds. *Le régime de Vichy et les Français.* Paris: Fayard, 1992.

Barber, John, and Mark Harrison. *The Soviet Home Front, 1941–1945: A Social and Economic History of the USSR in World War II.* New York: Longman, 1991.

Barghoorn, Frederick C. *Détente and the Democratic Movement in the USSR.* New York: Free Press, 1976.

Beda, A. M. *Sovetskaia politicheskaia kul'tura cherez prizmu MVD: Ot "moskovskogo patriotizma" k idee "Bol'shogo Otechestva" (1946–1958).* Moscow: Izdatel'stvo ob"edineniia Mosgorarkhiv, 2002.

Bennett, Gill. *The End of the War in Europe, 1945.* London: HMSO, 1996.

Bennett, Rab. *Under the Shadow of the Swastika: The Moral Dilemmas of Resistance and Collaboration in Hitler's Europe.* New York: New York University Press, 1999.

Berliner, Joseph. *Factory and Manager in the Soviet Union.* Cambridge, MA: Harvard University Press, 1957.

Bidlack, Richard. "Survival Strategies in Leningrad during the First Year of the Soviet-German War." In Thurston and Bonwetsch, *People's War*, 84–107.

Bogdan, Valentina. *Mimikriia v SSSR: Vospominaniia inzhenera 1935–1942 gody.* Frankfurt: Polyglott-Druck, 1981.

Boterbloem, Kees. *Life and Death under Stalin: Kalinin Province, 1945–1953.* Montreal: McGill-Queen's University Press, 1999.

Bourdieu, Pierre. *Outline of a Theory of Practice*. Translated by Richard Nice. Cambridge: Cambridge University Press, 1993.

Brandist, Craig. "Gramsci, Bakhtin and the Semiotics of Hegemony." *New Left Review* 216: 2 (1997): 94–109.

Brooks, Jeffrey. *Thank You, Comrade Stalin! Soviet Public Culture from Revolution to Cold War*. Princeton, NJ: Princeton University Press, 2000.

Brown, Kate. *A Biography of No Place: From Ethnic Borderland to Soviet Heartland*. Cambridge, MA: Harvard University Press, 2004.

Bubis, Edward, and Blair A. Ruble. "The Impact of World War II on Leningrad." In *The Impact of World War II on the Soviet Union*, edited by Susan J. Linz, 189–206. Totowa, NJ: Rowman and Allanheld, 1985.

Buckley, Mary. *Women and Ideology in the Soviet Union*. Ann Arbor: University of Michigan Press, 1989.

Bugai, N. F. "K voprosu o deportatsii narodov SSSR v 30–40-kh godakh." *Istoriia SSSR*, no. 6 (1989): 135–44.

Bugai, N. F., ed. *Iosif Stalin – Laverentiiu Berii: "Ikh nado deportirovat'." Dokumenty, fakty, kommentarii*. Moscow: Druzhba narodov, 1992.

Burowoy, Michael. *Manufacturing Consent: Changes in the Labor Process Under Monopoly Capitalism*. Chicago: University of Chicago Press, 1982.

Burton, Chris. "Medical Welfare During Late Stalinism: A Study of Doctors and the Soviet Health System, 1945–1953." Ph.D. diss., University of Chicago, 2000.

Butler, W. E. *Soviet Law*. London: Butterworths, 1988.

Calder, Angus. *The People's War: Britain 1939–1945*. New York: Pantheon Books, 1969.

Chapman, Janet. *Real Wages in Soviet Russia Since 1928*. Cambridge, MA: Harvard University Press, 1963.

Chomsky, Noam, and Edward Hermann. *Manufacturing Consent: The Political Economy of the Mass Media*. New York: Pantheon Books, 1988.

Clinard, Marshall. *The Black Market: A Study of White Collar Crime*. Montclair, NJ: Patterson Smith, 1969.

Conquest, Robert. *The Great Terror: Stalin's Purge of the 1930s*. New York: Collier Books, 1968.

Conway, Martin. *Collaboration in Belgium: Leon Degrelle and the Rexist Movement, 1940–1944*. New Haven: Yale University Press, 1993.

Dale, J., and P. Foster, eds. *Feminists and State Welfare*. London: Routledge, 1986.

Dallin, Alexander. *German Rule in Russia, 1941–1945*. New York: St. Martin's Press, 1957.

Darnton, Robert. "The Forbidden Best-Sellers of Pre-Revolutionary France." In *The French Revolution: The Essential Readings*, edited by Ronald Schechter, 106–37. Oxford: Oxford University Press, 2001.

Davies, Sarah. *Popular Opinion in Stalin's Russia: Terror, Propaganda, and Dissent, 1934–1941*. Cambridge: Cambridge University Press, 1997.

Deak, Istvan et al., eds. *The Politics of Retribution in Europe: World War II and Its Aftermath*. Princeton, NJ: Princeton University Press, 2000.

Dean, Martin. *Collaboration in the Holocaust: Crimes of the Local Police in Belorussia and Ukraine, 1941–44*. New York: St. Martin's Press, 2000.

———. "Where Did All the Collaborators Go?" *Slavic Review* 64: 4 (Winter 2005): 791–98.

De Certeau, Michel. *The Practice of Everyday Life*. 2nd ed. Translated by Steven Rendall. Los Angeles: University of California Press, 2002.

Diamond, Hanna. *Women and the Second World War in France 1939–1948: Choices and Constraints*. New York: Pearson Education, 1999.

Diefendorf, Jeffrey M., ed. *Rebuilding Europe's Bombed Cities*. New York: St. Martin's Press, 1990.

———. *In the Wake of War: The Reconstruction of German Cities After World War II*. New York: Oxford University Press, 1993.

Djilas, Milovan. *The New Class: An Analysis of the Communist System*. New York: Praeger, 1957.

Dower, John. *Embracing Defeat: Japan in the Wake of World War II*. New York: W. W Norton and Co./New Press, 1999.

Dunham, Vera. *In Stalin's Time: Middleclass Values in Soviet Fiction*. Durham, NC: Duke University Press, 1990.

Duskin, Eric. *Stalinist Reconstruction and the Confirmation of a New Elite*. New York: Palgrave, 2001.

Dutton, Paul V. "An Overlooked Source of Social Reform: Family Policy in French Agriculture, 1939–1945." *Journal of Modern History* 72: 2 (June 2000): 375–412.

Edele, Mark. "A 'Generation of Victors'? Soviet Second World War Veterans from Demobilization to Organization 1941–1956." Ph.D. diss., University of Chicago, 2004.

———. "Soviet Veterans as an Entitlement Group, 1945–1955." *Slavic Review* 65: 1 (2006): 111–37.

Ehrenburg, Ilya, and Vasily Grossman. *The Black Book: The Ruthless Murder of Jews by German-Fascist Invaders Throughout the Temporarily-Occupied Regions of The Soviet Union and in the Death Camps of Poland During the War of 1941–1945*. New York: Holocaust Publications, 1981.

Eley, Geoff. *Forging Democracy: The History of the Left in Europe, 1850–2000*. Oxford: Oxford University Press, 2000.

Ellman, Michael. "The 1947 Soviet Famine and the Entitlement Approach to Famines." *Cambridge Journal of Economics* 24: 5 (2000): 603–30.

Erickson, John. *The Road to Stalingrad*. London: Harper and Row, 1975.

Fieseler, Beate. "The Bitter Legacy of the 'Great Patriotic War': Red Army Disabled Soldiers under Late Stalinism." In Furst, *Late Stalinist Russia*, 46–61.

Filtzer, Donald. "The Regime and the Working Class During Late Stalinism, 1945–1953." Unpublished paper delivered at the American Association for the Advancement of Slavic Studies National Convention. St. Louis, MO, 20 November 1999.

————. *Soviet Workers and Late Stalinism: Labour and the Restoration of the Stalinist System after World War II*. Cambridge: Cambridge University Press, 2002.

————. *Soviet Workers and Stalinist Industrialization: The Formation of Modern Soviet Production Relations, 1928–1941*. Armonk, NY: M. E. Sharpe, 1986.

————. "Standard of Living versus Quality of Life: Struggling with the Urban Environment in Russia during the Early Years of Post-War Reconstruction." In Fürst, *Late Stalinist Russia*, 81–102.

Fineman, Martha. "Masking Dependency: The Political Role of Family Rhetoric." In *The Subject of Care: Feminist Perspectives on Dependency*, edited by Eva Feder Kittay and Ellen K. Feder, 215–44. Lanham, MD: Rowman and Littlefield Publishers, 2002.

Fishman, Sarah et al., eds. *France at War: Vichy and the Historians*. New York: Oxford University Press, 2000.

Fitzpatrick, Sheila. "Ascribing Class: The Construction of Social Identity in Soviet Russia." *Journal of Modern History* 65: 4 (1993): 745–70.

————. *Everyday Stalinism: Ordinary Life in Extraordinary Times. Soviet Russia in the 1930s*. New York: Oxford University Press, 1999.

————. "Postwar Soviet Society: The 'Return to Normalcy,' 1945–1953." In *The Impact of World War II on the Soviet Union*, edited by Susan J. Linz, 129–56. Totowa, NJ : Rowman and Allanheld, 1985.

————. "Stalin and the Making of the New Elite, 1928–1939." *Slavic Review* 38: 3 (1979): 377–402.

————. *Stalin's Peasants: Resistance and Survival in the Russian Village after Collectivization*. Oxford: Oxford University Press, 1994.

Fredman, Sandra. *Women and the Law*. Oxford: Oxford University Press, 1997.

Freeden, Michael. *Ideology: A Very Short Introduction*. Oxford: Oxford University Press, 2003.

Friedrich, Klaus-Peter. "Collaboration in a 'Land without a Quisling': Patterns of Cooperation with the Nazi German Occupation Regime in Poland during World War II." *Slavic Review* 64: 4 (Winter 2005): 711–46.

Furst, Juliane, ed. *Late Stalinist Russia: Society Between Reconstruction and Reinvention*. London: Routledge, 2006.

Ganson, Nicholas. "Famine of Victors: The Soviet Hunger of 1946–1947 in Historical and Global Perspective." Ph.D. diss., University of North Carolina-Chapel Hill, 2006.

Gartenschläger, Uwe. "Living and Surviving in Occupied Minsk." In Thurston and Bonwetsch, *People's War*, 13–28.

Geertz, Clifford. *The Interpretation of Cultures: Selected Essays*. New York: Basic Books, 1973.

Genovese, Elizabeth Fox, and Eugene D. Genovese. "The Political Crisis of Social History: A Marxian Perspective." *Journal of Social History* 10 (1976): 205–20.

Getty, J. Arch. "'Excesses Are not Permitted': Mass Terror and Stalinist Governance in the Late 1930s." *The Russian Review*, no. 1 (2002): 113–38.

———. *Origins of the Great Purges: The Soviet Communist Party Reconsidered, 1933–1938*. Cambridge: Cambridge University Press, 1985.

———. "State and Society Under Stalin: Constitutions and Elections in the 1930s." *Slavic Review* 50: 1 (Spring 1991): 18–35.

Getty, J. Arch, and Oleg Naumov. *The Road to Terror: Stalin and the Self-Destruction of the Bolsheviks, 1932–39*. New Haven: Yale University Press, 1999.

Gitelman, Zvi. "Soviet Reactions to the Holocaust, 1945–1991." In *The Holocaust in the Soviet Union: Studies and Sources on the Destruction of the Jews in the Nazi-Occupied Territories of the USSR, 1941–1945*, edited by Lucjan Dobroszycki and Jeffrey S. Gurock, 3–28. New York: M. E. Sharpe, 1993.

Goldman, Wendy. *Women At The Gates: Gender and Industry in Stalin's Russia*. Cambridge: Cambridge University Press, 2002.

———. *Women, the State, and Revolution: Soviet Family Policy and Family Life, 1917–1936*. New York: Cambridge University Press, 1993.

Gorbachev, Mikhail S. *Memoirs: Mikhail Gorbachev*. New York: Doubleday, 1996.

Gordon, Linda, ed. *Women, the State, and Welfare*. Madison: University of Wisconsin Press, 1990.

Gorlizki, Yoram, and Oleg Khlevniuk. *Cold Peace: Stalin and the Soviet Ruling Circle, 1945–1953*. Oxford: Oxford University Press, 2004.

Gorsuch, Anne. *Youth in Revolutionary Russia: Enthusiasts, Bohemians, Delinquents*. Bloomington: Indiana University Press, 2000.

Gross, Jan T. *Fear: Anti-Semitism in Poland After Auschwitz. An Essay in Historical Interpretation*. Princeton, NJ: Princeton University Press, 2006.

———. *Neighbors: The Destruction of the Jewish Community in Jedwabne, Poland*. Princeton, NJ: Princeton University Press, 2001.

———. *Polish Society under German Occupation: Generalgouvernement, 1939–44*. Princeton, NJ: Princeton University Press, 1979.

———. "A Tangled Web: Confronting Stereotypes Concerning Relations between Poles, Germans, Jews, Communists." In Deak et al., eds., *Politics of Retribution*, 74–130.

———. "Themes for a Social History of War Experience and Collaboration." In Deak et al., eds., *Politics of Retribution*, 15–36.

Grossman, Gregory. "The Second Economy of the USSR." *Problems of Communism* 26: 5 (1987): 25–40.

Gutman, Amy, ed. *Democracy and the Welfare State*. Princeton, NJ: Princeton University Press, 1988.

Hahn, Werner G. *Postwar Soviet Politics: The Fall of Zhdanov and the Defeat of Moderation, 1946–1953*. Ithaca, NY: Cornell University Press, 1982.

Hankiss, Elemér. "Games of Corruption: East Central Europe, 1945–1999." In *Political Corruption in Transition*, edited by Stephen Kotkin and Andras Sajó, 243–60. Budapest: Central European University Press, 2002.

Harvey, David. *The Condition of Post-Modernity: An Enquiry into the Origins of Social Change*. Oxford: Oxford University Press, 1989.

Hein, Carola et al., eds. *Rebuilding Urban Japan After 1945*. New York: Palgrave Macmillan, 2003.

Heinzen, James. "A 'Campaign Spasm': Graft and the Limits of the 'Campaign' against Bribery after the Great Fatherland War." In Furst, *Late Stalinist Russia*, 123–41.

———. "Graft and 'the Art of the Bribe' in the Late Stalin Period, 1943–1953: The View from the State and the View from Below." Unpublished paper delivered at the American Association for the Advancement of Slavic Studies National Convention. Salt Lake City, UT, 4 November 2005.

Hellbeck, Jochen. "Fashioning the Stalinist Soul: The Diary of Stepan Podlubnyi (1931–1939)." *Jahrbücher für Geschichte Osteuropas* 44: 3 (1996): 344–73.

Hessler, Julie. "A Postwar Perestroika: Toward a History of Private Enterprise in the USSR." *Slavic Review* 57: 3 (1998): 516–42.

———. *A Social History of Soviet Trade: Trade Policy, Retail Practices, and Consumption, 1917–1953*. Princeton, NJ: Princeton University Press, 2004.

Hilberg, Raul. *The Destruction of the European Jews*. New Haven: Yale University Press, 2003.

Hirschfeld, Gerhard, and Patrick Marsh, eds. *Collaboration in France: Politics and Culture during the Nazi Occupation, 1940–1944*. Oxford: Oxford University Press, 1989.

———. *Nazi Rule and Dutch Collaboration: The Netherlands under German Occupation, 1940–45*. Translated by Louise Willmot. Oxford: Oxford University Press, 1988.

Hoffmann, David. "Mothers in the Motherland: Stalinist Pronatalism in its Pan-European Context." *Journal of Social History* 34: 1 (2000): 35–54.

———. *Peasant Metropolis: Social Identities in Moscow, 1929–1941*. Ithaca, NY: Cornell University Press, 1994.

———. *Stalinist Values: The Cultural Norms of Soviet Modernity, 1917–1941*. Ithaca, NY: Cornell University Press, 2003.

Hoffman, Stanley. "Collaborationism in France during World War II." *Journal of Modern History* 40: 3 (September 1968): 375–95.

Holquist, Peter. "Anti-Soviet *Svodki* From the Civil War: Surveillance as a Shared Feature of Russian Political Culture." *Russian Review* 56: 3 (1997): 445–50.

———. "'Information Is the Alpha and Omega of Our Work': Bolshevik Surveillance in Its Pan-European Context." *Journal of Modern History* 69: 3 (1997): 415–50.

————. *Making War, Forging Revolution: Russia's Continuum of Crisis, 1914–1921.* Cambridge: Cambridge University Press, 2002.

Hooper, Cynthia. "A Darker 'Big Deal': Concealing Party Crimes in the Post-Second World War Era." In Furst, *Late Stalinist Russia,* 142–63.

Hough, Jerry. *Soviet Leadership in Transition.* Washington, DC: Brookings Institution, 1980.

Hough, Jerry, and Merle Fainsod. *How the Soviet Union is Governed.* Cambridge, MA: Harvard University Press, 1979.

Hunt, Lynn. *The Family Romance of the French Revolution.* Berkeley: University of California Press, 1992.

Jones, Gareth Stedman. *Languages of Class: Studies in English Working-Class History, 1832–1982.* Cambridge: Cambridge University Press, 1983.

Johnston, Timothy. "Subversive Tales?: War Rumours in the Soviet Union, 1945–1947." In Furst, *Late Stalinist Russia,* 62–78.

Karol, K. S. *Solik: Life in the Soviet Union, 1939–1946.* New York: Pluto Press, 1986.

Kaplan, Cynthia S. "The Impact of World War II on the Party." In Linz, *Impact of World War II,* 157–87.

————. *The Party and Agricultural Crisis Management in the USSR.* Ithaca, NY: Cornell University Press, 1987.

Kenez, Peter. *The Birth of the Propaganda State: Soviet Methods of Mass Mobilization, 1917–1929.* Cambridge: Cambridge University Press, 1985.

————. *Civil War in South Russia, 1919–1920: The Defeat of the Whites.* Berkeley: University of California Press, 1977.

Kenney, Padraic. *Rebuilding Poland: Workers and Communists, 1945–50.* Ithaca, NY: Cornell University Press, 1997.

Kharkhordin, Oleg. *The Collective and the Individual in Russia: A Study of Practices.* Berkeley: University of California Press, 1999.

Kirschenbaum, Lisa. "'Our City, Our Hearth, Our Families': Local Loyalties and Private Life in Soviet World War II Propaganda." *Slavic Review* 59: 4 (Winter 2000): 825–47.

Klier, John D., and Shlomo Lambroza. *Pogroms: Anti-Jewish Violence in Modern Russian History.* Cambridge: Cambridge University Press, 1992.

Klitgaard, Robert E. *Controlling Corruption.* Berkeley: University of California Press, 1988.

Koenker, Diane P. *Republic of Labor: Russian Printers and Soviet Socialism, 1918–1930.* Ithaca, NY: Cornell University Press, 2005.

Kolakowski, Leszek. *The Presence of Myth.* Chicago: University of Chicago Press, 1989.

Kotkin, Stephen. *Magnetic Mountain: Stalinism as a Civilization.* Berkeley: University of California Press, 1995.

Kotkin, Stephen, and András Sajó, eds. *Political Corruption in Transition: A Skeptic's Handbook.* Budapest: Central European University Press, 2002.

Koven, Seth, and Sonya Michel, eds. *Mothers of a New World: Maternalist Politics and the Origins of Welfare States*. New York: Routledge, 1993.

Kozhina, Elena. *Through the Burning Steppe: A Memoir of Wartime Russia, 1942–1943*. New York: Riverhead Books, 2000.

Kravchenko, Victor. *I Chose Justice*. London: Scribner's, 1951.

Kravis, Irving B., and Joseph Mintzes. "Soviet Union: Trends in Prices, Rations, and Wages." *Monthly Labor Review* 34: 2 (1947): 32–48.

Krysko, W. W. *Witness to the Birth of Political Anti-Judaism*. New York: Vantage Press, 1999.

Kuretsidis-Haider, Claudia, and Winfried R. Garscha, eds. *Keine "Abrechnung": NS-Verbrechen, Justiz und Gesellschaft in Europa nach 1945*. Leipzig-Vienna: Akademische Verlagsanstalt, 1998.

Kuromiya, Hiroaki. *Freedom and Terror in the Donbas: A Ukrainian-Russian Borderland, 1870s–1990s*. New York: Cambridge University Press, 1998.

Lapalombara, Joseph. "Structural and Institutional Aspects of Corruption." *Social Research* 64: 2 (1994): 325–50.

Lapidus, Gail Warshofsky. *Women in Soviet Society: Equality, Development, and Social Change*. Berkeley: University of California Press, 1978.

Ledeneva, Alena, Stephen Lovell, and Andrei Rogachevskii, eds. *Bribery and Blat in Russia: Negotiating Reciprocity from the Middle Ages to the 1990s*. London: University of London Press, 2000.

Leder, Mary. *My Life in Stalinist Russia: An American Woman Looks Back*. Bloomington: Indiana University Press, 2001.

Lenin, V. I. *Collected Works*. Moscow: Progress Publishers, 1964.

Lenoe, Matthew. *Agitation, Propaganda, and the "Stalinization" of the Soviet Press, 1922–1930*. Pittsburgh: University of Pittsburgh Press, 1998.

Linz, Susan J., ed. *The Impact of World War II on the Soviet Union*. Totowa, NJ: Rowman and Allanheld, 1985.

Lloyd, Christopher. *Collaboration and Resistance in Occupied France: Representing Treason and Sacrifice*. New York: Palgrave Macmillan, 2003.

Loza, Dmitry. *Fighting for the Soviet Motherland*. Edited and translated by James F. Gebhardt. Lincoln: University of Nebraska Press, 1998.

McCagg, William O. *Stalin Embattled, 1943–1948*. Detroit: Wayne State University Press, 1978.

Magnúsdóttir, Rósa. "Keeping Up Appearances: How the Soviet State Failed to Control Popular Attitudes Toward the United States of America, 1945–1959." Ph.D. diss., University of North Carolina-Chapel Hill, 2006.

Martin, Terry. "The Origins of Soviet Ethnic Cleansing." *Journal of Modern History* 70: 4 (December 1998): 831–61.

Mazower, Mark. *Dark Continent: Europe's Twentieth Century*. New York: Vintage Books, 1999.

Medvedev, Roy. *All Stalin's Men*. Translated by Harold Shukman. New York: Blackwell, 1984.

————. *Let History Judge: The Origins and Consequences of Stalinism*. New York: Columbia University Press, 1989.

Medvedev, Roy, and Dmitri Ermakov. *"Seryi Kardinal" M. A. Suslov: Politicheskii portret*. Moscow: Izd-vo "Respublika," 1992.

Medvedev, Roy, and Zhores Medvedev. *Khrushchev: The Years in Power*. New York: Columbia University Press, 1978.

Mendelsohn, John, ed. *The Holocaust #18: Punishing the Perpetrators of the Holocaust. The Ohlendorf and Weizsaecker Cases*. New York: Garland, 1982.

Merridale, Catherine. *Ivan's War: Life and Death in the Red Army, 1939–1945*. New York: Metropolitan Books, 2006.

————. *Night of Stone: Death and Memory in Twentieth-Century Russia*. New York: Viking, 2000.

Millar, James R. *The Soviet Economic Experiment*. Edited by Susan J. Linz. Urbana: University of Illinois Press, 1990.

Miller, Judith. *One, by One, by One: Facing the Holocaust*. New York: Simon and Schuster, 1990.

Miry, Raoul. "The Black Market." In *Belgium Under Occupation*, edited by Jan-Albert Goris, 64–83. New York: Moretus Press, 1947.

Morkovin, V. K. "Rabochie Dona v poslevoennyi period, 1946–1950." Kandidatskaia diss., Rostov State University, 1972.

Naiman, Eric, ed. *Everyday Life in Early Soviet Russia*. Bloomington: Indiana University Press, 2006.

————. *Sex in Public: The Incarnation of Early Soviet* Ideology. Princeton, NJ: Princeton University Press, 1997.

Nakachi, Mie. "Population, Politics, and Reproduction: Late Stalinism and Its Legacy." In Furst, *Late Stalinist Russia*, 23–45.

Narodnoe khoziaistvo Rostovskoi oblasti v 9-oi piatiletke: Statisticheskii sbornik. Rostov-on-Don: Rostov State University, 1976.

"Nastoiashchii tovarishch" (True Comrade). *Don*, no. 11 (1948): 182–93.

Nove, Alec. *An Economic History of the USSR*. New York: Penguin Books, 1969.

Novick, Peter. *The Resistance versus Vichy: The Purge of Collaborators in Liberated France*. New York: Columbia University Press, 1968.

"Obshchestvennaia atmosfera posle voiny (1945–1946)." *Svobodnaia mysl'*, no. 6 (April 1992): 2–18.

O'Rourke, Shane. *Warriors and Peasants: The Don Cossacks in Late Imperial Russia*. New York: St. Martin's Press, 2000.

Patolichev, N. S. *Ispytanie na zrelost'*. Moscow: Politizdat, 1977.

Penter, Tanja. "Collaboration on Trial: New Source Material on Soviet Postwar Trials against Collaborators." *Slavic Review* 64: 4 (Winter 2005): 782–90.

Petroff, Serge. *The Red Eminence: A Biography of Mikhail A. Suslov*. Clifton, NJ: Kingston Press, 1988.

Petrone, Karen. *Life Has Become More Joyous, Comrades: Celebrations in the Time of Stalin*. Bloomington: Indiana University Press, 2000.

Piat' let spustia. Rostov-on-Don: Rostov State University, 1948.

Piotrowski, Tadeusz. *Poland's Holocaust: Ethnic Strife, Collaboration with Occupying Forces and Genocide in the Second Republic, 1918–1947*. Jefferson, NC: McFarland Press, 1998.

Poliakov, S. E. *Mify i real'nost' sovremennoi psikhologii*. Moscow: Editorial URSS, 2004.

Pollard, Miranda. *Reign of Virtue: Mobilizing Gender in Vichy France*. Chicago: University of Chicago Press, 1998.

"Postanovlenie Soveta Ministrov SSSR: O poriadke provedeniia organizovannogo nabora rabochikh." In *Resheniia partii i pravitel'stva po khoziaistvennym voprosam, 1917–1967 gody*, edited by K. U. Chernenko and M. S. Smirtiukov, 117–25. Moscow: Izd-vo Politicheskoi literatury, 1967–88.

Pred, Allan. *Making Histories and Constructing Human Geographies: The Local Transformation of Practice, Power Relations, and Consciousness*. Boulder, CO: Westview Press, 1990.

Qualls, Karl. "Imagining Sevastopol: History and Postwar Community Construction, 1942–1953." *National Identities* 5: 2 (July 2003): 123–39.

—————. "Localism During National Reconstruction: A Case Study of Post-War Sevastopol, 1944–1953." Unpublished paper delivered at the American Association for the Advancement of Slavic Studies National Convention. St. Louis, MO, 20 November 1999.

Raleigh, Donald J. *Experiencing Russia's Civil War: Politics, Society, and Revolutionary Culture in Saratov, 1917–1922*. Princeton, NJ: Princeton University Press, 2002.

—————. *Provincial Landscapes: The Local Dimensions of Soviet Power*. Pittsburgh: University of Pittsburgh Press, 2001.

Reichman, Henry. "The Rostov General Strike of 1902." *Russian History* 9: 1 (1982): 67–85.

Rigby, T. H. *Communist Party Membership in the U.S.S.R., 1917–1967*. Princeton, NJ: Princeton University Press, 1968.

Rimmel, Lesley A. "Another Kind of Fear: The Kirov Murder and the End of Bread Rationing in Leningrad." *Slavic Review* 56: 3 (1997): 481–99.

—————. "Svodki and Popular Opinion in Stalinist Leningrad." *Cahiers du Monde russe* 40 (1999): 217–34.

Rittersporn, Gábor Tamás. *Simplifications staliniennes et complications sovietiques: Tensions sociales et conflits politiques en U.R.S.S.* Paris: Editions des archives contemporaines, 1988.

Rossman, Jeffrey. *Worker Resistance Under Stalin: Class and Revolution on the Shop Floor*. Cambridge, MA: Harvard University Press, 2005.

Rostovskaia oblast' za 50 let. Rostov-on-Don: Rostov State University, 1967.

Sasoon, A. A., ed. *Women and the State: The Shifting Boundaries of Public and Private*. London: Hutchinson Education, 1987.

Scanlan, James. *Marxism in the USSR: A Critical Survey of Current Soviet Thought*. Ithaca, NY: Cornell University Press, 1985.

Schwartz, Harry. *Russia's Postwar Economy*. New York: Syracuse University Press, 1947.

Schwarz, Solomon M. *Labor in the Soviet Union*. New York: Praeger, 1951.

Scott, James C. *Domination and the Arts of Resistance: Hidden Transcripts*. New Haven: Yale University Press, 1990.

————. *Seeing Like a State: How Certain Schemes to Improve the Human Condition Have Failed*. New Haven: Yale University Press, 1998.

Scott, Joan Wallach. *Gender and the Politics of History*. New York: Columbia University Press, 1988.

————. "Gender: A Useful Category of Historical Analysis." *American Historical Review* 91 (1986): 1053–75.

Sen, Amartya. *Poverty and Famines: An Essay on Entitlement and Deprivation*. Oxford: Clarendon Press, 1981.

Seniavskii, S. L., and M. I. Khlusov. "Industrial'nye kadry SSSR v 1946–1955 godakh." *Voprosy istorii* 10: 4 (1965): 15–37.

Shchemalaev, N. N. et al. *Rostsel'mash*. Rostov-on-Don: Rostov State University, 1968.

Sholokhov, Mikhail. *Quiet Flows the Don*. Translated by Robert Daglish. Edited by Brian Murphy. New York: Carroll and Graf Publishers, 1996.

Siegelbaum, Lewis H. *Stakhanovism and the Politics of Productivity in the USSR, 1935–1941*. Cambridge: Cambridge University Press, 1988.

Siegelbaum, Lewis H., and Ronald Grigor Suny, eds. *Making Workers Soviet: Power, Class, and Identity*. Ithaca, NY: Cornell University Press, 1994.

————. "Soviet Norm Determination in Theory and Practice, 1917–1941." *Soviet Studies* 36: 1(1984): 45–68.

Skrjabina, Elena. *After Leningrad: From the Caucasus to the Rhine (9 August 1942–25 March 1945). A Diary of Survival During World War II*. Carbondale, IL: Southern Illinois University Press, 1978.

————. *Siege and Survival: The Odyssey of a Leningrader*. Translated by Norman Luxenburg. Carbondale, IL: Southern Illinois University Press, 1971.

Smirnov, V. "Rabochie kadry tiazhelogo mashinostroeniia SSSR v 1946–1958 godakh." *Istoricheskie zapiski* 71: 3 (1964): 17–62.

Solzhenitsyn, Aleksandr. *Gulag Archipelago*. 2 vols. Translated by Thomas P. Whitney. New York: Harper and Row, 1974.

Taylor, Lynne. *Between Resistance and Collaboration: Popular Protest in Northern France, 1940–45*. New York: St. Martin's Press, 2000.

Thane, Pat, and Gisela Bock, eds. *Maternity and Gender Politics: Women and the Rise of the European Welfare States, 1880s–1950s*. New York: Routledge, 1991.

Thompson, E. P. *The Making of the English Working Class*. New York: Pantheon Books, 1963.

Thurston, Robert W. "Fear and Belief in the USSR's 'Great Terror.'" *Slavic Review* 45: 2 (1986): 213–34.

————. *Life and Terror in Stalin's Russia, 1934–1941*. New Haven: Yale University Press, 1996.

Thurston, Robert W., and Bernd Bonwetsch, eds. *The People's War: Responses to World War II in the Soviet Union*. Urbana: University of Illinois Press, 2000.

Tolz, Vera. "New Information about the Deportation of Ethnic Groups in the USSR during World War 2." In *World War 2 and the Soviet People: Selected Papers from the Fourth World Congress for Soviet and East European Studies, 1990*, edited by John Garrard and Carol Garrard, 161–83. New York: St. Martin's Press, 1993.

Treadgold, Donald. *Twentieth Century Russia*. 9th ed. Boulder, CO: Westview Press, 2000.

Treml, Vladimir, and Michael Alexeev. "The Growth of the Second Economy in the Soviet Union and Its Impact on the System." In *The Postcommunist Economic Transformation: Essays in Honor of Gregory Grossman*, edited by Robert W. Campbell, 221–47. Boulder, CO: Westview Press, 1994.

Tumarkin, Nina. *The Living and the Dead: The Rise and Fall of the Cult of World War II in Russia*. New York: Basic Books, 1994.

Viola, Lynne, ed. *Contending with Stalinism: Soviet Power and Popular Resistance in the 1930s*. Ithaca, NY: Cornell University Press, 2002.

Viola, Lynne et al., eds. *Riazanskaia derevnia v 1929–1930 gg.: Khronika golovo-kruzheniia dokumentov i materialy*. Translated from English by Elena Osokina. Moscow: ROSSPEN, 1998.

Volin, Lazar. *Survey of Soviet Russian Agriculture*. Washington, DC: U.S. Department of Agriculture, 1951.

Volkov, I. M. *Trudovoi podvig Sovetskogo krest'ianstva v poslevoennye gody: Kolkhozy SSSR v 1946–1950 godakh*. Moscow: Mysli, 1972.

Voznesensky, N. A. *The Economy of the USSR during World War II*. Washington, DC: Public Affairs Press, 1948.

Vozrozhdenie Sovetskogo Dona, 1943 — February 14 — 1946. Rostov-on-Don: Rostov State University, 1946.

Weiner, Amir. "The Making of a Dominant Myth: The Second World War and the Construction of Political Identities within the Soviet Polity." *The Russian Review* 55: 4 (October 1996): 638–60.

————. *Making Sense of War: The Second World War and the Fate of the Bolshevik Revolution*. Princeton, NJ: Princeton University Press, 2000.

Werth, Alexander. *Russia at War, 1941–1945*. New York: Dutton, 1964.

Westwood, J. N. *A History of Russian Railways*. London: G. Allen and Unwin, 1964.

White, Hayden. *The Content of the Form: Narrative Discourse and Historical Representation*. Baltimore: Johns Hopkins University Press, 1987.

Wimberg, Ellen. "Socialism, Democratism and Criticism: The Soviet Press and the National Discussion of the 1936 Draft Constitution." *Soviet Studies*, no. 2 (1992): 313–32.

Wingfield, Nancy M., and Maria Bucur. *Gender and War in Twentieth-Century Eastern Europe*. Bloomington: Indiana University Press, 2006.

Wynn, Charters. *Workers, Strikes and Pogrom: The Donbas-Dnieper Bend in Late Imperial Russia, 1870–1905*. Princeton, NJ: Princeton University Press, 1992.

Zaleski, Eugene. *Stalinist Planning for Economic Growth, 1933–1952*. Chapel Hill: University of North Carolina Press, 1980.

Zhak, Mariia S. Unpublished and Untitled Memoir.

Zima, V. F. *Golod v SSSR 1946–1947 godov: Proiskhozhdenie i posledstviia*. Moscow: Rossiiskaia akademiia nauk, 1996.

Zubkova, Elena. "Obshchestvennaia atmosfera posle voiny (1945–1946)." *Svobodnaia mysl'* 6: 12 (1992): 3–18.

———. *Obshchestvo i reformy, 1945–1964*. Moscow: Rossiia Molodaia, 1993.

———. *Russia After the War: Hopes, Illusions, and Disappointments, 1945–1957*. Translated by Hugh Ragsdale. Armonk, NY: M. E. Sharpe, 1998.

Zverev, A. G. *Zapiski ministra*. Moscow: Politizdat, 1973.

Zvezdin, Z. K., L. S. Rogachevskaia, and D. A. Baevskii, eds. *Politicheskii i trudovoi pod"em rabochego klassa SSSR (1928–1929 gg.): Sbornik dokumentov*. Moscow: Gosudarstvennoe izdatel'stvo, 1956.

Zweiniger-Bargielowska, Ina. *Austerity in Britain: Rationing, Controls, and Consumption, 1939–1955*. Oxford: Oxford University Press, 2000.

Index

Abramian, Karina 172
Afanas'ev, S. P. 89
Akhmatova, Anna 285
Akimenko, V. I. 71, 74, 202, 272–73
Aleksandriuk, Petr Il'ich 65, 98, 164–65,
    168, 222, 258, 259n60, 268–70, 273–74
Alekseevich, Svetlana 155n31
Alexander III (Romanov) 19
Alexeev, Michael 182n13, 183n14
Andreev, A. A. 26
Anisimov, Captain K. 267–68, 270–71
Anisimov, V. 53
Anti-Semitism (or anti-Semitic; See also
    Judeo-commune syndrome) 6, 17,
    22, 31, 37, 116–17, 118n28, 134, 140–
    43, 170, 171n101, 175n123, 177, 283
Aralova, L. G. 238–39
Armenians 1, 19–20, 25, 33, 35, 124–25,
    133, 139, 141n150, 143, 172
Aseev, A. M. 130–31
Asmolov Tobacco Factory (see also: Don
    State Tobacco Factor or DGTF) 17,
    25n38
Auschwitz 117n24

Baltic states 157
Barghoorn, Frederick 212n1
Bataisk 1, 23
Belarus (or Belarusan) 147n11, 175n122
Belgium 181
Bel'kov, Nikolai 154
Berlin 4n10, 5, 41, 86, 149, 286
Black cat (*chernaia koshka*—crime gang)
    50–51, 54, 70–71, 75
Black Sea 17, 24n37
Bock, Gisela 113n6, 114n11
Bogdan, Sergei 27–28
Bogdan, Valentina 27–28, 29n52, 30n58,
    31–32, 35, 141, 175n123, 177

Bolshevik 7, 20, 22, 24, 26, 32, 36, 66–67,
    78, 81, 84, 90–91, 104–05, 110–11,
    141, 151, 176, 195, 197, 209, 214n9,
    218n27, 221–23, 229, 236, 241, 244,
    250, 256, 285
Bolshevik Revolution (including the
    anniversary of, November 7) 78, 81,
    84, 90–91, 104–05, 110–11, 214n9,
    221, 229, 285
Bonds (or Bond Drives) 67n101, 80–81,
    85, 89, 105–07, 109–11, 121, 153, 189,
    209, 283
Bostandzhian, A. K. 124–25
Boterbloem, Kees 147n11, 148n14,
    166n75
Brandist, Craig 212n1
Britain (or British) 5, 21, 28–29, 42, 45, 78,
    114, 115n13, 181, 287
Brest-Litovsk (Treaty) 20
Brezhnev, Leonid 182, 281
"Brezhnev generation" 223, 280
Brooks, E. Willis 231n81
Brown, Kate 148n13, 171n101
Budenny, S. M. 22
Byba, Klavdiia 122

Caucasus 4, 18n6, 19, 30n59, 32, 36
Central Asia 44, 80
Central Party Control Commission 258
Chamberlain, Neville 28–29
Chechen 149n19
Cherkassk (also Starocherkassk) 19n13
Chernysheva, Svetlana P. 69, 74, 105,
    173, 233, 272, 273n125
China 18
Civil War 5n15, 12n37, 17, 20, 23–24,
    26n43, 32, 39, 65, 78, 117, 153,
    176n124, 211, 221, 287

Cold War 4, 75, 105, 149, 157, 180, 212–13, 285–86

Collaboration 5n13, 6, 8, 15, 126, 144–79, 190, 245, 252, 270, 278

Communist Party of the Soviet Union (CPSU) 1, 4, 11, 42, 103, 157, 180n3, 213, 216–17, 226, 229, 232, 234, 237, 241, 244, 246–47, 261, 267, 276–77, 279–80

Constitution (1918; See also Stalin Constitution, 1936) 214n10

Council of Nationalities 216

Council of the Union 216

Crime 6, 39–40, 42, 44, 50–51, 54, 62–64, 66, 69–71, 75, 129, 132, 182n12, 186, 215, 228, 234–35, 249

Crimean Tartars 149n19

Czechoslovakia 29, 44n20, 76n157, 213

Darnton, Robert 211n166

Dean, Martin 147n11, 157n34

Denikin, A. I. 24

Djilas, Milovan 10n29, 285n7

Donbass Region 38

Don Cossacks (or Cossacks) 3–4, 16–17, 19–20, 23–24, 26, 29–32, 85n32, 141–42, 151, 153, 157, 169–71, 174–79, 222–23

Don River 1, 4, 16, 47

Don State Tobacco Factory (*Donskaia Gosudarstvennaia Tabachnaia Fabrika* or DGTF) 25, 73, 84–85, 93, 98, 104, 130, 138–39, 159, 209, 233

Double burden 115–16, 128–29, 282

Dubrovin, Ivan F. 255

Dunham, Vera 247n12

Dvinskii, Boris A. 27, 58, 74, 81, 94, 148n14, 161, 221–22, 268, 271

Efimov, Aleksandr 224

Emel'ianenko, S. I. 105, 173–75, 236, 271

Ehrenburg, Ilya 35

Eisenstein, Sergei 173n110

Einsatzgruppen 34, 36

Ely, Geoff 213n4

Ermolenko, Aleksandra 68, 272

Ermolenko, Genadii 1n2, 71, 74, 105, 141, 172–73, 202–04, 234, 272

Etkind, Alexander 36

Eurasia (or Eurasian) 6, 41, 78, 112–13, 116, 118

Europe (or European) 5, 27, 41, 72, 77n1, 114, 116–17, 145–46, 147n11, 149, 171n104, 181, 213, 220, 241, 278, 282, 286

Evdokimov, E. G. 27

Ezhov, N. I. 27, 226n55, 266n96

Fabrichno-zavodskoe obuchenie (FZOs) 45, 48–49, 54, 59–62, 66–67, 99–100, 123, 169n91, 241

Family Law (or Legislation; 1944) 118–19, 130, 136

"Family rhetoric" 112–13, 119, 123, 126, 128, 134–35, 138–39, 142–44, 146, 223, 226, 285

Famine 5, 15, 17, 22–23, 32, 40–45, 48, 52, 53n27, 55n33, 63–64, 66, 67n105, 72–76, 103, 105, 107, 111, 138–39, 184–85, 203, 205, 209, 224, 229n65, 265, 263, 279, 282–83, 284, 286

Fedorova, Mariia A. 120–21, 125

Fedunov, Nikolai 124, 219

Fieseler, Beate 131n91

Filtzer, Donald 46n30, 61n69, 71n134, 88n45, 109n140, 149n20

Fineman, Martha 113n4

Finland 29, 44n20, 76n157

First Five-Year Plan (1928–32) 24–25, 44n22, 80, 281

Fitzpatrick, Sheila 14n42, 115n14, 130, 182n10, 183n18, 184n22, 186n32, 213n15, 216n19, 286

Fomenko, Vladimir 85

Fourth Five-Year Plan (1946–50) 48, 69, 80, 83–84, 89–90, 221

France 5n13, 12n37, 29, 44n20, 76n157, 113n4, 114, 137n129, 145–46, 148n15, 171n104, 211n166, 213

    Vichy France 5n13, 114, 145–46, 148n15

Fredman, Sandra 115n12

Garkushenko, K. G. 225, 241

Georgia (or Georgians) 19, 142, 204

German (and Germany; see also Nazi) 1, 4n10, 20, 23n32, 25, 29–39, 41, 58n59,

64, 72, 80, 82, 85–86, 91, 97–98, 112, 114, 124–26, 134, 136, 140–42, 145–46, 147n11, 148–56, 158–81, 192, 198, 213, 218–20, 222, 228, 238–42, 248, 257, 269n108, 271, 281, 286
West Germany 213
Gestapo 34, 151–52, 156, 158, 160, 166–67, 170
Getty, J. Arch 13n40, 214–15, 226n55, 229, 248n15, 266n96
Gitelman, Zvi 36, 118n30
Glebov-Avilov, N. P. 26
Gogoberidze, L. D. 26
Goncharov, A. G. 86
Gorbachev, Mihail 16, 27n48, 287
Great Fatherland War (see World War II)
Greeks 19
Gross, Jan 117n24
Grossman, Gregory 185n27

Hankiss, Elemér 246n5
Heinzen, James 247n12, 262n78, 267n104
Hellbeck, Jochen 13
Hessler, Julie 182, 198, 201
Hitler, Adolph 3, 29, 34, 142, 151, 162, 174n119, 239
    Hitlerite (or Hitlerist) 33, 134, 153, 218
Hoffman, David 212n3, 215n14
Holocaust 116, 118, 125n59, 175n122
Hooper, Cynthia 247n12, 249, 256n44, 258, 264
Hoover, Herbert 41, 44n20, 76
Hungary (or Hungarian) 174, 245
Hunt, Lynn 113n4

Iakovlev, Vadim 1
Iankovskii, I. A. 254–55
Ingush 149n19
International Women's Day (March 8) 121–22, 127, 138
Italy 171n104, 213
Izvestiia 117, 122, 126

Japan (or Japanese) 41, 78, 137n129, 181, 237, 286
Jews (or Jewish) 1, 10, 17, 19–22, 25, 29n54, 31–32, 34–37, 116–18, 123–26, 133–35, 139–43, 148n15, 160, 172, 181, 283
Judeo-commune syndrome 116, 140–42, 283

K., Nina Nikitichna 68–69, 102, 105, 156–57, 272
Kaganovich, Lazar 219
Kalabukhin, A. S. 260
Kaledin, General Aleksei 20
Kalinin, Mikhail 158
Kalinin Paper Mill 72–73
Kalymuks 149n19
Kaplan, Cynthia 246n10
Karachay-Balkars 149n19
Karol, K. S. 3, 16, 24, 26n43, 29–30, 31n61, 33, 38–39, 68, 77, 101–02, 109–10, 135–36, 140–43, 175n123, 176n124, 177, 180, 184n20, 202–05, 210, 234, 237, 242, 278, 281, 287
    Klava (K. S. Karol's wife) 37–38, 101, 102n104, 142, 176n124, 202n125, 203, 234
    Kolia (K. S. Karol's friend) 3, 16, 39, 101, 135, 203n127, 204, 210, 234, 274, 278, 281
Karotskova, Ekaterina 74, 175
Kenney, Padraic 42n9, 116n21, 181n7, 204n134, 214n7, 263n83
Kharkov 16, 19n12
Kielce, Poland 116
Kiromiya, Hiroaki 147, 148n13 166n75
Klitgaard, Robert 245n5
Kobilev, A. I. 87n41, 95, 131, 258
Koenker, Diane 5n15, 215n14
Koliadin, V. 284
Komsomol (Communist Youth League) 3n5, 28–29, 48, 55, 158n38, 238
Kononov, Leonid 174
Korean War 41n4
Korolev, A. I. 87
Kotkin, Stephen 245n3
Kozhin, A. A. 267
Kozhina, Elena 175–78
Krasikova, Anastasia K. 57, 122, 223, 228, 231, 258, 260, 265
Krasnodar (Krasnodarskii krai) 195, 222

Krasnov, Ataman Petr 176n124
Krasnyi Aksai 25, 49, 57, 59–60, 89n52, 97, 99, 168, 227n56, 229n64, 268
Khrushchev, Nikita 178, 278, 281, 287
Kravchenko, Victor 26n43
Krysko, W. W. 18–23
Kuban Territory 19n12
Kuban Cossacks 20, 24, 30n58, 176n124
Kucherenko, Nikolai P. 222, 235, 237
Kugusheva, L. G. 150
Kursk 16

Lapalombara, Joseph 245
Leder, Abram 31, 34–35
Leder, Mary 13n40, 16, 29, 31, 34–35, 136, 140, 143, 178
Lenin, Vladimir (or Leninist) 18, 24, 83, 85n30, 97, 162, 183, 221, 223–24, 233, 244, 248, 256, 277–78, 285
Leningrad 30n59, 36, 38, 154, 175–77, 285
Lewis, Jane 115n13
Łódź, Poland 29, 116, 263n83

Makarov, I. F. 262
Makhno, Nestor (Makhnovtsi) 21
Malenkov, Georgii 226n55
Malinovskii, Marshall R. 219
Marshall Plan 286
Marxism (or Marxist) 9n26, 45n23, 75, 78, 244
Marxism-Leninism 2, 7n21, 8, 167, 230, 244, 246, 251, 260
May Day 81, 83–84, 91, 96, 105, 110, 120, 221, 272n117, 274n129
Mazower, Mark 112n2, 114n8, 171n104
Medvedev, Roy 25–26
Mensheviks 244
Merridale, Catherine 75n155, 102n106, 117, 125n60, 154n28, 228n58, 281
Meskhetians 149n19
Mikoyan, Anastas 225
Mikoyan Shoe Factory 25, 49, 72, 82, 94, 96, 98–99, 108, 139n139, 190, 198, 206, 209, 257, 260, 263n84, 275
Minin, P. I. 247n13
Miry, Raoul 181
Moldavia (or Moldavian) 173

Molotov, Viacheslav 29–30, 32–33, 104–05, 110, 225
Mongolia 18
Moscow 16, 26, 27n47, 29, 31, 72, 107n130, 131–32, 135, 198, 200, 204, 206, 213n6, 219, 221, 226n55, 230, 259, 267–72
Moscow University 221
Mother Heroine (Award) 72, 119, 276, 282
Motherland (*Rodina*) 32, 67n101, 83, 85, 95, 113n4, 119n34, 120–23, 125, 147, 152–55, 158–59, 165, 167, 171, 173n110, 176, 190, 219, 224
Mozheiko, A. I. 266n97

Nakhichevan' 19–20, 25, 124
Nazi (or Nazism) 1, 4, 29–30, 32–38, 77, 118, 124, 126, 133–34, 139–41, 144–47, 149–51, 156, 158–60, 162–63, 167–73, 175n122, 176, 178, 193, 213n6, 218n25, 219, 226, 237, 242
Nazi-Soviet Non-Aggression Pact (1939) 29, 77
Netherlands 172n104
New Economic Policy (NEP) 182–83, 287
Nicholas II (Romanov) 19
NKVD (secret police) 13n40, 25–28, 50, 62, 70, 87, 134, 148n14, 174, 239
Nomenklatura 3, 9–10, 76, 144, 158, 161, 236, 247, 249–50, 265n92, 277, 279–80
Norway 172n104
Novocherkassk 19n13, 51, 151–53, 158n35, 170, 176n124
Nuremburg trials 32–34

Ohlendorf, Otto 34
Order No. 270 ("Not a Step Back Order") 33, 148
Order of Lenin 221
Orel 16
Osaka 41
Ovchinnikov, G. F. 26

Pacherskaia, Olga 273–74
Pale of Settlement 19, 25
Palestine 140

Parshin, P. 269n108
Partisans 1, 34–35, 37, 107, 117n25, 124,
    148n14, 152, 166n78, 170n98, 172,
    219, 222, 224
Pastushenko, N. I. 56, 95, 127, 159, 161,
    169–70
Patolichev, N. S. 16, 268, 270, 273–74, 277
Pavlov, Ivan P. 238
Peasant (or peasants) 8, 10, 17, 20, 22–23,
    30n59, 39, 43, 109, 120, 151, 171n101,
    174, 189n51, 212–14, 217, 222, 236,
    243, 246n11, 247n11, 277, 280
Penter, Tanja 118n28, 220n33
Petrone, Karen 212n3, 215n13
Petrovskii, Iurii Alekseevich 273n125,
    274n129
Pianiatsev, Oleg 70, 105, 141, 173
Piatigorsk 30n59, 36, 37n79, 37n81
Pogroms 17, 116
Poland (or Polish) 29, 42, 44n20, 76n157,
    81n1, 116–17, 181, 204n134, 213–14,
    228, 263n83
    Polish Peasant Party 213n6, 214
    Polish Provisional Government of
        National Unity 213
    Polish Socialist Party 213n6
    Polish Worker's Party 181, 213n6
"Politics of myth" 78
"Politics of productivity" 77–81, 87–91,
    97, 100–01, 107–10, 279, 283
Ponomarev, Boris 234n90
Porcelain Goods Factory (Emal'posuda)
    55
Pototov, A. M. 194, 263
Pravda 52–53, 65, 106, 107n130, 110, 117,
    189, 223, 225
Presidium (of the Supreme Soviet)
    119n33, 216
Prisoners of War (or POWs) 1, 34, 77n1,
    147–48, 156–57, 159, 165, 168,
    169n95, 172n104, 173–75, 178, 278
Purges (1936–39) 17, 24–28, 35, 39, 115,
    215n17, 223, 244, 266n96, 272,
    273n124, 276, 278, 281
Pushkin, Alexander 69n115

Red Army 1, 3–4, 32–36, 37n79, 50, 56,
    64n89, 71, 81–82, 91, 96n85, 112, 117,
    119–20, 122–23, 134, 136, 141, 149,
    151–52, 154–55, 157, 162, 173, 175,
    177, 197, 213–14, 218–22, 248n16,
    249, 253n32, 262
Red Cross 41
Repko, N. I. 241
Revolution
    (1905) 17, 214
    (1917) 20, 22, 28, 49, 65, 67, 78, 81–85,
        90–91, 104–05, 110–11, 120, 140–
        41, 221, 223, 226, 229, 239, 285, 287
    (Stalin Revolution: see Stalin, Joseph)
Ribbentrop, Joachim von 29
Riga 18
Rigby, T. H. 116n19, 246n10, 246n11,
    249n17
Rimmel, Lesley 14
Roosevelt, Franklin Delano 238
Rossman, Jeffrey 108n135
Rostsel'mash 24–27, 39, 48–49, 52–55, 57,
    59–61, 69–70, 73–74, 78, 80, 83, 85–
    86, 89–92, 95, 97, 99n100, 100–02,
    104–05, 130, 174, 207, 209, 220, 222,
    225, 227n56, 235, 240, 251, 254, 268–
    69n108, 274–75
Rostov-Bataisk Dam 1
Rostov Art Institute 202
Rostov Medical Institute 47, 57, 129
Rostov Pedagogical Institute 162, 222,
    262
Rostov State University 27, 68, 173, 237
Rotterdam 41
Rumania (or Rumanian) 173–74
Rykunov, S. P. 130

Sajó, András 245n3
Schwartz, Harry 180n2
Scott, James 11n30
Scott, Joan 3n6, 112, 281
Sea of Azov 4, 17, 19, 24n37
Semenova, Svetlana 40n3, 68–69, 71, 140,
    172–73, 202, 272
Sen, Amartya 185n25
Seraphim, Peter 25
Sheboldaev, B. P. 26–27
Shevchenko, A. I. 63
Sholokhov, Mikhail A. 32, 222–23
Skrjabina, Elena 30n59, 36–37

Sluzhashchie 9, 246n11, 257
Smirtova, Z. S. 112
Smith, S. A. 10n26
Smolensk 248n15
Snake's Gulch (ravine) 34–35
Socialism (or Socialist) 1–2, 8, 29, 51,
    77n2, 79, 80n11, 81, 83–84, 85n30,
    89–90, 91n56, 95–96, 101, 107, 109–
    10, 180, 190, 203, 212–14, 218–19,
    223, 226–28, 232–37, 239, 241–43,
    285–86
Socialist Competition 79–81, 83–85, 89–
    90, 95–96, 101, 107, 109–10, 234
"Socialist Democracy" 79, 180n3, 212–13,
    217–18, 226–27, 232–35, 240–43, 285
Solzhenitsyn, Aleksandr 26n43, 28
Sorkin, Veniamin Isaakovich 124, 126
Source Lens 11, 13
Spielrein, Sabina 35–36
Stakhanovite (Stakhanovism) 49, 79,
    80n11, 81, 84, 107, 154, 221, 252, 274
Stakhurskii, Mikhail 117
Stalin, Joseph 3–5, 8, 13, 14n45, 15, 30, 33,
    39, 45n23, 73–78, 81, 83–85, 90–91,
    102–07, 109–11, 119, 122n45, 123–24,
    128, 140–42, 149, 155, 157, 162,
    169n95, 172n109, 175, 176n124,
    182n9, 183n15, 184, 214, 218–23, 225–
    26, 229, 233, 239–40, 242, 244, 246,
    247n13, 255, 259, 272–73, 276–78,
    285–87
    Stalingrad 4, 149, 151–53
    Stalinism (Stalinist) 2–3, 6–8, 11, 13, 15,
        17, 27n48, 44n22, 77, 79, 107, 110,
        118, 145, 147, 178, 183n13, 210,
        213–14, 218, 220, 226, 239, 244,
        256, 262, 271, 278–79, 281, 283,
        285–87
    de-Stalinization 3, 33, 281, 286
    Stalin Constitution (1936) 8, 13n40, 78,
        107, 212, 214–18, 226, 229, 235–36,
        243
    Stalin Revolution (1928–33) 183, 223–
        24, 278
Stavropol *krai* (territory) 16, 19n12, 27n48
Sudakov, V. A. 266–67
Supreme Soviet 99, 119n33, 137, 158,
    216–19, 221–29, 235, 237–38

Suslov, Mikhail A. 26–27
Svodki (Informant reports) 11–14, 73, 107,
    138–39, 208, 211, 248, 279

Taganrog 19, 221, 224
Tartars (or Tatarstan) 19, 149n19, 259n62
Tashkent 91, 117, 222
Thane, Pat 113n6, 114n11
Tokyo 41
Tolkachi (Suppliers) 246, 251, 256
Tolz, Vera 147n11
Treml, Vladimir 182n13, 183n14
Trotskyites 26–27
Truman, Harry 41, 44n20, 76
Tumarkin, Nina 155n31, 200n113
Turok, M. K. 263n85

Ukraine (or Ukrainian) 7n19, 21, 32, 38,
    44, 76, 117, 147, 157, 171n101, 200,
    228n61
United Nations 275
United Nations' Relief and
    Rehabilitation Administration
    (UNRRA) 76
United States (or US) 4–5, 180n2, 181, 287
Uspenskaia, T. D. 264
USSR (or Soviet Union) 2–5, 7n21, 8, 14,
    16, 25, 29–30, 32, 39, 40–44, 46, 51,
    53n27, 56, 68, 72, 76, 77n2, 78–79, 83,
    101–02, 104, 109, 112, 113n4, 116–17,
    120n37, 123–24, 141n150, 143, 145–
    48, 150n4, 157n34, 181–83, 185, 189,
    193, 202, 212, 214, 215n14, 216–19,
    226, 228n61, 232, 236, 239, 242, 244–
    45, 261, 278–80, 285–87

Vinnytsia Region, Ukraine 117
Viola, Lynne 12n37, 14
Voice of Rostov (*Golos Rostova*) 34–35,
    37n79, 162
Volkov, N. 268, 270
Volga German Autonomous Republic
    149
Voronezh 16, 19n12
Voroshilov, Kliment 219

Warsaw 41

Weiner, Amir 7n19, 78, 117, 147–48, 158n39
White Army (or Whites) 17, 20–24, 26n43, 117, 153, 176n124
World War I (or First World War) 12n37, 17–18, 20, 35–36, 39, 114, 156, 260
World War II (or the Great Fatherland War) 7n19, 8, 16–17, 21, 23–25, 29–30, 39, 41n4, 65, 78, 113n4, 114, 117, 123, 144–45, 156, 181–82, 213, 220n33

Yalta 213
Yugoslavia 76n157

Zakharov, M. A. 159
Zakharova, L. N. 126

Zhak, Mariia 17n5, 22, 35, 40, 69–70, 74, 105, 116n20, 140, 143, 148n14, 234, 237, 261n70, 271–73
Zhak, Sergei 35, 68, 70, 105, 116n20, 143
Zhak, Veniamin 35, 83–84, 105, 110, 116n20, 143, 271–72
Zhdanov, Andrei 4, 157, 260, 266n96, 285–86
Zhdanovshchina 285
Zhdanov, Iurii Andreevich 286n9
Zhelnin, Iura 123
Zhitomir 32
Zhukov, Marshal Gregory 70
Zlatko, I. I. 168
Zoshchenko, Mikhail 285
Zubkova, Elena 104n113, 238n116, 281
Zverev, A. G. 184